Alastair
Sawday's

Special Places
to Stay

British
Bed & Breakfast

4   Contents

British B&Bs just get better and better. We have over 140 new entries in this 19th edition, some shared with Canopy & Stars — a quixotic collection of huts, houses, even roof-top vehicles. One of my favourite memories of this year was fine-lunching on the verandah of a floating wooden cabin in, of all places, an Essex gravel pit.

Most of our new places are more conventionally magnificent: garden annexes and barns, grand manors, an eco-build in Scotland kept warm with their own sheep. The dazzling variety in these pages may make you want to retire young, and explore. (I've met people who've done just that — retired to explore Sawday's places all over Europe.)

B&B prices have risen over the last decade, but the value remains superb. I have just returned from a Welsh B&B

Photo: Tom Germain

with mighty trees for beams and a giant 15th-century bedroom. I took a moonlit hike up the hill behind the house, returning with a small herd of heifers gamboling around me. Magical, unexpected and yet typical.

The part played in these pages by those who live close to the land, off the land and for the land — is remarkable. It is no longer rare to be offered food grown at home, energy generated on the roof or down in the river, furniture built in the workshop and art created in your host's studio. Organic food has long been a passion of mine, and more and more B&Bs provide it, supporting a system that nourishes the land and sustains rural jobs. Going out on a limb has our full support.

It seems a lifetime ago that we were railing against nylon sheets and hatchet-jawed hosts. These are now largely history but there's a new obsession with luxury, sometimes at the expense of style, panache and character. Not so in these pages, where you will meet people swimming against the current and defying convention in their own very special ways.

A last word: it has been tough this last winter for some of our Somerset B&Bs, inundated by floodwater and the press. But they are recovered, and want to see you back. So put your wellies away and get on the road.

Alastair Sawday

It's simple. There are no rules, no boxes to tick. We choose places that we like and are fiercely subjective in our choices. We also recognise that one person's idea of special is not necessarily someone else's so there is a huge variety of places, and prices, in the book. Those who are familiar with our *Special Places* series know that we look for comfort, originality, authenticity, and reject the insincere, the anonymous and the banal. The way guests are treated comes as high on our list as the setting, the architecture, the atmosphere and the food.

Inspections

We visit every place in the guide to get a feel for how both house and owner tick. We don't take a clipboard and we don't have a list of what is acceptable and what is not. Instead, we chat for an hour or so with the owner and look round. It's all very informal, but it gives us an excellent idea of who would enjoy staying there. If the visit happens to be the last of the day, we may stay the night. Once in the book properties are re-inspected every four years or so, to keep things fresh and accurate.

Feedback

In between inspections we rely on feedback from our army of readers, as well as from staff members who are encouraged to visit properties across the series. This feedback is invaluable to us and we always follow up on comments. So do tell us whether your stay has been

a joy or not, if the atmosphere was great or stuffy, the owners cheery or bored. The accuracy of the book depends on what you, and our inspectors, tell us. A lot of the new entries in each edition are recommended by our readers, so keep telling us about new places you've discovered too. Please visit our site, www.sawdays.co.uk/recommend to tell us about your discoveries.

However, please do not tell us if the bedside light was broken, or the shower head was scummy. Tell the owner, immediately, and get them to do something about it. Most owners are more than happy to correct problems and will bend over backwards to help. Far better than bottling it up and then writing to us a week later!

Photo: Hillview Cottage, Somerset, entry 431

Subscriptions

Owners pay to appear in this guide. Their fee goes towards the high costs of inspecting, developing our website and producing an all-colour book. We only include places that we like and find special for one reason or another, so it is not possible for anyone to buy their way onto these pages. Nor is it possible for the owner to write their own description. We will say if the bedrooms are small, or if a main road is near. We do our best to avoid misleading people.

Disclaimer

We make no claims to pure objectivity in choosing these places. They are here simply because we like them. Our opinions and tastes are ours alone and this book is a statement of them; we hope you will share them. We have done our utmost to get our facts right but apologise unreservedly for any mistakes that may have crept in.

You should know that we don't check such things as fire regulations, swimming pool security or any other laws with which owners of properties receiving paying guests should comply. This is the responsibility of the owners.

Photo: Launceston Farm, Dorset, entry 172

Finding the right place for you

All these places are special in one way or another. All have been visited and then written about honestly so that you can take what you like and leave the rest. Those of you who swear by Sawday's books trust our write-ups precisely because we don't have a blanket standard; we include places simply because we like them. But we all have different priorities, so do read the descriptions carefully and pick out the places where you will be comfortable. If something is particularly important to you then do check when you book: a simple question or two can avoid misunderstandings.

Maps

Each property is flagged with its entry number on the maps at the front. These maps are a great starting point for planning your trip, but please don't use them as anything other than a general guide – use a decent road map for real navigation. Most places will send you detailed instructions once you have booked your stay.

Symbols

Below each entry you will see some symbols, which are explained at the very back of the book. They are based on the information given to us by the owners. However, things do change: bikes may be under repair or a new pool may have been put in. Please use the symbols as a guide rather than an absolute statement of fact and double-check anything that is important to you — owners occasionally bend their own rules, so it's worth asking

if you may take your child or dog even if they don't have the symbol.

Children – The 👶 symbol shows places which are happy to accept children of all ages. This does not mean that they will necessarily have cots, high chairs, etc. If an owner welcomes children but only those above a certain age, we have put these details at the end of their write-up. These houses do not have the child symbol, but even these folk may accept your younger child if you are the only guests. Many who say no to children do so not because they don't like them but because they may have a steep stair, an unfenced pond or they find balancing the needs of mixed age groups too challenging.

Pets – Our 🐕 symbol shows places which are happy to accept pets. It means they can sleep in the bedroom with you, but not on the bed. Be realistic about your pet – if it is

nervous or excitable or doesn't like the company of other dogs, people, chickens, children, then say so. Do let the owners know when booking that you intend to bring your pet – particularly if it is not the usual dog!

Owners' pets – The 🐈 symbol is given when the owners have their own pet on the premises. It may not be a cat! But it is there to warn you that you may be greeted by a dog, serenaded by a parrot, or indeed sat upon by a cat.

Quick reference indices

At the back of the book you'll find a number of quick reference indices that will help you choose the place that is just right for you.

Photo: Hanover House, Gloucestershire, entry 209

In this edition you'll find listings of properties where:
• at least one bedroom or bathroom is accessible for wheelchair users
• guests' pets can sleep in the bedroom (but not on the bed)
• children of all ages are welcome. Cots, highchairs etc are not necessarily available.

B&B Awards

We've chosen B&Bs that we think deserve a special mention. Our categories are:
• One of a kind;
• Favourite newcomers;
• Most praised breakfast;
• Old favourites.

More details are given on pages 14-17, and all the award winners have been stamped.

Types of places

Some houses have rooms in annexes or stables, barns or garden 'wings', some of which feel part of the house, some of which don't. If you have a strong preference for being in the throng or for being apart, check those details. Consider your surroundings when you are packing: large, ancient country houses may be cooler than you are used to; city places and working farms may be noisy at times; and that peacock or cockerel we mention may disturb you. Light sleepers should pack car plugs, and take a dressing gown if there's a separate bathroom (though these are sometimes provided).

Some owners give you a front door key so you may come and go as you please; others like to have the house empty between, say, 10am and 4pm. If you would prefer not to wander far during the day then look for the places that have the 'Stay all day' quick reference at the back of the book.

Sawday's Canopy & Stars   CANOPY&STARS

These are some of our more outdoor places. They could be anything from palatial treehouses to rustic wagons and everything in-between. The same standards of inspection and selection apply, but you might find things delightfully different to what you're used to. You could be clambering up a ladder to bed, throwing another log on the wood-burner or wheeling your luggage in a barrow, so take a look and keep your mind open to the outdoors.

These entries are highlighted with a green Canopy & Stars logo.

Rooms

Bedrooms – We tell you if a room is a double, twin/double (i.e. with zip and link beds), suite (with a sitting area), family or single. Most owners are flexible and can juggle beds or bedrooms; talk to them about what you need before you book. Staying in a B&B will not be like staying in a hotel; it is rare to be given your own room key and your bed will not necessarily be made during your stay, or your room cleaned. Make sure you are clear about the room that you have booked, its views, bathroom and beds, etc.

Bathrooms – Most bedrooms in this book have an en suite bath or shower room; we only mention bathroom details when they do not. So, you may get a 'separate' bathroom (yours alone but not en suite) or a shared bathroom. Under certain entries we mention that two rooms share a bathroom and are 'let to same party only'. Please do not assume this means you must be a group of friends to apply; it simply means that if you book one of these rooms you will not be sharing a bathroom with strangers. If these things are important to you, please check when booking. Bath/shower means a bath with shower over; bath and shower means there is a separate shower unit.

Sitting rooms – Most B&B owners offer guests the family sitting room to share, or they provide a sitting room specially for guests, but do not assume that every bedroom or sitting room has a TV.

Meals
Unless we say otherwise, a full cooked breakfast is included. Some owners – particularly in London – will give you a good continental breakfast instead. Often you will feast on local sausage and bacon, eggs from resident hens, homemade breads and jams. In some you may have organic yogurts and beautifully presented fruit compotes. Some owners are fairly unbending about breakfast times, others are happy to just wait until you want it, or even bring it to you in bed.

Apart from breakfast, no meals should be expected unless you have arranged them in advance. Although we don't say so on each entry – the repetition a few hundred times would be tedious – all owners who

Photo: The Old Store House, Powys, entry 680

provide packed lunch, lunch or dinner need ADVANCE NOTICE. And they want to get things right for you so, when booking, please discuss your diet and meal times. Meal prices are quoted per person, and dinner is often a social occasion shared with your hosts and other guests.

Do eat in if you can – this book is teeming with good cooks. And how much more relaxing after a day out to have to move no further than the dining room for an excellent dinner, and to eat and drink knowing there's only a flight of stairs between you and your bed. Very few of our houses are licensed, but most are happy for you to bring your own drink.

If you do decide to head out for supper, you can find recommendations of our favourite pubs on our *Special Places to Eat and Drink* microsite, see: www.sawdays.co.uk/pubs. If a B&B has a pub nearby, you can see this on their page on our website, too.

Prices and minimum stays
Each entry gives a price PER ROOM for two people. We also include prices for single rooms, and let you know if there will be any extra to pay, should you choose to loll in a double bed on your own.

The price range for each B&B covers a one-night stay in the cheapest room in low season to the most expensive in high season. Some owners charge more at certain times (during regattas or festivals, for example) and some charge less for stays of more than one night. Some owners ask for a two-night minimum stay and we mention this where possible. Most of our houses could fill many times over on peak weekends and during the summer; book early, especially if you have specific needs.

Booking and cancellation
You may not receive a reply to your booking enquiry immediately; B&Bs are not hotels and the owners may be away. When you speak to the owner double-check the price you will pay for B&B and for any meals.

Requests for deposits vary; some are non-refundable, especially in our London homes, and some owners may charge you for the whole of the booked stay in advance. Some cancellation policies are more stringent than others. It is also worth noting that some owners will take the money directly from your credit/debit card without contacting you to discuss it. Ask them to explain

their cancellation policy clearly before booking to avoid a nasty surprise.

Payment
Most of our owners take cash and UK cheques with a cheque card. Some take credit cards; if they do we have given them the appropriate symbol. Check that your particular credit card is acceptable.

Tipping
Owners do not expect tips. If you have been treated with extraordinary kindness, write to them, or leave a small gift. Please tell us, too – we love to hear, and we do note all feedback.

Arrivals and departures
Say roughly what time you will arrive (normally after 4pm), as most hosts like to welcome you personally. Be on time if you have booked dinner; if, despite best efforts, you are delayed, phone to give warning.

Closed
When given in months this means the whole of the month stated.

Photo: Ramsden Farm, Kent, entry 278

Sawday's
BED & BREAKFAST
INSPECTED & SELECTED
2014/15

We've chosen 12 absolute gems for our annual Sawday's B&B Awards. All our B&Bs are special, but these have been chosen as they stand out in one of these four categories. So set off to discover them – all offer individual stays in smashing places.

Award categories:

One of a kind

Favourite newcomers

Most praised breakfast

Old favourites

One of a kind

Sawday's has always celebrated individuality, generosity of spirit and a sense of fun. These inspiring B&Bs stood out this year – we hope you enjoy them as much as we do:

Entry 111

Fingals
Dittisham, Devon

Entry 283

Breedon Hall
Breedon-on-the-Hill, Derbyshire

Entry 534

Old Country Farm & The Lighthouse
Mathon, Worcestershire

Favourite newcomers

Discovering a new Special Place is always exciting. We delight in meeting new B&B owners, hearing their stories and helping them reach likeminded people who want to stay in B&Bs with personality and charm. We've highlighted all the new ones and love them all – here's a selection of our favourites:

Entry 578

Castle of Park
Banff, Aberdeenshire

Entry 595

Three Glens
Thornhill, Dumfries & Galloway

Entry 675

Pottery Cottage
Clyro, Herefordshire

Most praised breakfast

A good breakfast is a must! Many of our owners bake their own bread, cook the perfect egg from happy hens, press apples from the orchard and more. This year's winners bring you imaginative homemade spreads with great local and home-produced ingredients:

Entry 419

Pool House
Woolavington, Somerset

Entry 447

Old Reading Room
Mells, Somerset

Entry 449

Jericho
Mells, Somerset

Old favourites

We wanted to celebrate all that is best about our longest running and most loyal B&B owners. It's their boundless good humour and kindness that makes for an unforgettable stay in these fantastic B&Bs. Our old favourites are:

Entry 156

Fullers Earth
Cattistock, Dorset

Entry 204

Clapton Manor
Clapton-on-the-Hill, Gloucestershire

Entry 413

Bashfords Farmhouse
West Bagborough, Somerset

Vintage Vacations, Isle of Wight, entry 248

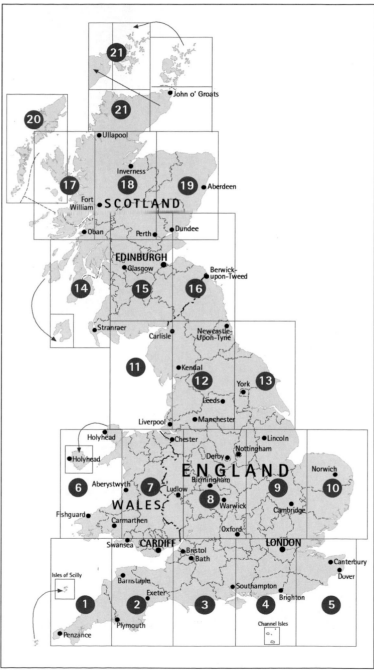

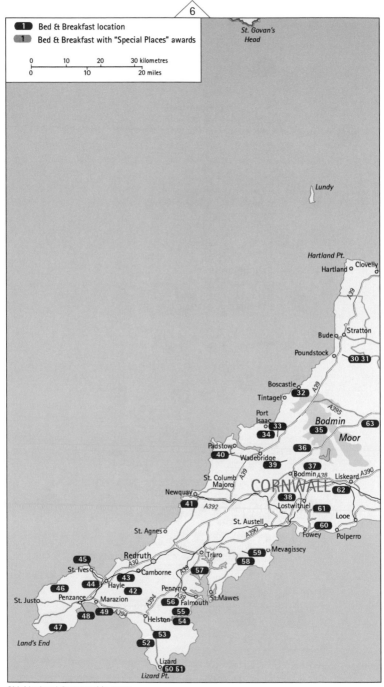

6

1 Bed & Breakfast location
1 Bed & Breakfast with "Special Places" awards

0   10   20   30 kilometres
0   10   20 miles

St. Govan's
Head

Lundy

Hartland Pt.
Hartland ○ Clovelly
Bude ○ ─ Stratton
Poundstock ○ ── **30 31**

Boscastle ○
Tintagel ○ **32**
Port
Isaac ○ **33**   **Bodmin**   **63**
34   **35**   **Moor**
Padstow ○   **36**
40
Wadebridge ○
39   **37**
St. Columb   Bodmin A38 Liskeard A390
Major ○   **CORNWALL**   **62**
Newquay ○
41 A392   Lostwithiel **61**
38   Looe
St. Agnes ○   **60**
Redruth   Fowey   Polperro
45   Truro ○   **59** Mevagissey
St. Ives ○   **57**   **58**
43 Camborne
44 Hayle
46   **42**   Penryn ○
St. Just ○   Penzance ○ Marazion   **56** Falmouth   St.Mawes
48 **49**   **55**
Helston ○ **54**
47   **53**
Land's End   **52**
Lizard
50 51
Lizard Pt.

©Maidenhead Cartographic, 2104

Map 2

21

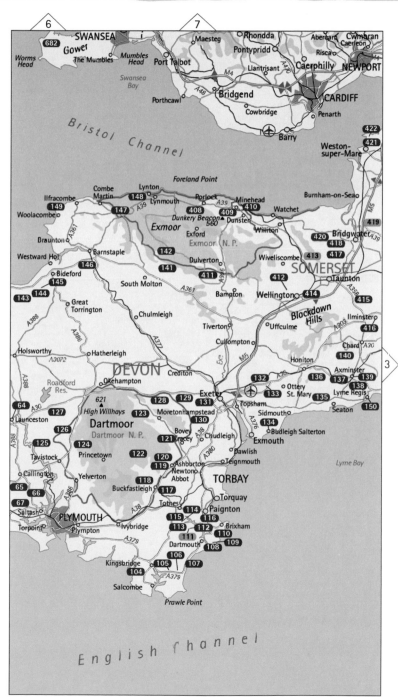

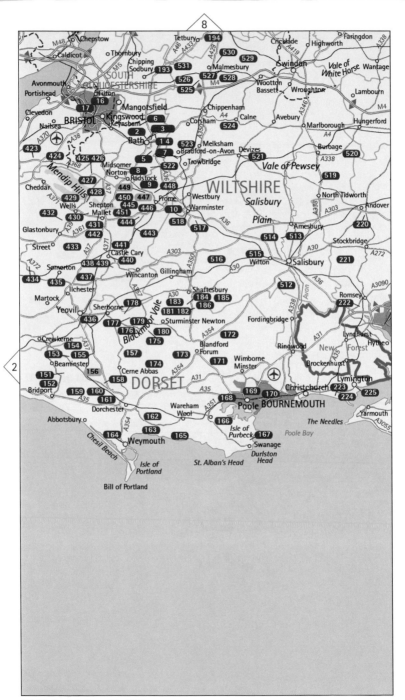

Map 4

23

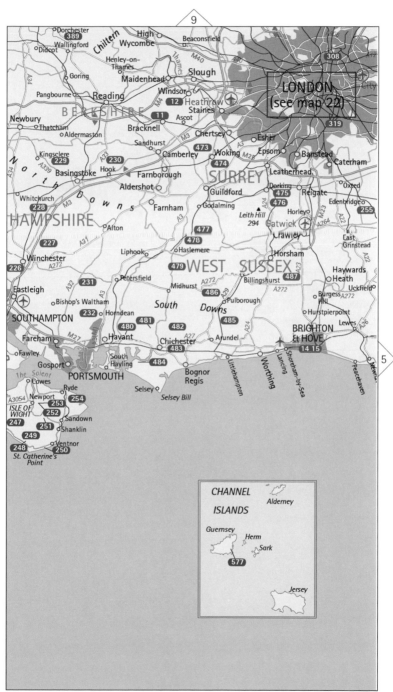

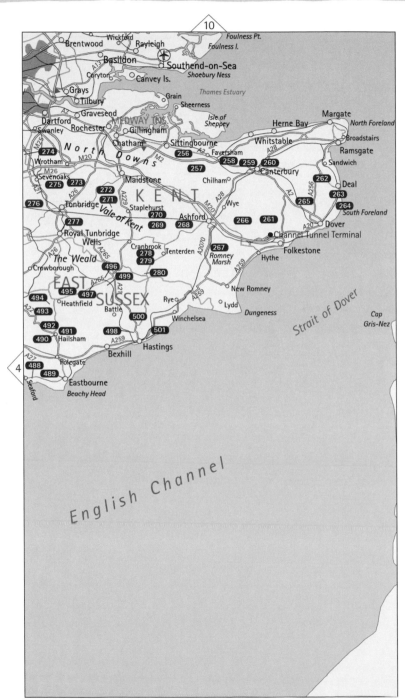

Map 6

25

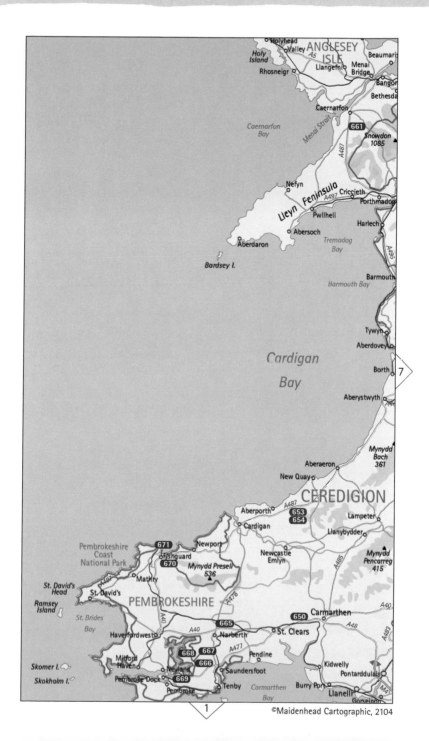

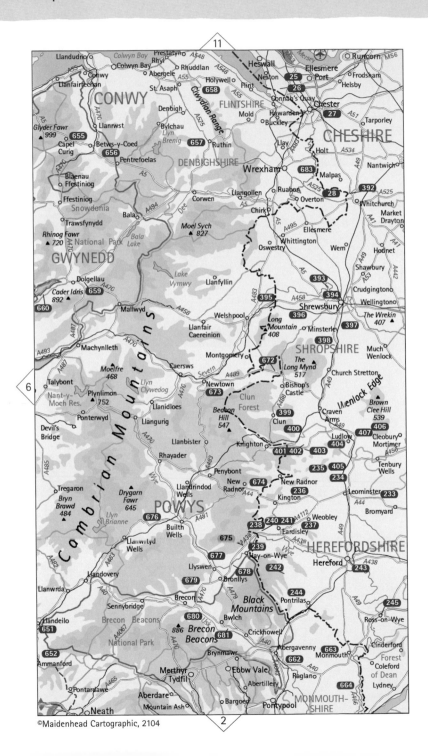

Map 8   27

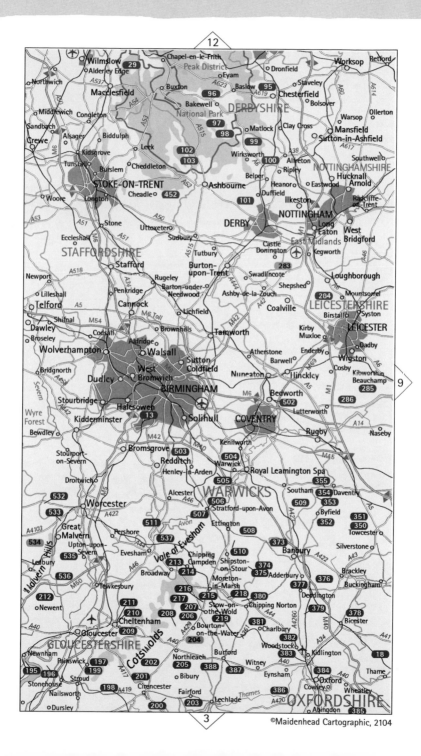

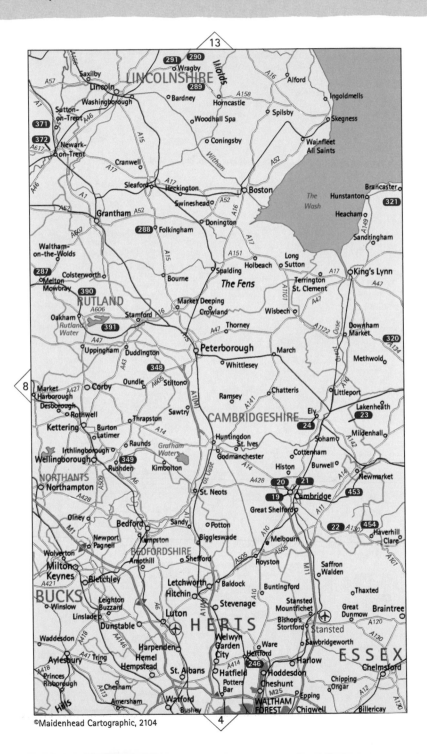

Map 10   29

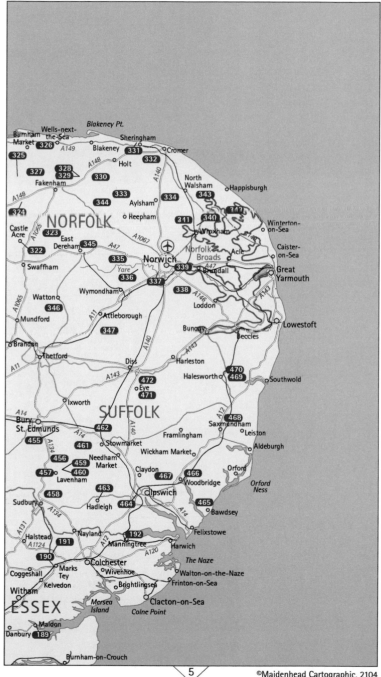

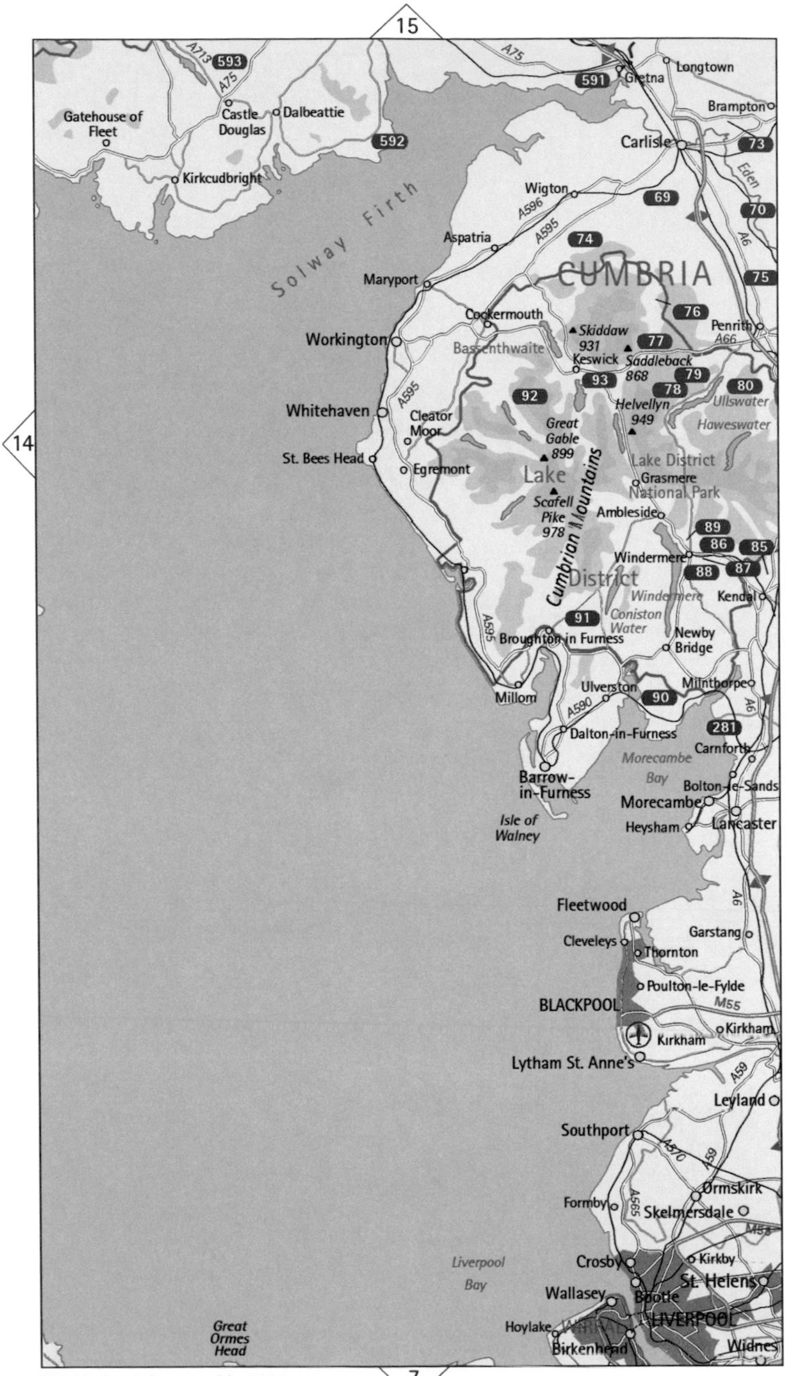

15

A713
A75
593
A75
591
Gretna
Longtown
Castle Douglas
Dalbeattie
Brampton
Gatehouse of Fleet
592
Carlisle
73
Kirkcudbright
Wigton
A596
69
Eden
70
Solway Firth
Aspatria
74
A595
CUMBRIA
75
Maryport
Cockermouth
76
Penrith
▲ Skiddaw 931
A66
Workington
Bassenthwaite
Keswick
Saddleback
868
77
Helvellyn
949
78
79
80
Ullswater
93
92
Whitehaven
A595
Cleator Moor
Great Gable
▲ 899
Haweswater
St. Bees Head
Egremont
Lake
Grasmere
Lake District National Park
Scafell Pike
978
Ambleside
Cumbrian Mountains
89
86
85
Windermere
88
87
District
Windermere
Kendal
91
Coniston Water
Newby Bridge
A595
Broughton-in-Furness
Millom
Ulverston
A590
90
Milnthorpe
A6
Dalton-in-Furness
281
Carnforth
Morecambe Bay
Barrow-in-Furness
Bolton-le-Sands
Morecambe
Isle of Walney
Heysham
Lancaster
A6
Fleetwood
Cleveleys
Thornton
Garstang
BLACKPOOL
Poulton-le-Fylde
M55
Kirkham
Kirkham
Lytham St. Anne's
A59
Leyland
Southport
A570
A59
Ormskirk
Formby
A565
Skelmersdale
M58
Liverpool Bay
Crosby
Kirkby
St. Helens
Wallasey
Bootle
LIVERPOOL
Great Ormes Head
Hoylake
Birkenhead
Widnes

14

7

Map 12   31

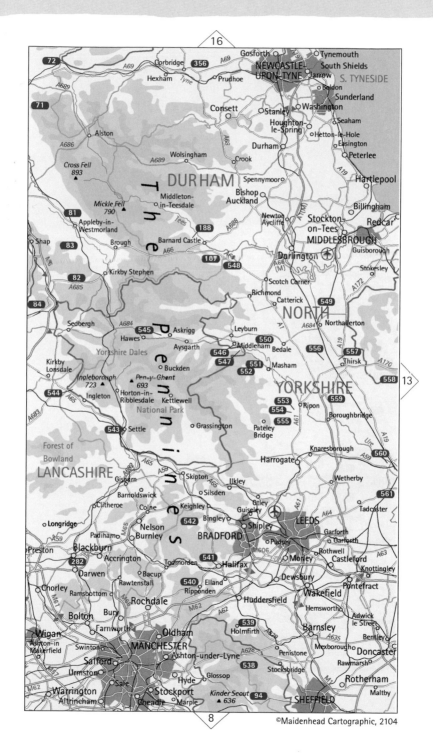

©Maidenhead Cartographic, 2104

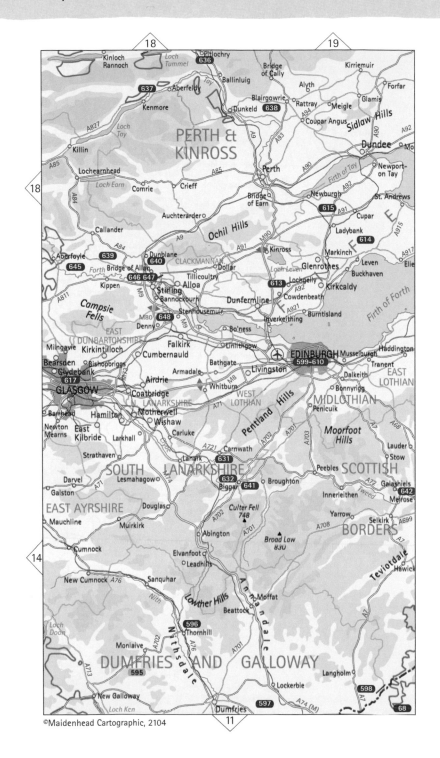

Map 16   35

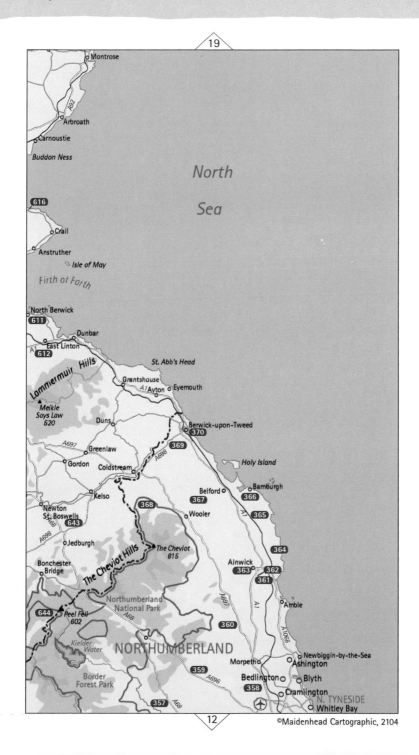

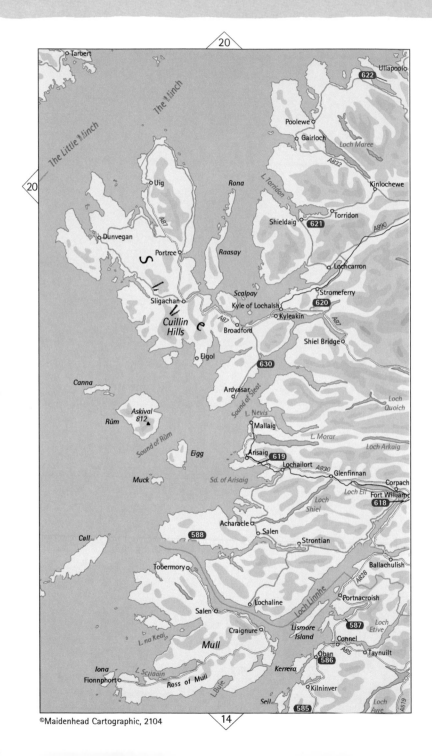

Map 18

37

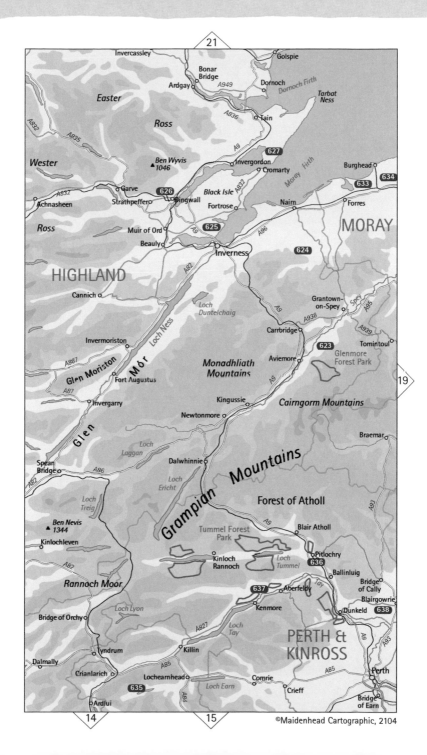

©Maidenhead Cartographic, 2104

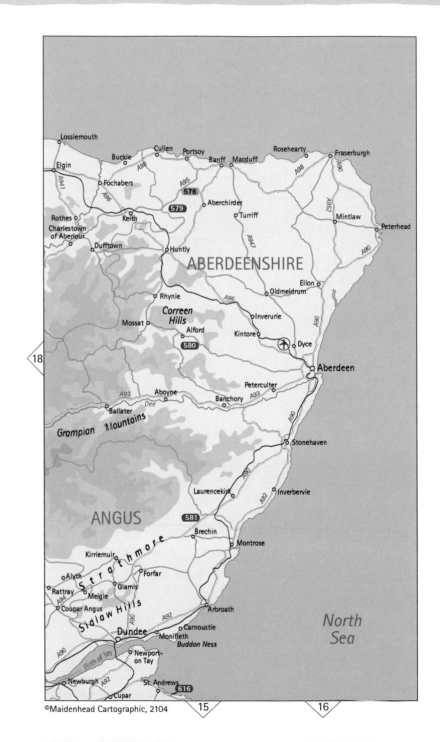

Map 20   39

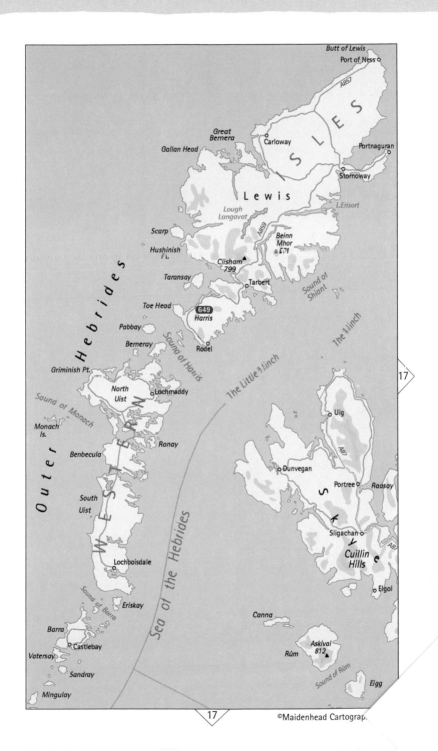

Butt of Lewis
Port of Ness
A857
ISLES
Great Bernera
Carloway
Gallan Head
Portnaguran
Stornoway
Lewis
Lough Langavat
L.Erisort
A859
Scarp
Beinn Mhor
Hushinish Pt.
Clisham
799
Taransay
Tarbert
Sound of Shiant
Toe Head
649
Harris
Pabbay
Berneray
Rodel
Sound of Harris
Griminish Pt.
North Uist
Lochmaddy
The Little Minch
The Minch
Uig
Sound of Monach
Monach Is.
Ronay
A87
Benbecula
Dunvegan
Portree
Raasay
South Uist
Sea of the Hebrides
Sligachan
Cuillin Hills
A87
Lochboisdale
Eriskay
Canna
Elgol
Barra
Vatersay
Castlebay
Askival
812
Sandray
Rùm
Sound of Rùm
Eigg
Mingulay

Hebrides
Outer
WESTERN
Skye

17

©Maidenhead Cartograp.

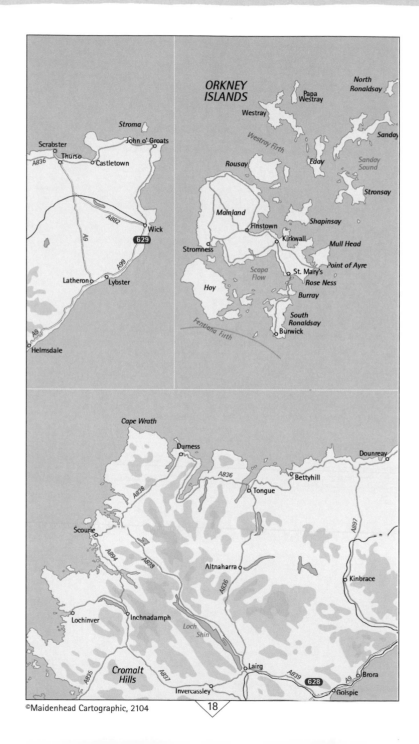

ORKNEY
ISLANDS

North
Ronaldsay

Papa
Westray

Westray

Stroma

John o' Groats

Scrabster

Thurso

Castletown

A836

Westray Firth

Sanday

Rousay

Eday

Sanday
Sound

Stronsay

A882

A9

Wick

Mainland

Finstown

Shapinsay

Kirkwall

Mull Head

629

Stromness

Point of Ayre

A99

Latheron

Lybster

Scapa
Flow

St. Mary's

Rose Ness

Hoy

Burray

Fentland Firth

South
Ronaldsay

A9

Helmsdale

Burwick

Cape Wrath

Durness

Dounreay

A836

Bettyhill

A838

Tongue

A897

Scourie

A894

A838

Altnaharra

A836

Kinbrace

Lochinver

Inchnadamph

Loch
Shin

A835

Cromalt
Hills

A837

Lairg

A839

628

A9

Brora

Invercassley

Golspie

Map 22

41

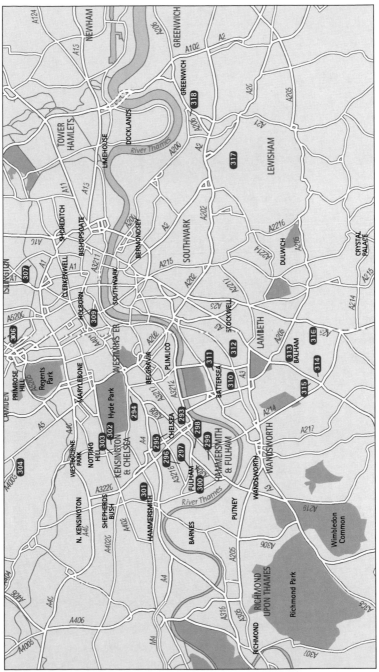

England

Bath & N.E. Somerset

Pitt House

You couldn't be closer to the centre, nor on a calmer street. This Grade I-listed, seven-storey house, once home to William Pitt the Younger, is now inhabited by a warm, creative couple with a wry sense of humour. Inside: Georgian splendour matched by 21st-century eccentricity. Find sanded floorboards, walls of pure white, dazzling marble busts, a cow hide rug, a tumble of classical and oriental styles... collectors of antiques will keel over in a state of bliss. Bedrooms (up four flights of stairs) are only marginally less exotic, and share a fabulous bathroom and sitting room. Breakfast is the finest of continental. Outstanding.

Rooms	2 doubles sharing bath/shower (separate shower): £90–£110. Singles £75–£80.
Meals	Continental breakfast. Pubs/restaurants 2-minute walk.
Closed	Rarely.

David & Sarah Bridgwater
Pitt House,
15 Johnstone Street, Bath,
Bath & N.E. Somerset BA2 4DH

Tel	+44 (0)1225 471580
Mobile	+44 (0)7710 124376
Email	david.j.bridgwater@btinternet.com

Entry 1   Map 3

Bath & N.E. Somerset

77 Great Pulteney Street

Elegant stone steps lead down past exotic ferns to a spacious garden flat in this broad street of grand Grade I-listed houses. Inside all is pale wood, modern art, bergère chairs and palms. Downstairs is a large, smart bedroom and bathroom with loads of books and its own door to a delightful small sunny garden. On fine mornings you breakfast here, or choose the gorgeous upstairs dining room: fine local bacon and sausages and fruit from the allotment. Ian is a keen cook so dinner will also be special, but there are lots of good places to eat – and shop – nearby. Henry may play the Northumbrian pipes for you if you ask nicely...

Minimum stay: 2 nights at weekends.

Rooms	1 double: £85–£110. Singles from £60.
Meals	Dinner £25. Packed lunch from £5.
Closed	Rarely.

Ian Critchley & Henry Ford
77 Great Pulteney Street,
Bath,
Bath & N.E. Somerset BA2 4DL

Tel	+44 (0)1225 466659
Email	critchford@77pulteneyst.co.uk
Web	www.77pulteneyst.co.uk

Entry 2   Map 3

Bath & N.E. Somerset

Sir Walter Elliot's House

Utterly wonderful hosts at this Grade I-listed house. On one of Bath's finest Regency terraces, it has been so beautifully restored that the BBC filmed it for *Persuasion*; Jane Austen Society members often stay. Up several stairs are bedrooms flooded with light, two with views over Sydney Gardens, one with a bathroom in marquina marble, cherrywood and ebony. Have breakfast in the convivial family kitchen, or in the plant-filled conservatory. For the adventurous, Mechthild will serve an Austrian alternative – cold meats and cheeses, fresh rye breads and homemade cakes. *Herrlich!*

Minimum stay: 2 nights at weekends.

Rooms	3 twin/doubles: £95-£155. Singles £90-£115.
Meals	Pub/restaurant 300 yds.
Closed	Rarely.

Mechthild & Julian Self von Hippel
Sir Walter Elliot's House,
95 Sydney Place, Bath,
Bath & N.E. Somerset BA2 6NE

Tel	+44 (0)1225 469435
Mobile	+44 (0)7737 793772
Email	visitus@SirWalterElliotsHouse.co.uk
Web	www.sirwalterelliotshouse.co.uk

Entry 3   Map 3

Bath & N.E. Somerset

The Georgian Stables

Minutes from Bath centre... enjoy independence in converted stables, or choose Sydney Room in the main house. Bedrooms are stylish and snug, all is white and airy with splashes of colour and shelves of books. The stables, of original stone, have a smart wet room and a cobbled terrace; both rooms have their own sitting room. Breakfast is served by Hilary's friendly housekeeper: homemade muesli, fruits, free-range eggs, pains au chocolat. A canal runs past the end of lovely gardens with unbeatable views. Opposite: acres of National Trust land and the Skyline Circular Walk; take a picnic, watch the hot-air balloons rise over the city.

Minimum stay: 2 nights at weekends.

Rooms	House – 1 double with sitting room; Stables – 1 double with sitting room: £90-£150.
Meals	Pubs/restaurants 8-minute walk.
Closed	Occasionally.

Hilary Cooper
The Georgian Stables,
41 Sydney Buildings, Bath,
Bath & N.E. Somerset BA2 6DB

Tel	+44 (0)1225 465956
Mobile	+44 (0)7798 810286
Email	thegeorgianstables@gmail.com

Entry 4   Map 3

Bath & N.E. Somerset

De Montalt Wood

Deep valley views, acres of gardens and woodland to roam, pretty places to sit and muse... all just a couple of miles from Bath. Charles and Ann's Victorian house is a smart family home with a comfortable country feel. Airy bedrooms have big beds with fine linen, a sofa, TV, and garden vistas; bathrooms are luxurious with rain showers and bottled scented things. You breakfast in the elegant dining room: a full English, poached haddock, fruits on the sideboard, lashings of coffee. There are lovely walks with good pubs on the way, bluebells fill the woods in spring and Bath brims with history, spa and good restaurants.

Rooms	1 double; 1 double with separate bath: £110–£120.
Meals	Pubs/restaurants 5-minute drive.
Closed	Christmas & New Year.

	Charles & Ann Kent
	De Montalt Wood,
	Summer Lane, Combe Down, Bath,
	Bath & N.E. Somerset BA2 7EU
Tel	+44 (0)1225 838001
Email	bookings@demontaltwood.co.uk
Web	www.demontaltwood.co.uk

Entry 5   Map 3

Bath & N.E. Somerset

The Power House

On top of Bath's highest hill lies Rikki's Bauhaus-inspired home, its glass walls making the most of a magical spot and a sensational view; on a clear day you can see the Welsh hills. In the vast open-plan living space downstairs – homely, inviting, inspiring – are treasures from a lifetime of travels: ancient Tuareg camel sacks, kitsch Art Deco pots, gorgeous Persian chests. Bedrooms are big, airy and light, with doors onto a huge balcony – and those views. Rikki is an incredible chef and uses the freshest and finest ingredients from Bath's farmers' market, ten minutes away. Breakfasts are superb.

Rooms	1 double; studio – 1 double: £100–£120. 1 single: £70. 2 further small doubles available, sharing bathrooms.
Meals	Dinner £25. Pubs/restaurants 3-minute drive.
Closed	Rarely.

	Rikki Howard
	The Power House,
	Brockham End, Lansdown, Bath,
	Bath & N.E. Somerset BA1 9BY
Tel	+44 (0)1225 446308
Email	rikkijacout@aol.com

Entry 6   Map 3

Old Mill Treehouse

A smartly designed cabin on stilts with a well-finished interior — clean and light — and lashings of luxury, including a wall-mounted TV. Six miles from Bath, Tony and Beverley's treehouse is in the grounds of their Old Mill; over the stream and down a winding path. You'll have the skies to yourselves (not counting the wildlife), but climb back down and great pub food is only a 5-minute walk away. This is handy as your kitchen facilities are limited to a wine cooler for a glass of bubbly on the balcony! It's a magical spot with views towards the village and a delicious breakfast is delivered each morning. Stylish and fun.

Minimum stay: 2 nights. Book through Sawday's Canopy & Stars online or by phone.

Rooms	Treehouse for 2: £140–£180. Extra camp bed available £10 per night.
Meals	Continental breakfast included.
Closed	Never.

Sawday's Canopy & Stars
Old Mill Treehouse,
The Old Mill, Wellow Lane,
Norton St Philip, Bath,
Bath & N.E. Somerset BA2 7NB
Tel   +44 (0)117 204 7830
Email   enquiries@canopyandstars.co.uk
Web   www.canopyandstars.co.uk/oldmill

Entry 7   Map 3

Pitfour House

Georgian gentility in a village near Bath. This is where the rector would live in an Austen novel: it's handsome, respectable, and the feel extends inside, where convivial hosts Frances (a keen cook) and Martin (keen gardener) put you at ease in their elegant home. The creamy guest sitting room gleams with period furniture, the dining room is panelled and parqueted, fresh flowers abound. The two bedrooms — one with en suite shower, one with a private bath — are compact but detailed with antiques. Take tea in the neat walled garden, admire the vegetable patch, then taste the spoils in one of Frances's fine suppers.

Minimum stay: 2 nights at weekends.

Rooms	1 twin/double; 1 twin/double with separate bath: £88–£98. Singles £25.
Meals	Dinner £28–£35. Restaurant 1.5 miles.
Closed	Rarely.

Frances Hardman
Pitfour House,
High Street,
Timsbury, Bath,
Bath & N.E. Somerset BA2 0HT
Tel   +44 (0)1761 479554
Email   pitfourhouse@btinternet.com
Web   www.pitfourhouse.co.uk

Entry 8   Map 3

Bath & N.E. Somerset

Hollytree Cottage

Meandering lanes lead to this 16th-century cottage, with roses round the door, a grandfather clock in the hall and an air of genteel tranquillity. The cottage charm has been updated with Regency mahogany and sumptuous sofas. The bedrooms have views over undulating countryside; pretty bathrooms have oils and lotions. On sunny days breakfast is in the lovely garden room looking onto a colourful ornamental patio, sloping lawns, a pond, flowering shrubs and trees. A place to come for absolute peace, birdsong and walks; the joys of elegant Bath are 20 minutes away and Julia knows the area well; let her help plan your trips.

Sorry no card payments.

Rooms	1 double, 1 twin, 1 four-poster: £85–£95. Singles £55–£60.
Meals	Pub/restaurant 0.5 miles.
Closed	Rarely.

Julia Naismith
Hollytree Cottage,
Laverton, Bath,
Bath & N.E. Somerset BA2 7QZ

Tel	+44 (0)1373 830786
Mobile	+44 (0)7564 196703
Email	jnaismith@toucansurf.com
Web	www.hollytreecottagebath.co.uk

Entry 9   Map 3

Bath & N.E. Somerset

New Entry — INSPECTED & SELECTED A SPECIAL PLACE

Reeves Barn

Drive under the huge willow to find prettily converted barns and an away-from-it-all feel. Artist Barbette welcomes you with tea and cakes — or prosecco and canapés if it's early evening. The independent studio room comes with big glass doors, soft colours, limed beams, a simple wet room with scented oils (and, if you pay extra, a mini kitchen for meals). Choose an English breakfast or a breakfast hamper — wake and eat when you want! The bedroom in the main barn has its own entrance and a lovely roll top tub. Snooze in the sun by pots of roses, curl up by the wood-burner. A sweet retreat, with Bath, Wells and Babington House close by.

Rooms	1 double; studio – 1 double with sitting room & kitchenette: £85–£105. Extra bed/sofabed available £10 per person per night.
Meals	Dinner, 3 courses, £35. Pub 2 miles.
Closed	Rarely.

Barbette Saunders
Reeves Barn,
17 Whitbourne Springs,
Corsley, Warminster,
Bath & N.E. Somerset BA12 7RF

Tel	+44 (0)1373 832106
Mobile	+44 (0)7796 687806
Email	barbettesaunders@gmail.com

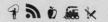

Entry 10   Map 3

Berkshire

Whitehouse Farm Cottage

In the quiet village of Binfield, an idyllic find: a 17th-century farmhouse with a gorgeous garden (NGS), and two charmingly converted buildings. Garden Cottage has a beamed drawing room downstairs and an immaculate gallery bedroom. The Forge – deliciously cosy – keeps the blacksmith's fireplace and overlooks an atmospheric courtyard garden with pebble mosaics. The single is in the house with its own cosy sitting room. Fabulous locally sourced breakfasts with freshly baked bread are served in the house by delightful Keir and Louise, film prop makers by profession. Hugely popular with guests and just about perfect!

Rooms	Garden Cottage – 1 double with sitting room; The Forge – 1 double with summerhouse: £85–£120. 1 single with sitting room: £75–£85.
Meals	Pubs/restaurants within 1 mile.
Closed	Occasionally.

	Keir & Louise Lusby
	Whitehouse Farm Cottage, Murrell Hill Lane, Binfield, Bracknell, Berkshire RG42 4BY
Tel	+44 (0)1344 423688
Mobile	+44 (0)7711 948889
Email	garden.cottages@ntlworld.com

Entry 11   Map 4

Berkshire

Gilbey's

Step up the stairs to your elegant top-floor studio; it's above a buzzy restaurant and in the heart of pretty Eton. Charming staff greet and look after you, and all is gleaming with rich autumn colours, cream carpets, immaculate linen, smart bathrooms and a rooftop view of Windsor Castle. Relax or work – there is a huge comfy sofa and flat-screen TV as well as useful desks. A generous continental breakfast is delivered to you: fresh bread and croissants, yogurts and fruit. There are interesting shops and galleries galore, you're a stroll from the college or river trips on the Thames, and Waterloo is 50 minutes by train.

Rooms	1 double: £175–£200.
Meals	Continental breakfast. Supper £18.50. Pubs/restaurants 300 yds.
Closed	Christmas.

	Caroline Gilbey
	Gilbey's, 82-83 High Street, Eton, Windsor, Berkshire SL4 6AF
Tel	+44 (0)1753 854921
Email	caroline@gilbeygroup.com
Web	www.gilbeygroup.com/eton

Entry 12   Map 4

Birmingham

Woodbrooke Quaker Study Centre

A pleasure to find ten tranquil acres (woodlands, lawns, lake and walled garden) so close to the centre of Birmingham – run by such special people. This impressive Georgian mansion was donated by George Cadbury to the Quakers in 1903, as a place for study and contemplation. And so it remains. There are corridors aplenty and public rooms big and small: a library, a silent room, a lovely new garden lounge, and a dining hall where organic buffet meals feature fruit and veg from the grounds. Bedrooms, spread over several buildings, are carpeted, comfortable, light and airy, and most have en suite showers. Welcoming, nurturing, historic.

Rooms	7 doubles, 7 twins (most rooms are en suite): £68. 45 singles (most rooms are en suite): £50.
Meals	Lunch £10. Dinner £10. Pubs/restaurants 15-minute walk.
Closed	Christmas & Boxing Day.

Becky Thomas
Woodbrooke Quaker Study Centre,
1046 Bristol Road, Selly Oak,
Birmingham B29 6LJ

Tel	+44 (0)121 472 5171
Email	enquiries@woodbrooke.org.uk
Web	www.woodbrooke.org.uk

Entry 13   Map 8

Brighton & Hove

4-5 Palmeira Square

Drift along Brighton seafront to find the Regency splendour of Hove's Palmeira Square. Susie welcomes you into her spacious ground-floor flat where rooms are flooded with light, ceilings are high and furnishings have pizzazz – kilims on bamboo floors, funky chandeliers, elegant antiques. Your bedroom overlooks a leafy courtyard at the back; Susie will give you either the lovely peppermint cool one, or the large plum-coloured one with a new wet room. She has lived in Portugal, Brazil and Bordeaux, works from home and delivers a delicious breakfast to your door, or at a pretty seat in the window bay – turn your head to catch the sea.

Minimum stay: 2 nights. Babies welcome but unsuitable for older children.

Rooms	1 double: £110-£140.
Meals	Continental breakfast. Pub/restaurant 500 yds.
Closed	Rarely.

Susie de Castilho
4-5 Palmeira Square,
Flat 1, Hove,
Brighton & Hove BN3 2JA

Tel	+44 (0)1273 719087
Mobile	+44 (0)7917 562771
Email	stay@2staybrighton.co.uk
Web	www.2staybrighton.co.uk

Entry 14   Map 4

Brighton & Hove

Bristol

The Art House Hove

Peaceful, close to the sea and in the heart of popular Hove, this Victorian villa is a friendly town treat. Bedrooms on the top floor are furnished in an eclectic style, mixing antique finds with quirky light-fittings; art books, flowers and splashes of colour complete the picture. Dexter and Liz give you a breakfast feast: muesli, fruit salad, patisseries fresh from the bakery, eggs, smoked salmon, hash browns. Liz runs mosaic courses in the garden studio and her wonderful work decorates the house. Dozens of cafés and bistros are on the doorstep; Brighton is a 15-minute amble along the promenade.

Minimum stay: 2 nights at weekends.

The Rooftop Rockets

Va va vroom… Four sleek, cleverly designed aluminium caravans — British-built, American-inspired — have landed on the top floor of Brooks Guesthouse! They've a 'grass' terrace with big plant pots, rooftop views, goose down duvets on five-foot wide beds (three have fold-down singles too), and surprising mod cons like swish Hansgrohe eco showers (with fluffy towels) and techy kit: iPod dock, TV, DVD. Breakfast in the hotel, then step out into Bristol central: St Nicholas Market for great food and bustle, elegant Georgian squares, the vibrant harbourside, cool galleries and restaurants. Something different and stylish.

Minimum stay: 2 nights. Book through Sawday's Canopy & Stars online or by phone.

Rooms	2 doubles sharing bath & 2 extra wcs with 1 single: £85-£95.
	1 single sharing bath & 2 extra wcs with 2 doubles: £65-£75.
	Supplement applies in high season.
Meals	Pubs/restaurants 0.5 miles.
Closed	Rarely.

Rooms	Caravan for 2: £109-£149; caravan for 4: £119-£169.
Meals	Breakfast included.
Closed	Never.

	Dexter Tiranti
	The Art House Hove,
	27 Wilbury Road,
	Hove,
	Brighton & Hove BN3 3PB
Tel	+44 (0)1273 775350
Email	enquiries@thearthousehove.co.uk
Web	www.thearthousehove.co.uk

	Sawday's Canopy & Stars
	The Rooftop Rockets,
	Brooks Guesthouse Bristol,
	Exchange Avenue,
	St Nicholas Market, Bristol BS1 1UB
Tel	+44 (0)117 204 7830
Email	enquiries@canopyandstars.co.uk
Web	www.canopyandstars.co.uk/brooksguesthouse

Entry 15   Map 4

Entry 16   Map 3

Bristol

9 Princes Buildings

A super city base with comfortable beds, charming owners and, without a doubt, the best views in Clifton. You're a hop from the elegant Suspension Bridge, restaurants, shops and pubs of the village and a ferry to whisk you to town or the station; yet all is quiet and the garden is large and leafy. You walk in to a big square hall; the drawing room has a peaceful feel and a veranda for the views. Bedrooms are sunny and traditional: one downstairs overlooks the garden, the top floor double is furnished more simply. Simon and Joanna give you a good, leisurely breakfast too: local sausages and bacon, homemade jams and marmalade.

Buckinghamshire

Long Crendon Manor

Masses of history and oodles of character at this timbered listed house with high chimneys, dating from 1187... no wonder film companies are keen to get through the arched entrance and into the courtyard! The vast dining room is a dramatic setting for breakfast: sausages from Sue's pigs, home-baked bread, plum and mulberry jam from the gardens. Windows on both sides bring light into the fire-warmed drawing room with leather sofas, gleaming furniture, family bits and bobs, pictures galore. Sleep soundly in comfortable, country-house style bedrooms (one with gorgeous yellow panelling). Peaceful.

Rooms	2 doubles, 1 twin/double; 1 twin/double with separate bath: £85–£87. Singles from £60.
Meals	Pub/restaurant 100 yds.
Closed	Rarely.

Rooms	1 double, 1 four-poster; 1 double with extra twin in dressing room sharing bath: £100–£200. Singles £80–£100.
Meals	Supper £30. Pubs/restaurants 3-minute walk.
Closed	Occasionally.

Simon & Joanna Fuller
9 Princes Buildings,
Clifton,
Bristol BS8 4LB
Tel   +44 (0)117 973 4615
Email   info@9pb.co.uk
Web   www.9princesbuildings.co.uk

Sue Soar
Long Crendon Manor,
Frogmore Lane,
Long Crendon, Aylesbury,
Buckinghamshire HP18 9DZ
Tel   +44 (0)1844 201647
Email   sue.soar@longcrendonmanor.co.uk
Web   www.longcrendonmanor.co.uk

Entry 17 Map 3

Entry 18 Map 8

Cambridgeshire

Cambridge University

Buses, bicycles and punting on the Cam: huge fun when you're in the heart of it all. Enter the Great Gate Tower of Christ's College to be wooed by tranquil, beautiful quadrangle gardens, breakfasts beneath portraits of hallowed masters, and a serene chapel. At smaller Sidney Sussex – 1598-old with additions – you can play tennis in gorgeous gardens, picnic on perfect lawns and start the day with rare-breed sausages. Churchill has a great gym, Downing has Quentin Blake paintings on the walls, St Catharine's has a candlelit chapel. Bedrooms (some shared showers) and lounges are functional; well-informed porters are your first port of call.

Rooms spread across 13 colleges.

Rooms	60 doubles; 206 twins: £75-£128. 804 singles: £44-£79. 3 apartments for 2-3: £85-£150.
Meals	Breakfast included. Some colleges offer dinner from £7. See website for details.
Closed	Mid-January to mid-March; May/June; October/November; Christmas. A few rooms available throughout year.

	University Rooms Cambridge University, Cambridge, Cambridgeshire
Web	www.universityrooms.com/en/city/cambridge/home

Entry 19   Map 9

Cambridgeshire

Duke House

Opposite Christ's Pieces, one of the city's oldest green spaces, and right in the centre: perfect! This house has been refurbished from top to toe and all is gleaming and generous. Settle into the guest sitting room (chandelier, Regency style furniture, calm colours) and sleep soundly under Irish goose down in beautiful bedrooms all named after dukes; top-floor's Cambridge suite has a romantic balcony. The lovely breakfast room has separate tables with fabric-backed chairs overlooking a little plant-filled courtyard; Liz serves an excellent organic and homemade spread. Shops, botanical garden, restaurants... a happy stroll.

Children over 10 welcome. Minimum 2 nights at weekends.

Rooms	3 doubles: £120-£150. 1 suite for 2 (extra sofabed available): £160-£195. Singles £105-£135.
Meals	Pubs/restaurants 5-minute walk.
Closed	Rarely.

	Liz Cameron Duke House, 1 Victoria Street, Cambridge, Cambridgeshire CB1 1JP
Tel	+44 (0)1223 314773
Email	info@dukehousecambridge.co.uk
Web	www.dukehousecambridge.co.uk

Entry 20   Map 9

Cambridgeshire

5 Chapel Street

Exemplary! Where: in a lovely, comfortable, refurbed Georgian house 20 minutes' walk from Cambridge centre. How: with warmth, pleasure, intelligence and local knowledge. Bedrooms have good quality mattresses, bedding and towels. Characterful pieces – an antique brass bed, a freestanding bath, oriental rugs – flowers, calm colours, garden views. The breakfasts: delicious, largely organic and local – fresh fruit salad, kedgeree with smoked Norfolk haddock, home baking (three types of bread; gluten free, no problem). If you'd like to swing a cat book the biggest room; borrow vintage bikes and thoroughly enjoy your break.

Minimum stay: 2 nights at weekends & high season usually. Children over 11 welcome.

Rooms	2 doubles; 1 twin: £95–£120. Singles £85–£95.
Meals	Pubs/restaurants 5-minute walk.
Closed	Rarely.

Christine Ulyyan
5 Chapel Street,
Cambridge,
Cambridgeshire CB4 1DY
Tel   +44 (0)1223 514856
Email   christine.ulyyan@gmail.com
Web   www.5chapelstreet.co.uk

Entry 21   Map 9

Cambridgeshire

Springfield House

The former school house hugs the bend of a river, its French windows opening to delightful rambling gardens with scented roses… and a yew garden, and a mulberry tree that provides fruit for breakfast. It's an elegant home reminiscent of another age, with fascinating history on the walls and big comfortable bedrooms for guests; one is reached by narrow stairs and has steps out to the garden. The conservatory, draped with a huge mimosa, is an exceptional spot for summer breakfasts, and the breakfasts are rather delicious. Good value and peaceful, yet close to Cambridge, of which Judith is a fund of knowledge.

Rooms	2 doubles; 1 twin/double with separate bath: £70–£85. Singles £45–£60.
Meals	Pubs 150 yds.
Closed	Rarely.

Judith Rossiter
Springfield House,
14-16 Horn Lane, Linton,
Cambridgeshire CB21 4HT
Tel   +44 (0)1223 891383
Email   springfieldhouselinton@gmail.com
Web   www.springfieldhouselinton.com

Entry 22   Map 9

Cambridgeshire

The Old Vicarage

Tug the bell pull and step inside a 19th-century parsonage with a labyrinth of rooms. Homemade flapjack and chocolates await, peaceful bedrooms are countrified and classy with stylish bathrooms – one a lovely en suite. Original artwork peppers every wall and is mostly for sale online. Take breakfast overlooking a big mature garden and brace yourself for a wonderful full English. Cats, dogs and chickens roam freely and if you're lucky you'll spot a proud peacock or muntjac deer within the trees. Explore Cambridge, walk Wicken Fen with its Konik ponies and birdlife, then stroll to one of the locals.

Rooms	1 twin/double; 1 double with separate bath: £90-£100. Singles £55-£60.
Meals	Pubs in village.
Closed	Christmas & New Year.

	Gill Pedersen
	The Old Vicarage,
	7 Church Street, Isleham, Ely,
	Cambridgeshire CB7 5RX
Tel	+44 (0)1638 780095
Email	gill@pedersen.co.uk
Web	www.oldvicarageisleham.co.uk

Entry 23   Map 9

Cambridgeshire

Peacocks B&B

Above their delightful riverside tearoom in the heart of Ely, George and Rachel have created two suites. Each has its own sitting room stocked with books and squashy sofas. Brewery House has a fireplace and river views; Cottage is cosy and pretty with flowery wallpaper. Both have goose down duvets and tea trays. Enjoy breakfast by the Aga: perhaps savoury crumpets, omelette or delicious Croque Madame. Browse the nearby antique centre, visit the cathedral, stroll out for dinner or explore Cambridge and the Fens; but make sure to leave time for tea – there are 70 kinds! The Peacocks are friendly and funny – lovely hosts.

Rooms	2 suites for 2, each with separate bath & wc: £125-£150.
Meals	Pubs/restaurants 3-minute walk. Tearoom closed Monday & Tuesday.
Closed	Rarely.

	Sundy Smith
	Peacocks B&B,
	65 Waterside, Ely,
	Cambridgeshire CB7 4AU
Mobile	+44 (0)7900 666161
Email	peacockbookings65@gmail.com
Web	www.peacockstearoom.co.uk

Entry 24   Map 9

Cheshire

Goss Moor

Crunch up the gravelled drive to the big white house, a beautifully run family home. Bedrooms are light, bright and decorated in creams and blues; bathrooms are spotless and warm. Be cosseted by fluffy bathrobes, biscuits, decanters of sherry – all is comfortable and inviting. After a day's exploring the Wirral and Liverpool, historic Chester and the wilds of north Wales – a short drive all – return to a kind welcome from Sarah. Expect a generous and delicious breakfast by the sunny bay window; in the summer, you are free to enjoy the garden and pool (not always heated!).

Rooms	1 twin/double; 1 double with separate bath: £80–£85. Singles £50–£55.
Meals	Occasional dinner with wine, £25. Pub/restaurant 2 miles.
Closed	Rarely.

Chris & Sarah White
Goss Moor,
Mill Lane, Willaston, Neston,
Cheshire CH64 1RG

Tel	+44 (0)151 327 4000
Mobile	+44 (0)7771 510068
Email	sarahcmwhite@aol.com
Web	www.gossmoor.co.uk

Entry 25   Map 7

Cheshire

Trustwood

Small and pretty and wrapped in beautiful country, Trustwood stands in peaceful gardens with National Trust woods at the end of the lane. Outside, sweetpeas flourish to the front, while lawns run down behind to a copse where bluebells thrive in spring. Inside, warm, fresh, contemporary interiors are just the ticket: super bedrooms, fabulous bathrooms, and a wood-burner and sofas in the sitting room. Free-range hens provide eggs for delicious breakfasts, Lin accounts for the lovely scones. As for the Wirral, much more beautiful than you probably imagine; coastal walks, botanic gardens and the spectacular Dee estuary all wait.

Rooms	2 doubles: £75. Singles £50.
Meals	Restaurants 2 miles.
Closed	Occasionally.

Lin & Peter Friend
Trustwood,
Vicarage Lane, Burton, Neston,
Cheshire CH64 5TJ

Tel	+44 (0)151 336 7118
Mobile	+44 (0)7550 012462
Email	lin@trustwood.freeserve.co.uk
Web	www.trustwood.freeserve.co.uk

Entry 26   Map 7

Cheshire

Cotton Farm

Only a four-mile hop from Roman Chester and its 900-year-old cathedral is this sprawling, red-brick farmhouse. Elegant chickens peck in hedges, ponies graze, lambs frisk and cats doze. The farm, run by conservationists Nigel and Clare, is under the Countryside Stewardship Scheme – there are wildflower meadows, summer swallows and 250 acres to roam. Farmhouse bedrooms are large, stylish and cosy with lovely fabrics, robes, a decanter of sherry and huge bath towels, but best of all is the relaxed family atmosphere. Breakfasts, with homemade bread, are delicious and beautifully presented.

Children over 10 welcome.

Rooms	2 doubles; 1 twin: £85.
	Singles £55-£60.
Meals	Pub 1.5 miles.
Closed	Rarely.

Clare & Nigel Hill
Cotton Farm,
Cotton Edmunds, Chester,
Cheshire CH3 7PG

Tel	+44 (0)1244 336616
Mobile	+44 (0)7840 682042
Email	information@cottonfarm.co.uk
Web	www.cottonfarm.co.uk

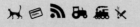

Entry 27   Map 7

Cheshire

Mulsford Cottage

Delicious! Not just the food (Kate's a pro chef) but the sweet whitewashed cottage with its sunny conservatory and vintage interiors, and the green Cheshire countryside that bubble-wraps the place in rural peace. Chat – and laugh – the evening away over Kate's superb dinners, lounge by the sitting room fire, then sleep deeply in comfy bedrooms: cane beds, a bright red chair, a vintage desk. The double has a roll top bath, the twin a tiny shower-with-a-view. Step out to birdsong and the 34-mile Sandstone Trail to Shropshire. Wales starts just past the hammock, at the bottom of the large and lovely garden.

Rooms	1 double; 1 twin with separate
	bath/shower: £80-£85.
	Singles £55.
Meals	Dinner from £18. Pub 1.5 miles.
Closed	Rarely.

Kate Dewhurst
Mulsford Cottage,
Mulsford, Sarn, Malpas,
Cheshire SY14 7LP

Tel	+44 (0)1948 770414
Email	katedewhurst@hotmail.com
Web	www.mulsfordcottage.co.uk

Entry 28   Map 7

Cheshire

Harrop Fold Farm

Artists, foodies and walkers adore this antique-filled farmhouse with soul-lifting views. On the edge of the Peak District, the oldest building on the farm dates from 1694 (Bonnie Prince Charlie visited here). The B&B part has a warm peaceful breakfast room, a stone-flagged sitting room, a spectacular studio. Fresh flowers, antique beds, fine fabrics, hot water bottles with chic covers, bathrooms with fluffy robes: you get the best. Gregarious Sue and daughter Leah hold art and cookery courses so the food too is outstanding. Bedrooms have stupendous views – and flat-screen TVs and DVDs just in case the weather spoils!

Minimum stay: 2 nights at weekends.

Rooms	2 doubles: £95. Singles from £60.
Meals	Cookery demo & dinner £60. Pub 1.9 miles.
Closed	Rarely.

	Sue Stevenson Harrop Fold Farm, Rainow, Macclesfield, Cheshire SK10 5UU
Tel	+44 (0)1625 560085
Email	stay@harropfoldfarm.co.uk
Web	www.harropfoldfarm.co.uk

Entry 29   Map 8

Cornwall

New Entry
INSPECTED & SELECTED
A SPECIAL PLACE

Higher Bakesdown

Listen to the distant sound of the sea... it's all you'll hear, apart from the odd honk of the geese. The pigs long gone, you stay in the converted piggery attached to the thatched cottage – a simple, whitewashed space with wood-burner, sweet snug bedroom and French windows onto a courtyard. Or you can choose a colourful gypsy caravan – to be that little bit closer to nature. Restaurateurs Kristy and Todd grow their own veg and breakfast (in the cottage) is a spread of hedgerow jelly, home-laid eggs and the full Cornish Monty with perhaps Hog's pudding or fluffy cheese omelette. Wildflower meadow and woodland, with a surfing beach close by.

Minimum stay: 2 nights.

Rooms	Annexe – 1 double with sitting room & kitchenette: £70-£80. 1 gypsy caravan for 2 (singles/couples only; March-Sept only; compost wc): £70; self-catering option available. Extra bed/sofabed £10 p.p.p.n.
Meals	Breakfast £10 per couple per day. Occasional dinner, 2 courses, £20. Pubs/restaurants 5 miles.
Closed	Christmas.

	Kristy Turner Higher Bakesdown, Marhamchurch, Bude, Cornwall EX23 0HJ
Tel	+44 (0)1288 341167
Email	info@laboucheccrcolc.co.uk
Web	www.higherbakesdown.co.uk

Entry 30   Map 1

Higher Bakesdown Gypsy Caravan

A vibrant, sunny camp centred around the brightly painted Gypsy Caravan and fenced off by strings of prayer flags fluttering in the breeze; you'll have the whole meadow to yourself, unless you count the donkey! Climb inside your cosy shelter with books and retro games under the bed and a welcome hamper waiting for you (award-winning chef Todd is available for evening meals when his restaurant in Launceston's not open). The camp is ingeniously eco-friendly with a thatched compost loo and a rainwater recovery hot shower in the nearby converted stable. Bring your bike; head for the beach to catch some waves – or simply stay put.

Minimum stay: 2 nights. Book through Sawday's Canopy & Stars online or by phone.

The Old Parsonage

A spellbinding coastline, secret coves, spectacular walks. All this and a supremely comfortable Georgian rectory with pretty gardens. Morag and Margaret are relaxed and welcoming hosts. Superb pitch pine floors and original woodwork add warmth and a fresh glow, the big engaging bedrooms (one on the ground floor) have a quirky, upbeat mix of furniture and furnishings, and the bathrooms are pampering. Breakfasts are wonderful: savoury mushrooms, Cornish oak-roasted mackerel, French toast with bacon... In front of the house the land slopes away to the Atlantic, just a five-minute walk across a SSSI. A peaceful retreat.

Minimum stay: 2 nights. Children over 12 welcome.

Rooms	Gypsy caravan for 2: £70.	Rooms	5 twin/doubles: £95–£115. Singles from £75.
Meals	Breakfast hamper included. Cooked breakfast from £10.	Meals	Packed lunch £5.95. Pub/restaurant 600 yds.
Closed	October–March.	Closed	November–February.

	Sawday's Canopy & Stars Higher Bakesdown Gypsy Caravan, Higher Bakesdown, Marhamchurch, Bude, Cornwall EX23 0HJ		**Morag Reeve & Margaret Pickering** The Old Parsonage, Forrabury, Boscastle, Cornwall PL35 0DJ
Tel	+44 (0)117 204 7830	Tel	+44 (0)1840 250339
Email	enquiries@canopyandstars.co.uk	Mobile	+44 (0)7890 531677
Web	www.canopyandstars.co.uk/ higherbakesdown	Email	morag@old-parsonage.com
		Web	www.old-parsonage.com

☝ 🖂 📶 🍾 🍴

Cornwall

Tremoren

Views stretch sleepily over the Cornish countryside. You might feel inclined to do nothing more than wander the lovely garden or snooze by the pool, but the surfing beaches, the Camel Trail and the Eden Project are so close. The stone and slate former farmhouse has been smartly updated and your airy ground-floor bedroom comes with soft colours, pretty china, crisp linen, a comfortable bathroom, and its own sitting room, snug with sofas, books, maps and TV. For summer, there's a flower-filled terrace, perfect for a pre-dinner drink. Lanie, bubbly and engaging, runs her own catering company – dinner will be delicious!

Rooms	1 double with sitting room: £90-£100.
Meals	Dinner, 4 courses, £26.
	Inns 0.5 miles.
Closed	Rarely.

Philip & Lanie Calvert
Tremoren,
St Kew, Bodmin,
Cornwall PL30 3HA
Tel   +44 (0)1208 841790
Email   la.calvert@btinternet.com
Web   www.tremoren.co.uk

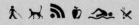

Entry 33   Map 1

Cornwall

The Corn Mill

This restored mill in a quiet Cornish valley is a relaxed and friendly home. Step inside and find a country cottage medley of flowers and family furniture, antique rugs and interesting market finds. Artist Suzie has her studio in a folly in the pretty garden; ducks and geese wander in the orchard. Cosy bedrooms have flowery fabrics, antique eiderdowns, warm blankets and good cotton; bathrooms are simple and fresh with fluffy towels. Breakfast well in the farmhouse kitchen on a locally sourced spread and bread fresh from the Rayburn. Exceptional coastal walking, music festivals, great beaches and Port Isaac are all nearby.

Rooms	1 double: £80.
	1 family room for 4: £80-£100.
Meals	Pub/restaurant 2 miles.
Closed	Christmas & New Year.

Susan Bishop
The Corn Mill,
Port Isaac Road,
Trelill, Bodmin,
Cornwall PL30 3HZ
Tel   +44 (0)1208 851079
Email   jemandsuzie@icloud.com

Entry 34   Map 1

Cornwall

Cornwall

The Barn at The Old Stables

The closer you inch down the lane to The Barn, the greener the fields become, the louder the spring-time bleating lambs. But that's all the noise here: this converted hay barn is a hubbub–free hideaway. Find a lavish double bedroom with fine touches: vast bathroom, sublime 'sink in' mattress and contemporary furniture made by Judith's son. Judith lives opposite and is most at home by her Aga, whipping up a delicious breakfast with local bacon or preparing extraordinary three–course dinners: after a day's walking or cycling the Camel Trail and Cornish coast, you can eat in the candlelit dining room, the valley unfolding beyond.

Minimum stay: 2 nights at weekends.

Higher Lank Farm

Families rejoice: you can only come if you have a child under five! Celtic crosses in the garden and original panelling hint at the house's 500-year history; bedrooms, newly decorated, have pocket sprung mattresses and large TVs. Nursery teas begin at 5pm, grown-up suppers are later and energetic Lucy will cheerfully babysit while the rest of you slink off to the pub. Farm-themed playgrounds are covered in safety matting and grass, there are piglets and chicks, eggs to collect, pony and trap rides, a sand barn for little ones and cream teas in the garden. Oh, and real nappies are provided!

Rooms	Barn – 1 double: £85-£105.
Meals	Dinner, 3 courses, £27.50.
	Pub/restaurant 5 miles.
Closed	Christmas & New Year.

Rooms	3 family rooms for 4: £100.
	Singles by arrangement.
Meals	Supper £23. Nursery tea £7.
	Pub 1.5 miles.
Closed	November–Easter.

	Judith Argent
	The Barn at The Old Stables,
	Helland, Bodmin,
	Cornwall PL30 4QE
Tel	+44 (0)1208 75543
Mobile	+44 (0)7786 558641
Email	juargent@hotmail.com
Web	www.thebarnincornwall.co.uk

	Lucy Finnemore
	Higher Lank Farm,
	St Breward,
	Bodmin,
	Cornwall PL30 4NB
Tel	+44 (0)1208 850716
Email	lucyfin@higherlankfarm.co.uk
Web	www.higherlankfarm.co.uk

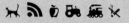

Entry 35   Map 1

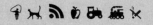

Entry 36   Map 1

Cornwall

Cabilla Manor

There's a treasure round every corner and an opera house in one of the barns. Instant seduction as you enter the old manor house out on the moor, brimful of interest and colour. Rich exotic rugs and cushions, artefacts from around the world, Louella's sumptuous hand-stencilled quilts, huge beds, coir carpets, garden flowers. There's a dining room crammed floor to ceiling with books, many of them Robin's (a writer and explorer) and a lofty conservatory for friendly meals overlooking a semi-wild garden – with tennis and elegant lawns. The views are heavenly, the generous hosts wonderful and the final mile of the approach thrillingly wild.

Cornwall

Koeschi

In the middle of ancient bluebell woods, an eco home extraordinaire! Designed by Pete and Celia's nephew it teems with great features: a green roof covered in wild flowers, timbers from their woods, solar and wood-burner heating, wool insulation. You have your own part of the house, all clean lines and comfort, with a terrace leading into the woodland – woodpeckers and tree creepers keep you company. Wake for sourdough toast, local bangers and bacon, very good coffee. Pete, a sculptor, has his studio next door (have a tour, book a course), it's a hop to the Eden Project and Fowey fishing... and the peace is blissful.

Rooms	1 double; 1 double with separate bath & shower: £90. 1 double, 1 twin sharing bath & shower (let to same party only): £90. Singles £45.
Meals	Dinner, 3 courses with wine, £35. Pub 4 miles. Restaurant 8-10 miles.
Closed	Christmas.

Rooms	1 suite for 2 with separate bath/shower & sitting room: £80-£100. Singles £70.
Meals	Pubs/restaurants 0.5 miles.
Closed	Rarely.

Robin & Louella Hanbury-Tenison
Cabilla Manor,
Mount, Bodmin,
Cornwall PL30 4DW
Tel   +44 (0)1208 821224
Mobile   +44 (0)7770 664218
Email   louella@cabilla.co.uk
Web   www.cabilla.co.uk

Celia Robbins
Koeschi,
Lanlivery,
Bodmin,
Cornwall PL30 5BX
Tel   +44 (0)1208 871029
Email   celia@petegrahamcarving.co.uk
Web   www.cornwallecohome.co.uk

Entry 37   Map 1

Entry 38   Map 1

Cornwall

Menkee

From this handsome Georgian farmhouse there are long views towards the sea; you're 20 minutes away from the coastal path and wild surf but you may not want to budge. Gage and Liz are deliciously unstuffy and look after you well: newspapers and a weather forecast appear with a scrumptious breakfast, your gorgeously comfortable bed is turned down in the evening and walkers can be dropped off and collected. The elegant house is filled with beautiful things, gleaming furniture, fresh flowers, roaring fires and pretty fabrics – all you have to do is slacken your pace and wind down.

Minimum stay: 2 nights in high season.

Rooms	1 double; 1 twin: £80–£90. Singles from £40.
Meals	Pub/restaurant 3 miles.
Closed	Rarely.

Gage & Liz Williams
Menkee,
St Mabyn, Wadebridge,
Cornwall PL30 3DD

Tel	+44 (0)1208 841378
Mobile	+44 (0)7999 549935
Email	gagewillms@aol.com
Web	www.cornwall-online.co.uk/menkee

Entry 39   Map 1

Cornwall

Molesworth Manor

It's a splendid old place, big enough to swallow hordes of people, peppered with art and interesting antiques. There are palms and a play area in the garden, two charming drawing rooms with an honesty bar and open fires for cosy nights, a carved staircase leading to bedrooms that vary in style and size – His Lordship's at the front, the Maid's in the eaves – and bathrooms that are lovely and pampering. The whiff of homemade muffins and a delicious breakfast lures you downstairs in the morning, Padstow and its food delights will keep you happy when you venture out. A superb bolthole run by Geoff and Jessica, youthful and fun.

Rooms	7 doubles, 1 twin/double; 1 twin with separate shower room: £85–£125. Singles by arrangement.
Meals	Pubs/restaurants 2 miles.
Closed	November–January. Open off-season by arrangement for larger parties.

Geoff French & Jessica Clarke
Molesworth Manor,
Little Petherick, Padstow,
Cornwall PL27 7QT

Tel	+44 (0)1841 540292
Email	molesworthmanor@aol.com
Web	www.molesworthmanor.co.uk

Entry 40   Map 1

Cornwall

Cornwall

Myrtle Cottage

A proper cottage – beautifully kept, low-ceilinged and light – in a traditional Cornish village with a good foodie pub. Rooms, with distant sea views, are invitingly cosy: uneven white walls, prettily quilted beds, pale-carpeted or varnished creaking boards, flowers fresh from the garden. Sue does great breakfasts: homemade bread, muffins and preserves, local eggs and bacon, in the dining room, the sun room, or out on the patio. There are games and toys for tots and maps for walkers to borrow. You're a 15-minute stroll from the South West Coast Path so near many outstanding beaches; Porth Joke's a favourite. Lovely.

Drym Farm

Rural, but not too deeply: the Tate at St Ives is a 15-minute drive. The 1705 farmhouse, beautifully revived, is surrounded by ancient barns, a dairy and a forge, fascinating to Cornish historians. Jan arrived in 2002, with an enthusiasm for authenticity and simple, stylish good taste. French limestone floors in the hall, eclectic art on the walls, a roll top bath, a *bateau lit*, an antique brass bed. Paintwork is fresh cream and taupe. There are old fruit trees and young camellias, a TV-free sitting room with two plump sofas and organic treats at breakfast. Charming and utterly peaceful.

Rooms	1 double; 1 twin with separate bath: £75-£80. Singles £55-£65.
Meals	Dinner £21. Pubs/restaurants 0.5 miles.
Closed	Rarely.

Rooms	2 doubles: £90-£100. Singles from £60.
Meals	Pubs/restaurants within 1-4 miles.
Closed	Rarely.

	Sue Stevens
	Myrtle Cottage,
	Trevail, Cubert, Newquay,
	Cornwall TR8 5HP
Tel	+44 (0)1637 830460
Mobile	+44 (0)7763 101076
Email	enquiries@myrtletrevail.co.uk
Web	www.myrtletrevail.co.uk

	Jan Bright
	Drym Farm,
	Drym, Praze-an-Beeble,
	Camborne,
	Cornwall TR14 0NU
Tel	+44 (0)1209 831039
Email	drymfarm@hotmail.co.uk
Web	www.drymfarm.co.uk

Entry 41   Map 1

Entry 42   Map 1

Cornwall

Cornwall

House at Gwinear

An island of calm, this grand old rambling house sits in bird-filled acres but is only a short drive from St Ives. The Halls are devoted to the encouragement of the arts and crafts which is reflected in their lifestyle. Find shabby chic with loads of character and no stuffiness – fresh flowers on the breakfast table, a piano in the corner, rugs on polished floors, masses of books. In a separate wing is your cosy bedroom and sitting room, with a fine view of the church from the bath. The large lawned gardens are there for bare-footed solace, and you can have breakfast in the Italianate courtyard on sunny days.

Penquite

A doll's house of a B&B in a constellation of Cornwall's best attractions, set in a quiet village overlooking the Hayle estuary and bird reserve. A doctor's house from 1908, it oozes Arts and Crafts with chunky stone walls, sloping roof, winding stairs and polished oak enhanced by Stephanie's ceramics. There's a snug, bay-windowed sitting room; a private suite of cute bedrooms in the eaves; a mature garden of lofty pines, palms and summer house; a generous continental spread on the terrace or light-filled dining room. Stroll to pubs and deli, or past a golf course to the coastal path and St Ives Bay views.

Rooms	1 twin/double with separate bath & sitting room: £80.
Meals	Supper, 2 courses with wine, £25. Pub 1.5 miles.
Closed	Rarely.

Rooms	1 family room for 3; 1 single with extra z-bed (let to same party only): £85-£110.
Meals	Continental breakfast. Restaurant 2-minute walk.
Closed	Rarely.

	Charles & Diana Hall
	House at Gwinear,
	Gwinear,
	St Ives,
	Cornwall TR27 5JZ
Tel	+44 (0)1736 850444
Email	charleshall@btinternet.com

	Stephanie Pace
	Penquite,
	Vicarage Lane, Lelant,
	St Ives, Cornwall TR26 3EA
Tel	+44 (0)1736 755002
Email	stephaniepace@hotmail.com
Web	www.penquite-seasidesuite-cornwall.com

Entry 43   Map 1

Entry 44   Map 1

Cornwall

11 Sea View Terrace

In a smart row of Edwardian villas, with stunning harbour and sea views, is a delectable retreat. Sleek, softy coloured interiors are light and gentle on the eye – an Italian circular glass table here, a painted seascape there. Bedrooms are perfect with crisp linen and vistas of whirling gulls from private terraces; bathrooms are state of the art. Rejoice in softly boiled eggs with anchovy and chive-butter soldiers for breakfast – or continental in bed if you prefer. Grahame looks after you impeccably and design aficionados will be happy.

Children over 12 welcome.

Cornwall

Keigwin Farmhouse

Off the glorious coast road to St Ives, in two walled acres overlooking the sea, is a very old farmhouse lived in by Gilly. Walk to the beach at Portheras Cove, dine well at Gurnard's Head, return to little whitewash-and-pine bedrooms with views that make you want to get out your paints, and a big shared bathroom with a massive old bath, fresh with organic cotton towels. A treat: Gilly's scones on arrival, eggs from her hens, stacks of books above the stairs and an arty feel – wide floorboards, creamy colours, family pieces, sculptures, ceramics, glass. A relaxed, delightful – and musical instrument-friendly – B&B.

Rooms	3 suites for 2: £100-£135. Singles from £75.
Meals	Dinner, with wine, from £25 (groups only). Packed lunch from £15. Pubs/restaurants 5-minute walk.
Closed	Rarely.

Rooms	2 doubles sharing 2 baths with 1 single (let to same party only): £75. 1 single sharing 2 baths with 2 doubles (let to same party only): £35.
Meals	Pubs/restaurants 3 miles.
Closed	Rarely.

	Grahame Wheelband
	11 Sea View Terrace,
	St Ives,
	Cornwall TR26 2DH
Tel	+44 (0)1736 798440
Mobile	+44 (0)7973 953616
Email	info@11stives.co.uk
Web	www.11stives.co.uk

	Gilly Wyatt-Smith
	Keigwin Farmhouse,
	Keigwin, Morvah,
	Penzance,
	Cornwall TR19 7TS
Tel	+44 (0)1736 786425
Email	sleep@keigwinfarmhouse.co.uk
Web	www.keigwinfarmhouse.co.uk

Entry 45   Map 1

Entry 46   Map 1

Cornwall

Cove Cottage

Down a long lane to a rose-clad cottage in the most balmy part of Cornwall... peace in a private cove. Your own door leads up steps to a gorgeous suite with luxurious linen on an antique four-poster, art, sofas... and a flowery balcony with spectacular views of the sea and subtropical gardens. Settle in happily to the sound of the waves. Sue is friendly and serves a great breakfast in the garden room: home-laid eggs, homemade jams and their own honey. The Penwith peninsula hums with gardens, galleries and stunning sandy beaches; Minack Theatre and Lamorna are close. Return for a salad supper of lobster or crab. Paradise!

Cornwall

Venton Vean

Everything at Venton Vean is tip-top. Immensely helpful owners Philippa and David moved from London with their family and have transformed a dilapidated Victorian house into a supremely cool and elegant B&B. Moody colours, mid-century design classics and interesting reclamation finds make for a stunning and eclectic interior. Food is a passion — expect freshly ground coffee in your room and some of the most tantalising breakfasts around: Mexican, Spanish, even a good old full English will have you dashing down in the morning. Arty Penzance is a joy as is the craggy-coved beauty all around.

Rooms	1 suite for 2: £120-£130.
Meals	Cold platter £12.50.
	Dinner, in low season, £30.
	Pub/restaurant 3 miles.
Closed	Rarely.

Rooms	4 doubles: £75-£95.
	1 family room for 4: £110-£140.
	Singles from £60.
Meals	Dinner, 3 courses, from £20.
	Packed lunch from £5.
	Cream tea £4.
Closed	Rarely.

	Sue White
	Cove Cottage,
	St Loy, St Buryan, Penzance,
	Cornwall TR19 6DH
Tel	+44 (0)1736 810010
Email	thewhites@covecottagestloy.co.uk
Web	www.covecottagestloy.co.uk

	Philippa McKnight
	Venton Vean,
	Trewithen Road, Penzance,
	Cornwall TR18 4LS
Tel	+44 (0)1736 351294
Email	info@ventonvean.co.uk
Web	www.ventonvean.co.uk

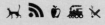

Entry 47 Map 1

Entry 48 Map 1

Cornwall

Ednovean Farm

There's a terrace for each fabulous bedroom (one truly private) with views to the wild blue yonder and St Michael's Mount Bay, an enchanting outlook that changes with the passage of the day. Come for peace, space and the best of eclectic fabrics and colours, pretty lamps, Christine's sculptures, fluffy bathrobes and handmade soaps. The beamed open-plan sitting/dining area is an absorbing mix of exotic, rustic and elegant; have full breakfast here (last orders nine o'clock) or continental in your room. A footpath through the field leads to the village; walk to glorious Prussia Cove and Cudden Point, or head west to Marazion.

Minimum stay: 4 nights in high season. Over 16s welcome.

Rooms	2 doubles, 1 four-poster: £95–£130.
Meals	Pub 5-minute walk.
Closed	Rarely.

Christine & Charles Taylor
Ednovean Farm,
Perranuthnoe, Penzance,
Cornwall TR20 9LZ

Tel	+44 (0)1736 711883
Email	info@ednoveanfarm.co.uk
Web	www.ednoveanfarm.co.uk

Entry 49   Map 1

Cornwall

Bay House

Perched on the edge of the map, high on rugged, seapink-tufted cliffs, Bay House is as close to the sea as you can get. Rooms are spacious (one with a bay window), the dining room defers to stunning sunsets and the attention to detail is immaculate. Expect fine original artwork and antiques, Ralph Lauren dressing gowns, designer linen, Molton Brown lotions, iPod docks and DVD players. Scramble down to secluded beaches, stroll to the famous Lizard Lighthouse or relax to the sound of the surf in the beautiful garden under rustling palms and hovering kestrels. Breakfast is outstanding – with John's homemade bread and jams.

Rooms	2 twin/doubles: £120–£160.
Meals	Pubs/restaurants 5-minute walk.
Closed	Christmas.

Carla Caslin
Bay House,
Housel Bay, The Lizard,
Cornwall TR12 7PG

Tel	+44 (0)1326 290235
Mobile	+44 (0)7740 168805
Email	carla.caslin@btinternet.com
Web	www.mostsoutherlypoint.co.uk

Entry 50   Map 1

Cornwall

Landewednack House

The pug dogs will greet you enthusiastically and Susan will give you tea and biscuits in the drawing room of this extremely pretty and immaculate house. Antony the chef keeps the wheels oiled and the food coming – treat yourself to green crab soup or succulent lobster; the wine cellar holds over 2,000 bottles so there's plenty of choice. Upstairs to smart, sumptuous roomy bedrooms and tip-top bathrooms; the twin room is smaller and not all have sea views, but everything you could possibly need is there, from robes to brandy. The pool area is stunning, the garden is filled with interest and it's a three-minute walk to the sea.

Minimum stay: 2 nights July & August.

Rooms	4 doubles; 1 twin: £110–£190. Singles £85. Dogs £10 per night.
Meals	Dinner, 3 courses, £38.
Closed	Rarely.

	Susan Thorbek
	Landewednack House,
	Church Cove,
	The Lizard, Helston,
	Cornwall TR12 7PQ
Tel	+44 (0)1326 290877
Email	luxurybandb@landewednackhouse.com
Web	www.landewednackhouse.com

Entry 51 Map 1

Cornwall

Halftides

Hugely enjoyable and special, surrounded by three acres with dazzling views down the coast and out to sea. Fresh funky bedrooms, not huge but filled with light, have gorgeous fabrics, crisp bedding, dreamy views; bathrooms (one a small pod-shower in the room) are sleek in glass and chrome. Susie is great fun, an artist and chef and gives you a delicious organic breakfast in the pretty, airy dining room. Take the coastal path north or south, visit the working harbour in the village, head for a swim down the private path to the beach below. A perfect place to relax and unwind.

Minimum stay: 2 nights. Children over 3 welcome.

Rooms	1 double; 1 double with separate bath: £100–£120. 1 single sharing bath (let with double to same party only): £35–£55.
Meals	Dinner, 2-3 courses with wine, £30–£35. Pub within walking distance.
Closed	February.

	Charles & Susie Holdsworth Hunt
	Halftides,
	Laflouder Lane, Mullion, Helston,
	Cornwall TR12 7HU
Tel	+44 (0)1326 241935
Mobile	+44 (0)7970 821261
Email	halftides@btinternet.com
Web	www.halftides.co.uk

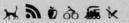

Entry 52 Map 1

Cornwall

Halzephron House

The coastal path runs through the grounds and the view is to die for — you can see St Michael's Mount on a clear day. Be greeted by homemade biscotti and organic coffee roasted in Cornwall: lovely Lucy and Roger are foodies as well as designers. The suite is contemporary, quirky and full of charm: space, art and bowls of wild flowers, velvet sofa and a big antique French bed; drift off under goose down to the sound of the waves. The drawing room leads onto a deck overlooking the garden and the sea; soak up the stunning sunsets. You can walk to three amazing beaches, a 13th-century church, a golf course and a gastropub. Heaven.

Cornwall

The Hen House

A generous, peaceful oasis. Sandy and Gary are warmly welcoming, and have oodles of local information on places to visit, eat and walk — with OS maps on loan. Ground floor rooms, in individual barns, are spacious and colourful with bright fabrics, king-size beds and stable doors to the courtyard. Relax in the hot tub in the wildflower meadow, bask on the sun loungers, wander by the ponds and watch the ducks' antics; the central courtyard is fairy-lit at night. Scrumptious locally sourced breakfasts are served in the dining chalet surrounded by birdsong. Tai-chi in the meadow, reiki and reflexology in the Serpentine Sanctuary... bliss.

Minimum stay 2 nights. Children over 12 welcome.

Rooms	1 suite for 2 with sitting room: £110–£130. Extra bed/sofabed available £30–£45 per person per night.
Meals	Pub 0.25 miles.
Closed	Rarely.

Rooms	3 doubles in 3 barns: £80–£90. Singles £70.
Meals	Pub/restaurant 1 mile.
Closed	Rarely.

	Lucy Thorp
	Halzephron House,
	Gunwalloe, Helston,
	Cornwall TR12 7QD
Mobile	+44 (0)7899 925816
Email	info@halzephronhouse.co.uk
Web	www.halzephronhouse.co.uk

	Sandy & Gary Pulfrey
	The Hen House,
	Tregarne, Manaccan, Helston,
	Cornwall TR12 6EW
Tel	+44 (0)1326 280236
Mobile	+44 (0)7809 229958
Email	henhouseuk@btinternet.com
Web	www.thehenhouse-cornwall.co.uk

Entry 53   Map 1

Entry 54   Map 1

Cornwall

Trerose Manor

Follow winding lanes through glorious countryside to find the prettiest, listed manor house, a warm family atmosphere and welcoming tea in the beamed kitchen. Large, light bedrooms, one with floor-to-ceiling windows, sit peacefully in your own wing and have views over the stunning garden. All are dressed in pretty colours, have comfy seats for garden gazing and smartly tiled bathrooms. A sumptuous breakfast can be taken outside in summer, there are wonderful walks over fields to river or beach and stacks of interesting places to visit. Lovely.

Rooms	2 doubles, 1 twin/double: £120–£130. Singles £80.
Meals	Pubs/restaurants within walking distance.
Closed	Rarely.

Tessa Phipps
Trerose Manor,
Mawnan Smith,
Falmouth,
Cornwall TR11 5HX
Tel   +44 (0)1326 250784
Email   info@trerosemanor.co.uk
Web   www.trerosemanor.co.uk

Entry 55   Map 1

Cornwall

Bosvathick

A huge old Cornish house that's been in Kate's family since 1760 – along with Indian rugs, heavy furniture, ornate plasterwork, pianos, portraits... even a harp. Historians will be in their element: pass three Celtic crosses dating from the 8th century before the long drive finds the imposing house (all granite gate posts and lions) and a rambling garden with grotto, lake, pasture and woodland. Bedrooms are simple and traditional, full of books and antiques; bathrooms are spick and span, one small and functional, one large. Come to experience a 'time warp' and charming Kate's good breakfasts. Close to Falmouth University, too.

Post code has been changed from TR11 5RD; Sat Nav will find new post code if updated.

Rooms	2 twin/doubles: £90. 2 singles: £45–£70.
Meals	Supper, from £25. Packed lunch £5–£10. Pubs 2 miles.
Closed	Rarely.

Kate & Stephen Tyrrell
Bosvathick,
Constantine,
Falmouth,
Cornwall TR11 5RZ
Tel   +44 (0)1326 340103
Email   kate@bosvathickhouse.co.uk
Web   www.bosvathickhouse.co.uk

Entry 56   Map 1

Cornwall

Trevilla House

Come for the position: the sea and Fal estuary wrap around you, and the King Harry ferry gives you an easy reach into the glorious Roseland peninsula. Inside find comfortable airy bedrooms with homemade quilts on the beds – the twin with a sofa and old-fashioned charm, the double with stunning sea views. Jinty rustles up delicious locally sourced breakfasts and homemade jams, and you eat in the sunny conservatory that looks south over the sea. Trelissick Gardens is just next door; with other gardens not far away. The Maritime Museum, Eden, Tate, cycling, watersports and coastal walks are all close by.

Rooms	1 double, 1 twin: £85-£95. 1 single, sharing bath (let to same party only): £50-£55. Singles £50-£55.
Meals	Pubs/restaurants 1-2 miles.
Closed	Christmas & New Year.

Jinty & Peter Copeland
Trevilla House,
Feock, Truro,
Cornwall TR3 6QG

Tel	+44 (0)1872 862369
Mobile	+44 (0)7791 977621
Email	jinty@trevilla.com
Web	www.trevilla.com

Entry 57   Map 1

Cornwall

Hay Barton

Giant windows overlook many acres of farmland, and Jill and Blair look after you so well! Breakfasts are special with the best local produce, homemade granola, yogurt and more. Arrive for tea and lovely home-baked cake, laid out in a comfortable guest sitting room with a log fire and plenty of books and maps. Bedrooms are fresh and pretty with garden flowers, soft white linen on big beds and floral green walls. Gloriously large panelled bathrooms have long roll top baths and are painted in earthy colours. You can knock a few balls around the tennis court, and you're near to good gardens and heaps of places to eat.

Minimum stay: 2 nights in summer.

Rooms	3 twin/doubles: £80. Singles £60.
Meals	Pubs 1-2 miles.
Closed	Rarely.

Jill & Blair Jobson
Hay Barton,
Tregony, Truro,
Cornwall TR2 5TF

Tel	+44 (0)1872 530288
Mobile	+44 (0)7813 643028
Email	jill.jobson@btinternet.com
Web	www.haybarton.com

Entry 58   Map 1

Cornwall

Ashby Villa

Lesley is friendly and outgoing and invites you for a cream tea in the kitchen of her Edwardian home. The village is lively but the Dog House, just for guests, is peacefully tucked behind, overlooking gardens and fields. Comfy bedrooms have a roll top tub or power shower, cosy rugs on tiled floors, local art, French country furniture and a shared terrace; one wood-lined studio has a wood-burner and its own patio. Zip over to the conservatory for a tasty breakfast and John's homemade bread. The Roseland Peninsula has secret coves and Truro is close. Return with fish for your own barbecue, then relax in the candlelit conservatory. Bliss.

Cornwall

Tredudwell Manor

Winding lanes lead to this handsomely refurbished Queen Anne style house. Surrounded by lawns and mature trees the views are south to the sea and the total peace is just the tonic. Inside is a marble bar for more reviving and the mix of sofas, mini-ottomans, parquet floors with Persian rugs and family portraits make for a genteel atmosphere. First floor bedrooms are large enough to waltz in with toile de Jouy wallpaper, antiques and views. In the roof space are more compact but delightful rooms – uncluttered and calm with low beams, shuttered windows and modern bathrooms. Breakfast is a treat with the best produce from nearby Fowey.

Rooms	Dog House – 1 double: £75.
	Dog House – 1 family room for 3: £85.
	Dog House – 2 studios for 2, each with extra sofabed & kitchenette: £90-£95.
Meals	Light meals and BBQ available. Pub in village. Picnic hamper on request.
Closed	Rarely.

Rooms	6 doubles: £80-£120.
	1 family room for 4: £120-£160.
	Singles from £50.
Meals	Pubs/restaurants 2 miles.
Closed	Rarely.

Lesley Black
Ashby Villa,
Fore Street,
Tregony, Truro,
Cornwall TR2 5RW
Tel   +44 (0)1872 530189
Email   blacklesley5@aol.com
Web   www.cornwallvillagebedandbreakfast.co.uk

Justin & Valérie Shakerley
Tredudwell Manor,
Lanteglos,
Fowey,
Cornwall PL23 1NJ
Tel   +44 (0)1726 870226
Email   justin@tredudwell.co.uk
Web   www.tredudwell.co.uk

Entry 59   Map 1

Entry 60   Map 1

Cornwall

Collon Barton

Come for the lofty position on a grassy hillside, the heartlifting views over unspoilt countryside and the pretty creekside village of Lerryn. This 18th-century house is a working sheep farm and an artistic household (sculptures galore, and family portraits). Anne and Iain give you eggs from their happy chickens in the old dairy, now a large, light breakfast room. Traditional airy bedrooms come in pink or blue and there's an elegant drawing room. On sunny days, Anne welcomes you with tea in the summer house. Wonderful riverside and coastal walks and good gardens abound; the Eden Project is 20 minutes away.

Pets by arrangement.

Rooms	1 twin/double, 1 twin/double with dressing room & extra beds: £80. Singles £50.
Meals	Pub 10-minute walk.
Closed	Rarely.

	Anne & Iain Mackie
	Collon Barton,
	Lerryn,
	Lostwithiel,
	Cornwall PL22 0NX
Tel	+44 (0)1208 872908
Mobile	+44 (0)7721 090186
Email	annemackie@btconnect.com

Entry 61   Map 1

Cornwall

Trussel Barn

Views shoot off in all directions and landscaped gardens drop to the valley below, where the little branch line runs alongside the river linking Liskeard and Looe... fabulous. Ex-yacht skipper Richard and talented cook Kathy are full of plans for their new enterprise, and give you four comfortable, carpeted rooms (two are huge) with firm mattresses and new furniture. Bathrooms shine and breakfast is worth waking up for – full English, homemade everything and delicious preserves. After a day discovering Eden Project or coast, look forward to drinks on the great terrace – or a sink-into sofa and a roaring fire.

Rooms	1 double with separate bath: £60–£90. 1 suite for 2: £90. 1 twin, sharing bath with 1 double & 1 single (let to same party only): £60–£90. 1 single, sharing bath with 1 double & 1 twin (let to same party only): £50.
Meals	Dinner £20. Pubs/restaurants within 3 miles.
Closed	Rarely.

	Richard Shields & Kathy Williams
	Trussel Barn,
	St Keyne, Liskeard,
	Cornwall PL14 4QL
Tel	+44 (0)1579 340450
Mobile	+44 (0)7785 350552
Email	trusselbarn@btinternet.com
Web	www.trusselbarn.com

Entry 62   Map 1

Cornwall

Hornacott

The garden, in its lovely valley setting, has seats in little corners poised to catch the evening sun — perfect for a pre-dinner drink. The peaceful house is named after the hill and you have a private entrance to your airy suite: a room with a large bed plus a lofty sitting room with a balcony and windows that look down onto the wooded valley. With CD player, music, chocolates and magazines you are truly self-contained. Jos, a kitchen designer, and Mary-Anne love having guests and living the slow life — busily! — and give you top-notch local produce and free-range eggs for breakfast.

Rooms	1 twin with separate shower: £70. 1 suite for 2: £100. Singles £50. Children under 12: £25.
Meals	Dinner, 3 courses, £20. BYO. Pubs/restaurants 4.5 miles.
Closed	Christmas.

Jos & Mary-Anne Otway-Ruthven
Hornacott,
South Petherwin, Launceston,
Cornwall PL15 7LH
Tel   +44 (0)1566 782461
Email   otwayruthven@btinternet.com
Web   www.hornacott.co.uk

🌱 🐈 🐕 👶 🚲 ✖

Entry 63   Map 1

Cornwall

New Entry
INSPECTED & SELECTED
A SPECIAL PLACE

Beechgrove

A striking Victorian home in this historic market town with views across to mysterious Bodmin Moor. Richard and Jane, relaxed and friendly hosts, give you dinner using local and seasonal produce, often with home-grown fruit and vegetables and served on fine china. Stoke up with a delicious traditional, or more adventurous, breakfast with plenty of choice and homemade preserves and bread. Sleep peacefully in the very private guest suite upstairs with its super-king bed and extra single, its comfy sitting room, soft robes and a smart bathroom; the feel is spacious and contemporary, the colours restful. A hidden gem.

Rooms	1 suite for 2 with sitting room & adjoining single for 1-4 (let to same party only & extra small bed available): £90. Singles £60.
Meals	Dinner, 2-3 courses, £19.50-£25. Pubs/restaurants 10-minute walk.
Closed	Rarely.

Jane & Richard Herman
Beechgrove,
47a Dunheved Road, Launceston,
Cornwall PL15 9JF
Tel   +44 (0)1566 779455
Email   enquiries@beechgrovecornwall.co.uk
Web   www.beechgrovecornwall.co.uk

👶 📖 📶 👶 ✖

Entry 64   Map 2

Cornwall

Cadson Manor

This lovely old manor, with spectacular views across the Lynher valley, has been in the Crago family for generations. Chatty and friendly Brenda looks after you well; expect flowers, log fires, homemade cakes and delicious breakfasts with eggs from the hens. Everything shines, from the slate hall floor and antique furniture to the pretty china and talkative parrot. Fish in the lake, picnic in the grounds or walk Cadson Bury among Highland cattle. Bedrooms and bathrooms have hotel comfort, rich drapes and thoughtful extras. Historic houses, gardens, the Eden Project, golf and the coast are all close, and the walks are sublime.

Minimum stay: 2 nights in high season.

Rooms	2 doubles (en suite); 1 double, 1 twin sharing bath when let to same party, otherwise have exclusive use of bath: £98–£115. Singles £75.
Meals	Pub/restaurant 3 miles.
Closed	Occasionally.

	Brenda Crago
	Cadson Manor,
	Callington,
	Cornwall PL17 7HW
Tel	+44 (0)1579 383969
Email	brenda.crago@btconnect.com
Web	www.cadsonmanor.co.uk

Entry 65   Map 2

Cornwall

Pentillie Castle

So many temptations: woodland gardens that tumble down to the Tamar, a walled Victorian kitchen garden still being restored, a magnificent Victorian bathing hut... and Pentillie beef cattle, uniquely theirs, grazing either side of the great drive up to the handsome house. Bedrooms are smart, spacious and deeply comfortable, bathrooms pamper. Ted and Sarah, with daughter Sammie, have mastered that delicate balancing act between luxury and stuffiness, bringing out one and banishing the other. It's the sort of place where you gasp at the perfection of it all and then throw your shoes off before diving into the sofa.

Rooms	8 twin/doubles: £130–£195. 1 four-poster: £185–£210.
Meals	Dinner, 3 courses, £30. Pubs/restaurants 15-minute drive.
Closed	Rarely.

	Sammie Coryton
	Pentillie Castle,
	St Mellion, Saltash,
	Cornwall PL12 6QD
Tel	+44 (0)1579 350044
Email	contact@pentillie.co.uk
Web	www.pentillie.co.uk

Entry 66   Map 2

Cornwall

Lantallack Farm

You will be inspired here, in generous Nicky's heart-warming old Georgian farmhouse. Find a straw-yellow sitting room with a log fire, books to read and a grand piano; views are breathtaking across countryside, streams and wooded valley. Bedrooms have deliciously comfy beds; Polly's Bower, a romantic hideaway in the old cider barn, is a charming open-plan space with whitewash and old beams, wood-burner and freestanding tub. Breakfast in the walled garden on fine days: apple juice from the orchard and bacon and sausages from down the road. There are 40 acres to explore, a leat-side trail and a heated outdoor pool. Marvellous.

Minimum stay: 2 nights.

Rooms	1 double; Polly's Bower: 1 double with sitting area & kitchen: £100–£135.
Meals	Supper on request in Polly's Bower, £25. Pubs/restaurants 1 mile.
Closed	Rarely.

	Nicky Walker Lantallack Farm, Landrake, Saltash, Cornwall PL12 5AE
Tel	+44 (0)1752 851281
Email	enquiries@lantallack.co.uk
Web	www.lantallackgetaways.co.uk

🐈 📶 🦫 🏊 🚂 🍷 ✂

Entry 67   Map 2

Cumbria

Mallsgate Hall

Moss-walled lanes wend through wonderful scenery to this intriguing 17th-century fortified manor house and busy working farm. The aim is for self-sufficiency and Christopher and Ilona (he an environmental law barrister) pour energy into the place. Estate produce stars in meals by Ilona's cousin Alice, a Ballymaloe-trained cook. You eat in the Library or Great Hall, sleep in the big vault-ceilinged bedroom (children in a small bunk-bedded room), and bathe in the equally beamed and comfortably old-fashioned bathroom. The gardens – overlooked by the pretty Georgian façade – are a joy. Bring jumpers, wellies and wander!

Rooms	1 double (bunk room available for 2 children, sharing bath with double): £120. Singles £80. Children £30.
Meals	Supper, 2 courses, £25. Pubs 3 miles.
Closed	Rarely.

	Ilona Boyle Mallsgate Hall, Roweltown, Carlisle, Cumbria CA6 6LX
Tel	+44 (0)1697 748292
Email	ilonaboyle@gmail.com
Web	www.mallsgate.co.uk

🍷 🐕 🚜 🚲

Entry 68   Map 15

Hawksdale Lodge

Spring heaven! Bowl along blissfully quiet roads while sheep bleat and daffs bob in the breeze. This is a supremely comfortable B&B at any time of the year though and your hosts look after you with great charm from their stunning 1810 gentleman farmer's house with pretty garden. Home baking and local produce at breakfast, sumptuously dressed bedrooms with plenty of space and seating, warm and inviting bathrooms with proper windows. The National Park is only six miles away for strenuous walking and cycling, the northern Lakes and fells beckon, Hadrian's Wall is near. Return to something homemade and delicious. Lovely.

Minimum stay: 2 nights in high season.

Drybeck Farm

An easy, slow pace infuses Drybeck Farm. Eat breakfast – your first morning's hamper is a feast of good local things – watching wildlife on the Eden river. Choose from three spaces which Steve and Paula have lavished with care and craftsmanship: Evelyn's a cosy, comfortable wagon for two with full-length bed, fire-pit and cooking tripod. Croglin's an 18ft yurt for four, decorated with beautiful fabrics, sheepskins and vintage pieces. 21-foot Arwen sleeps 6 and is similarly gorgeously decked-out. You're off the Lakes' tourist trail, Carlisle is nearby and there's plenty to keep you occupied on the farm – a lovely place.

Bookings start on a Monday or Friday. Book through Sawday's Canopy & Stars online or by phone.

Rooms	1 double; 1 double with separate bath: £95-£150. Easter £135 (min. 2 night stay) & New Year £150. Singles £70-£100.
Meals	Dinner, 2 courses, from £15. Pubs/restaurants less than 1 mile.
Closed	Christmas.

Rooms	Yurt for 4 (1 double, 2 single futons): £101-£120. Yurt for 6 (1 double, 4 single futons): £114-£124. Wagon for 2: £63-£72. Extra futons available. Dogs £20.
Meals	Breakfast included on the 1st morning.
Closed	December-March.

	Lorraine Russell Hawksdale Lodge, Dalston, Carlisle, Cumbria CA5 7BX
Mobile	+44 (0)7810 641892
Email	enquiries@hawksdalelodge.co.uk
Web	www.hawksdalelodge.co.uk

	Sawday's Canopy & Stars Drybeck Farm, Drybeck Farm, Armathwaite, Carlisle, Cumbria CA4 9ST
Tel	+44 (0)117 204 7830
Email	enquiries@canopyandstars.co.uk
Web	www.canopyandstars.co.uk/drybeck

Cumbria

Sirelands

Sirelands, once a gardener's cottage, stands among rhododendrons and trees on a sunny slope, a stream trickling by: a stunning spot. The Carrs have lived here for years and the house has a relaxed and homely feel. Enjoy a chatty aperitif then home-grown produce at dinner on a polished table; retire to the sitting room, delightful with log basket, honesty bar, flowers and books. Sash windows overlook the wooded garden, visited by roe deer and a wide variety of birds. Bedrooms and bathrooms are pleasant, peaceful and spotless; one loo has an amazing view! Friendly Angela loves cooking and treats you to tea and homemade cake.

Rooms	1 double with separate bath/shower; 1 twin: £100. Singles £50-£60.
Meals	Dinner, 2-3 courses, £22-£27.50. Pubs within 5 miles.
Closed	Christmas & New Year.

David & Angela Carr
Sirelands,
Heads Nook,
Brampton, Carlisle,
Cumbria CA8 9BT
Tel   +44 (0)1228 670389
Mobile +44 (0)7748 101513
Email   carr_sirelands@btconnect.com

Entry 71   Map 12

Cumbria

Willowford Farm

Lauren and Liam are enthusiastic about their organic farm and their guests. Two single-storey stone byres have been converted environmentally with thermafleece wool in the roof and a wood-burning boiler for heated slate floors. In one byre: the bedrooms, fresh, stylish, with slate floors and lofty beams, perhaps windows looking onto the farmyard, or skylights for the stars. In the other: a cosy sitting room with views of sheep and hills, and tables for meals of home-reared lamb and beef, and tasty veggy dishes; or head off to the pub! Hadrian's Wall, forts, museums and walks are all here – and Millie the sheepdog gives a welcome to visiting dogs.

Rooms	5 twin/doubles: £80-£85. Singles £55-£60.
Meals	Packed lunch £6. Lunch & dinner £6-£16 at owners' pub 1 mile away; owners can provide transport.
Closed	Christmas.

Liam McNulty & Lauren Harrison
Willowford Farm,
Gilsland,
Brampton,
Cumbria CA8 7AA
Tel   +44 (0)1697 747962
Email stay@willowford.co.uk
Web   www.willowford.co.uk

Entry 72   Map 12

Cumbria

Chapelburn House

Yomp in the most dramatic scenery close to the best bits of Hadrian's Wall, then head for Chapelburn House. Matt and Katie are young, charming, unflappable, food is reared happily then cooked with more flavour than fuss. Honey is from their bees, bread is home-baked. You have a sitting room with an open fire, lots of books and squishy sofas, and a south-facing garden room for summer dreaming. Bedrooms are deeply comfortable and bathrooms (one definitely not for fatties!) brand spanking new. Children are more than welcome to join in. This would delight exhausted refugees from London, too.

Rooms	2 doubles: £70-£90.
Meals	Dinner, 3 courses, £25. Packed lunch £5-£7.50. Restaurant 5 miles.
Closed	Christmas & New Year.

Matthew & Katie McClure
Chapelburn House,
Low Row,
Brampton,
Cumbria CA8 2LY
Tel   +44 (0)1697 746595
Email   stay@chapelburn.com
Web   www.chapelburn.com

Entry 73   Map 11

Cumbria

Boltongate Old Rectory

This lovely old rectory has superb fell views and a warm, friendly heart. Step in and feel instantly at home – it's an absolute treat to stay. Find a beautiful mix of antique and contemporary pieces, handmade Harris mattresses, big chunky sofas, Farrow & Ball colours and natural fabrics. The treats continue at table: Gill is passionate about sourcing organic and local ingredients, and everything is homemade and delicious; David knows his wines and you eat by candlelight in a 16th-century room. They're relaxed and charming and create a fabulous house-party feel. Red squirrels are happily well-fed too – and stunning Skiddaw awaits.

Rooms	1 double, 1 twin/double; 1 double with separate bath: £120-£130. Singles from £95.
Meals	Dinner, 3 courses, £35. Pub 10-minute drive.
Closed	Sundays & Mondays. December/January.

Gill & David Taylor
Boltongate Old Rectory,
Boltongate, Ireby, Wigton,
Cumbria CA7 1DA
Tel   +44 (0)1697 371647
Mobile   +44 (0)7763 242969
Email   boltongate@talk21.com
Web   www.boltongateoldrectory.com

Entry 74   Map 11

Cumbria

Lazonby Hall

The pinky sandstone façade rises, château-like, from bright flowers, box hedges, crunchy gravel: enchanting. Views, from sash windows and garden folly, yawn over the Eden valley to the Pennines. Step past pillars to panelled, antique-filled rooms of heavy curtains, marble fires, mahogany and oils. Formal, yet not daunting – the Quines and their dachshunds bring life, flexibility, and delicious Cumbrian breakfasts. Wake to birdsong and garden views. This sweet area of winding lanes and dry stone walls is near the north Lakes, Penrith, Carlisle, Scotland, ripe for exploration by foot, bike, canoe or train.

Rooms	2 doubles; 1 double, 1 twin sharing bath: £80-£130. Singles £75-£100.
Meals	Supper, 3 courses, £25-£50. Pub/restaurant 2 miles.
Closed	Rarely.

Mr & Mrs Quine
Lazonby Hall,
Lazonby, Penrith,
Cumbria CA10 1BA
Tel   +44 (0)1768 870800
Email   info@lazonbyhall.co.uk
Web   www.lazonbyhall.co.uk

Entry 75   Map 11

Cumbria

Johnby Hall

You are ensconced in the quieter part of the Lakes and have independence in this Elizabethan manor house – once a fortified Pele tower, now a family home. The bedrooms are airy and each has its own sitting room with books, children's videos, squashy sofas, pretty fabrics and whitewashed walls. Beds have patchwork quilts, windows have stone mullions and all is peaceful. Henry gives you sturdy breakfasts, and good home-grown suppers by a roaring fire in the great hall; he and Anna can join you or leave you in peace. Children will have fun: hens and pigs to feed, garden and woods to roam, garden toys galore. Walks from the door are sublime.

Rooms	1 twin/double, 1 family room for 4, each with sitting room: £120-£125. Singles £85-£88. Extra bed/sofabed available £20 per person per night.
Meals	Supper, 2 courses, £20. Pub 1 mile.
Closed	Rarely.

Henry & Anna Howard
Johnby Hall,
Johnby, Penrith,
Cumbria CA11 0UU
Tel   +44 (0)17684 83257
Email   bookings@johnbyhall.co.uk
Web   www.johnbyhall.co.uk

Entry 76   Map 11

Cumbria

Robyns Barn

Wow, fabulous views – fells and mountains in every direction including Blencathra, the most climbed fell in the Lakes. Robyns Barn is attached to the main house, and it's all yours. Step into a large, welcoming open-plan space: limewashed walls, big oak table, beams, antique pine, toasty wood-burner and plenty of DVDs, books and games. Inviting bedrooms, upstairs, have sheepskins on wooden floors. Wake when you want – Kathryn leaves a continental breakfast with homemade bread, muesli, fruit, yogurts; there's a farm shop close by serving excellent cooked breakfasts too. The garden is a blank canvas... plans are afoot.

Minimum stay: 2 nights. Children over 8 welcome.

Rooms	Barn – 1 double with sitting/dining room & kitchenette; 1 twin (let to same party only): £70–£90.
Meals	Continental breakfast. Supper £15. Pubs/restaurants 1 mile.
Closed	Rarely.

Adrian & Kathryn Vaughan
Robyns Barn,
Lane Head Farm, Troutbeck,
Keswick, Penrith, Cumbria CA11 0SY

Tel	+44 (0)1768 779841
Email	robynsbarn@hotmail.co.uk
Web	www.robynsbarn.co.uk

Entry 77   Map 11

Cumbria

Lowthwaite

Leave your worries behind as you head up the lanes to the farmhouse tucked into the fell. Jim, ex-hiking guide, and Danish Tine moved back from Tanzania with their daughters in 2007 and give you four peaceful bedrooms in the view-filled barn wing. Handsomely chunky twin beds are of recycled dhow wood, crisp light bathrooms sport organic soaps and you wake to the smell of homemade bread; breakfasts are fine Scandinavian and English inspired spreads. In a garden full of bird feeders and pheasants a stream trickles through one of the guest terraces, and there are endless fells to explore. A treat for peace-seekers and families.

Rooms	2 twin/doubles: £60–£90. 2 family rooms for 4: £60–£90. Singles £40–£70.
Meals	Packed lunch £6. Dinner £18–£27. Pubs 2.5 miles.
Closed	Christmas.

Tine & Jim Boving Foster
Lowthwaite,
Matterdale, Penrith,
Cumbria CA11 0LE

Tel	+44 (0)1768 482343
Email	info@lowthwaiteullswater.com
Web	www.lowthwaiteullswater.com

Entry 78   Map 11

Cumbria

Greenah

Tucked into the hillside off a narrow lane, this 1750s smallholding is surrounded by fells, so is perfect for walkers. Absolute privacy for four friends or family with your own entrance to a beamed and stone-flagged sitting room with wood-burning stove, creamy walls and cheery floral curtains. Warm bedrooms have original paintings, good beds, hot water bottles, bathrobes and a sparkling bathroom with a loo with a remarkable view. Malcolm is a climber; Marjorie is totally committed to organic food so you get a fabulous breakfast, and good advice about the local area. Fell walking is not compulsory!

Children over 8 welcome.

Rooms	1 double, 1 twin, sharing shower (let to same party only): £92-£95. Singles £60-£65.
Meals	Pubs/restaurants 3 miles.
Closed	November–January.

Marjorie & Malcolm Emery
Greenah,
Matterdale, Penrith,
Cumbria CA11 0SA

Tel	+44 (0)1768 483387
Mobile	+44 (0)7767 213667
Email	info@greenah.co.uk
Web	www.greenah.co.uk

Entry 79   Map 11

Cumbria

Whitbysteads

Swing into the yard of a gentleman's farmhouse at the end of a drive lined with gorse, stone walls and sheep. It's a working farm, so lots going on with four-wheel drives, dogs, busy hens and relaxed bustle. Victoria does styles and period charm well: warm rugs, flowery sofas with plain linen armchairs, modern family paintings. Bedrooms have colourful wallpapers and quilts, lots of art and comfort; bathrooms are wonderfully vintage, eclectic and big. Great hosts who make you feel instantly at home here; enjoy the breathtaking views over the fells – easy for the M6 too. Dress up in the evening for dinner at Sharrow Bay.

Rooms	1 double; 1 double, 1 twin sharing bath (let to same party only): £90-£110. Singles £45.
Meals	Dinner from £20. Children's tea £5. Pub 0.5 miles.
Closed	Rarely.

Victoria Lowther
Whitbysteads,
Askham, Penrith,
Cumbria CA10 2PG

Tel	+44 (0)1931 712284
Mobile	+44 (0)7976 276961
Email	victoria@whitbysteads.org
Web	www.whitbysteads.org

Entry 80   Map 11

Cumbria

Kirkby Thore Hall

A gorgeous, imposing village house with 14th-century beginnings, architectural treats and kind, helpful hosts. Walk straight in to a large hall/dining room with roaring fire, gleaming antiques and interesting pictures. You breakfast here on Cranstons of Penrith sausages, local farm eggs and homemade jam; a library with a desk and your own sitting room are just next door. Two bedrooms upstairs are huge with beamed ceilings (one like an up-turned boat), some exposed stone, light-filled windows, pretty fabrics; bathrooms are spotless. This valley is quiet, with gentler hills than the Lakes, and you are near the Pennines too.

Stays of 2 nights or more £84. Extra bed available.

Rooms	1 double, 1 twin/double: £90.
Meals	Dinner, 2-3 courses, £18-£22. Restaurant 0.5 miles.
Closed	Rarely.

Christine & David Tucker
Kirkby Thore Hall,
Kirkby Thore,
Penrith,
Cumbria CA10 1XN
Tel   +44 (0)17683 62989
Email   manxhorizon@btinternet.com
Web   www.kirkbythorehall.co.uk

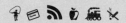

Entry 81   Map 12

Cumbria

Kelleth Old Hall

Glorious unimpeded views of fields, cows and the Howgill Fells from this fun and characterful B&B. Charlotte — chutney enthusiast, writer of three novels — has moved into an ancient manor (the fourth owner in 400 years); now it glows with paintings, antiques and books. Short steep stairs lead from 17th-century flagstones to a big canopied brass bed and yellow silk curtains at mullion windows. All is warm, charming, inviting, and that includes the roll top bath beneath a vaulted ceiling. Fuel up on a Cumbrian breakfast, return to a delicious dinner of exotic flavours. Near the A685 but peaceful at night.

Rooms	1 double with extra single bed: £80-£90. Singles £60-£65.
Meals	Dinner, 2-3 courses, £18-£22. Pub/restaurant 5 miles.
Closed	Occasionally.

Charlotte Fairbairn
Kelleth Old Hall,
Kelleth, Penrith,
Cumbria CA10 3UG
Tel   +44 (0)1539 623344
Mobile   +44 (0)7754 163941
Email   charlottefairbairn@hotmail.co.uk
Web   www.kelletholdhall.co.uk

Entry 82   Map 12

Cumbria

Drybeck Hall

Looking south to fields, woodland and beck this Grade II* listed, 1679 farmhouse has blue painted mullion windows and exposed beams. Expect a deeply traditional home with good furniture, an open fire and pictures of Anthony's predecessors looking down on you benignly; the family has been in the area for 800 years. Comfortable bedrooms have pretty floral fabrics and oak doors; bathrooms are simple but sparkling. Lulie is relaxed and charming and a good cook: enjoy a full English with free-range eggs in the sunny dining room, and home-grown vegetables and often game for dinner. A genuine slice of history.

Rooms	1 double, 1 twin: £90. Singles £45.
Meals	Dinner, 3 courses, £25. Pub/restaurant 4 miles.
Closed	Rarely.

Lulie & Anthony Hothfield
Drybeck Hall,
Appleby-in-Westmorland,
Cumbria CA16 6TF

Tel	+44 (0)1768 351487
Email	lulieant@aol.com
Web	www.drybeckhall.co.uk

Entry 83   Map 12

Cumbria

Lapwings Barn

In the back of most-beautiful-beyond, down narrow lanes, this converted barn is a gorgeous retreat for two – or four. Delightful generous Gillian and Rick give you privacy and an upstairs sitting room with log stove, sofa and a balcony with views. Bedrooms downstairs (separate entrances) are pleasingly rustic with beams and modern stone-tiled bathrooms. Breakfast is delivered: sausages and bacon from their Saddlebacks, eggs from their hens, superb homemade bread and marmalade. Stroll along lowland tracks, watch curlews and lapwings, puff to the top of Whinfell. Ambleside and Beatrix Potter's house are near. One of the best.

Rooms	Barn – 2 twin/doubles & sitting room: £60–£90. Singles from £35.
Meals	Packed lunch £5. Pub/restaurant 3.5 miles.
Closed	Rarely.

Rick & Gillian Rodriguez
Lapwings Barn,
Whinfell, Kendal,
Cumbria LA8 9EQ

Tel	+44 (0)1539 824373
Mobile	+44 (0)7901 732379
Email	stay@lapwingsbarn.co.uk
Web	www.lapwingsbarn.co.uk

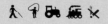

Entry 84   Map 12

Cumbria

Summerhow House

In four acres of fine landscaping and fun topiary is a large and inviting home of flamboyant wallpapers and shades of aqua, lemon and rose. Stylish but laid-back, grand but unintimidating, both house and hosts are a treat. Bedrooms have gilt frames and marble fireplaces, Molton Brown goodies and garden views, there are two sitting rooms to retreat to and breakfasts to delight you – fruits from the orchard, eggs from Sizergh Castle (John's family home). Two miles from Kendal: hop on the train to the Lakes. Walkers, sailors, skiers, food-lovers, dog-lovers will be charmed... aspiring actors too (talk to Janey!).

Rooms	1 double; 1 twin: £80–£120.
	Singles £50–£69.
Meals	Pub/restaurant 1.5 miles.
Closed	Occasionally.

	Janey & John Hornyold-Strickland
	Summerhow House,
	Shap Road,
	Kendal,
	Cumbria LA9 6NY
Tel	+44 (0)1539 720763
Email	stay@summerhowbedandbreakfast.co.uk
Web	www.summerhowbedandbreakfast.co.uk

Entry 85   Map 11

Cumbria

Parsonage House

The lane to this handsome Lakeland stone house is bordered by fields and fells, a beck runs through the garden and hens wander in the orchard. Step into a long hall with polished oak and Persian rugs, and be greeted as friends by Jeni and Steve. Their deeply comfortable home embraces you with log fires, books, family photographs, beautiful fabrics, excellent bedrooms and lots of art by Jeni. Morning sun streams into the dining room, and breakfast is served at separate linen-clad tables: fruits, granolas and a full cooked Cumbrian with local sausages and bacon. You can stroll to the pub for a good supper.

Minimum stay: 2 nights. Children over 12 welcome.

Rooms	3 doubles: £85–£120.
Meals	Restaurants 400 yds.
Closed	Rarely.

	Jeni & Steve Calvert
	Parsonage House,
	Kings Garth, Ings, Kendal,
	Cumbria LA8 9PU
Mobile	+44 (0)7881 385129/
	+44 (0)7881 382892
Email	parsonagehousebb@gmail.com
Web	www.parsonagehouse.co.uk

Entry 86   Map 11

Cumbria

Gillthwaite Rigg

All is calm and ordered in this airy and tranquil Arts and Crafts house. Come for nature and to be surrounded by lake and fell countryside – you may spot a badger or deer in the garden! Find panelled window seats, gleaming oak floors, leaded windows, wooden latched doors and motifs moulded into white plaster. Bedrooms with original fireplaces and large comfy beds have an uncluttered simplicity and views. Banks of books, wood-burners, proper Cumbrian breakfasts and kind, affable hosts add cheer. Rhoda and Tony are passionate about wildlife and conservation; there are acres to roam and their biomass boiler is fuelled from their woodland.

Babies & children over 6 welcome.

Rooms	1 double; 1 twin/double: £75–£90. Singles £60.
Meals	Pubs/restaurants 1 mile.
Closed	Christmas & New Year.

Rhoda M & Tony Graham
Gillthwaite Rigg,
Heathwaite Manor,
Lickbarrow Road, Windermere,
Cumbria LA23 2NQ

Tel	+44 (0)1539 446212
Mobile	+44 (0)7765 415934
Email	tonyandrhodagraham@hotmail.com
Web	www.gillthwaiterigg.co.uk

Entry 87   Map 11

Cumbria

Gilpin Mill

Come to be seriously spoiled. Down leafy lanes is a pretty white house by a mill pond, framed by pastures and trees. Steve took a year off to build new Gilpin Mill, and Jo looks after their labs and guests – beautifully. In the country farmhouse sitting room oak beams span the ceiling and a slate lintel sits above the log fire. Bedrooms are equally inviting: beds are topped with duck down, luscious bathrooms are warm underfoot. Alongside is a lovely old barn where timber was made into bobbins; in the mill pond is a salmon and trout ladder and a dam, soon to provide power for the grid. And just six cars pass a day!

Children over 10 welcome.

Rooms	3 twin/doubles: £90–£110. Singles £60–£70.
Meals	Pub 2.5 miles.
Closed	Christmas.

Jo & Steve Ainsworth
Gilpin Mill,
Crook,
Windermere,
Cumbria LA8 8LN

Tel	+44 (0)1539 568405
Email	info@gilpinmill.co.uk
Web	www.gilpinmill.co.uk

Entry 88   Map 11

Cumbria

Fellside Studios

Off the beaten tourist track, a piece of paradise in the Troutbeck valley: seclusion, stylishness and breathtaking views. Prepare your own candlelit dinners, rise when the mood takes you, come and go as you please. The flower beds spill with heathers, hens cluck, and there's a decked terrace for continental breakfast in the sun – freshly prepared by your gently hospitable hosts who live in the attached house. In your studio apartment you get oak floors, slate shower rooms, immaculate kitchenettes with designer touches, DVD players, comfy chairs, luxurious towels. Wonderful.

Minimum stay: 2 nights.

Rooms	1 double, 1 twin/double, each with kitchenette: £80–£100. Singles £50–£60.
Meals	Continental breakfast. Pub/restaurant 0.5 miles.
Closed	Rarely.

Monica & Brian Liddell
Fellside Studios,
Troutbeck,
Windermere,
Cumbria LA23 1NN

Tel	+44 (0)1539 434000
Email	brian@fellsidestudios.co.uk
Web	www.fellsidestudios.co.uk

Entry 89   Map 11

Cumbria

Broughton House

Down lanes edged with dry stone walls and hedges, with distant views of the Lakeland mountains... what peace! You feel instantly at home too, in a house full of books and colour. Bedrooms come with a jar of Cate's homemade brownies, a bowl of fruit and a deep mattress: a brass bed in one, privacy in the wing, snug simplicity in Ben's Cabin. Wake to fresh juice, pancakes, homemade bread, local bacon and sausages, smoked salmon and scrambled eggs. Muffin the dog, Minty the cat, a host of hens and a large garden all add to the charm. Perfect for cycling, a hop from lake Windermere and eating out in pretty Cartmel is a treat.

Rooms	2 doubles: £90. 1 cabin for 2 (1 double, 1 single, kitchen & yurt sitting room): £60–£70. Singles £50.
Meals	Pub 1 mile.
Closed	29 November – 27 December.

Cate Davies
Broughton House,
Field Broughton,
Grange-over-Sands,
Cumbria LA11 6HN

Tel	+44 (0)1539 536439
Email	info@broughtonhousecartmel.co.uk
Web	www.broughtonhousecartmel.co.uk

Entry 90   Map 11

Cumbria

Cockenskell Farm

The house and hill farm garden with its wild rhododendrons and damson orchard sits at the southern end of Lake Coniston and the views are glorious. Inside find beamed rooms, art and antique pine; bedrooms have pretty patchwork covers and lovely wallpapers. Relax with a book in the conservatory, stroll through the magical, bird-filled garden or tackle a bit of the Cumbrian Way which meanders through the fields to the back. On sunny days Sara will give you breakfast in the conservatory. History seeps from every pore, the place glows with loving care and to stay here is a treat.

Children over 12 welcome.

Rooms	1 twin; 1 twin with separate bath: £90. Singles from £45.
Meals	Packed lunch £7.50. Pubs 2-4 miles.
Closed	November-February.

	Sara Keegan
	Cockenskell Farm,
	Blawith, Ulverston,
	Cumbria LA12 8EL
Tel	+44 (0)1229 885217
Mobile	+44 (0)7909 885086
Email	keegan@cockenskell.co.uk
Web	www.cockenskell.co.uk

Entry 91 Map 11

Cumbria

New House Farm

The large comfy beds, the extravagant baths, the linen, the fabrics, the pillows – comfort par excellence! The renovation is impressive, too; the plasterwork stops here and there to reveal old beam, slate or stone. A trio of the bedrooms are named after the mountain each faces; Swinside brings the 1650s house its own spring water. The breakfast room has a wood-burner, hunting prints and polished tables for Hazel's breakfasts to fuel your adventures, the sitting room sports fireplaces and brocade sofas, and walkers will fall gratefully into the hot spring spa. Luxurious, and huge fun.

Children over 6 welcome.

Rooms	2 doubles, 1 twin/double; Stables – 2 four-posters: £110-£170. Singles £60-£85.
Meals	Lunch from £6 (Apr-Nov). Dinner, 3-5 courses, £32-£38. Packed lunch £8. Afternoon tea £5. Pubs 2.5 miles.
Closed	Rarely.

	Hazel Thompson
	New House Farm,
	Lorton,
	Cockermouth,
	Cumbria CA13 9UU
Mobile	+44 (0)7841 159818
Email	hazel@newhouse-farm.co.uk
Web	www.newhouse-farm.com

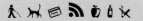

Entry 92 Map 11

Cumbria

Howe Keld

Dismiss all thoughts of the chintzy Keswick guest house: David and Val have swept through with carpets made of Herdwick sheep wool, local wood and slate, bedroom furniture made by a local craftsman and contemporary wallpapers and fabrics. It's luxurious but not flashy, and there's a cosy sitting room crammed with info on the area; theatre, shops and restaurants are all within strolling distance (choose rooms at the front if you need total quiet). Fill up at breakfast on home-baked bread, freshly made smoothies or a jolly good fry-up. A friendly, supremely comfortable place.

Minimum stay: 2 nights at weekends, 3 on bank holidays.

Rooms	13 doubles: £90-£130.
	1 single: £50-£95.
Meals	Pub/restaurant 300 yds.
Closed	Part of December including
	Christmas. Most of January
	excluding New Year.

David Fisher
Howe Keld,
5/7 The Heads,
Keswick,
Cumbria CA12 5ES

Tel	+44 (0)1768 772417
Email	david@howekeld.co.uk
Web	www.howekeld.co.uk

Derbyshire

Underleigh House

A Derbyshire longhouse in Brontë country built by a man called George Eyre. The position is unbeatable – field, river, hill, sky – but the stars of the show are Philip and Vivienne, dab hands at spoiling guests rotten. There's a big sitting room with maps for walkers, a dining room hall for hearty breakfasts, and tables and chairs scattered about the garden. Back inside, bedrooms vary in size, but all have super beds, goose down duvets and good views; a couple have doors onto the garden, the suites have proper sitting rooms. Fantastic walks start from the front door, Castleton Caves are on the doorstep and Chatsworth is close.

Minimum stay: 2 nights at weekends. Children over 12 welcome.

Rooms	3 doubles: £90-£95.
	2 suites for 2: £105-£110.
	Singles £75-£90.
Meals	Packed lunches £6.
	Pubs/restaurants 0.5 miles.
Closed	Christmas & January.

Philip & Vivienne Taylor
Underleigh House,
Lose Hill Lane, Hope,
Hope Valley,
Derbyshire S33 6AF

Tel	+44 (0)1433 621372
Email	underleigh.house@btconnect.com
Web	www.underleighhouse.co.uk

Brampton Barn Shepherd's Hut

Modelled on a traditional shepherd's hut with simple country furnishings and painted match boarding, a wood-burner, full-sized double bed and chairs with deep feather cushions – here you also have electric lighting and in the converted barn next door, a private kitchen area and washroom complete with flushing toilet and hot shower. The hut has become part of Brenda and Jeremy's farm and they'll happily advise on what to do and where to walk in this rich area of the Peak District. They can provide you with farm produce and both continental and traditional breakfast provisions, including their own honey. Very friendly.

Book through Sawday's Canopy & Stars online or by phone.

River Cottage

Well-travelled Gilly and John have restored their large house – built in the 1740s – and given it a fresh modern twist. Interiors are light and airy, with mirrors, antiques and immaculate fabrics giving each room a charm of its own. Attention to detail includes Gilly's legendary breakfasts – and five types of tea. Outside: a lovely tiered garden with the river Wye running through; easy to ignore the busy A6 when settled here with a glass of wine. Ashford-in-the-Water is one of the prettiest villages in the Peaks, fishing can be arranged and you are ten minutes from Chatsworth – there's a bus stop right outside the door.

Minimum stay: 2 nights at weekends Easter-October.

Rooms	Shepherd's hut for 2: £70.
Meals	Breakfast from £5 per person.
Closed	Christmas.

Rooms	3 doubles; 1 double with separate bath: £100–£125. Singles £85–£110.
Meals	Pubs 800 yds.
Closed	Mid-December to mid-February.

	Sawday's Canopy & Stars
	Brampton Barn Shepherd's Hut,
	Brampton Hall, Old Brampton,
	Chesterfield, Derbyshire S42 7JG
Tel	+44 (0)117 204 7830
Email	enquiries@canopyandstars.co.uk
Web	www.canopyandstars.co.uk/
	bramptonbarn

	Gilly & John Deacon
	River Cottage,
	Buxton Road,
	Ashford-in-the-Water, Bakewell,
	Derbyshire DE45 1QP
Tel	+44 (0)1629 813327
Email	info@rivercottageashford.co.uk
Web	www.rivercottageashford.co.uk

Entry 95   Map 8   Entry 96   Map 8

Derbyshire

The Lodge at Dale End House

One of those places where you get your own annexe – in this case, the former milking parlour of the listed farmhouse. It certainly has scrubbed up nicely. The ground-floor bedroom has a finely dressed antique bed and magnificent chandelier while the well-equipped kitchen is a boon if you don't fancy venturing out for supper. Friendly, helpful Sarah takes orders for breakfasts – eggs from her hens, local sausages and bacon – and delivers to your door. No open fire but cosy underfloor heating warms you after a blustery yomp in any direction. Bring your four-legged friends – canine or equine – to this happy house.

Rooms	Lodge – 1 double with kitchen/dining/sitting room: £85-£95.
Meals	Pubs/restaurants 2.5 miles.
Closed	Rarely.

Sarah & Paul Summers
The Lodge at Dale End House,
Gratton, Bakewell,
Derbyshire DE45 1LN

Tel	+44 (0)1629 650380
Email	thebarn@daleendhouse.co.uk
Web	www.daleendhouse.co.uk

Entry 97   Map 8

Derbyshire

Old Shoulder of Mutton

The lively village of Winster is mega-pretty; the Old Shoulder of Mutton, once a pub, sits in its middle. Steven and Julie are welcoming and their home is as cosy as can be. Find a warm contemporary and traditional mix, framed clay pipes (found during renovations), a charming drawing room, luxurious bedrooms and snazzy en suite bathrooms. Breakfast is by the wood-burner: feast on eggs Benedict, homemade jam, local bacon and the famous Derbyshire oatcakes. There's a lovely and unexpected garden at the back; Bakewell, with its legendary Monday market and Chatsworth House, is a short drive, and the walking is dreamy.

Children over 12 welcome. Minimum stay: 2 nights.

Rooms	2 doubles, 1 twin/double: £95-£140.
Meals	Pubs in village.
Closed	Rarely.

Steven White
Old Shoulder of Mutton,
West Bank,
Winster, Matlock,
Derbyshire DE4 2DQ

Tel	+44 (0)1629 650005
Email	steven@theoldshoulderofmutton.co.uk
Web	www.oldshoulderofmutton.co.uk

Entry 98   Map 8

Derbyshire

Manor Farm

Between two small dales, close to great houses (Chatsworth, Hardwick Hall, Haddon Hall), lies this cluster of ancient farms and church; welcome to the 16th century! Simon and Gilly, warm, delightful and fascinated by the history, have restored the east wing to create big, beamy rooms in the old hayloft and a pretty garden room on the ground floor; a cosy and quaint bedroom overlooks the church. Wake to a scrumptious breakfast in the cavernous Elizabethan kitchen. There's a 'book exchange' in the old milking parlour and a lovely garden with sweeping views across the valley and distant hills.

Children over 6 welcome.

Rooms	1 double, 2 twin/doubles: £80-£90. 1 family room for 2-4: £80-£140. Singles £55-£70.
Meals	Pubs within 10-minute drive.
Closed	Rarely.

Simon & Gilly Groom
Manor Farm,
Dethick, Matlock,
Derbyshire DE4 5GG
Tel   +44 (0)1629 534302
Mobile +44 (0)7944 660814
Email   gilly.groom@w3z.co.uk
Web   www.manorfarmdethick.co.uk

Entry 99   Map 8

Derbyshire

Mount Tabor House

On a steep hillside between the Peaks and the Dales, a chapel in a pretty village with a peaceful aura and great views. Enter a hall where light streams through stained-glass windows – this is a relaxed, easy place to stay with a distinctive and original interior, a log-burner to keep you toasty and a sweet dog called Molly. Fay is charming and generous and breakfast, in a dining room with open stone walls, is delicious: mainly from the village shops and as organic as possible; you can eat on the balcony in summer. Walk to the pub for dinner, come home to a fabulous wet room and a big inviting bed.

Usually minimum stay: 2 nights at weekends.

Rooms	1 twin/double: £90-£95. Extra bed/sofabed available £10-£30 per person per night.
Meals	Occasional dinner £25. Pub 100 yds.
Closed	Rarely.

Fay Whitehead
Mount Tabor House,
Bowns Hill, Crich,
Matlock,
Derbyshire DE4 5DG
Tel   +44 (0)1773 857008
Mobile +44 (0)7813 007478
Email   mountabor@msn.com

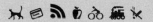

Entry 100   Map 8

Derbyshire

Park View Farm

An extravagant refuge after a long journey, run by hospitable hosts. Daringly decadent, every inch of this Victorian farmhouse brims with flowers, sparkling trinkets, polished brass, plump cushions and swathes of chintz. Bedrooms with beautiful views dance in swirls of colour, frills, gleaming wood, lustrous glass, buttons and bows; fresh eggs, fresh fruits, homemade breads and their own rare-breed sausages accompany the grand performance. Have afternoon tea on the vine covered terrace, roam the 370 organic acres. Kedleston Hall Park provides a stunning backdrop.

Rooms	2 four-posters; 1 four-poster with separate bath: £85-£90. Singles £65.
Meals	Pub/restaurant 1 mile.
Closed	Christmas.

Linda Adams
Park View Farm,
Weston Underwood, Ashbourne,
Derbyshire DE6 4PA
Tel +44 (0)1335 360352
Mobile +44 (0)7771 573057
Email enquiries@parkviewfarm.co.uk
Web www.parkviewfarm.co.uk

Entry 101   Map 8

Derbyshire

Alstonefield Manor

Country manor house definitely, but delightfully understated and cleverly designed to look natural. This family home, sitting in walled gardens, is high in the hills above Dovedale. Local girl Jo spoils you with homemade scones and tea when you arrive, served on the lawns or by the fire in the elegant drawing room. Beautiful bedrooms have antiques, flowers, lovely fabrics, painted floors and garden views; wood panelled bathrooms have showers or a roll top tub. Wake to birdsong – and a candlelit breakfast with local bacon and Staffordshire oatcakes. After a great walk, stroll across the village green for supper at The George. A joy.

Minimum stay: 2 nights. Children over 12 welcome.

Rooms	1 double, 2 doubles, each with separate bath: £110-£150. Singles from £95.
Meals	Pub 100 yds.
Closed	Christmas & occasionally.

Robert & Jo Wood
Alstonefield Manor,
Alstonefield,
Ashbourne,
Derbyshire DE6 2FX
Tel +44 (0)1335 310393
Email stay@alstonefieldmanor.com
Web www.alstonefieldmanor.com

Entry 102   Map 8

Derbyshire

Beechenhill Farm

Perched bang in the middle of the Peak District. Sustainable thinking has created this progressive family run, organic farm. Sue, an artist renowned for Swedish folk art, set targets to reduce their carbon footprint — so successfully she now guides others. Feed chickens, watch cows come home for milking, sit in a hot tub or eccentric sauna cave, even get married in a beautifully romantic hall. All is country-cosy, dotted with animal collections, tapestries and local art; views flood bedrooms (the family one has a pocket shower room). Organic breakfasts are a treat, and nippers will love Sue's adventure maps. Unwind and replenish...

Minimum stay: 2 nights. Children over 3 welcome.

Rooms	1 double: £88-£90. 1 family room for 3-4: £88-£130. Singles £52.
Meals	Pubs 2 miles.
Closed	November-March.

Sue Prince
Beechenhill Farm,
Ilam Moor Lane, Ilam,
Derbyshire DE6 2BD
Tel   +44 (0)1335 310274
Email   stay@beechenhill.co.uk
Web   www.beechenhill.co.uk

Entry 103   Map 8

Devon

Seaview House

Morning sun pours into the dining room... tuck in to breakfast to the sound of seagulls and classical music. Your host is fun and well-travelled, and this house has heaps of personality: driftwood carvings above an open fire, a charcoal nude, a Rajasthani mirror embroidery hanging, white sofas, polished antiques and French style painted furniture. Your ground floor bedroom has a richly dressed bed, the bathroom a cheery seaside feel. Enjoy views from the living rooms to Bigbury Bay and Thurlestone Rock, walk to great beaches and across the river to Burgh Island; there's a cliff-top golf club and Kingsbridge and Salcombe (full of boats and cafés) are a short drive.

Rooms	1 twin/double: £75. Singles £60.
Meals	Pub 0.25 miles.
Closed	Rarely.

J Meredith
Seaview House,
Thurlestone,
Kingsbridge,
Devon TQ7 3NE
Mobile   +44 (0)7711 704193
Email   jan.meredith1@gmail.com

Entry 104   Map 2

Devon

Keynedon Mill

Welcome to an ancient stone mill, and beautiful rooms in the old miller's house. There's a big friendly kitchen with stone floors and a cheerful red Aga, a beamed dining room with a long polished table, a guest sitting room with a wood-burner, and a pretty garden with a stream running through – picnic, read, enjoy a glass of wine in peaceful corners. Elegant bedrooms have superb beds, antique linen curtains, fresh flowers, morning tea trays and garden views. A delicious breakfast of home-baked bread and local produce will set you up for the day: walk the coastal path, discover secluded coves.

Minimum stay: 2 nights. Children over 8 welcome.

Rooms	2 doubles, each with separate bath/shower; 1 twin: £90–£110. 1 family room for 3: £110. Singles £55–£75.
Meals	Picnics and lunches by arrangement. Pub 0.5 miles.
Closed	Rarely.

Stuart & Jennifer Jebb
Keynedon Mill,
Sherford, Kingsbridge,
Devon TQ7 2AS

Tel	+44 (0)1548 531485
Mobile	+44 (0)7775 501409
Email	bookings@keynedonmill.co.uk
Web	www.keynedonmill.co.uk

Entry 105   Map 2

Devon

Stokenham House

Lovely Stokenham House gazes at the sea and the bird-rich Slapton Ley. Iona and Paul – an energetic and thoughtful, creative couple – have made a super South Hams base: huge chill-out cushions on the lawn, summerhouse in the pretty banked garden, BBQ by the pool. It's grand yet laid-back, with a fine drawing room, big conservatory and a family-friendly feel. Learn to cook or grow veg, invite friends for dinner, host your own party: Iona is a superb cook. The funky large annexe suite is very private; generous bedrooms in the house are decked in vintage fabrics and papers, and have single rooms off.

Dogs welcome in downstairs room.

Rooms	1 twin/double, sharing separate bath with single; 1 suite for 2: £120. 1 family room for 4 (extra beds available): £120–£210. 1 single sharing bath with twin/double: £45. Child over 5: £35. Cots & highchairs available.
Meals	Dinner from £30. Pubs/restaurants 2-minute walk.
Closed	Rarely.

Iona & Paul Jepson
Stokenham House,
Stokenham, Kingsbridge,
Devon TQ7 2ST

Tel	+44 (0)1548 581257
Mobile	+44 (0)7720 443132
Email	ionajepson@googlemail.com
Web	www.stokenhamhouse.co.uk

Entry 106   Map 2

Devon

Strete Barton House

Contemporary, friendly, exotic and exquisite: French sleigh beds and Asian art, white basins and black chandeliers, and a garden with sofas for the views. So much to love – and best of all, the coastal path outside the door. Your caring hosts live the dream, running immaculate B&B by the sea, in an old manor house at the top of the village. Breakfasts are exuberantly local (village eggs, sausages from Dartmouth, honey from the bay), there's a wood-burner in the sitting room, warm toasty floors and Kevin and Stuart know exactly which beach, walk or pub is the one for you. Heavenly.

Minimum stay: 2 nights in summer.

Rooms	3 doubles, 1 twin/double; 1 twin/double with separate shower: £105-£140. Cottage: 1 suite & sitting room: £150-£160.
Meals	Pub/restaurant 50 yds.
Closed	Rarely.

Stuart Litster & Kevin Hooper
Strete Barton House,
Totnes Road, Strete,
Dartmouth, Devon TQ6 0RU
Tel   +44 (0)1803 770364
Email   info@stretebarton.co.uk
Web   www.stretebarton.co.uk

Entry 107   Map 2

Devon

Nonsuch House

The photo says it all! You are in your own crow's nest, perched above the flotillas of yachts zipping in and out of the estuary mouth: stunning. Kit and Penny are great fun and look after you well; ex-hotelier Kit smokes his own fish fresh from the quay and produces brilliant dinners. Further pleasures lie across the water... and a five-minute walk brings you to the ferry that transports you, and your car, to the other side. Breakfasts in the conservatory are a delight, bedrooms are big and comfortable, and fresh bathrooms sparkle.

Minimum stay: 2 nights at weekends. Over 10s welcome.

Rooms	1 double; 3 twin/doubles: £115-£170. Singles £90-£145.
Meals	Dinner, 3 courses, £37.50 (not Tues/Wed/Sat). Pub/restaurant 5-minute walk & short boat trip.
Closed	Rarely.

Kit & Penny Noble
Nonsuch House,
Church Hill, Kingswear,
Dartmouth, Devon TQ6 0BX
Tel   +44 (0)1803 752829
Email   enquiries@nonsuch-house.co.uk
Web   www.nonsuch-house.co.uk

Entry 108   Map 2

Devon

Brightwater House

Hearts will soar: you're right up in the crow's nest here and feeling smugly private, with breathtaking views over the yacht-spotted river to Dartmouth and the Naval College. Painter Susie's 1930s house is splashed with sunlight from three sides in the tiled conservatory with Lloyd Loom chairs, fresh flowers, shelves of books; you breakfast heartily here while boat-watching. The bedroom has its own entrance from the garden terrace (down steep steps), and is small and pretty with white painted furniture, pale silk curtains and Susie's paintings; the bathroom is modern, new and fresh with cream stone tiles. Beguiling.

Low season 5% discount breaks (3-6 nights).

Rooms	1 twin: £105-£125.
	Singles £95-£115.
Meals	Pubs/restaurants 5-minute walk.
Closed	Rarely.

Susie Bennett
Brightwater House,
Higher Contour Road, Kingswear,
Dartmouth, Devon TQ6 0DE
Tel   +44 (0)1803 752898
Email   sben2121@yahoo.co.uk
Web   www.brightwaterhouse.co.uk

Entry 109   Map 2

Devon

Kaywana Hall

With glossy modern lines and sparkling glass in its own wooded valley, this is a 'Grand Designs' project in the making. All is smart and contemporary from the great oil paintings and slate and wooden floors to the ultra-crisp bed linen and immaculate bathrooms. The bedrooms are separate from the main house and up steps; one has views over the pool, and all have private terraces. The feel is spacious and uncluttered but warm and cosy, too. Friendly Tony gives you delicious locally sourced choices at breakfast, you can hop on the ferry for Dartmouth and close by are regattas, gardens to visit, beaches and steam train and river trips.

Minimum stay: 2 nights.

Rooms	2 doubles, 1 twin/double: £140-£165.
	Singles £120-£155.
Meals	Pub/restaurant 0.5 miles.
Closed	1 December – 1 March.

Anthony Pithers & Gordon Craig
Kaywana Hall,
Higher Contour Road, Kingswear,
Dartmouth, Devon TQ6 0AY
Tel   +44 (0)1803 752200
Email   res@kaywanahall.co.uk
Web   www.kaywanahall.co.uk

Entry 110   Map 2

Devon

Fingals

Welcome back to an institution from our first B&B book. We call it an 'institution' not because it has been going so long that some of the original guests' grandchildren now take their girlfriends, but because it has always been beyond categorisation. Richard and Sheila are moving back into their Queen Anne manor farmhouse and winding down – but as ever doing it their own way. Stay in a best hotel room, or self-cater in rooms nattily converted into apartments. The old laissez-faire atmosphere remains: honesty bar, wood-panelled dining room (dinner on occasion), grass court, pool and gym. Not your run-of -the-mill B&B… but nor are Richard and Sheila.

Minimum stay: 2 nights at weekends.

Rooms	3 doubles: £110-£210. Self-catering: 1 for 2; 1 for 4; 1 for 5; 1 for 6: £300-£1200 per week. Extra bed/sofabed available £15 p.p.p.n.
Meals	Dinner £36. Pub 1 mile; restaurants 6 miles.
Closed	Mid-January to mid-March.

Sawday's
BED & BREAKFAST

One of a kind

	Richard & Sheila Johnston
	Fingals,
	Dittisham,
	Dartmouth,
	Devon TQ6 0JA
Tel	+44 (0)1803 722398
Email	info@fingals.co.uk
Web	www.fingals.co.uk

Entry 111   Map 2

Devon

Kerswell Farmhouse

Close to Totnes yet out in the wilds, this house and barn sit on a ridge with glorious views to Dartmoor. Twelve years ago the Devon longhouse was in poor repair: you'd never know now! All has been transformed by oak – seasoned and new – while the front sports a gorgeous conservatory. Graham sells British art (on fabulous display), Nichola is an interior designer, together they run truly welcoming B&B. Bedrooms are super-comfortable with electronic slatted blinds, bathrooms are state of the art, and the suite comes with its own slice of garden. Books and DVDs are on tap, food and wines are a serious treat.

Children over 12 welcome.

Rooms	2 doubles: £105-£140. Barn: 1 twin/double: £105-£140. Barn: 1 suite: £140. 1 single with separate bath: £65-£105. Dinner, B&B £80-£100 per person.
Meals	Dinner £30. Restaurants 2 miles.
Closed	22 December – 6 January.

	Graham & Nichola Hawkins
	Kerswell Farmhouse,
	Kerswell, Cornworthy,
	Totnes, Devon TQ9 7HH
Tel	+44 (0)1803 732013
Mobile	+44 (0)7503 335507
Email	gjnhawkins@rocketmail.com
Web	www.kerswellfarmhouse.co.uk

Entry 112   Map 2

Devon

Devon

Riverside House

The loveliest 18th-century house with the tidal river estuary bobbing past with boats and birds; dip your toes in the water while sitting in the garden. Felicity, an artist, and Roger, a passionate sailor, give you pretty bedrooms with paintings, poetry, little balconies, wide French windows and binoculars; spot swans at high tide, herons (perhaps a kingfisher) when the river goes down. Stroll to the pub for quayside barbecues and jazz in summer; catch the ferry from Dittisham to Agatha Christie's house; discover delightful Dartmouth. Kayaks and inflatables are welcome by arrangement.

Minimum stay: 2 nights at weekends.

The Old Parsonage

Marilyn's relaxed Georgian house shines with light and polish. It's beautiful inside and out: bedrooms with luxurious linen and quilts, chocolates and tea trays; bathrooms with scented lotions, robes and slippers; a walled garden with rare-breed hens and rows of produce. Breakfast is set with pretty china and place mats on a crisp table cloth: fruit salad, a continental choice or a full English cooked on the Aga. A spreading magnolia provides a delightful breakfast spot in summer. Walks and beaches are good; lively Totnes and Dartington are close. Return, and settle with a book on a huge sofa next to the open fire. Bliss.

Rooms	1 double; 1 double with separate shower: £80–£95. Singles £75. Extra bed/sofabed available £30 per person per night.
Meals	Pubs 100 yds.
Closed	Rarely.

Rooms	2 doubles; 1 double with separate bath/shower: £95. Singles £65.
Meals	Pubs/restaurants 1 mile.
Closed	Rarely.

	Felicity & Roger Jobson Riverside House, Tuckenhay, Totnes, Devon TQ9 7EQ
Tel	+44 (0)1803 732837
Mobile	+44 (0)7710 510007
Email	felicity.riverside@hotmail.co.uk
Web	www.riverside-house.co.uk

	Marilyn Harvey The Old Parsonage, Harbertonford, Totnes, Devon TQ9 7TP
Tel	+44 (0)1803 732121
Email	info@theoldparsonagedevon.com
Web	www.theoldparsonagedevon.com

Entry 113   Map 2

Entry 114   Map 2

Devon

Avenue Cottage

The tree-lined approach is steep and spectacular; the cottage sits in 11 wondrous acres of rhododendron, magnolia and wild flowers with a lily-strewn pond, grassy paths and lovely views over the river. Find a quiet spot in which to read or simply sit and absorb the tranquillity. Richard is a gifted gardener, and the archetypal gardener's modesty and calm have penetrated the house itself – it is uncluttered, comfortable and warmed by a log fire. The old-fashioned twin room has a big bathroom with a walk-in shower and a balcony with sweeping valley views; the pretty village and pub are a short walk away.

Rooms	1 twin/double (en suite); 1 double sharing shower room with owner: £70–£90. Singles £45–£55.
Meals	Pub 0.25 miles.
Closed	Rarely.

	Richard Pitts
	Avenue Cottage,
	Ashprington, Totnes,
	Devon TQ9 7UT
Tel	+44 (0)1803 732769
Mobile	+44 (0)7719 147475
Email	richard.pitts@btinternet.com
Web	www.avenuecottage.com

Entry 115   Map 2

Devon

Stoke Gabriel Lodgings

Deep in dreamy Devon countryside – but up, up high, free, above the river Dart – a deliciously simple, shiny new house where balconies gulp in long light views and large rooms are shot with rich raspberry, deep turquoise and purple hues. David and Helen's enthusiasm is infectious, both for their home (white walls, oak floors, silk and swish fittings) and village (millpond, jetty, pubs, café and ancient yew). So let them spoil you: cream tea on arrival, smoked salmon for breakfast, an open fire in the family sitting room, a crossword in the conservatory. With these hosts, with this view, you won't want to go home.

Rooms	2 doubles; 1 twin/double: £90–£100. Singles £60–£65
Meals	Pubs/restaurants within walking distance.
Closed	Rarely.

	Helen & David Littlefair
	Stoke Gabriel Lodgings,
	Badger's Retreat, 2 Orchard Close,
	Stoke Gabriel, Totnes,
	Devon TQ9 6SX
Tel	+44 (0)1803 782003
Mobile	+44 (0)7785 710225
Email	info@stokegabriellodgings.com

Entry 116   Map 2

Devon

Kilbury Manor

You can stroll down to the Dart from the garden and onto their little island, when the river's not in spate! Back at the Manor – a listed longhouse from the 1700s – are four super-comfortable bedrooms, the most private in the stone barn. Your genuinely welcoming hosts (with dogs Dillon and Buster) moved to Devon to renovate a big handsome house and open it to guests. Julia does everything beautifully so there's organic smoked salmon and delicious French toast for breakfast, baskets of toiletries by the bath, the best linen on the best beds and a drying room for wet gear – handy if you've come to walk the Moor. Spot-on B&B.

Rooms	1 double; 1 double with separate bath; Barn – 2 doubles: £75-£90. Singles from £65.
Meals	Pubs/restaurants 1.5-4 miles.
Closed	Rarely.

Julia & Martin Blundell
Kilbury Manor,
Colston Road,
Buckfastleigh,
Devon TQ11 0LN

Tel	+44 (0)1364 644079
Email	info@kilburymanor.co.uk
Web	www.kilburymanor.co.uk

Entry 117   Map 2

Devon

Mitchelcroft

Saunter down mown paths through meadow grass... The wooden verandah has pots of flowers, the pond attracts dragonflies and the magnificent garden is full of wildlife. Michael has done some stylish redesigning of this 1960s bungalow – and he and Deborah have created a friendly home. Bedrooms come with king-size beds, good linen, an abundance of flowers and personal touches; each has its own outside spot – sleep out on the terrace if you fancy some stargazing! Marvel at panoramic views while you tuck into a breakfast of fruits, cereals, nuts and the full works. Dartmoor National Park beckons, and it's a five-minute walk to a good pub.

Minimum stay: 2 nights at weekends & in high season.

Rooms	3 doubles: £80-£100. Singles £60.
Meals	Light supper available. Pub 5-minute walk. Hosted weekends with dinner & guided walking/cycling tours (min. 6).
Closed	November-March.

Deborah Owen
Mitchelcroft,
Scoriton, Buckfastleigh,
Devon TQ11 0HU

Tel	+44 (0)1364 631336
Mobile	+44 (0)7841 342070
Email	mitchelcroft@hotmail.co.uk
Web	www.mitchelcroft.co.uk

Entry 118   Map 2

Devon

Agaric Rooms at Tudor House

A merchant's townhouse now happily given over to rooms for the Agaric Restaurant. Sophie and Nick are young, fun and very clever: in these mostly large, individually styled rooms, fabrics are plush, colours rich and bathrooms have roll tops, robes and smart towels; the ground floor double has a striking wet room. A breakfast room is cool with leather and palms; full English or anything else you want is served here. Don't come without booking into the restaurant for fabulous modern British cooking – then stagger two steps down the street to your well-earned bed. Ashburton bustles with good food shops, antiques and books.

Rooms	2 doubles: £120.
	1 family room for 4: £140–£170.
	1 single: £58–£70.
Meals	Owners' restaurant next door.
	Packed lunch from £10 for 2.
Closed	Rarely.

Sophie & Nick Coiley
Agaric Rooms at Tudor House,
36 North Street, Ashburton,
Devon TQ13 7QD

Tel	+44 (0)1364 654478
Email	eat@agaricrestaurant.co.uk
Web	www.agaricrestaurant.co.uk

Entry 119   Map 2

Devon

Penpark

Clough Williams-Ellis of Portmeirion fame did more than design an elegant house; he made sure it communed with nature. High on a hill overlooking the valley, light pours in to this lovely house from every window, and the views stretch across rolling farmland to Dartmoor and Hay Tor. The big double has a comfy sofa and its own balcony; the spacious private suite has arched French windows to gardens, pretty woodland beyond, and an extra room for young children. All is traditional and comforting: antiques, heirlooms, African carvings, silk and fresh flowers, richly coloured rugs. Your charming, generous hosts look after you well.

Rooms	2 twin/doubles, each with separate
	bath/shower: £76–£84.
	1 family room for 4 with separate
	shower (ground floor garden room,
	dogs welcome): £76–£84.
	Singles by arrangement.
Meals	Pubs/restaurants 3 miles.
Closed	Rarely.

Madeleine & Michael Gregson
Penpark,
Bickington, Ashburton,
Devon TQ12 6LH

Tel	+44 (0)1626 821314
Email	maddy@penpark.co.uk
Web	www.penpark.co.uk

Entry 120   Map 2

Devon

Highfield House

Come for complete peace in the Dartmoor National Park and be bowled over by the views from the glorious garden. Helen is charming and her smart contemporary house gleams; light floods in through huge windows and the south-facing terrace runs the length of the house. Large bedrooms with armchairs are sumptuous, one has its own roof terrace with views of the moor; bathrooms are sparkling and modern. The birds sing, the pale oak floors are heated from below and the locally sourced breakfast is generous. Wonderful walks start at the end of the garden and the pretty village has a friendly pub serving good food.

Minimum stay: 2 nights. Children over 12 welcome.

Rooms	1 double, 2 twin/doubles: £80–£90. Singles £75–£85.
Meals	Pub 300 yds. Restaurants within 5 miles.
Closed	1 November – 14 February.

Helen Waterworth
Highfield House,
Mapstone Hill, Lustleigh, Newton
Abbot, Devon TQ13 9SE
Tel   +44 (0)1647 277577
Email   helen@highfieldhousedevon.co.uk
Web   www.highfieldhousedevon.co.uk

Entry 121   Map 2

Devon

Corndonford Farm

An ancient Devon longhouse and an engagingly chaotic haven run by warm and friendly Ann and Will, along with their Dartmoor ponies. Steep, stone circular stairs lead to bedrooms: bright colours, a four-poster with lacy curtains, gorgeous views over the cottage garden and a bathroom with a beam to duck. A place for those who want to get into the spirit of it all – maybe help catch an escaped foal, chatter to the farm workers around the table; not for fussy types or Mr and Mrs Tickety Boo! Delicious Aga breakfasts and good for walkers too – the Two Moors Way is on the doorstep.

Under 10s by arrangement.

Rooms	1 four-poster; 1 twin with separate bath: £80. Singles £40.
Meals	Pub 2 miles.
Closed	Rarely.

Ann & Will Williams
Corndonford Farm,
Poundsgate,
Newton Abbot,
Devon TQ13 7PP
Tel   +44 (0)1364 631595
Email   corndonford@btinternet.com

Entry 122   Map 2

Devon

Cyprian's Cot

A charming 16th-century terraced cottage filled with beams and burnished wood. The old stone fireplace is huge, the grandfather clock ticks, the views are stunning and Shelagh is warm and welcoming. Guests have their own sitting room with a crackling fire; up the narrow stairs and into cosy bedrooms – a small double and a tiny twin. Tasty breakfasts, served in the dining room, include free-range eggs, sausages and bacon from the local farm and garden fruits. Discover the lovely town with its pubs, fine restaurant and interesting shops. With the Dartmoor Way and the Two Moors Way on the doorstep, the walking is wonderful too.

Rooms	1 twin; 1 double with separate bath: £65-£75. Singles £32-£35.
Meals	Pubs/restaurants 4-minute walk.
Closed	Rarely.

Shelagh Weeden
Cyprian's Cot,
47 New Street, Chagford,
Newton Abbot,
Devon TQ13 8BB

Tel	+44 (0)1647 432256
Email	shelaghweeden@btinternet.com
Web	www.cyprianscot.co.uk

Entry 123   Map 2

Devon

New Entry
INSPECTED & SELECTED
A SPECIAL PLACE

Rose Cottage

On a quiet country road on the edge of Peter Tavy is a pretty slate-hung cottage and a garden full of birds: Pippin's delight. Enter to find a dining room with a shining wooden floor, a fine Georgian table and a smart Aga to keep things cosy. Bedrooms are sunny; 'Blue Room' and 'Rose Room' have lovely fabrics, watercolours, luxuriously comfy king-size beds and TVs; the sweet twin shares a bathroom with 'Rose' so is perfect for families. After a generous breakfast, pull on your boots and stride onto Dartmoor – or visit Pippin's favourite gardens. Then it's home to a delicious dinner – and hot water bottles on chilly nights.

Minimum stay: 2 nights at weekends. Babes in arms and children over 8 welcome.

Rooms	1 double; 1 double, 1 twin sharing bath (let to same party only): £70. Singles £40.
Meals	Dinner, 2 courses, £20. Pubs/restaurants 0.5 miles.
Closed	Christmas.

Pippin Clarke
Rose Cottage,
Peter Tavey,
Tavistock,
Devon PL19 9NP

Tel	+44 (0)1822 810500
Email	rose.pippin@gmail.com
Web	rosecottagedartmoor.co.uk/

Entry 124   Map 2

Devon

Wonwood Barton

A Thomas Hardy feel here... with stone barns wrapping around a pretty courtyard. In the middle is the Roundhouse, where you have breakfast – huge table, toasty stove and a bar in the corner. The two independent ground floor rooms each have a wood-burner and sweet seating area, old beams and high ceilings, painted furniture and jaunty cushions; views stretch across the Tamar and beyond to Cornwall. Claudine and Bill (and their labradors) are charming and look after you well. Tamar Valley is stunning and so unspoilt; head off for walks, cycling, canoeing and good gardens. Return to snuggle by your fire – supper can be made for you too.

Minimum stay: 2 nights at weekends & in high season.

Rooms	1 double, 1 twin/double: £80–£90.
Meals	Dinner, 2-3 courses, £15–£20. Pubs/restaurants 1 mile.
Closed	Rarely.

Claudine & Bill Sparks
Wonwood Barton,
Lamerton, Tavistock,
Devon PL19 8SE

Tel	+44 (0)1822 870533
Mobile	+44 (0)7970 128229
Email	booking.wonwood@gmail.com
Web	www.wonwoodbarton.com

Entry 125   Map 2

Devon

Burnville House

Granite gateposts, Georgian house, rhododendrons, beechwoods and rolling fields of sheep: that's the setting. But there's more. Beautifully proportioned rooms reveal subtle colours, elegant antiques, squishy sofas and bucolic views, stylish bathrooms are sprinkled with candles, there are sumptuous dinners and pancakes at breakfast. Your hosts left busy jobs in London to settle here, and their place breathes life – space, smiles, energy. Swim, play tennis, walk to Dartmoor from the door, take a trip to Eden or the sea. Or... just gaze at the moors and the church on the Tor and listen to the silence, and the sheep.

Rooms	3 doubles: £85–£95. Singles £65.
Meals	Dinner from £23. Pub 2 miles.
Closed	Rarely.

Victoria Cunningham
Burnville House,
Brentor, Tavistock,
Devon PL19 0NE

Tel	+44 (0)1822 820443
Mobile	+44 (0)7881 583471
Email	burnvillef@aol.com
Web	www.burnville.co.uk

Entry 126   Map 2

Jacob's Hut

In glorious, peaceful Devon, with views to Thrushelton church, is this lovingly handcrafted shepherd's hut. It's light, simple and uncluttered, with a pretty dresser and binoculars to help you identify your feathered neighbours. You can see the pond through the stable door or sit outside under the weeping willows and look out for kingfishers. There's a private shower room 60 yards away, attached to Josephine and Gordon's house; they deliver your breakfast to the summerhouse whenever you want. You can rustle up a meal there to eat by the fire, or head out for dinner; there are good pubs locally, and a farm shop (great pasties!).

Minimum stay: 2 nights. Book through Sawday's Canopy & Stars online or by phone.

Rooms	Shepherd's hut for 2: £80.
Meals	Breakfast hamper included. Full English from £5 per person.
Closed	November–March.

Sawday's Canopy & Stars
Jacob's Hut,
Lewdown,
Okehampton,
Devon EX20 4QY

Tel	+44 (0)117 204 7830
Email	enquiries@canopyandstars.co.uk
Web	www.canopyandstars.co.uk/jacobshut

Entry 127   Map 2

Higher Eggbeer Farm

Over 900 years old and still humming with life. A farming menagerie share the rambling gardens, and children can't believe their luck: ponies to shampoo, kittens to play with, piglets to feed. Sally Anne and sons, Alistair and Robin, are wonderful hosts: friendly, artistic, fun and slightly wacky. It's an adventure to stay so keep an open mind as the house is a historic gem and undeniably rustic. Huge fireplaces, interesting art, books, piano, wellies, muddle and lived-in charm; the family are happy to babysit too. Be wrapped in peace in one of two wings, immersed in a panorama of forest, hills and fields of waving wheat.

Rooms	East Wing – 1 double, 1 twin sharing bath/shower (let to same party only); West Wing – 2 doubles, 1 twin sharing baths & 2nd wc: £65–£95. West Wing – 1 single sharing baths & 2nd wc with 2 doubles & 1 twin: £55–£65.
Meals	Restaurants 5-minute walk.
Closed	Rarely.

Sally Anne Selwyn & Alistair Scott Lawson
Higher Eggbeer Farm,
Cheriton Bishop, Exeter,
Devon EX6 6JQ

Tel	+44 (0)1647 24427
Mobile	+44 (0)7850 136131
Email	ascottlawson@gmail.com
Web	www.higher-eggbeer.co.uk

Entry 128   Map 2

Brook Farmhouse

Tuck yourself up in the peace and quiet of Paul and Penny's whitewashed, thatched cottage, surrounded by glorious countryside. Inside find your own charming sitting room with a huge inglenook, good antiques, fresh flowers, and comfy sofa and chairs; breakfast here on homemade apple juice, eggs from the owners' hens and delicious local bacon and sausages. Up the ancient spiral stone stairs is your warm, beamed bedroom with smooth linen, chintzy curtains, lots of cushions. You are near Dartmoor and can reach Devon beaches and the north Cornish coast; perfect for hearty walkers, birdwatchers, surfers and picnic-lovers.

Rooms	1 double with separate bath: £80–£85. Singles £55–£65.
Meals	Pub 2 miles.
Closed	Rarely.

Paul & Penny Steadman
Brook Farmhouse,
Tedburn St Mary,
Exeter,
Devon EX6 6DS
Tel +44 (0)1647 270042
Email penny.steadman@btconnect.com
Web www.brook-farmhouse.co.uk

New Entry
INSPECTED & SELECTED
A SPECIAL PLACE

Coombe Farmhouse

Old and new blend perfectly here in this 400-year-old whitewashed farmhouse. Fenella and Simon's friendly thatched home is filled with books, beams and wonky stairs, polished wood and contemporary art. Your own private entrance opens into a guest sitting room with two cottagey bedrooms up above. Food is good! For breakfast, maybe pancakes or an egg, bacon, sausage extravaganza, with organic juice from garden apples and homemade soda bread. Supper starts with drinks and canapés by the log-burner. Cycle rides, walks, Dartmoor and arty Totnes are all on tap; children will love the Breeze hut – Pete and Dazzle the ponies too.

Children over 8 welcome.

Rooms	1 double; 1 twin with separate shower: £75–£90. Singles £60–£65.
Meals	Dinner, BYO, £35. Pubs/restaurants 20-minute walk.
Closed	Rarely.

Fenella Hughes
Coombe Farmhouse,
Higher Ashton,
Exeter,
Devon EX6 7QS
Tel +44 (0)1647 253434
Mobile +44 (0)7557 307571
Email fenellahughes@hotmail.co.uk

Devon

Devon

Old Orchard Shepherd's Hut

The epitome of simple, homely elegance: hand-stitched white curtains and roses entwined around the door. This hill-top hut looks down on Andy's lovely apple orchard. Order breakfast whenever you like, involve yourself in the life of this organic community farm or simply unwind by the wood-burner or by the fire-pit – watching the sun set across the valley. It's been an entirely local project: the hut made from nearby timber, the wrought-iron curtain rods forged on site. If you fancy getting out and about, being just outside Exeter is good for exploring Devon, for walks on Dartmoor or surfing off the coast.

Minimum stay: 2 nights. Book through Sawday's Canopy & Stars online or by phone.

Larkbeare Grange

Expectations rise as you follow the tree-lined drive to the immaculate Georgian house... to be warmly greeted with homemade cakes. The upkeep is perfect, the feel is chic and the whole place exudes well-being. Sparkling sash windows fill big rooms with light, floors shine and the grandfather clock ticks away the hours. Expect the best: good lighting, goose down duvets, luxurious fabrics and fittings, a fabulous suite for a small family, flexible (and delicious) breakfasts and lovely views from the bedrooms at the front. Charlie, Savoy-trained, and Julia are charming and fun and there are bikes to borrow. Exceptional B&B!

Rooms	Shepherd's hut for 2: £75–£80.
Meals	Breakfast included.
Closed	November–March.

Rooms	2 doubles, 1 twin/double: £110–£140.
	1 suite for 4: £170–£195.
	Singles £85–£120.
Meals	Pub 1.5 miles.
Closed	Rarely.

	Sawday's Canopy & Stars
	Old Orchard Shepherd's Hut,
	West Town Farm, Ide,
	Exeter, Devon EX2 9TG
Tel	+44 (0)117 204 7830
Email	enquiries@canopyandstars.co.uk
Web	www.canopyandstars.co.uk/
	oldorchard

	Charlie & Julia Hutchings
	Larkbeare Grange,
	Larkbeare, Talaton,
	Exeter, Devon EX5 2RY
Tel	+44 (0)1404 822069
Mobile	+44 (0)7762 574915
Email	stay@larkbeare.net
Web	www.larkbeare.net

Entry 131 Map 2

Entry 132 Map 2

Devon

Lower Allercombe Farm

Horses in the paddock and no-frills bedrooms at this down-to-earth, very friendly B&B. Don't expect twinsets and pearls; Susie, ex-eventer, may greet you in two-tone jodhpurs instead. She and Lizzie (her terrier) live at one end of the listed longhouse, you at the other. There's a sitting room with horsey pictures and wood-burner, and bedrooms upstairs that reflect the fair price. You'll feast on home eggs and tomatoes in the morning, and rashers from award-winning pigs. Very handy for Exeter, the south coast and Dartmoor; the airport is ten minutes away, the A30 is one mile.

Rooms	1 double, 1 twin; 1 double with separate bath: £60–£80. Singles £50.
Meals	Pub/restaurant 2 miles.
Closed	Rarely.

Susie Holroyd
Lower Allercombe Farm,
Rockbeare, Exeter,
Devon EX5 2HD

Tel	+44 (0)1404 822519
Mobile	+44 (0)7800 636961
Email	holroyd.s@gmail.com
Web	www.lowerallercombefarm.co.uk

Entry 133   Map 2

Devon

Rosehill Rooms and Cookery

A stunning original veranda runs along this fine listed Victorian house, opening to a rose-filled cottage garden and seats for the sun. Sharon and Willi, natural, warm and friendly, give you stylish, upbeat bedrooms with seaside names, garden views and sofas; bathrooms with slate style floors gleam. Nip downstairs for a delicious breakfast of porridge with honey and cream, muffins, croissants, a full English, a choice of seven mueslis… generous to a fault. Exeter and Sidmouth are close; the coastal path, the beach and bustling Budleigh are a stroll. You can book a winter cookery day too – popular with locals!

Minimum stay: 2 nights.

Rooms	4 doubles: £100–£125.
Meals	Pubs/restaurant 5-minute walk.
Closed	Rarely.

Willi & Sharon Rehbock
Rosehill Rooms and Cookery,
30 West Hill,
Budleigh Salterton,
Devon EX9 6BU

Tel	+44 (0)1395 444031
Email	info@rosehillroomsandcookery.co.uk
Web	www.rosehillroomsandcookery.co.uk

Entry 134   Map 2

Devon

Glebe House

Set on a hillside with fabulous views over the Coly valley, this late-Georgian vicarage is now a heart-warming B&B. The views will entice you, the hosts will delight you and the house is filled with interesting things. Chuck and Emma spent many years at sea – he a Master Mariner, she a chef – and have filled these big light rooms with cushions, kilims and treasured family pieces. There's a sitting room for guests, a lovely conservatory with vintage vine, peaceful bedrooms with blissful views and bathrooms that sparkle. All this, two sweet pygmy goats, wildlife beyond the ha-ha and the fabulous coast a hike away.

Minimum stay: 2 nights July & August weekends & bank holidays.

Rooms	1 double, 1 twin/double: £80. 1 family room for 4: £80–£110. Singles £50.
Meals	Dinner, 3 courses, £25. Pubs/restaurants 2.5 miles.
Closed	Christmas & New Year.

Emma & Chuck Guest
Glebe House,
Southleigh, Colyton,
Devon EX24 6SD
Tel   +44 (0)1404 871276
Mobile +44 (0)7867 568569
Email emma_guest@talktalk.net
Web   www.guestsatglebe.com

Entry 135   Map 2

Devon

West Colwell Farm

Devon lanes, pheasants, bluebell walks *and* sparkling B&B. The Hayes clearly love what they do; ex-TV producers, they have converted this 18th-century farmhouse and barns into a snug and stylish place to stay. Be charmed by original beams and pine doors, heritage colours and clean lines. Bedrooms are very private and luxurious, two have terraces overlooking the wooded valley and the most cosy is tucked under the roof. Linen is tip-top, showers are huge and breakfasts (Frank's pancakes, lovely bacon, eggs from next door) are totally flexible. A welcoming glass of wine, starry night skies, beaches nearby, peace all around. Bliss.

Rooms	3 doubles: £85–£95. 10% discount for 3 nights or more. Singles £70.
Meals	Restaurants 3 miles.
Closed	1 December – 28 February.

Frank & Carol Hayes
West Colwell Farm,
Offwell,
Honiton,
Devon EX14 9SL
Tel   +44 (0)1404 831130
Email stay@westcolwell.co.uk
Web   www.westcolwell.co.uk

Entry 136   Map 2

Devon

Barton View

The feel is contemporary with a hint of brocante and breakfast is… whenever! There's a happy self-catering twist to this bright B&B. As well as a pretty bedroom and shower room, you've a sitting room – sofa and leather chair by the log-burner – and a kitchen area stocked with good homemade and local breakfast choices and all the kit for you to rustle it up. The Magranes, in the adjoining house, are relaxed and on hand to pop in. Views are of 15th-century Shute Barton and richly rolling AONB countryside. Train and bike here, walk along the Jurassic Coast from Beer to Branscombe, be a birder – and try the many good eateries in the area.

Minimum stay: 2 nights. Reduced rates for stays longer than 2 nights. Book 4 nights and get a 5th for free.

Rooms	1 double (apartment with sitting room & kitchen area, child's bed available): £95.
Meals	Pub 30-minute walk.
Closed	Rarely.

Paddy & Di Magrane
Barton View,
Shute, Axminster,
Devon EX13 7QR

Tel	+44 (0)1297 35197
Email	paddymagrane@onetel.com
Web	www.bartonview.co.uk

Entry 137 Map 2

Devon

The Stables

Herb garden, veg patch, forests and a wild swimming lake… head down the track to this organic farm and education centre – an inspirational place. You stay in their eco converted stables – solar panels, natural spring water, timbers from the land. Bedrooms are simple and white, the living area is big with high rafters, long communal table and a seating area. Breakfast is laissez-faire (brought over to you or ingredients provided) and all is homemade, home-grown and seasonal. Lots to do too: a wooden yoga stage for early bird sessions, natural remedy courses, a zip-wire (book well in advance)… and walks galore.

Rooms	2 twin/doubles; 1 twin/double with separate bath: £100. Singles £50.
Meals	Pubs/restaurants 1-3 miles.
Closed	Rarely.

Zoe Haigh
The Stables,
Trill Farm, Musbury, Axminster,
Devon EX13 8TU

Tel	+44 (0)1297 631113
Email	zoe@trillfarm.co.uk
Web	www.trillfarm.co.uk

Entry 138 Map 2

Devon

Antonia Fraser

A lively weekly market and River Cottage Canteen just over the road... you're right in the heart of town. Next door to Antonia's art gallery, step into a relaxed home full of art and colour; you'll be welcomed with tea and cake, and given a key so you can come and go. Large bedrooms in elegant tones have lamps next to comfy beds, rugs on original boards, period fireplaces and masses of paintings; bathrooms are charming. Hop down for breakfast and good coffee in the rich yellow sitting/dining room: more wonderful art, blue painted chest, oval table, a pot of flowers. Antonia can suggest art events, coastal walks, gastro pubs and more.

50% deposit on booking.

Rooms	1 double, 1 twin/double: £95–£120. Extra bed available at no charge.
Meals	Pubs/restaurants within walking distance.
Closed	Occasionally.

Antonia Fraser
Antonia Fraser,
7 West Street, Axminster,
Devon EX13 5NX

Tel	+44 (0)1297 598702
Mobile	+44 (0)7788 840542
Email	antoniaf@onetel.com
Web	www.antoniafraserbandb.co.uk

Entry 139   Map 2

Devon

Applebarn Cottage

A tree-lined drive leads to a long white wall, and a gate opening to an explosion of colour – the garden. Come for a deliciously restful place and the nicest, most easy-going hosts; the wisteria-covered 17th-century cottage is full of books, paintings and fresh flowers. Bedrooms – one in an extension that blends in beautifully – are large, traditional, wonderfully comfortable, and the views down the valley are sublime. Patricia trained as a chef and dinners at Applebarn are delicious and great fun. Breakfast, served in a lovely oak-floored dining room, includes honey from the neighbour's bees.

Minimum stay: 2 nights.

Rooms	2 suites for 2: £78–£83. Dinner, B&B option (dinner & aperitif) £41.50–£67 per person.
Meals	Dinner, 3 courses with aperitif, £28.
Closed	November to mid-March.

Patricia & Robert Spencer
Applebarn Cottage,
Bewley Down,
Axminster,
Devon EX13 7JX

Tel	+44 (0)1460 220873
Email	paspenceruk@yahoo.co.uk
Web	www.applebarn.wordpress.com

Entry 140   Map 2

Devon

Sannacott

On the southern fringes of Exmoor you're in peaceful rolling hills, hidden valleys and a Designated Dark Sky area. The Trickeys breed horses from their Georgian style farmhouse; find roaring log fires, antiques, pretty fabrics, fresh flowers and a relaxed feel. Bedrooms are traditional and comfortable (one in an annexe), some with views over the garden and countryside. Generous breakfasts include homemade bread and jams and organic or local goodies. There's a pretty bird-filled garden to wander, walkers can enjoy the North Devon coastal path, birdwatchers and riders will be happy and there are well-known gardens to visit.

Pets by arrangement. Stabling available and arrangements can be made for riding to West Liscombe B&B.

Rooms	1 double, 1 twin/double sharing bath/shower (let to same party only); annexe – 1 twin with kitchenette: £80. Singles £45.
Meals	Occasional dinner, 3 courses, £25. Pub 2.5 miles.
Closed	Rarely.

Clare Trickey
Sannacott,
North Molton,
Devon EX36 3JS

Tel	+44 (0)1598 740203
Email	mct@sannacott.co.uk
Web	www.sannacott.co.uk

👨‍🦽 🚶 ♿ 🐕 📶 👶 🚜

Entry 141   Map 2

Devon

Tabor Hill Farm

From nearly 1,000-feet up the moorland views roll away to the south and down to the church spire in the village. Bring walking boots, perhaps even your horse, and enjoy being well away from it all in this beautiful Exmoor National Park spot. Smart rooms come with super-comfortable Hypnos beds, new oak floors and a stylish country feel; bathrooms are modern and spotless. A woodburner warms the dining room and you may tinkle the Bechstein if you wish as sociable Astley fries eggs from her own hens. There are trails to walk, romantic Exmoor to explore, a wildlife hide and the clearest night skies. Wonderful.

Children over 14 welcome. Pets by arrangement.

Rooms	1 double, 1 twin: £80. Singles £50.
Meals	Dinner £20. Pubs/restaurants 2-6 miles.
Closed	Rarely.

Astley Shilton Barlow
Tabor Hill Farm,
Heasley Mill, South Molton,
Devon EX36 3LQ

Tel	+44 (0)1598 740528
Email	taborhillfarm@btinternet.com
Web	www.taborhillfarm.co.uk

🐕 📶 👶 🚜 ✗

Entry 142   Map 2

Devon

Leworthy Barton

Biscuits, scones, sweet vases of hedgerow flowers. Breakfasts are left for you to cook and come courtesy of Rupert's Tamworth pigs and happy hens; bread and jams are homemade, wellies and waxed jackets are on tap. Rupert is a busy farmer and designer who chooses to give guests what he would most like himself. So... you have the whole of the stables, tranquil, beautifully restored and with field and sky views. Downstairs is open-plan, with kitchen and log-burner; up are sloping ceilings, wooden floors, big bed, soft towels. It's cosy yet spacious, stylish yet homely, and the Atlantic coast is the shortest drive.

Rooms	Barn – 1 double with sitting room & kitchen: £80-£100. Singles £60.
Meals	Pub 3 miles.
Closed	Rarely.

Rupert Ashmore
Leworthy Barton,
Woolsery,
Bideford,
Devon EX39 5PY
Tel +44 (0)1237 431140

Entry 143　Map 2

Devon

Beara Farmhouse

The moment you arrive at the whitewashed farmhouse you feel the affection your hosts have for their home and gardens. Richard is a lover of wood and a fine craftsman – every room echoes his talent; he also created the pond that's home to mallards and geese. Ann has laid brick paths, stencilled, stitched and painted, all with an eye for colour; bedrooms and guest sitting room are delectable and snug. Open farmland all around, sheep, pigs and hens in the yard, the Tarka Trail on your doorstep and hosts happy to give you 6.30am breakfast should you plan a day on Lundy Island. Guests love this place.

Minimum stay: 2 nights at weekends, bank holidays & June-September.

Rooms	1 double, 1 twin: £80. Singles by arrangement.
Meals	Pub 1.5 miles.
Closed	20 December – 5 January.

Ann & Richard Dorsett
Beara Farmhouse,
Buckland Brewer,
Bideford,
Devon EX39 5EH
Tel +44 (0)1237 451666
Web www.bearafarmhouse.co.uk

Entry 144　Map 2

Devon

South Yeo

Down windy lanes with tall grassy banks and the smell of the sea is a lovely Georgian country house with two walled gardens and barns at the back. You'll fall for this place the moment you arrive, and its owners: Jo runs an interiors business; Mike keeps the cattle and sheep that graze all around. Bedrooms are inviting; the double, overlooking the valley, has a cream French bed, a pretty quilted cover, a claw-foot bath and a little sitting room (adjoining) with TV. There's an elegant drawing room with a real fire too. Delicious breakfasts with home-laid eggs and homemade jams are brought to a snug room that catches the morning sun.

Devon

Hollamoor Farm

If it's a civilised retreat you're after then head to where the Taw and Torridge meet... to Tarka country, and this rambling 300-year-old farm. Roses ramble, swallows swoop and there are 500 acres to explore. One bedroom is in a barn next to the house and combines stone rusticity and country house grandeur with aplomb; the soft furnishings are exquisite. The bedroom in the house is equally plush and both have fun bathrooms. There's a huge fireplace in the dining room and a well-loved sitting room where you can meet the Wreys (past and present). A real family home where the door is always open – elegant informality at its very best.

Rooms	1 double with sitting room; 1 twin/double with separate bath: £85–£105. Singles £75.
Meals	Pub 1.5 miles.
Closed	Rarely.

Rooms	1 twin/double with separate bath; barn – 1 twin/double: £90. Singles £48.
Meals	Dinner, 3 courses, £30. Pubs/restaurants 3 miles.
Closed	Rarely.

	Joanne Wade
	South Yeo,
	Yeo Vale, Bideford,
	Devon EX39 5ES
Tel	+44 (0)1237 451218
Mobile	+44 (0)7766 201191
Email	stay@southyeo.com
Web	www.southyeo.com

	Sir George & Lady Caroline Wrey
	Hollamoor Farm,
	Tawstock,
	Barnstaple,
	Devon EX31 3NY
Tel	+44 (0)1271 373466
Mobile	+44 (0)7766 700904
Email	carolinewrey@gmail.com

Entry 145   Map 2

Entry 146   Map 2

Devon

Beachborough Country House

Welcome to this gracious 18th-century rectory with stone-flagged floors, lofty windows, wooden shutters and glorious rugs. Viviane is vivacious and spoils you with dinners and breakfasts from the Aga; dine in the elegant dining room before a twinkling fire. Hens cluck, horses whinny but otherwise the peace is deep. Ease any walker's pains away in a steaming roll top tub; lap up country views from big airy bedrooms. There's a games room for kids in the outbuildings and a stream winds through the garden – a delicious three acres of vegetables and roses. Huge fun.

Devon

North Walk House

Sea views, brass bedsteads and big rooms at this calm retreat, perfectly positioned on a cliff-top path – super for walkers and foodies. Ian and Sarah welcome you with homemade cake in a cosy guest lounge, and give you light bedrooms with sparkling bathrooms and seductive beds. Enjoy the coastal and Exmoor walks, or genteel Lynton and Lynmouth; return to log fire and armchairs. Take your tea on a sea-view terrace, or be tempted by Sarah's four-course dinner, seasonal and mostly organic. Everything here has been carefully thought out, from the welcome to the décor and the refreshments: arrive, unpack, unwind…

Rooms	2 doubles; 1 twin/double (extra single available): £80–£90. Singles £55. Up to 3 extra beds available, please enquire for price.
Meals	Dinner, 2-3 courses, from £19. Catering for house parties. Pub 3 miles.
Closed	Rarely.

Rooms	4 doubles; 1 twin: £80–£150. Singles £50–£100.
Meals	Dinner, 4 courses, from £27. Pub/restaurant 0.25 miles.
Closed	Rarely.

	Viviane Clout
	Beachborough Country House,
	Kentisbury,
	Barnstaple,
	Devon EX31 4NH
Tel	+44 (0)1271 882487
Mobile	+44 (0)7732 947755
Email	viviane@beachboroughcountryhouse.co.uk
Web	www.beachboroughcountryhouse.co.uk

	Ian & Sarah Downing
	North Walk House,
	North Walk,
	Lynton,
	Devon EX35 6HJ
Tel	+44 (0)1598 753372
Email	walk@northwalkhouse.co.uk
Web	www.northwalkhouse.co.uk

Entry 147   Map 2

Entry 148   Map 2

Devon

Victoria House

Beachcombers, surfers and walkers will be in their element here. You stay in the beach-hut annexe with a big romantic deck facing the sea; complete with funky daybed and a magnificent view. The owners live next door in the Edwardian seaside villa: Heather is lively and fun; she and David are ex-RAF. They go out of their way to give you the best tour de force breakfasts – fruits, yogurts, waffles, eggs Benedict or the full Monty. Sip a sundowner on the deck or stir yourself to go further; you are on the coastal road to Woolacombe (of surfing and kite-surfing fame) and the beach is a ten-minute walk. A top spot for couples.

Check-in 4pm-9pm, unless arranged. Special diets catered for.

Rooms	1 double: £100-£115. Siingles £70-£80.
Meals	Pubs/restaurants 200 yds.
Closed	Rarely.

Heather & David Burke
Victoria House,
Chapel Hill, Mortehoe,
Woolacombe,
Devon EX34 7DZ

Tel	+44 (0)1271 871302
Email	heatherburke59@fsmail.net
Web	www.victoriahousebandb.co.uk

Entry 149   Map 2

Dorset

Arty BnB By the Sea

Hugh & Candida – busy, travelled artists and environmentalists – make this place very special. You'll be at ease in a blink if you go for easy-going, arty, ramshackling in places, inspiring in others. Revel in the creativity of it all, from Hugh's bold paintings and wallpaper to great homemade bread and jam. You share the dining room, the lawn and veranda (with a nod to Cape Cod), looking sideways to the sea and Golden Cap, and could help in the veg garden. Rooms don't have sea views but plenty of comfort and charm; one has a handsome four-poster; both have brand new shower rooms. Plenty to do in Lyme on foot; forget the car.

Rooms	2 doubles: £100.
Meals	Restaurant 5-minute walk.
Closed	Rarely.

Candida & Hugh Dunford Wood
Arty BnB By the Sea,
The Little Place, Silver Street,
Lyme Regis,
Dorset DT7 3HR

Mobile	+44 (0)7932 677540
Email	hugh@dunfordwood.com
Web	www.artybnbbythesea.com

Entry 150   Map 2

Dorset

Pear Tree Farm

Four miles from bustling Bridport, this traditional, pretty Dorset farmhouse is reached with care down secret narrow lanes and surrounded by deep valleys. A keen traveller and garden designer, Emma's home brims with interesting art, antiques, rugs, comfy old armchairs and books; there is an extraordinary collection of glass walking sticks. The garden is a true delight and blissful views from flowery and timeless bedrooms will charm you. Wake to a breakfast of local bacon and home-laid eggs in the kitchen, take off on walks from the door, or on the coast. Bridport Literary Festival is a joy and this is a good area for food.

Rooms	1 twin/double, 1 twin sharing bath (let to same party only): £75–£80. Singles £50.
Meals	Pubs/restaurants within 4 miles.
Closed	Christmas & Easter.

Emma Poë
Pear Tree Farm,
Loscombe, Bridport,
Dorset DT6 3TL
Tel   +44 (0)1308 488223
Email poe@gotadsl.co.uk
Web   www.peartreefarmbedandbreakfast.co.uk

Entry 151   Map 3

Dorset

No 27

In a peaceful side street in Bridport is an historic artisan's house with masses of charm. Find walls painted in chalky hues, flagstones toasty underfoot, painted floorboards topped with kilims, and books, paintings, antiques and flowers. Juliet invites you to use the house like a home, and breakfasts are generous, delicious and served around a large table in the kitchen extension; admire the garden from a wall of glass. Explore the pubs, seafood restaurants and market stalls of Bridport, the beaches of Lyme Regis and the wonderful Jurassic Coast; come home to fresh, airy bedrooms, both with views to garden and hills.

Minimum stay: 2 nights on weekdays. Children over 10 welcome.

Rooms	1 double; 1 double with separate bath: £100–£120.
Meals	Supper from £15. Pubs/restaurants in town.
Closed	Rarely.

Juliet Lewis
No 27,
27 Barrack Street, Bridport,
Dorset DT6 3LX
Tel   +44 (0)1308 426378
Email julietalewis@gmail.com
Web   www.no27bridport.co.uk

Entry 152   Map 3

Dorset

Urless Farm

In its own beautiful valley, this extended, refurbished 19th-century family house does seriously smart B&B. You'll want to linger over breakfast – local bacon, their hens' eggs, homemade jams, their own tomato sauce – in the light-filled orangery with breathtaking views across rich farmland to the distant Mendips. Luxuriate in traditional bedrooms with antiques and colourful rugs on polished floors; sensors control the lighting in peerless bathrooms with heated floors. Watch for wildlife by the ponds in the large, well-kept grounds. It's a short walk to a good pub and Dorset's delights surround you.

Over 16s welcome.

Rooms	2 doubles, 1 twin; 1 double with separate shower: £100–£120.
Meals	Pubs/restaurants 15-minute walk.
Closed	Rarely.

Charlotte Hemsley
Urless Farm,
Corscombe, Dorchester,
Dorset DT2 0NP
Tel   +44 (0)1935 891528
Email   charlie@urless.co.uk
Web   www.urlessdorset.com

Entry 153   Map 3

Dorset

Wooden Cabbage House

Leafy lanes and a private drive lead you to Martyn and Susie's beautifully restored hamstone house, hidden in rolling West Dorset. Leave the hubbub behind, savour the stunning valley views, relax in this spacious stylish home amongst flowers, fine antiques and paintings. Cosy bedrooms have country-house charm. A delicious breakfast is served in the gorgeous garden room – home-grown fruits, local eggs and sausages – and French windows open to a productive potager and terraced gardens. Local walks are good and the Jurassic coast is half an hour away; return to comfy sofas by the log fire. Fabulous hosts – nothing is too much trouble.

Minimum stay: 2 nights at weekends.

Rooms	2 doubles, 1 twin: £100–£110. Singles from £80.
Meals	Dinner, 3 courses with wine, £40. Supper, 2 courses with wine, £30. Pubs/restaurants 3 miles.
Closed	Rarely.

Martyn & Susie Lee
Wooden Cabbage House,
East Chelborough, Dorchester,
Dorset DT2 0QA
Tel   +44 (0)1935 83362
Email   relax@woodencabbage.co.uk
Web   www.woodencabbage.co.uk

Entry 154   Map 3

Dorset

Old Forge

Snug in a stream-tickled hamlet, deep in Hardy country, this B&B is as pretty as a painting – and wonderfully peaceful. That is, until owner Judy starts to giggle: she is full of smiles and laughter. This is a happy place, a real country home, a no-rules B&B. The one guest double, sharing the former forge with a self-catering pad for two, is neat, warm and cosy with yellow hues, thick carpets and trinkets from travels. The 17th-century farmhouse opposite is where you breakfast: Prue Leith-trained Judy serves a neighbour's eggs and a friend's sausages, in an eclectically furnished room with bucolic views to garden, meadows and hills.

Rooms	Old Forge – 1 double: £80–£90. Extra person £15.
Meals	Restaurant 1.5 miles.
Closed	Rarely.

Judy Thompson
Old Forge,
Lower Wraxall Farmhouse,
Lower Wraxall, Dorchester,
Dorset DT2 0HL

Tel	+44 (0)1935 83218
Email	judyjthompson@hotmail.co.uk
Web	www.lowerwraxall.co.uk

Entry 155   Map 3

Dorset

Fullers Earth

Such an English feel: the village with pub, post office and stores, the rose-filled walled garden with fruit trees beyond, the tranquil church view. This listed house – its late-Georgian frontage added in 1820 – is a treat: flowers and white linen, a lovely sitting room where you settle with tea and cake by the fire, roomy bedrooms with comfortable beds, books and views. At breakfast enjoy perfect compotes and jams from the garden, homemade muesli and local produce. Friendly Ian and Wendy will plan great walks with you in this AONB, the Jurassic coast is 20 minutes away and you can walk to the pub through the garden.

Rooms	1 double; 1 double sharing bath/shower room with single (let to same party only): £85–£95. 1 single sharing bath/shower room with double (let to same party only): £40.
Meals	Pub in village.
Closed	Christmas.

2014/15
Sawday's
BED & BREAKFAST

Old favourite

Wendy Gregory
Fullers Earth,
Cattistock, Dorchester,
Dorset DT2 0JL

Tel	+44 (0)1300 320190
Mobile	+44 (0)7792 654543
Email	stay@fullersearth.co.uk
Web	www.fullersearth.co.uk

Entry 156   Map 3

Dorset

Holyleas House

In a lovely village, a fabulous house, comfortable, peaceful and easy – and Tia and her two friendly dogs give the warmest welcome. You breakfast by a log fire in an elegant dining room in winter, on free-range eggs, bacon and sausages from the farmers' market, homemade jams and marmalade. Sleep in light, softly coloured bedrooms with lovely views across well-tended gardens; bathrooms are spotless. Walkers and explorers will be happy to roam the Dorset Downs, then return to a roaring fire and a cosy book in the drawing room.

Minimum stay: 2 nights in high season & at weekends.

Dorset

Tudor Cottage

There are gentle walks from this thatched cottage along the river Frome valley, and rugged coastal paths nearby for heartier souls. Return to homemade scones, a sitting room with lots of art and a roaring fire on chilly days – architecture buffs will swoop upon the 16th-century over mantle and ancient stone archway. Sleep soundly in crisp white linen with thick fabrics at the windows (you are on the road but it's quiet at night); bathrooms are gleaming. Charming Louise can make anybody feel at home and cooks delicious breakfasts and suppers from local ingredients. Fossils abound and you can track down public gardens too.

Children over 12 welcome.

Rooms	1 double: £80-£90.
	1 family room for 3: £100-£120.
	1 single with separate bath: £40.
Meals	Pub a short walk.
Closed	Christmas & New Year.

Rooms	1 double, 1 twin: £85-£95.
	Singles £75.
Meals	Supper £25. Afternoon tea £5
	(included on arrival).
	Pub 2 miles.
Closed	Rarely.

	Tia Bunkall
	Holyleas House,
	Buckland Newton, Dorchester,
	Dorset DT2 7DP
Tel	+44 (0)1300 345214
Mobile	+44 (0)7968 341887
Email	tiabunkall@holyleas.fsnet.co.uk
Web	www.holyleashouse.co.uk

	Louise Clarke
	Tudor Cottage,
	9 Dorchester Road, Frampton,
	Dorchester, Dorset DT2 9NB
Tel	+44 (0)1300 320382
Mobile	+44 (0)7970 282151
Email	stay@tudorcottagedorset.co.uk
Web	www.tudorcottagedorset.co.uk

Entry 157   Map 3

Entry 158   Map 3

Dorset

INSPECTED & SELECTED
New Entry
A SPECIAL PLACE

Manor Farm

Pheasants stroll along grassy lanes, kestrels fly overhead and this stunning stone manor house is a delight. Ashley is easy-going and you have your own wing as well as a private courtyard next to the orangery; take a book and sit by the koi ponds. Bedrooms come in comfy country style; the Rose suite with antique linen and pretty wallpaper is charming. The dining room gleams with antiques, silver and flowers; feast on a breakfast of home-laid eggs, homemade jams and local sausages. Climb Eggardon Hill, visit Bridport and Sherborne; Lyme Regis and the Jurassic Coast are a short drive. Friendly lurchers add to the relaxed feel.

Minimum stay: 2 nights. Coarse fishing available on estate lake.

Rooms	1 double, 1 twin, each with separate bath/shower: £120-£150. 1 suite for 2: £150-£175. Singles £80. Extra bed/sofabed available £50 per person per night.
Meals	Pubs within 3 miles.
Closed	Rarely.

	Ashley Stewart Manor Farm, West Compton, Dorchester, Dorset DT2 0EY
Tel	+44 (0)1300 320400
Email	ashley@manorfarmwestcompton.com
Web	www.westcomptonmanor.co.uk

Entry 159   Map 3

Dorset

Manor Farm

You are high up on the chalk hills that fall to the Jurassic Coast. Tessa's family have lived in the flint and stone house since 1860 and it is crammed with history: solid antiques, books galore, pictures, maps and photographs. From all the windows views soar to sheep-dotted hills. You can settle by the wood-burner in the snug, and your Aga-cooked breakfast or supper is served in the handsome dining room, or the garden in summer; cooking is one of Tessa's passions. Bedrooms are without frills but clean and comfortable; the bathroom is large and sparkling. Outdoor heaven is yours; find a pet pig called Pork!

Rooms	1 double, 1 twin sharing bath (let to same party only): £70-£100.
Meals	Dinner, 2-3 courses, from £15. Pub/restaurant 4 miles.
Closed	Rarely.

	Tessa Russell Manor Farm, Compton Valence, Dorchester, Dorset DT2 9ES
Tel	+44 (0)1308 482227
Mobile	+44 (0)7818 037184 (signal unreliable)
Email	tessa.nrussell@btinternet.com
Web	www.manor-farm.uk.com

Entry 160   Map 3

Dorset

Dorset

Whitfield Farm Cottage

Jackie and David are warm, delightful hosts, and their pretty thatched 18th-century cottage is full of charm. A delicious breakfast is served in the large beamed kitchen, or in the walled courtyard on sunny days, and the garden brims with roses, lavender and sweet peas. Bedrooms are immaculate; one, in blue and white, opens onto the garden; the sitting room is cosy and comfy with inglenook fireplace and window seats. Dorchester is close, you're eight miles from the stunning Jurassic Coast, and you can enjoy a day's fishing on the river Frome (licences are sometimes available).

Minimum stay: 2 nights at weekends.

Yoah Cottage

Rose and Furse are ceramic sculptors; she makes delicate, sometimes humorous, pieces, he creates bold animals and birds; their thatched, rambling house is a jaw-dropping gallery of modern art, ceramics and fabrics. The prettiest of cottage gardens brims with colour and scent – lots of seats and a summerhouse for sitting and admiring. Originally two cottages, you sleep on one side in lovely bedrooms under the eaves, sharing (with friends or family) a bathroom and a sitting room with log fire. Breakfast (full English, homemade jams) is next to the couple's studio. Such warm-hearted, artistic owners – and you're deep in Hardy country.

Minimum stay: 2 nights.

Rooms	1 twin/double, 1 twin: £80–£85. Singles £50.
Meals	Pubs/restaurants 1.25 miles.
Closed	Christmas & Easter.

Rooms	1 double, 1 twin sharing bath (let to same party only): £70–£90. Singles £40–£50.
Meals	Pub/restaurant next door.
Closed	Christmas & Easter.

	Jackie & David Charles
	Whitfield Farm Cottage,
	Poundbury Road,
	Dorchester,
	Dorset DT2 9SL
Tel	+44 (0)1305 260233
Email	dcharles@gotadsl.co.uk
Web	www.whitfieldfarmcottage.co.uk

	Furse & Rosemary Swann
	Yoah Cottage,
	West Knighton,
	Dorchester,
	Dorset DT2 8PE
Tel	+44 (0)1305 852087
Email	roseswann@tiscali.co.uk
Web	www.yoahcottage.co.uk

Entry 161   Map 3

Entry 162   Map 3

Dorset

Marren

On the Dorset coastal path overlooking Weymouth Bay – a blissful spot for Jurassic Coast adventures. The owners have transformed this 1920s house, set in six acres of terraced and wooded garden, and their style reflects their penchant for natural materials and country life. Bedrooms are elegant and comfortable; one has a door onto the garden; from the other you can marvel at the sun setting over the sea. Enjoy superb spreads of farm produce and homemade bread, then head off to the secluded beach below and a turquoise sea swim. There's a sense of slow living here. Leave the low-slung Morgan at home: the track is steep!

Minimum stay: 2 nights at weekends. Children over 12 welcome.

Rooms	2 doubles: £95–£135.
Meals	Pub 1 mile.
Closed	Rarely.

Peter Cartwright
Marren,
Holworth, Dorchester,
Dorset DT2 8NJ

Tel	+44 (0)1305 851503
Mobile	+44 (0)7957 886399
Email	marren@lineone.net
Web	www.marren.info

Entry 163   Map 3

Dorset

Old Harbour View

Perch in the bow-fronted window and gaze down on the harbour where the fishing boats dock. What a position – at the heart of Old Weymouth. As for the house, built in 1805, it is uniquely 12 feet wide, yet all is spacious inside, and brimming with light. Imagine stained-glass windows, huge gilt mirrors, fragrant lilies, amusing etchings and posters, sumptuous sofas, and the most delightful hosts. Boat trips, seafood restaurants galore... then it's back home to ivory-white beds in soft-carpeted rooms. Wake to Anna's breads and jams, and locally-smoked haddock: outstanding breakfasts served on lovely china.

Ask about permits for parking, on booking. Minimum stay: 2 nights.

Rooms	1 double, 1 twin/double: £98. Singles £76.
Meals	Pubs/restaurants within walking distance.
Closed	Rarely.

Peter Vincent
Old Harbour View,
12 Trinity Road,
Weymouth,
Dorset DT4 8TJ

Tel	+44 (0)1305 774633
Email	info@oldharbourview.co.uk
Web	www.oldharbourviewweymouth.co.uk

Entry 164   Map 3

Dorset

Lulworth House

Down through hills, wild heaths and pine forests to beautiful Lulworth. Carole and John's home is set back from this popular cove in a peaceful lane; artist and garden designer, their 1980s house is a creative treasure, inside and out. The garden has a tropical feel with banana trees, ferns, deep borders and abundant grapes over a pergola. Inside is a sparkling white canvas dotted with colour: paintings, glass vases, antique desk, an old grandfather clock, cubist furniture. Garden bedrooms are delightful – one opens to its own terrace; breakfast is upstairs in the stunning open-plan living space. Walks galore from the door.

Rooms	1 double; 1 double with separate shower room: £85-£110.
Meals	Pubs/restaurants within walking distance.
Closed	Occasionally.

John & Carole Bickerton
Lulworth House,
Bindon Road,
West Lulworth, Wareham, Dorset
BH20 5RU
Tel   +44 (0)1929 406192
Email   info@lulworthhousebandb.co.uk
Web   www.lulworthhousebandb.co.uk

Entry 165   Map 3

Dorset

Gold Court House

Anthea and Michael have created a mood of restrained luxury and uncluttered, often beautiful, good taste in their Georgian townhouse. Restful bedrooms have antiques, beams, linen armchairs, radios and TVs. There's an eye-catching collection of aquamarine glass, interesting art, and a large drawing room and pretty walled garden in which to relax after a day out. Views are soft and lush yet you are in the small square of this attractive town with cafés and galleries a short walk. Your hosts are delightful – "they do everything to perfection," says a guest; both house and garden are a refuge.

Children over 10 welcome.

Rooms	1 double; 2 twin/doubles, each with separate bath: £85. Singles £60.
Meals	Restaurants 50 yds.
Closed	Rarely.

Anthea & Michael Hipwell
Gold Court House,
St John's Hill,
Wareham,
Dorset BH20 4LZ
Tel   +44 (0)1929 553320
Email   info@goldcourthouse.co.uk
Web   www.goldcourthouse.co.uk

Entry 166   Map 3

Dorset

The Old Post Office

The stunning coastal path comes past the front door of this restored bungalow on a private cliff-top estate. Clamber down to a hidden beach and a short walk will take you to Swanage. The house glows with warm colour and a friendly, informal feel. Comfortable sunny bedrooms have painted furniture and French windows onto an inviting veranda, set with rocking chairs and candles. Toasty bathrooms sparkle. Artist Rowena and rare-book dealer David look after you very well; Rowena loves to cook and chat and breakfast is local and delicious, with mushrooms, herby potatoes and eggs from Arabella the hen. To stay is a treat!

Minimum stay: 2 nights at weekends during high season.

Rooms	1 double with separate bath; 1 twin: £90. Singles £60.
Meals	Pub/restaurant 0.3 miles.
Closed	Rarely.

Rowena Bishop
The Old Post Office,
4 Ballard Estate, Swanage,
Dorset BH19 1QZ

Tel	+44 (0)1929 422041
Mobile	+44 (0)7976 356013
Email	rowena@outwardbound.plus.com
Web	www.oldpostofficeswanage.co.uk

Entry 167   Map 3

Dorset

Bering House

Fabulous in every way. Renate's attention to detail reveals a love of running B&B: the fluffy dressing gowns and bathroom treats, the biscuits, fruit and sherry… she and John are welcoming and delightful. Expect pretty sofas, golden bath taps, a gleaming breakfast table, and a big sumptuous suite with views across sparkling Poole harbour to Brownsea Island and Purbeck Hills. Breakfasts are served on blue and white Spode china: exotic fruits with Parma ham, smoked salmon with poached eggs and muffins, kedgeree, smoked haddock gratin, warm figs with Greek yogurt and honey: the choice is superb. An immaculate harbourside retreat.

Rooms	1 twin/double: £85. 1 suite for 2 with kitchenette: £100. Singles £75-£90.
Meals	Pub 400 yds. Restaurant 500 yds.
Closed	Rarely.

Renate & John Wadham
Bering House,
53 Branksea Avenue,
Hamworthy,
Poole,
Dorset BH15 4DP

Tel	+44 (0)1202 673419
Email	johnandrenate1@tiscali.co.uk

Entry 168   Map 3

Dorset

The Park 24

All is lush, leafy and quiet, yet a mere stroll from the centre. The garden teems with lavender and agapanthus in summer, and tea on the terrace is glorious. Chris and Fiona's Edwardian home has a relaxing open house feel; the elegant sitting room gleams with beautiful antiques and flowers, and a log fire in winter keeps you toasty. Cosy chic ground-floor bedrooms have ultra sleek shower rooms. Chat away at the refectory table while Fiona cooks breakfast, tuck into porridge with cinnamon and cream. Work it off on the beach, then back for a summerhouse nap – and a possible sighting of a sweet spaniel nosing through the undergrowth!

Minimum stay: 2 nights at busy times.

Dorset

7 Smithfield Place

Valerie adores large mirrors – which she paints and distresses herself – rich fabrics, real wood, dainty antiques. She also delights in looking after guests, so no detail is missed in her elegant home, from the gorgeous bathroom to a 'full works' breakfast – taken in the spanking new breakfast room or on a sunny patio. Built in 1880 as a worker's cottage, the house sits on a quiet cul-de-sac off Winton's thriving high street, two miles from Bournemouth town centre with easy public transport. The garden is lit up in spring by blooming camellias and cherry blossom, and the whole house sparkles – as does your charming hostess.

Rooms	2 doubles: £88–£135. Singles from £70.
Meals	Pub/restaurant 1 mile.
Closed	Rarely.

Rooms	1 double: £80. Singles £55.
Meals	Packed lunch £15. Pub/restaurant 100 yds.
Closed	Christmas.

Chris & Fiona Dixon-Box
The Park 24,
24 Meyrick Park Crescent,
Talbot Woods, Bournemouth,
Dorset BH3 7AQ

Tel   +44 (0)1202 296473
Mobile +44 (0)7740 425623
Email   info@thepark24.co.uk
Web   www.thepark24.co.uk

Valerie Johns
7 Smithfield Place,
Winton,
Bournemouth,
Dorset BH9 2QJ

Tel   +44 (0)1202 520722
Mobile +44 (0)7743 481671
Email   valeriejohns@btinternet.com
Web   www.smithfieldplace.co.uk

Entry 169   Map 3

Entry 170   Map 3

Dorset

The Old Mill

Ancient willow trees cast shade over stretches of lawn as kingfishers flit from branch to branch. A secret paradise unfurls before you, as through the Mill's gardens the Stour and its tributaries flow, their banks a-shimmer with hostas, irises, day lilies, gunneras and ferns. Find privacy and independence in your own comfortably contemporary bolthole above the detached garage; a chandelier sparkles in the sun, a mini kitchen hides behind louvre doors, and relaxed Caroline brings you a fine continental breakfast. Walk across the water meadows to little Spetisbury for a pint; discover the delights of Brownsea Island and Blandford Forum.

Minimum stay: 2 nights at weekends during high season & bank holidays.

Rooms	1 family room for 2 (self-contained with sofabed & kitchenette): £95. Singles £80 (mid-week only). £12 per child per night.
Meals	Continental breakfast. Pubs/restaurants 3 miles.
Closed	Rarely.

	Caroline Ivay
	The Old Mill,
	Spetisbury, Blandford Forum,
	Dorset DT11 9DF
Tel	+44 (0)1258 456014
Mobile	+44 (0)7786 096803
Email	c.ivay@btinternet.com
Web	www.theoldmillspetisbury.com

Entry 171   Map 3

Dorset

Launceston Farm

Farmhouse chic in the most glorious of surroundings. The bedrooms, all named after the fields, are an exquisite blend of contemporary and traditional; two have roll tops in the room itself. Take tea by the open fire or find a secluded spot in the ornamental, walled gardens. Breakfast and candlelit dinner are farm-sourced and deliciously rustic. Sarah, who was born in this listed house, provides a truly relaxing stay; son Jimi's organic farm tours are a must and there are footpaths through the surrounding AONB from the door. You will leave this country retreat feeling completely rejuvenated.

Children over 12 welcome. Dogs welcome in the warm boot room.

Rooms	4 doubles, 2 twin/doubles: £100–£125. Singles £70–£125.
Meals	Dinner, 3 courses, £30 (Mon & Fri only). Pub 10-minute walk.
Closed	Rarely.

	Sarah Worrall
	Launceston Farm,
	Tarrant Launceston,
	Blandford Forum,
	Dorset DT11 8BY
Tel	+44 (0)1258 830528
Email	info@launcestonfarm.co.uk
Web	www.launcestonfarm.co.uk

Entry 172   Map 3

Dorset

Stickland Farmhouse

Charming Dorset... welcome to a soft, delightful thatched cottage in an enviably rural setting. Sandy and Paul have poured love into this listed farmhouse and garden, the latter bursting with lupins, poppies, foxgloves, clematis, delphiniums. Sandy gives you delicious breakfasts with homemade muesli, eggs from the hens and soda bread from the Aga. Pretty, cottagey bedrooms have crisp white dressing gowns and lots of books and pictures – one room opens onto your own seating area in the garden. The village has a good pub, and Cranborne Chase, rich in barrows and hill forts, is close by.

Minimum stay: 2 nights at weekends in summer. Children over 10 welcome.

Rooms	2 doubles, 1 twin: £70-£75. Singles £60.
Meals	Pub 3-minute walk.
Closed	Rarely.

Sandy & Paul Crofton-Atkins
Stickland Farmhouse,
Winterborne Stickland, Blandford
Forum, Dorset DT11 0NT

Tel	+44 (0)1258 880119
Mobile	+44 (0)7932 897774
Email	sandysticklandfarm@gmail.com
Web	www.sticklandfarmhouse.co.uk

Entry 173   Map 3

Dorset

INSPECTED & SELECTED — New Entry — A SPECIAL PLACE

Higher Melcombe Manor

You will thrill to this manor house of local stone and far-reaching views. Lorel and Michael are delightful, their home supremely comfortable and relaxed. The two acres appear to blend into the countryside, Highland cattle are sometimes seen grazing in the pastures and the garden is a colourful work in progress. Chic bedrooms have sumptuous linens, chalky white walls and painted furniture; bathrooms are simply stunning. There's a guest kitchen on the landing, and a big sitting room with duck egg blue sofas, bean bags, books and TV. Stretch out with a Bucks Fizz, a hot chocolate or whatever you fancy: you'll be pampered here.

Minimum stay: 2 nights. Check-in 5pm-6pm.

Rooms	3 doubles: £120. Singles from £75.
Meals	Supper, £15. Pub 1.5 miles.
Closed	Christmas.

Lorel Morton & Michael Woodhouse
Higher Melcombe Manor,
Melcombe Bingham,
Dorset DT2 7PB

Tel	+44 (0)1258 880251
Mobile	+44 (0)7973 920119
Email	lorel@lorelmorton.com
Web	www.highermelcombemanor.co.uk

Entry 174   Map 3

Dorset

Munden House

This is a super B&B – a couple of farm cottages and assorted outbuildings beautifully stitched together. It's run with great warmth by Colin and Annie, who buy and sell colourful rugs and have travelled the world to do it. Outside, long views shoot off over open country; inside, airy interiors, pretty bedrooms and lots of colour. The garden studios are bigger and more private; one has a galleried bedroom above a lovely sitting room. Annie cooks fantastic food – local meat, fish from Brixham – but her vegetarian dishes will seduce die-hard carnivores. You eat at smartly dressed tables; breakfast is on the terrace in good weather.

Rooms	2 doubles, 3 garden studios for 2, 1 four-poster, 1 twin/double: £90–£130. Singles from £70.
Meals	Dinner, 3 courses, £27. Pub 0.5 miles.
Closed	Christmas.

Annie & Colin Fletcher
Munden House,
Mundens Lane,
Alweston, Sherborne,
Dorset DT9 5HU
Tel +44 (0)1963 23150
Email stay@mundenhouse.co.uk
Web www.mundenhouse.co.uk

Entry 175   Map 3

Dorset

Glebe House

Clematis and wisteria cover much of the mellow brickwork of this spacious and uncluttered 1950s house, down a quiet lane in a tiny hamlet in the heart of stunning Blackmore Vale. From the hall look through to the mature pretty garden; it's open house and David and Barbara love having guests to stay. Enjoy tea and scones in the garden room, neat-as-a-pin bedrooms and bathrooms, and wide views from every window. Tuck into all sorts of tasty choices at breakfast, by the fire in the dining room. Magnificent castle and abbey are close, and walks from the door are outstanding – you could stay a week and never do the same one twice!

Rooms	1 double; 1 twin/double: £65–£80. Singles £50.
Meals	Pub/restaurant within 1 mile.
Closed	Rarely.

David & Barbara Fifield
Glebe House,
Folke, Sherborne,
Dorset DT9 5HP
Tel +44 (0)1963 210337
Mobile +44 (0)7980 864033
Email glebe.house@hotmail.com
Web www.glebehouse-dorset.co.uk

Entry 176   Map 3

Holt Cottage

The house stands on high ground and views are fabulous. Richard and Annabel give you a big welcome and two super suites in the cottage a step away. One upstairs, one down, each has its own sitting room, and private entrance so you can come and go as you please. All is sparkling and inviting, with elegant prints on the walls. Bedrooms have wonderful mattresses, good linen and flowers; find fluffy towels and lots of potions in immaculate bathrooms. Delicious breakfast by the Aga in the large beamed kitchen: fruit salad, local bacon and sausages, home-laid eggs; Annabel brings a continental breakfast to your suite if you prefer.

Caundle Barn

Take the pretty route… ramble through rich pasture, tiny hamlets and woodland to reach this attractive 17th-century stone barn. All is spotless, from the oak stairs and galleried landing to the antiques and exquisite curtains; Sarah has blended old and new beautifully. Your bedroom is sunny and sumptuous; the little shower room has scented oils and luxurious towels. Sarah cooks with the seasons and you'll enjoy homemade marmalade, fruits, local eggs, bacon and sausages. Views and walks are sublime, Sherborne is fun, there are gourmet pubs galore and Poppy the Jack Russell adds her charm to this friendly home.

Rooms	Cottage – 1 double, 1 twin/double, each with sitting room: £95–£110. Singles from £80.
Meals	Pub/restaurant 1 mile.
Closed	Rarely.

Rooms	1 double: £80. Singles £50.
Meals	Pubs/restaurants 4 miles.
Closed	Rarely.

Richard & Annabel Buxton
Holt Cottage,
Alweston, Sherborne,
Dorset DT9 5JF
Tel +44 (0)1963 23014
Mobile +44 (0)7766 583344
Email annabelbuxton@hotmail.com
Web www.holtcottagedorset.com

Sarah Howes
Caundle Barn,
Purse Candle,
Sherborne,
Dorset DT9 5DY
Tel +44 (0)1963 251264
Email howes20@btinternet.com

Entry 177   Map 3

Entry 178   Map 3

Dorset

Golden Hill Cottage

Deep in the countryside lies Stourton Caundle and this charming thatched cottage. You have the peace and privacy of your own sitting room, traditionally furnished with antiques, paintings and open fire; up a private stair is your carpeted twin room with its own shower room. Anna, courteous and kind, brings you splendid platefuls of local bacon and sausage, homemade jams and Dorset honey for breakfast; nothing is too much trouble for these hosts. There are glorious walks from the village, a good pub that serves food (check when the kitchen's open) and real ales, and Sherborne, Montacute and Stourhead for landscape, culture and history.

Babes in arms welcome.

Rooms	1 twin with sitting room: £80–£90. Singles £50.
Meals	Pubs/restaurants within 3 miles.
Closed	Rarely.

Anna & Andrew Oliver
Golden Hill Cottage,
Stourton Caundle,
Sturminster Newton,
Dorset DT10 2JW
Tel +44 (0)1963 362109
Email anna@goldenhillcottage.co.uk
Web www.goldenhillcottage.co.uk

Entry 179   Map 3

Dorset

Lower Fifehead Farm

A passion for cooking here! The dramatic dining room has church pews at an oak refectory table; the log fire will be lit in winter, and you can eat on the terrace in summer. Hearty breakfasts include bacon and sausages from home-reared pigs. devilled mushrooms or eggs Benedict; Jessica makes the bread and preserves, and there's always freshly squeezed orange juice. It's a gorgeous house too – it's been in Jasper's family for over 20 years and shines with pretty fabrics, antiques, hand-painted furniture, vintage pieces, rich colour – and seriously comfortable brass beds. Don't miss the candlelit dinners.

Minimum stay: 2 nights at weekends.

Rooms	2 doubles, 1 twin/double: £75–£95. Singles from £55.
Meals	Dinner, 2-3 courses, £20-£30. Pubs/restaurants 2 miles.
Closed	Christmas & New Year.

Jessica Miller
Lower Fifehead Farm,
Fifehead St Quinton,
Sturminster Newton,
Dorset DT10 2AP
Tel +44 (0)1258 817335
Email lowerfifeheadfm@gmail.com
Web www.lowerfifeheadfarm.co.uk

Entry 180   Map 3

The Old Forge, Fanners Yard

Step back in time in this beautifully restored forge: retro signs, museum pieces, ponies in the paddock and a simpler, slower way of life... Tim and Lucy's smallholding gives you a taste of harmonious living with the seasons, and they recycle everything. This includes Tim's classic cars, a cosy gypsy caravan and a vintage shepherd's hut. The attic bedrooms are snug — Lucy's quilts, country antiques, sparkling bathrooms, flowers — and their breakfasts are renowned: eggs from their hens, organic bacon and sausages, home-grown jams, apple juice straight from the orchard. A happy place, a tonic to stay.

Children over 8 welcome.

Rosie & Sam

Both very special and immaculately restored... You've Rosie, a 1934 gypsy caravan with a big, snug bed and stacks of traditional character: painted chest of drawers, brass kettle — and discreet heating. And Sam, the shepherd's hut, with its wood-burner and decking porch and all the Old Forge vintage charm (and some mod cons like mains power). Lucy made the patchwork curtains and her award-winning breakfasts are a joy too: local bacon and sausages, their hens' eggs, homemade marmalade and apple juice from your neighbouring orchard. Watch the sun set over the fields, or stroll through the woods for supper. A great escape.

Minimum stay: 2 nights. Book through Sawday's Canopy & Stars online or by phone.

Rooms	1 double with separate bath: £60–£95. 1 family room for 3: £70–£125. Gypsy caravan – 1 double, shepherd's hut – 1 double, each with shower/wc close by: £60–£95. Singles £60–£75
Meals	Pub/restaurant within 1 mile.
Closed	Rarely.

Rooms	Gypsy caravan for 2; shepherd's hut for 2: £95.
Meals	Breakfast included.
Closed	November–March.

Tim & Lucy Kerridge
The Old Forge,
Fanners Yard,
Compton Abbas, Shaftesbury,
Dorset SP7 0NQ

Tel	+44 (0)1747 811881
Email	theoldforge@ymail.com
Web	www.theoldforgedorset.co.uk

Sawday's Canopy & Stars
Rosie & Sam,
The Old Forge, Fanners Yard,
Compton Abbas, Shaftesbury,
Dorset SP7 0NQ

Tel	+44 (0)117 204 7830
Email	enquiries@canopyandstars.co.uk
Web	www.canopyandstars.co.uk/ theoldforge

Entry 181   Map 3

Entry 182   Map 3

Dorset

Lawn Cottage

In a quiet village in the Blackmore Vale, the path to this spacious cottage is lined with tulips and vegetables. Easy-going June is a collector of pretty things; fine sketches and watercolours, antiques and china blend charmingly with soft colours and zingy kilims. There's a delightful, sunny, en suite bedroom downstairs, with a private entrance and touches of toile de Jouy, and a double room upstairs. Breakfast is served in the big kitchen or out in the cottage garden; the tiny sitting room is a perfect snug. Visit Sherborne for its abbey, castle and smart shops; walk from the gate to Duncliffe Woods. Perfect Dorset B&B!

Rooms	1 twin/double; 1 double with separate bath: £70. Singles £40.
Meals	Pub/restaurant 1 mile.
Closed	Rarely.

June Watkins
Lawn Cottage,
Stour Row, Shaftesbury,
Dorset SP7 0QF

Tel	+44 (0)1747 838719
Mobile	+44 (0)7809 696218
Email	enquiries@lawncottagedorset.co.uk
Web	www.lawncottagedorset.co.uk

Entry 183   Map 3

Dorset

St Andrews Farm East

Deeply rural bliss! The part-thatched house is lovely: roses and clematis around the door, its tranquil garden keenly tended. The approach is pure Hardy: up a no through lane, verges rampant with wild flowers, old walls penning tiny cottage gardens, the pond where cartwheels were washed. Then there's Diana's creation – as designer and seamstress – of the elegant interiors. Bleached oak timbers frame the superb, chandeliered master bedroom. More gentle cream, antiques and flowers in the second charming double. Traditional, cosseting bathrooms too. Breakfasts are terrific – orchard fruit salad a speciality. Luxurious and friendly.

Rooms	1 double; 1 double with separate bath: £75-£85. Singles £50-£60.
Meals	Pubs/restaurants 1 mile.
Closed	Rarely.

Diana Man
St Andrews Farm East,
Bedchester,
Shaftesbury,
Dorset SP7 0JU

Tel	+44 (0)1747 812242
Email	mrsdianaman@hotmail.com
Web	www.bedchester.net

Entry 184   Map 3

Dorset

Rose Cottage

You are buried deep in a quiet corner here, just perfect for long walks: return to a pot of tea and homemade cake on the terrace overlooking the glorious garden. Bedrooms are light and charming with vintage painted furniture; loll in big beds with cushions and crisp white sheets. Views over the garden are fabulous: masses of colour with climbing roses, sweet peas, wild flowers, orchards and more. Breakfast is a mostly organic treat, with Rose Cottage honey and summer compotes, served in an elegant dining room with glowing furniture and dollops of morning sunshine. Amanda, warm and welcoming, looks after you very well indeed.

Babies & children over 8 welcome.

Rooms	1 twin/double; 1 twin/double with separate bath/shower: £80–£90. Singles £50.
Meals	Snacks & packed lunch available. Pub/restaurant 1 mile.
Closed	Christmas, New Year.

	Giles & Amanda Vardey
	Rose Cottage,
	Watery Lane, Donhead St Mary,
	Shaftesbury,
	Dorset SP7 9DF
Tel	+44 (0)1747 828449
Email	amanda@rosecottage.uk.com
Web	www.rosecottage.uk.com

Entry 185   Map 3

Dorset

Glebe Farm

You're in Dorset's highest village – views from the house sprawl for miles. Ian farms 1,000 acres, Tessa does shoot catering and is a part-time model. Their home, newly built, comes with green oak, soaring ceilings and walls of glass that frame spectacular views ("Emmerdale meets Grand Designs" to quote a happy guest). Aga-cooked breakfasts include local bacon and home-laid eggs, while bedrooms, one up, one down, have warm colours, big beds, beautiful views, super bathrooms. The Wessex Ridgeway starts in the village, so follow it over to magnificent Hambledon Hill, an Iron Age hill fort. Dine on the terrace in summer.

Over 14s welcome.

Rooms	2 twin/doubles: £100–£120. Singles from £60.
Meals	Dinner, 2 courses, £25 (by prior arrangement). Pubs 2 miles.
Closed	Christmas & New Year.

	Tessa & Ian Millard
	Glebe Farm,
	High Street, Ashmore, Salisbury,
	Dorset SP5 5AE
Tel	+44 (0)1747 811974
Mobile	+44 (0)7799 858961
Email	stay@glebefarmbandb.co.uk
Web	www.glebefarmbandb.co.uk

Entry 186   Map 3

Durham

The Coach House

There's so much to gladden your heart – the cobbled courtyard that evokes memories of its days as a coaching inn, the river running through the estate, the drawing room's log fire, the delicious breakfasts, the blackberry crumbles with cream... and Peter and Mary, your kind, unstuffy, dog-adoring hosts (they have one well-behaved one). All your creature comforts are attended to in this small, perfect, English country house: lined chintz, pure cotton linen, cushioned window seats looking onto a lovely garden, heated towel rails, cut flowers. Friendly, delightful, and the perfect stepping stone to Scotland or the south.

Rooms	1 twin/double; 1 twin/double with separate bath/shower: £90. Singles £60.
Meals	Dinner, 3 courses, £25. Pub/restaurants within 3 miles.
Closed	Rarely.

Peter & Mary Gilbertson
The Coach House,
Greta Bridge,
Barnard Castle,
Durham DL12 9SD

Tel	+44 (0)1833 627201
Email	info@coachhousegreta.co.uk
Web	www.coachhousegreta.co.uk

Entry 187   Map 12

Durham

Cooper House Farm

Lucy's clever and original use of vibrant colours, combined with antique and vintage pieces, produces astonishing results! And there are lots of wonderful pictures of cows. Hearty breakfasts are served at one large table in the kitchen with orange Aga, juke box and jolly sofas. Stoke up on homemade bread and jams, eggs from their hens – walk it off furiously in the glorious Dales or amble along the river; perhaps visit Barnard Castle. Return to hugely comfortable colourful bedrooms with pastoral views, warm shining bathrooms, a guests' sitting room with a roaring fire and three gentle dogs.

Children over 7 welcome.

Rooms	1 twin/double; 1 twin/double with separate bath: £95. Singles £55.
Meals	Pubs/restaurants 1-3 miles.
Closed	Rarely.

Lucy Blackmore
Cooper House Farm,
Cotherstone,
Barnard Castle,
Durham DL12 9QR

Tel	+44 (0)1833 650187
Email	contact@cooperhouse.org.uk
Web	www.cooperhouse.org.uk

Entry 188   Map 12

Essex

32 The Hythe

The Thames barge in all her glory: the Gibbs' garden runs almost into the river Blackwater where these majestic old craft are moored and the mudflats are a birdwatcher's dream. Summer breakfast on the deck – local smoked kippers and free-range eggs – watching the barges sail up the river is a rare treat. Beneath wide limpid skies this sensitively extended fisherman's cottage looks out to 12th-century St Mary's at the back where Kim and Gerry ring the Sunday bells. It's immaculate and comfortable inside, an inspired mix of modern and antique lit by myriad candles, among other romantic touches.

Children over 14 welcome.

Rooms	1 double; 1 double with separate bath: £90. Singles £70.
Meals	Pub 100 yds.
Closed	Christmas & Boxing Day.

	Kim & Gerry Gibbs 32 The Hythe, Maldon, Essex CM9 5HN
Tel	+44 (0)1621 859435
Mobile	+44 (0)7753 135108
Email	gibbsie@live.co.uk
Web	www.thehythemaldon.co.uk

Entry 189   Map 10

Essex

Caterpillar Cottage

Traditional brick and clapboard, dormer windows, tall chimney – this looks like the real thing. But Caterpillar Cottage was built in 2004 – in the grounds of Patricia's former grand 14th-century house. Filled with fine furniture, family photographs and *objets* from far-flung travels, it invites relaxation. The double-height, vaulted sitting room brims with sofas and books, logs crackle on chilly nights. Bedrooms are simple and comfortable; a travel cot and camp bed can be put up in the family room. Patricia, a lively grandmother, adores children. Enjoy the big peaceful garden with pretty terrace and vine-covered pergola.

Camp bed & travel cot available.

Rooms	1 double with separate bath/shower: £70-£75. 1 triple: £75-£85. 10% off for 3 nights or more. Singles from £40.
Meals	Packed lunch available. Pubs 50 yds.
Closed	Rarely.

	Patricia Mitchell Caterpillar Cottage, Fordstreet, Aldham, Colchester, Essex CO6 3PH
Tel	+44 (0)1206 240456
Email	bandbcaterpillar@tiscali.co.uk
Web	www.caterpillarcottage.co.uk

Entry 190   Map 10

Essex

Hill House

The Romer-Lees recently converted this listed brick Coach House and it's rather special: light and airy with pale beams, oatmeal carpets and merry gingham blinds. Downstairs is a private entrance hall; upstairs is a generous open-plan bedroom/living area with a queen-sized bed and en suite bathroom. On the other side of the room, separated by the stairs, are two cream sofas that open into double beds, a TV, DVDs and board games. No garden but you get a balcony with stunning views across the Colne Valley, breakfast (all the usuals plus bacon and sausages from the owners' rare-breed pigs) is served here on warm days. Cambridge is close.

Rooms	Coach House – 1 suite for 2 with sitting room & sofabeds (can sleep up to 6 people): £95-£120. Extra bed/sofabed available £15 per person per night.
Meals	Pub/restaurant 5-minute walk.
Closed	Rarely.

	Hattie Romer-Lee
	Hill House,
	Chappel Hill, Chappel,
	Colchester, Essex CO6 2DX
Tel	+44 (0)1787 221561
Mobile	+44 (0)7802 601144
Email	hattieromerlee@yahoo.co.uk
Web	www.hillhousechappel.com

Entry 191   Map 10

Essex

Emsworth House

Unexpectedly tranquil is this 1937 vicarage, with wide views over the Stour and some wonderful light for painting. Penny, an artist, is a flexible and generous host and you can laze or picnic in her two-acre garden. This is Constable country – great for walking and you are near Frinton beach, golf, sailing and riding. Return to comfy sofas and chairs, open fires and good books, and well decorated bedrooms with a country feel and the odd African throw or splash of colour. There's heaps of lovely art and a garden full of birds. Penny has camp beds and high chairs and a can-do attitude. Great fun.

Rooms	1 double, 1 twin; 1 double with separate bath: £70-£85. Singles from £55.
Meals	Pub/restaurant 0.5 miles.
Closed	Rarely.

	Penny Linton
	Emsworth House,
	Ship Hill, Station Road, Bradfield,
	Manningtree, Essex CO11 2UP
Tel	+44 (0)1255 870860
Mobile	+44 (0)7767 477771
Email	emsworthhouse@hotmail.com
Web	www.emsworthhouse.co.uk

Entry 192   Map 10

The Moda House

A fine house and a big B&B, but one that retains a deeply homely feel; Duncan and Jo are hugely well-travelled and have filled it with pictures and artefacts from all over the world. Bedrooms differ (three are in a neat annexe) but all are cosy and well decorated with lovely colours, good fabrics, pocket sprung mattresses and bright bathrooms with thick towels. Breakfast – locally sourced, cooked on the Aga and brought to round tables – sets you up for the day and you are a mile from the Cotswold Way. Return to a basement sitting room with comfy armchairs and lots of books, and a bustling town full of restaurants and shops.

Minimum stay: 2 nights over busy weekends & minimum 3 nights during Badminton.

Ashley Barn

On the edge of a hamlet... a beautifully restored, traditional converted barn. Huge doorways and floor to ceiling timber-framed windows let the light flood in. You have your own entrance and can come and go as you please. Your suite has good linen, plump pillows, flowers and views onto the garden; the roomy bathroom is gleaming. Walk through for breakfast by a log fire in the huge dining hall in the main barn: local sausages and bacon, eggs from the hens on pretty Poole pottery; Amanda is happy to cook dinner too. Badminton Horse Trials are a hop, Cirencester too; return for a wander round the rose garden, and a snooze by the fire.

Rooms	8 doubles: £82–£95. 3 singles: £62–£67.
Meals	Pubs/restaurants within 100 yards.
Closed	Rarely.

Rooms	1 double: £100–£110. Singles £75.
Meals	Dinner, 3 courses, £25. Pub/restaurant 5-minute drive.
Closed	Rarely.

	Duncan & Jo MacArthur The Moda House, 1 High Street, Chipping Sodbury, Gloucestershire BS37 6BA
Tel	+44 (0)1454 312135
Email	enquiries@modahouse.co.uk
Web	www.modahouse.co.uk

	Amanda Montgomerie Ashley Barn, Ashley, Tetbury, Gloucestershire GL8 8SU
Tel	+44 (0)1666 575156
Mobile	+44 (0)7785 505548
Email	amanda@montgomerie.org
Web	www.ashleybarn.co.uk

Entry 193   Map 3

Entry 194   Map 3

Gloucestershire

Grove Farm

Boards creak and you duck, in a farmhouse of the best kind: simple, small-roomed, stone-flagged, beamed, delightful. The walls are white, the polished furniture is good and there are pictures everywhere. In spite of great age (16th century), it's light, with lots of pretty windows. The 400 acres are farmed organically and Penny makes award-winning cheese and a grand breakfast – continental at busy times. Stupendous views across the Severn estuary to the Cotswolds, the Forest of Dean on the doorstep, and woodland walks carpeted with spring flowers. And there is simply no noise – unless the guinea fowl are in voice.

Rooms	1 double; 1 twin/double with separate bath: £45-£80. Singles £40.
Meals	Packed lunch £5. Pub 2 miles.
Closed	Rarely.

Penny & David Hill
Grove Farm,
Bullo Pill, Newnham,
Gloucestershire GL14 1EA

Tel	+44 (0)1594 516304
Mobile	+44 (0)7990 877984
Email	davidaghill48@gmail.com
Web	www.grovefarm-uk.com

Entry 195   Map 8

Gloucestershire

Frampton Court

Deep authenticity in this magnificent Grade I-listed house. The manor of Frampton on Severn has been in the family since the 11th century and although Rollo and Janie look after the estate, it is cooking enthusiasts Polly and Craig who greet you on their behalf and look after you. There are exquisite examples of decorative woodwork and, in the hall, a cheerful log fire; perch on the Mouseman fire seat. Bedrooms are traditional with antiques, panelling and long views. Beds have fine linen, one with embroidered Stuart hangings. Stroll around the ornamental canal, soak up the old-master views. An architectural masterpiece.

Children over 10 welcome.

Rooms	1 double, 1 twin/double, 1 four-poster: £150-£200.
Meals	Dinner, on request, £29-£40. Pub across the green. Restaurant 3 miles.
Closed	Christmas.

Polly Dugdale & Craig Kempson
Frampton Court,
Frampton on Severn,
Gloucestershire GL2 7EX

Tel	+44 (0)1452 740267
Email	framptoncourt@framptoncourtestate.co.uk
Web	www.framptoncourtestate.co.uk

Entry 196   Map 8

Gloucestershire

Mayfield Studio

A small lane runs past the studio, and oak doors open to a stylish interior. Slate floors are warmed from beneath and the double height ceiling lends an airy feel. A limewashed staircase leads to a mezzanine bedroom of uncluttered simplicity with views across the valley. Quirky industrial lighting, stone walls, 1930s woodcut prints, and Ercol furniture all marry superbly. There's no garden – although with permission you may use Sara's next door, choose to stay on a B&B or self-catering basis, with breakfasts delivered or left for you as you wish. Walk to Laurie Lee's favourite pub or dine locally, it's all on your doorstep.

Minimum stay: 2 nights at weekends.

Rooms	Studio – 1 double (extra bed available): £100–£125. Extra bed/sofabed available £40 per person per night.
Meals	Breakfast arranged on booking. Pubs/restaurants 2-4-minute walk.
Closed	Rarely.

Sara Kirby
Mayfield Studio,
Vicarage Street,
Painswick, Stroud,
Gloucestershire GL6 6XP
Tel   +44 (0)1452 814858
Email   sara.kirby@mac.com

Entry 197   Map 8

Gloucestershire

Well Farm

Perhaps it's the gentle, unstuffy attitude of Kate and Edward. Or the great position of the house with its glorious views across the valley. Whichever, you'll feel comforted and invigorated by your stay. It's a real family home and you get both a fresh, pretty bedroom that feels very private and the use of a comfortable, book-filled sitting room opening to a flowery courtyard; Kate is an inspired gardener. Sleep soundly on the softest of pillows, wake to the deep peace of the countryside and the delicious prospect of eggs from their own hens, local sausages and good bacon. The area teems with great walks – lovely pubs too.

Rooms	1 twin/double with sitting room: £90.
Meals	Dinner from £20. Pubs nearby.
Closed	Rarely.

Kate & Edward Gordon Lennox
Well Farm,
Frampton Mansell, Stroud,
Gloucestershire GL6 8JB
Tel   +44 (0)1285 760651
Email   kategl@btinternet.com
Web   www.well-farm.co.uk

Entry 198   Map 8

Gloucestershire

St Annes

Step straight off the narrow pavement into a sunny hall and a warm and welcoming family home. Iris and Greg have made their pretty 17th-century house, in the heart of this lovely bustling village, as eco-friendly as possible. Comfy bedrooms are charming; the four-poster room has a tiny en suite shower room. Farmers' market breakfasts are a feast and Rollo the dog loves children. Painswick is known as 'the Queen of the Cotswolds': enjoy superb walks through orchid meadows and beechwoods carpeted with bluebells; visit good pubs on the way. Great value.

Minimum stay: 2 nights at weekends April-September.

Rooms	1 double, 1 twin, 1 four-poster: £70–£75. Singles £50. Dogs £5. Extra bed in double room £20.
Meals	Packed lunch £6. Pubs/restaurants in village.
Closed	Rarely.

Iris McCormick
St Annes,
Gloucester Street,
Painswick,
Gloucestershire GL6 6QN

Tel	+44 (0)1452 812879
Email	iris@st-annes-painswick.co.uk
Web	www.st-annes-painswick.co.uk

Entry 199   Map 8

Gloucestershire

The Old Rectory

English to the core – and to the bottom of its lovely garden, with a woodland walk and plenty of quiet places to sit. You sweep into the circular driveway to a yellow labrador welcome. This beautiful 17th-century high gabled house is comfortably lived-in with an understated décor, antiques, creaky floorboards and a real sense of history. The bedrooms, one with a garden view, have good beds, a chaise longue or an easy chair; bathrooms are vintage and functional but large. Caroline is calm and competent and serves breakfasts with organic eggs and local bacon at the long table in the rich red dining room. A welcoming place.

Rooms	1 double, 1 twin/double (extra bed available): £85–£100. Extra bed & cot for children available. Singles £60–£100.
Meals	Pub 200 yds.
Closed	December/January.

Roger & Caroline Carne
The Old Rectory,
Meysey Hampton,
Cirencester,
Gloucestershire GL7 5JX

Tel	+44 (0)1285 851200
Email	carolinecarne@cotswoldwireless.co.uk
Web	www.meyseyoldrectory.co.uk

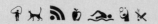

Entry 200   Map 8

Gloucestershire

The Old Bear

Step through the cool antiques showroom into a beautiful old house. Anne-Marie. charming and Danish, and Allan have filled their home with colour, polished antiques (of course) and vases of flowers. Upstairs to huge bedrooms with a sofa and armchair or two, books and tea tray with fresh coffee; beds have fine linen and bathrooms are pretty. Breakfast is at a lovely long sycamore table, with blue and white china in the dresser, gorgeous linen curtains at the window (looking onto the road); feast on French pastries, homemade jams, a neighbour's eggs, local bacon and sausages. Passing cars but quiet at night, so you sleep well.

Rooms	2 doubles (Z-beds & extra small double available): £95. Singles £75.
Meals	Pub/restaurant 1 mile.
Closed	Christmas.

Anne-Marie Hare
The Old Bear,
Perrotts Brook,
Cirencester,
Gloucestershire GL7 7BP
Tel   +44 (0)1285 831131
Email   annemarie.eaton1@btinternet.com
Web   www.hares-antiques.com

Entry 201   Map 8

Gloucestershire

The Guest House

You get your own new timber-framed house with masses of light and space, a terrace, and spectacular valley and woodland views. The living room has wooden floors, lovely old oak furniture and French windows onto the rose-filled garden. Sue brims with enthusiasm and is a flexible host: breakfast can be over in her kitchen or continental in yours. Look forward to the eggs from the hens and delicious dinners with produce from the veg patch. The bedroom is a charming up-in-the-eaves room with oriental rugs, colourful linen and a big comfy bed; your fresh, simple wet room is downstairs. A peaceful, secluded place.

Rooms	Cottage 1 double, sitting room & kitchenette: £130-£150. £260-£875 for a 2-7 night break.
Meals	Dinner, 2 courses, from £15; 3 courses, from £20. Pub 1 mile.
Closed	Rarely.

Sue Bathurst
The Guest House,
Manor Cottage, Bagendon,
Cirencester,
Gloucestershire GL7 7DU
Tel   +44 (0)1285 831417
Email   heritage.venues@virgin.net
Web   www.cotswoldguesthouse.co.uk

Entry 202   Map 8

Great Farm

Three riverside spots here, all named after the wildlife. Otter is a *Swallows and Amazons*-style haven, Nightingale is romantic with a claw-foot tub, and Barn Owl's two bowtop wagons with chill-out pod are perfect for families; fairy lights glow on the decking. Each feels very private, with a flushing loo, a hot shower or a bath, a covered outdoor kitchen, a fire-pit for toasting marshmallows. Leonie can bring you a breakfast hamper, and you can walk along the river bank to pretty Lechlade, with pubs, antique shops and row boats for hire. For adventurous chefs there are crayfish in the river – and traps provided!

Minimum stay: 2 nights. Book through Sawday's Canopy & Stars online or by phone.

Clapton Manor

Karin and James's 16th-century manor is as all homes should be: loved and lived-in. And, with three-foot-thick walls, rich Persian rugs on flagstoned floors, sit-in fireplaces and stone-mullioned windows, it's gorgeous. The garden, enclosed by old stone walls, is full of birdsong and roses. One bedroom has a secret door leading to a fuchsia-pink bathroom; the other room, smaller, has a Tudor stone fireplace and wonderful garden views. Wellies, dogs, a comfy guest sitting room with lots of books… and breakfast by a vast fireplace: homemade bread, award-winning marmalade and eggs from the hens. A happy, charming family home.

Rooms	Shepherd's hut camp for 2; railway wagon for 2: £90–£95. Gypsy caravan camp for 6: £115–£140.	Rooms	1 double, 1 twin/double: £110–£130. Singles from £100.
Meals	Breakfast hampers from £18 for 2.	Meals	Pub/restaurants within 15-minute drive.
Closed	November–March.	Closed	Rarely.

2014/15
Sawday's
BED & BREAKFAST

Old favourite

Sawday's Canopy & Stars
Great Farm,
Thatched Cottage, Whelford,
Fairford, Gloucestershire

Tel	+44 (0)117 204 7830
Email	enquiries@canopyandstars.co.uk
Web	www.canopyandstars.co.uk/ greatfarm

Karin & James Bolton
Clapton Manor,
Clapton-on-the-Hill,
Gloucestershire GL54 2LG

Tel	+44 (0)1451 810202
Mobile	+44 (0)7967 144416
Email	bandb@claptonmanor.co.uk
Web	www.claptonmanor.co.uk

Gloucestershire

Calcot Peak House

A treat to stay in such a handsome old house with such relaxed owners – lovely Alex is full of enthusiasm for her B&B enterprise. There's an excellent butcher in Northleach so breakfasts are tip-top, and the bedrooms are a sophisticated mix of traditional and contemporary: Farrow & Ball colours, rich florals, fresh flowers, and fluffy white robes for trots to the bathroom. You also have your own charming drawing room: tartan carpet, pink sofas, family oils. Outside: 19 acres for Dexie the dog and a bench on the hill for the view. Tramp the Salt Way, dine in Cirencester, let the owls hoot you to sleep.

Dogs very welcome to sleep in utility room (comfortable and warm!) but not in bedrooms.

Rooms	1 double, 1 twin sharing bath & drawing room (let to same party only, children's room available): £95. Singles £80.
Meals	Pub 2 miles.
Closed	Rarely.

Tom & Alexandra Pearson
Calcot Peak House,
Northleach,
Cheltenham,
Gloucestershire GL54 3QB
Tel   +44 (0)1285 721047
Email   pearsonalex5@gmail.com

Entry 205   Map 8

Gloucestershire

Rectory Farmhouse

Once a monastery, now a farmhouse with style. Passing a development of converted farm buildings to reach the Rectory's warm Cotswold stones makes the discovery doubly exciting. More glory within: Sybil, a talented designer, has created something immaculate, fresh and uplifting. A wood-burner glows in the sitting room, bed linen is white, walls cream; beds are superb, bathrooms sport cast-iron slipper baths and power showers and views are to the church. Your hosts are naturally friendly; Sybil used to own a restaurant and her breakfasts – by the Aga or in the conservatory under a rampant vine – are a further treat.

Over 14s welcome.

Rooms	2 doubles: £104–£110. Singles £85–£95.
Meals	Pubs/restaurants 1 mile.
Closed	Christmas & New Year.

Sybil Gisby
Rectory Farmhouse,
Lower Swell,
Stow-on-the-Wold, Cheltenham,
Gloucestershire GL54 1LH
Tel   +44 (0)1451 832351
Email   rectoryfarmhouse@yahoo.com
Web   www.rectoryfarmhouse.yolasite.com

Entry 206   Map 8

Gloucestershire

The Mews

Down the cobbled mews, a beautifully presented mews house – luxury and parking in the heart of Stow. Hostess Jan has her own self-contained space so is on hand to help, and gives you breakfast in a big, light, multi-purpose living room – metallic grey kitchen units at one end, a triptych mirror at the other, and a large sofa. Up the black, grey and cream stair carpet is a super-private bedroom on the first floor: a circular mirror floating above an immaculate bed, a wall of wardrobes, a mews' view, and a fabulous state-of-the-art bathroom. Old Stow, stuffed with galleries and antique shops, is a charming, civilised Cotswolds base.

Minimum stay: 2 nights at weekends.

Rooms	1 double: £90-£100. Singles £70-£90.
Meals	Pub/restaurant within walking distance.
Closed	Rarely.

Jan Winters
The Mews,
1 Fox Lane, Digbeth Street,
Stow-on-the-Wold,
Cheltenham,
Gloucestershire GL54 1BN

Mobile	+44 (0)7767 206923
Email	jan@themews-stowonthewold.com
Web	www.themews-stowonthewold.com

Entry 207   Map 8

Gloucestershire

Aylworth Manor

Set in a peaceful Cotswolds valley and surrounded by attractive gardens, John and Joanna's gorgeous manor is immaculate. Sit beside the wood-burner in the comfy snug or play the piano in a grand drawing room, rich with art and family photos: your hosts have that happy knack of making you feel instantly at home. Large sunny bedrooms come with garden and valley views, perfect linen on seriously cushy beds, antiques and lavish bathrooms. Wake refreshed for breakfast in the dining room: homemade bread, eggs from the ducks and hens, coffee in a silver pot. The Windrush Way passes the gate at the end of the drive. What a treat!

Children over 12 welcome.

Rooms	1 double; 1 twin/double with separate bath: £90-£110. Singles £60.
Meals	Pub 1 mile.
Closed	Rarely.

John & Joanna Ireland
Aylworth Manor,
Naunton,
Cheltenham,
Gloucestershire GL54 3AH

Tel	+44 (0)1451 850850
Mobile	+44 (0)7768 810357
Email	enquiries@aylworthmanor.co.uk
Web	www.aylworthmanor.co.uk

Entry 208   Map 8

Gloucestershire

Hanover House

The former home of Elgar's wife, in a Victorian terrace in Cheltenham's heart, is warm, elegant, inviting and surprisingly peaceful. There are big trees all around and the river Chelt laps at the foot of the garden. Inside, find a graceful period décor enlivened by exuberant splashes of colour; the delectable drawing room, with pale walls and a trio of arched windows, is the perfect foil for great art, books and rugs. Bedrooms are beautiful in vibrant red and amber; bathrooms are simply stylish. Breakfast is superb and served in the dining room window. Best of all are Veronica and James: musical, well-travelled, irresistible.

Gloucestershire

Detmore House

Down a private drive, surrounded by seven acres, this smart shiny house has been the home of poets, artists and writers. Gill carries on the creativity with her cooking, interior design, jewellery, gardening and chickens; she and Hugh are easy natural hosts. Supremely comfortable bedrooms have a smart hotel feel, bathrooms are immaculate and you and your dinner party guests will be spoiled with organic produce from the garden. There are wide lawns and mature trees and you can lap up the views across Charlton Hills from lots of lovely sitting spots. Cheltenham and the Cotswold Way are on the doorstep.

Rooms	1 double, 1 twin; 1 double with separate bath: £100–£120. Singles £70.
Meals	Pubs/restaurants 200 yds.
Closed	Rarely.

Rooms	2 twin/doubles, 1 twin: £85–£95. 1 family room for 3: £120–£150. Singles from £65.
Meals	Dinner from £28.50 (for groups of 6+). Packed lunch £6. Pub 1 mile.
Closed	Christmas & New Year.

	Veronica & James Ritchie Hanover House, 65 St George's Road, Cheltenham, Gloucestershire GL50 3DU
Tel	+44 (0)1242 541297
Email	info@hanoverhouse.org
Web	www.hanoverhouse.org

	Gill Kilminster Detmore House, London Road, Charlton Kings, Cheltenham, Gloucestershire GL52 6UT
Tel	+44 (0)1242 582868
Email	gillkilminster@btconnect.com
Web	www.detmorehouse.com

Entry 209   Map 8

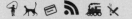

Entry 210   Map 8

Gloucestershire

The Courtyard Studio

This smart first-floor studio, attractive in reclaimed red brick, is reached via its own wrought-iron staircase; you are beautifully private. The friendly owners live next door, and will cook you a delicious breakfast in the house, or leave you a continental one in your own fridge. Find a clever, compact, contemporary space with a light and uncluttered living area, a mini window seat opposite two very comfortable boutiquey beds, fine linen, wicker armchair, and a patio area for balmy days. A 20-minute walk brings you to the centre of Cheltenham and you're a two-minute canter from the races.

Minimum stay: 2 nights.

Rooms	Studio – 1 twin: £85.
Meals	Restaurants/pubs within 1 mile.
Closed	Rarely.

John & Annette Gill
The Courtyard Studio,
1 The Cleevelands Courtyard,
Cleevelands Drive,
Cheltenham,
Gloucestershire GL50 4QF
Tel   +44 (0)1242 573125
Mobile   +44 (0)7901 978917
Email   courtyardstudio@aol.com

Entry 211   Map 8

Gloucestershire

Pauntley Court

If a rural hideaway is what you seek then beat a path here and prepare to be enchanted. The house is a historical corker and was home to the Whittington family for 300 years – Dick is reputed to have been born here. Plush traditional rooms with beautiful beds look over unspoilt countryside; smart bathrooms have Neal's Yard toiletries. Breakfast in the ballroom on fresh local produce, some from the garden, and enjoy the special juice of the day. Surrounded by romantic gardens you can wander at will amidst the yew 'ruins' or gaze at Pan over a glass of Chablis. Delightful Melissa adds the finishing touch to a blissful place.

Fishing & stable available.

Rooms	2 twin/doubles: £100–£120. Singles £80.
Meals	Pub 6 miles.
Closed	Rarely.

Mark & Melissa Hargreaves
Pauntley Court,
Pauntley Court Drive,
Redmarley, Gloucester,
Gloucestershire GL19 3JA
Tel   +44 (0)1531 828627
Mobile   +44 (0)7798 865979
Email   melissa@pauntleycourt.com
Web   www.pauntleycourt.com

Entry 212   Map 8

Gloucestershire

Seymour House

A gorgeous golden house, right on the high street of one of the Cotswolds' prettiest towns. It was a hotel until your hosts returned it to a family home, with two children and a dog it is most welcoming and appealing. There's a generous walled garden that slopes upwards at the back, and a long sash-window'd drawing room at the front, elegant and inviting: magazines and open fire at one end, breakfast tables at the other. Sarah loves to cook so expect the best. Bedrooms have madly comfortable beds, rich cream towels, delicious linen, a country-house feel. Nearby there are markets and gardens galore.

Over 10s welcome.

Rooms	3 doubles, 2 twin/doubles: £120–£130. Singles £80. Sunday–Thursday: 2 night stays £220.
Meals	Pubs/restaurants within walking distance.
Closed	Rarely.

Sarah Taylor
Seymour House,
High Street,
Chipping Campden,
Gloucestershire GL55 6AG

Tel	+44 (0)1386 840064
Email	sarah@seymourhousebandb.co.uk
Web	www.seymourhousebandb.co.uk

Entry 213   Map 8

Gloucestershire

The Court

Just off the high street this huge honey-hued Jacobean house has been in the family since it was built in 1624 by Sir Baptist Hicks. Dogs sound the alarm when you knock… step inside to find a relaxed faded splendour. Delicate ornaments sit on exquisite antiques, family portraits and spectacular oils line the walls; up winding stairs, bedrooms (all with TVs) have comfy beds, books, a mix of beautiful and functional furniture and breathtaking views of rooftops or gardens. Jane's friendly housekeeper cooks your Aga breakfast – eggs and jams are from the garden. The walking is superb, Hidcote and Kiftsgate are close. Great value.

Rooms	3 doubles: £70–£100. 2 doubles, sharing bath (let to same party only): £60 1 single, 1 double sharing bath (let to same party only): from £50.
Meals	Pub/restaurant 30 yds.
Closed	Christmas, Easter, Whitsun bank holiday & half term.

Jane Glennie
The Court,
Calf Lane,
Chipping Campden,
Gloucestershire GL55 6JQ

Tel	+44 (0)1386 840201
Email	j14glennie@aol.com
Web	www.thecourtchippingcampden.co.uk

Entry 214   Map 8

Gloucestershire

Wren House

Barely two miles from Stow-on-the-Wold, this peaceful house sits charmingly on the edge of a tiny hamlet. It was built before the English Civil War and Kiloran spent two years stylishly renovating it; the results are a joy. Downstairs, light-filled, elegant rooms with glowing rugs on pale Cotswold stone; upstairs, delicious bedrooms, spotless bathrooms and a doorway to duck. Breakfast in the vaulted kitchen is locally sourced and organic, where possible, and the well-planted garden, in which you are encouraged to sit, has far-reaching views. Explore rolling valleys and glorious gardens; Kiloran can advise.

Minimum stay: 2 nights.

Rooms	1 twin/double; 2 twin/doubles, each with separate bath/shower: £110. Singles from £85. Well-behaved dogs welcome, one at a time, and only downstairs, £25.
Meals	Pubs/restaurants 1 mile.
Closed	Rarely.

	Mrs Kiloran McGrigor Wren House, Donnington, Stow-on-the-Wold, Gloucestershire GL56 0XZ
Tel	+44 (0)1451 831787
Mobile	+44 (0)7802 676673
Email	enquiries@wrenhouse.net
Web	www.wrenhouse.net

Entry 215   Map 8

Gloucestershire

Donnington Manor

Through the pillared entrance find a slice of English life – old-fashioned grandeur in the Cotswolds. Kat and Henry, affable and interesting, keep their own chickens, bake their own bread, and breakfasts are delicious. Bedrooms (floral drapes, sinks in the room) have high ceilings and wonderful views, bathrooms (baths not showers) are a leisurely size and the drawing room and snug are to share: cosy log fires and paintings of ancestors. In summer, the natural gardens come into their own and the views from the terrace reach for miles. Walkers rejoice: the Heart of England Way runs right by.

Rooms	1 double, 1 twin, each with separate bath: £100–£140. Singles £75.
Meals	Pub/restaurant 2 miles.
Closed	Rarely.

	Katherine & Henry Dennis Donnington Manor, Donnington, Moreton-in-Marsh, Gloucestershire GL56 0YB
Mobile	+44 (0)7913 461551
Email	katdnns@gmail.com

Entry 216   Map 8

Gloucestershire

Windy Ridge House

Everyone loves Windy Ridge. It's comfortable, it's cosy, it's run by cheerful staff and it's well positioned for touring the Cotswolds. Nick's father was in construction and built this in traditional style using the finest timbers and stone; it's seen much refurbishment since then, including a smart French-bedded room with beautiful glass lamps, upbeat art and a modern bathroom. There's a proper four-man lift, a pine-panelled drawing room and polished things at every turn. Take a book to a velveteen sofa and help yourself from the honesty bar; visit the arboretum, the prize-winning gardens and the summer heated pool.

Rooms	2 doubles; 1 double, 1 twin/double, each with separate bath: £110-£120. Singles £90-£110. Extra bed/sofabed available £15-£20 per person per night.
Meals	Pub 100 yds.
Closed	Rarely.

Nick & Jennifer Williams
Windy Ridge House,
Longborough,
Moreton-in-Marsh,
Gloucestershire GL56 0QY

Tel	+44 (0)1451 830465
Email	nick@windy-ridge.co.uk
Web	www.windy-ridge.co.uk

Entry 217   Map 8

Gloucestershire

The Old School

So comfortable and filled with understated style is this 1854 Cotswold stone house. Wendy and John are generous, beds are huge, linen is laundered, towels and robes are fluffy. Your own mini fridge is carefully hidden and pretty lamps cast a warm glow. Best of all is the upstairs sitting room: a chic, open-plan space with church style windows letting light flood in and super sofas, good art, lovely fabrics. A wood-burner keeps you toasty, Wendy is a grand cook and all is flexible. A gorgeous, relaxing place to stay – on the A44 but peaceful at night – that positively hums with hospitality. Guests say "even better than home!"

Rooms	3 doubles, 1 twin/double: £120-£150. Singles £96-£120. Extra bed/sofabed available £20-£40 per person per night.
Meals	Dinner, 4 courses, £32. Supper, 2 courses, £18. Supper tray £12. Pub 0.5 miles.
Closed	Rarely.

Wendy Veale & John Scott-Lee
The Old School,
Little Compton, Moreton-in-Marsh,
Gloucestershire GL56 0SL

Tel	+44 (0)1608 674588
Mobile	+44 (0)7831 098271
Email	wendy@theoldschoolbedandbreakfast.com
Web	www.theoldschoolbedandbreakfast.com

Entry 218   Map 8

Hampshire

Vinegar Hill Pottery

A sylvan setting, stylish pottery, a young and talented family. The cobalt blues and rich browns of David's ceramics fill the old stables of a Victorian manor house. Take pottery courses (one hour to a long weekend) or just enjoy the creative Mexican-inspired décor. A narrow staircase spirals up to a modern loft: crisp whites, cathedral ceiling with sunny windows, brilliant shower. The ground-floor garden suite has a patio (with a gorgeous Showman's wagon!), sitting room, painted bed and optional children's beds. Lucy brings breakfast to your room. Stroll to the beach: stretch out and you almost touch the Isle of Wight.

Minimum stay: 2 nights at weekends April-October; 3 on bank holidays.

Rooms	1 double: £85.
	1 suite for 2-4: £95.
	Showman's wagon for 2 with separate wet room (available in summer): £80. Singles from £60.
Meals	Pub/restaurant 0.25 miles.
Closed	Rarely.

Lucy Rogers
Vinegar Hill Pottery,
Vinegar Hill, Milford on Sea,
Hampshire SO41 0RZ

Tel	+44 (0)1590 642979
Email	info@vinegarhillpottery.co.uk
Web	www.vinegarhillpottery.co.uk

Entry 223   Map 3

Hampshire

Bay Trees

The Isle of Wight and the Needles loom large as you approach Milford on Sea: the beach is shingle, the views are amazing. Mark and Sarah have become dab hands at B&B and welcome you in to a sun-filled conservatory with Ercol elm and beech tables and chairs; the home-bakes and award-winning breakfasts are delicious. Comfortable bedrooms, with good linen, are spotless and warm; bathrooms ooze white towels. One room opens to the lush garden: magnolias, weeping willow and pond; and chickens that lay your breakfast eggs! With Mark's background in hospitality and Sarah's passion for cooking the service here is second to none.

Usually minimum stay: 2 nights at weekends.

Rooms	1 double, 1 four-poster;
	1 family room for 3: £100-£115.
	Singles £80-£90.
Meals	Restaurants 100 yds.
Closed	Rarely.

Mark & Sarah Clayson
Bay Trees,
8 High Street, Milford on Sea,
Lymington, Hampshire SO41 0QD

Tel	+44 (0)1590 642186
Email	mark.clayson@btinternet.com
Web	www.baytreebedandbreakfast.co.uk

Entry 224   Map 3

Hampshire

Broadcroft

Down a leafy lane, and tucked behind a long serpentine wall... Heather and Billy's happy home is full of art, porcelain, antiques and traditional furnishings. Your comfy bedrooms are in a separate wing and face south overlooking the lovely garden. Breakfast is in the conservatory – a colourful spot with grandchildren's drawings and Heather's collection of wire/pottery chickens topping the window sills. Tuck into a continental or full English, and homemade compote. The garden teems with bulbs in spring, colour all year round; Billy grows all his veg in big tubs. Lymington is fun: restaurants, shops and a great Saturday market.

Very pet friendly with secure garden. Minimum stay: 2 nights preferred at weekends.

Rooms	1 double, 1 twin sharing bath (let to same party only): £70-£80. Both rooms as a family suite for 4: £140-£155. Singles £55-£60.
Meals	Pubs/restaurants 0.5 miles.
Closed	Rarely.

Heather Howard
Broadcroft,
28 Broad Lane, Lymington,
Hampshire SO41 3QP

Tel	+44 (0)1590 672741
Email	whoward@uwclub.net
Web	www.broadcroft-lymington.co.uk

Entry 225   Map 3

Hampshire

Brymer House

Complete privacy in a B&B is rare. Here you have it, just a 12-minute walk from town, cathedral and water meadows. Relax in your own half of a Victorian townhouse immaculately furnished and decorated, and with a garden to match – all roses and lilac in the spring. Breakfasts are sumptuous, there's a log fire in the guests' sitting room and fresh flowers abound. An 'honesty box' means you may help yourselves to drinks. Bedrooms are small and elegant, with antique mirrors, furniture and bedspreads; bathrooms are warm and spotless. Guy and Fizzy have charmed Special Places guests for many years.

Children over 7 welcome.

Rooms	1 double; 1 twin: £80-£90. Singles £60-£65. Extra bed/sofabed available £20 per person per night.
Meals	Pubs/restaurants nearby.
Closed	Rarely.

Guy & Fizzy Warren
Brymer House,
29-30 St Faith's Road, St Cross,
Winchester, Hampshire SO23 9QD

Tel	+44 (0)1962 867428
Email	brymerhouse@aol.com
Web	www.brymerhouse.co.uk

Entry 226   Map 4

Bridge House

A beautifully tended garden, with a paved breakfast area, surrounds this 1920s family home and the Grettons couldn't be more hospitable: tea, cake and good talk on arrival; stacks of local knowledge. Family photos and evidence of Michael's naval career personalise the elegant sitting room, with its open fire and doors onto the garden. Bedrooms – 'Yellow' and 'Blue' – are comfortable, pretty, immaculate, and the double overlooks the garden. Steph's breakfasts are a happy mix of good things homemade and local. The old Watercress Line is nearby, Winchester is a draw and have you been to Jane Austen's Chawton?

Weston Farm

Country life at its loveliest: a beautifully restored Georgian house and farm; fresh-laid eggs; a donkey and pony in the paddock, and generous, helpful hosts who will fetch you off the London train. Horse and hound wallpaper gallops over the hall, the sitting room has wood panelling, sash windows and a giant marble fireplace; comfortable bedrooms have writing desks, pretty curtains and white linen. A footpath traces the 800-acre arable farm so roam free over water meadows. Stroll to the typical Hampshire village of Micheldever (thatched cottages, handsome church) for dinner – or it's eight miles to historic Winchester.

Rooms	1 double; 1 twin with separate bath: £80-£90. Singles £65 (in twin room only).
Meals	Pubs/restaurants 5-minute drive.
Closed	Rarely.

Rooms	1 twin/double, 1 four-poster: £80. Singles £50.
Meals	Pub 1.5 miles.
Closed	Christmas.

Stephanie & Michael Gretton
Bridge House,
Chillandham Lane,
Martyr Worthy, Winchester,
Hampshire SO21 1AS
Tel   +44 (0)1962 779379
Email   bh@itchenvalleybandb.com
Web   www.itchenvalleybandb.com

Laura Stevens
Weston Farm,
Weston Down Lane, Weston Colley,
Winchester, Hampshire SO21 3AG
Tel   +44 (0)1962 774791
Mobile +44 (0)7999 816417
Email   westonfarmbandb@googlemail.com
Web   www.westonfarmaccommodation.co.uk

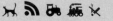

Entry 227   Map 4

Entry 228   Map 4

Hampshire

Browninghill Farm

Complete independence here: your own prettily converted threshing barn down an oak-lined lane. Hattie lives in the farm next door and looks after you well; breakfasts and dinners are rustled up for you in your little kitchen – eggs from the hens, homemade bread and jams and local produce. The attractive dining/sitting space has a soaring ceiling, beams, a duck egg blue dresser holding cheerful crockery and a picture window with views across the fields. Bedrooms (one up, one down) are cosy with comfy feather pillows and white linen; bathrooms are small yet perfect with robes and big towels. Snug and romantic.

Minimum stay: 2 nights.

Rooms	Barn – 1 double: £110. 1 single: £50.
Meals	Supper, 2 courses, £25. Pubs/restaurants 0.5 miles.
Closed	Rarely.

Hattie Pigot
Browninghill Farm,
Browninghill Green, Baughurst,
Tadley, Hampshire RG26 5JZ

Tel	+44 (0)1189 815537
Mobile	+44 (0)7789 431220
Email	hattie@browninghillfarm.com
Web	www.browninghillfarm.com

Entry 229   Map 4

Hampshire

Little Cottage

Just 45 minutes from Heathrow but the peace is deep, the views are long and the wildlife thrives – watch fox and deer, listen out for the rare nightjar. Chris and Therese grow summer salads and soft fruits and give you superb home cooking; eat in a big conservatory filled with greenery. Guests have a lovely sitting room with an eclectic mix of modern and antique furniture, and a pretty terrace overlooks the garden; bedrooms, likewise, are on the ground-floor, fresh and light, the double with distant views. Perfect for walkers and those who seek solace from urban life but don't want to stray too far.

Minimum stay: 2 nights at weekends (April-October). Over 12s welcome.

Rooms	1 double, 1 twin/double: £75-£90. 1 single: £50.
Meals	Dinner from £25. Pub 1.5 miles.
Closed	Christmas, New Year & occasionally.

Chris & Therese Abbott
Little Cottage,
Hazeley Heath, Hartley Wintney,
Hook, Hampshire RG27 8LY

Tel	+44 (0)1252 845050
Mobile	+44 (0)7721 462214
Email	info@little-cottage.co.uk
Web	www.little-cottage.co.uk

Entry 230   Map 4

Shafts Farm

The 1960s farmhouse has many weapons in its armoury: a tremendous South Downs thatched-village setting, owners who know every path and trail, comfortable generous bedrooms and a stunning rose garden designed by David Austin Roses (parterres, obelisks, meandering paths). The two bedrooms are fresh in cream, florals and plaids, each with a shower room with heated floors to keep toes toasty. Homemade granola, garden fruit and the full English make a fine start to the day; the airy, cane-furnished conservatory is the place for afternoon tea and a read. Your hosts are both geographers and have an intriguing display of maps.

Wriggly Tin Shepherd's Huts

Settle in to the slow lane in this wooded corner of Hampshire and hole-up in one of Alex's cleverly converted huts. All are off-grid, in gentle colours, with locally found enamel kitchenware and furnishings, log-burners and campfires. Beacon, and Butser, on the other side of the meadow, share an ingeniously designed shower and compost loo. Boundary is the new kid on the block, big enough for a family of four, with a fresh, spring green theme and plenty of Alex's creative touches. So – get happily back to basics near Hambledon, where cricket was born and where three major South Downs National Park walking trails meet.

Bookings start on a Monday, Wednesday or Friday. Book through Sawday's Canopy & Stars online or by phone.

Rooms	2 twins: £90. Singles £50.
Meals	Pubs/restaurants 500 yds.
Closed	Rarely.

Rooms	Shepherd's huts for 2-4: £75–£115. Extra single bunk available in Beacon, £15 per night.
Meals	Breakfast hampers from £20 for 2. Supper from £8.50 per person.
Closed	November–April.

Rosemary Morrish
Shafts Farm,
West Meon,
Petersfield,
Hampshire GU32 1LU
Tel   +44 (0)1730 829266
Email   info@shaftsfarm.co.uk
Web   www.shaftsfarm.co.uk

Sawday's Canopy & Stars
Wriggly Tin Shepherd's Huts,
Wriggly Tin, 15 Beckless Cottages,
Brook Lane, Hambledon,
Hampshire PO7 4TF
Tel   +44 (0)117 204 7830
Email   enquiries@canopyandstars.co.uk
Web   www.canopyandstars.co.uk/
         wrigglytin

Entry 231   Map 4

Entry 232   Map 4

Herefordshire

Grendon Manor

The best of traditional meets modern country living: this 16th-century manor house is a super mix of the very old and very new. A working sheep and cattle farm is wrapped around it and you can walk over fields and down to a pretty Norman church. Jane is easy company and looks after you well. Guests in their own wing will rejoice in bedrooms with old beams, crisply comfortable linen and new bathrooms, while the guest sitting room downstairs has marvellous dark oak panelling, rich colours and glowing lamps. A farmhouse-tasty breakfast sets you up for beautiful Herefordshire walks, and Ludlow is close.

Rooms	2 doubles, 1 twin: £100. Singles £50.
Meals	Dinner £25 (groups only). Pub/restaurant 2 miles.
Closed	Rarely.

Jane Piggott
Grendon Manor,
Bredenbury, Bromyard,
Herefordshire HR7 4TH
Tel   +44 (0)1885 482226
Mobile   +44 (0)7977 493083
Email   jane.piggott@btconnect.com
Web   www.grendonmanor.com

Entry 233   Map 7

Herefordshire

Bunns Croft

The timbers of this medieval yeoman's house are quite possibly a thousand years old. Little of the structure has ever been altered and it is sheer delight. Stone floors, rich colours, a piano, dogs, books, cosy chairs – all give a homely, warm feel. Cruck-beamed bedrooms are snugly small, the stairs are steep, and the twin's bathroom has its own sweet fireplace. The countryside is 'pure', too, with 1,500 acres of National Trust land a short hop away. Anita is charming, loves to look after her guests, grows her own fruit and vegetables and makes fabulous dinners. Just mind your head.

Rooms	1 twin; 1 double, sharing bath with 2 singles (let to same party only): £80-£90. 2 singles sharing bath with 1 double (let to same party only): £40. Dinner, B&B £65-£70 per person.
Meals	Dinner, 3 courses, £25. Pub 7 miles.
Closed	Rarely.

Anita Syers-Gibson
Bunns Croft,
Moreton Eye,
Leominster,
Herefordshire HR6 0DP
Tel   +44 (0)1568 615836

Entry 234   Map 7

Herefordshire

Pear Tree Farm

Steve and Jill are friendly, lively and keen to tell the story of their history-steeped 17th-century farmhouse and surrounds. Bedrooms have tip-top linen and traditional furniture complemented by Steve's artisan handmade pieces; the ground floor room has a kitchen area opening onto the garden; morning tea is delivered. Lovely Ludlow provides for the table, fruits are from the garden, eggs are free-range and bread and marmalade homemade. You can snooze in the orchard hammock, have afternoon tea on a garden bench, and the terracotta-painted sitting room is a cosy, book-filled spot for a cocktail before dinner. Hay-on-Wye is close.

Minimum stay: 2 nights.

Rooms	1 double, 1 twin/double; 1 double with separate bath: £105. Singles £90.
Meals	Dinner £37.50. Pubs/restaurants 0.5 miles.
Closed	Rarely.

Steve Dawson & Jill Fieldhouse
Pear Tree Farm,
Wigmore,
Leominster,
Herefordshire HR6 9UR

Tel	+44 (0)1568 770140
Email	info@peartree-farm.co.uk
Web	www.peartree-farm.co.uk

Entry 235   Map 7

Herefordshire

Staunton House

This handsome Georgian rectory has a traditional, peaceful feel. Step into light, colourful and well-proportioned rooms that brim with family photographs, antiques, china and masses of books. The original oak staircase leads to inviting bedrooms with comfortable beds, pretty fabrics and garden posies; the blue room looks onto garden and pond. Wander through the beautiful garden, drive to Hay or Ludlow, stride across ravishing countryside, play golf near Offa's Dyke; return to Rosie and Richard's lovely home to relax in their drawing room before enjoying a delicious dinner in the elegant dining room. You will be well looked after here.

Rooms	1 double, 1 twin/double: £85-£95. Singles from £55.
Meals	Dinner, 3 courses, £27.50. Pub/restaurant 2.5 miles.
Closed	Rarely.

Rosie & Richard Bowen
Staunton House,
Staunton-on-Arrow, Pembridge,
Leominster, Herefordshire HR6 9HR

Tel	+44 (0)1544 388313
Mobile	+44 (0)7780 961994
Email	rosbown@aol.com
Web	www.stauntonhouse.co.uk

Entry 236   Map 7

Herefordshire

Garnstone House

Come for peace and quiet in the Welsh Marches, good food and lovely, humorous, down-to-earth hosts. The atmosphere is easy, and the furniture a lifetime's accumulation of eclectic pieces and pictures of horses, hounds and country scenes. After dinner and good conversation, climb the picture-lined stairs to a comfortable, pretty bedroom in soft colours – either a twin or a double – and a bathroom that is properly old-fashioned. Delicious breakfasts (homemade jams and eggs from the hens), tasty dinners and a stunning garden to explore – the variety and colour of the springtime flowers are astonishing and the clematis is a glory.

Rooms	1 double, 1 twin sharing bath (let to same party only): £90–£100. Singles from £50.
Meals	Dinner from £25. Pub/restaurant 1 mile.
Closed	Rarely.

Dawn & Michael MacLeod
Garnstone House,
Weobley,
Herefordshire HR4 8QP
Tel   +44 (0)1544 318943
Email   macleod@garnstonehouse.co.uk
Web   www.garnstonehouse.co.uk

Entry 237   Map 7

Herefordshire

Hall's Mill House

Quiet lanes bring you to this most idyllic spot – a stone cottage in a light and open valley. The sitting room is snug with wood-burner and sofas but the kitchen is the hub of the place – delicious breakfasts and dinners are cooked on the Aga. Grace, chatty and easy-going, obviously enjoys living in her modernised mill house. Rooms are small, fresh, with exposed beams and slate sills; only the old mill interrupts the far-reaching, all-green views. Drift off to sleep to the sound of the Arrow burbling by – a blissful tonic for walkers and nature lovers. Great value, too.

Children over 4 welcome.

Rooms	1 double; 1 double, 1 twin sharing bath: £60–£70. Singles £30–£35.
Meals	Dinner from £15. Pub/restaurant 3 miles.
Closed	Christmas.

Grace Watson
Hall's Mill House,
Huntington,
Kington,
Herefordshire HR5 3QA
Tel   +44 (0)1497 831409
Email   hallsmillhouse@hotmail.co.uk

Entry 238   Map 7

Tinto House

Bang in the centre of Hay-on-Wye, opposite the clock tower, amid a sea of bookshops, this beautiful Georgian townhouse brims with period features and original art. John and Karen have decorated their home with love: in the dining room, John's eye-catching paintings set off oak antiques, bookshelves, a fireplace; bedrooms bear mementos of France; one room holds art exhibitions. The garden, on the Wye's banks, is resplendent with roses and sculptures. Breakfast on local sausages and compotes from home-grown fruit before hitting the Black Mountains or Hay's independent shops. Perfect for lovers of outdoor and armchair pursuits.

Minimum stay: 2 nights at weekends.

New Inn Brilley

Daphne is delightful, and spiritual and kind. Her ancient drovers inn shines brightly in the hills above Hay with its tattered Tibetan flags, wonky overgrown garden and words of wisdom at every turn. Enter a kingdom of peace, sleep in the house or the yurt, help yourself to supper or let yourself be cooked for. Spotless bedrooms (up steep steps) are pink or yellow, one with a teeny, sweet bathroom, one without (but Daphne can provide a potty). Homemade yogurt and plum jam at breakfast with eggs from her bantams, a warm and history-filled house crammed with collectibles and with views from every window. Unusual and uplifting.

Pets by arrangement.

Rooms	2 doubles, 1 twin; 1 double with separate bath: £90–£100. Singles £65–£85.
Meals	Packed lunch £6.50. Pub/restaurant 100 yds.
Closed	Christmas & New Year.

Rooms	2 doubles sharing bath: £55–£65. 1 yurt for 6 with separate shower room: £70–£90. Singles £40.
Meals	Dinner with dessert £12.50. Pub 4 miles.
Closed	Rarely.

	Karen Clare
	Tinto House,
	13 Broad Street, Hay-on-Wye,
	Herefordshire HR3 5DB
Tel	+44 (0)1497 821556
Mobile	+44 (0)7985 559355
Email	tintohouse13@gmail.com
Web	www.tinto-house.co.uk

	Daphne Tucker
	New Inn Brilley,
	Brilley, Whitney-on-Wye,
	Hereford,
	Herefordshire HR3 6HE
Tel	+44 (0)1497 831284
Email	karmadaphne@onetel.com
Web	www.newinnbrilley.co.uk

Entry 239   Map 7

Entry 240   Map 7

New Inn Brilley Glamping

The Yurt and Wagon — on a hillside meadow with fabulous mountain views — share showers and loos and are full of charm; simple and comfortable with quirky, pretty touches, handmade furniture, woollen blankets, down duvets. The Rising Sun cabin is equally inventive, seductive and tucked away with facilities of its own. Daphne will even cook your breakfast! And her warm, creative energy pervades the wild garden, meditation space, converted 'cow shed' kitchen and dining room, self-catering and B&B in her former pub. Sheep and fowl roam freely and so can you — perfect for an emotional, spiritual and nutritional tune-up.

Minimum stay: 2 nights. Book through Sawday's Canopy & Stars online or by phone.

Yew Tree House

Sue and John's gorgeous 19th-century home is surrounded by gardens bejewelled with roses and fruit trees — plus stunning views across the Golden Valley to Hay Bluff. Meet these delightful people over tea and homemade cake in a tastefully decorated guest sitting room with comfy sofas, an open fire and shelves groaning with books. Generous bedrooms in pretty pastels are supremely comfortable, bathrooms have plenty of fluffy towels. Wake to the smell of baking bread, hasten to the dining room for a delicious breakfast of local produce. Dore Abbey's down the road, and Hay-on-Wye a half-hour jaunt. The countryside is glorious.

Rooms	Yurt for 6 (1 double, bunks, sofabed): £70-£90. Wagon for 2: £75-£85. Cabin for 2: £95.
Meals	Breakfast from £6 per person.
Closed	Rarely.

Rooms	1 double, 1 twin, 1 suite for 3: £80-£95.
Meals	Dinner, 3 courses, £25. Pub/restaurant 3.5 miles.
Closed	Rarely.

	Sawday's Canopy & Stars New Inn Brilley Glamping, Brilley, Whitney-on-Wye, Hereford, Herefordshire R3 6HE
Tel	+44 (0)117 204 7830
Email	enquiries@canopyandstars.co.uk
Web	www.canopyandstars.co.uk/newinnbrilley

	John & Susan Richardson Yew Tree House, Batcho Hill, Vowchurch, Hereford, Herefordshire HR2 9PF
Tel	+44 (0)1981 251195
Email	enquiries@yewtreehouse-hereford.co.uk
Web	www.yewtreehouse-hereford.co.uk

Entry 241   Map 7

Entry 242   Map 7

Herefordshire

East Friars

Laid back, lively and on the banks of the river Wye... Polly and Roger's family house will scoop you up and make you feel at home. Find a jumble of books, music and art in every corner, comfy armchairs in the lived-in sitting room and generous sunny bedrooms. Watch swans and ducks from the conservatory or terrace, while you tuck into Polly's local, seasonal, yummy breakfast with homemade bread and marmalade; she's a chef and holds pop-up restaurant nights in the conservatory too. Fish from the pontoon, borrow a canoe, bounce on trampolines, stroll to the city centre. Ted Hughes the Jack Russell and Bea the Cockerton love guests too!

Caravan available for extra guests.

Rooms	1 twin/double: £65.
	1 family room for 4: £80–£120.
	Dinner, B&B £50–£55 per person.
	Extra bed/sofabed available £20 per person per night.
Meals	Pubs/restaurants 10-minute walk.
Closed	Rarely.

Polly Ernest
East Friars,
Greyfriars Avenue,
Hereford,
Herefordshire HR4 0BE
Tel   +44 (0)1432 276462
Email   polly@eastfriars.co.uk
Web   www.eastfriars.co.uk

Entry 243   Map 7

Herefordshire

Rock Cottage

Birds, books and beautiful Black Mountain views highlighted by morning sun, turning to an inky black line at dusk; the cottage glows. There's an instant feeling of warmth and friendliness as you step into the snug hall; find rich autumnal colours, old rugs, a big wood-burner and comfy sitting rooms. Local art and photos line the walls, bedrooms have sumptuous beds, perfect linen and garden posies. You eat (very well) en famille at the communal oak table, or out on the pretty terrace. Thoughtful Chris and Sue will take you to hear the dawn chorus and there are food and literary festivals, bookshops and walks galore.

Minimum stay: 2 nights. Pets by arrangement.

Rooms	2 doubles: £70–£90.
Meals	Packed lunch £6.
	Dinner, 1 course, £15; 3 courses, £23.
	Pub/restaurant 4 miles.
Closed	Christmas & New Year.

Chris & Sue Robinson
Rock Cottage,
Newton St Margarets,
Hereford,
Herefordshire HR2 0QW
Tel   +44 (0)1981 510360
Email   robinsrockcottage@googlemail.com
Web   www.rockcottagebandb.co.uk

Entry 244   Map 7

Herefordshire

The Coach House

Pots of flowers by the front door and Farne the friendly terrier greet you. Iola and Michael are warm, friendly, and give you a continental breakfast of homemade breads and preserves, eggs from Michael's hens, croissants from the local bakery. Their house is airy and pleasing with comfy sofas and an open fire in the sitting room, a huge dining room overlooking farmland and an inviting bedroom with painted beams, good linen and a bookcase full of novels. Sit in the garden and admire the glorious views to the south; head off for Ross-on-Wye, Ledbury, the music festival in Malvern, Cheltenham races and Wye valley walks.

Rooms	1 double: £85. Singles £55.
Meals	Continental breakfast. Pubs/restaurants 1 mile.
Closed	Rarely.

Iola & Michael Fass
The Coach House,
Old Gore,
Ross-on-Wye,
Herefordshire HR9 7QT
Tel +44 (0)1989 780339
Email iolafass@btinternet.com
Web www.thecoachhousebandb.com

Entry 245   Map 7

Hertfordshire

Number One

It's worth hopping out of bed for Annie's breakfast: luxury continental with raspberry brioche or the full delicious Monty. Her house is a sparkling Aladdin's cave of mirrors, bunches of white twigs with birds atop, candles, cherubs, painted wooden floors, big open fires and generous bunches of roses. Bedrooms are lavishly done; nifty bathrooms have Italian tiles – and more roses! Close to the centre, this good-looking Georgian terrace house featured in Pevsner's guide to Hertfordshire, and the market town is busy with theatre, shops and galleries. Return for a gourmet dinner in the magical courtyard garden – when the sun is shining!

Children over 12 welcome.

Rooms	2 twin/doubles; 1 double with separate bath/shower: £105–£130.
Meals	Dinner £40. BYO. Pubs/restaurants 5-minute walk.
Closed	Rarely.

Annie Rowley
Number One,
1 Port Hill, Hertford,
Hertfordshire SG14 1PJ
Tel +44 (0)1992 587350
Mobile +44 (0)7770 914070
Email annie@numberoneporthill.co.uk
Web www.numberoneporthill.co.uk

Entry 246   Map 9

Northcourt

A Jacobean manor in matchless grounds: 15 acres of terraced gardens, exotica and subtropical flowers. The house is magnificent too; huge but a lived-in home with big comfortable guest bedrooms in one of the wings. The formal dining room has separate tables, where delicious homemade bread and jams, garden fruit, honey and local produce are served. There's a snooker table in the library, a chamber organ in the hall and a grand piano in the vast music room. Groups are welcome and John offers garden tours. The peaceful village is in lovely downland – and you can walk from the garden to the Needles.

Vintage Vacations

Funky family escapes with a retro difference! The Scout Hall has a fifties-inspired interior and a balcony with magnificent views. No fighting over the Elvis bedroom... And, 10-minutes' walk away is The Mission with stained glass and a sunken bath in the Victorian baptismal font. The former has a fab roof space living area which opens out onto that balcony with its long views to the Needles. The latter a magnificent mezzanine with two large bedrooms floating in its roof space, and vintage finds: cinema seats, an English Rose kitchen, satin bedspreads. Sit out, barbecue, walk up to the lighthouse, down to the coastal path.

Bookings start on Mondays, Wednesdays and Fridays. Book through Sawday's Canopy & Stars online or by phone.

Rooms	3 twin/doubles: £78-£105. Singles £50-£68.
Meals	Pub 3-minute walk through gardens.
Closed	Rarely.

Rooms	2 cabins for 8 (2 doubles, 1 twin/double, 1 bunk room): £125-£327.
Meals	Breakfast ingredients to cook provided.
Closed	Never.

John & Christine Harrison
Northcourt,
Shorwell,
Isle of Wight PO30 3JG
Tel   +44 (0)1983 740415
Mobile   +44 (0)7955 174699
Email   christine@northcourt.info
Web   www.northcourt.info

Sawday's Canopy & Stars
Vintage Vacations,
Church Place, Chale,
Isle of Wight PO38 2HB
Tel   +44 (0)117 204 7830
Email   enquiries@canopyandstars.co.uk
Web   www.canopyandstars.co.uk/
            vintagevacations

Entry 247   Map 4

Entry 248   Map 4

Isle of Wight

Gotten Manor

Miles from the beaten track and bordered by old stone barns, the guest wing of this Saxon house is charmingly simple. Up steep stone steps (you must be nimble!) and through a low doorway find big bedrooms in laid-back rustic, funky French style: beams, limewashed stone, wooden floors, Persian rugs and a sweet window. Sleep on a rosewood bed and bathe by candlelight – in a roll top tub in your room. Friendly, informal Caroline serves breakfast in the old creamery: homemade yogurts, compotes and organic produce. There's a walled garden and a guest living room with cosy wood-burner.

Minimum stay: 2 nights at weekends. Over 12s welcome.

Rooms	2 doubles: £85-£100. Singles by arrangement.
Meals	Pub 1.5 miles.
Closed	Rarely.

Caroline Gurney-Champion
Gotten Manor,
Gotten Lane, Chale,
Isle of Wight PO38 2HQ

Tel	+44 (0)1983 551368
Mobile	+44 (0)7746 453398
Email	as@gottenmanor.co.uk
Web	www.gottenmanor.co.uk

Entry 249   Map 4

Isle of Wight

Lisle Combe

How many gardens sport tall palms, miniature donkeys and lawns that slope down to woods, fields and beach – with Botanic Gardens next door? The grounds are huge, the position is uplifting and upper rooms have views of the sea. Author Alfred Noyes lived here in the 1930s and the feel is timeless; today grandson Robert, wife Ruth and their young family, run gentle, charming, traditional B&B. After a day exploring Ventnor and all the coves and beaches, return to carpeted corridors, faded satin sofas, delightful gilt-framed oils and old-fashioned tranquillity. Bedrooms are homely, lofty, with floral cotton bedspreads.

Minimum stay: 2 nights July & August.

Rooms	1 double; 1 double, 1 triple, both with separate bath/shower: £75-£100. Child £25.
Meals	Pubs/restaurants 2 miles.
Closed	December-February.

Robert & Ruth Noyes
Lisle Combe,
Undercliff Drive, St Lawrence,
Ventnor,
Isle of Wight PO38 1UW

Tel	+44 (0)1983 852582
Email	enquiries@lislecombe.co.uk
Web	www.lislecombe.co.uk

Entry 250   Map 4

Redway Farm

Immerse yourself in the rolling landscape of the sunny Arreton Valley... up a winding lane find a handsome, south-facing Georgian farmhouse and friendly Linda. Bedrooms are quiet, large, light and sumptuous with thick mattresses, gorgeous linen and lovely views over the gardens; warm bathrooms sparkle. Downstairs is delightful with antiques, roaring fires and fresh flowers. You breakfast on fresh croissants from the Aga – or the full works with eggs from the hens, in the sun-filled morning room or the dining room with wood-burner. Explore acres of bird-sung garden, cycle to sandy beaches. Bliss.

Arreton Manor

A dream of a manor... Jacobean, grand and gorgeous. Owned by a parade of English monarchs, including Edward the Confessor and Henry VIII, it rests peacefully in five acres of landscaped gardens. Snooze by a fire in the atmospheric Old Hall, breakfast in the wonderful dining room: ancient oak panelling, polished table and gilt-framed pictures of nobility. Gleaming bedrooms have rich fabrics and excellent linen. Wake for Julia's award-winning breakfast: local sausages and bacon, famous Arreton tomatoes, homemade jams. Village pubs are a stroll, festival sites a short drive; it's a treat to stay in this friendly, very special home.

Rooms	2 doubles, each with separate bath: £89-£99. Singles £69-£79.
Meals	Pub 3 miles.
Closed	Rarely.

Rooms	2 doubles: £115-£130.
Meals	Pubs 5-minute walk.
Closed	Rarely.

Linda James
Redway Farm,
Budbridge Lane, Merstone,
Newport,
Isle of Wight PO30 3DJ
Tel   +44 (0)1983 865228
Mobile +44 (0)7775 480830
Email   lindajames.redway@gmail.com
Web   www.bedbreakfast.redwayfarm.co.uk

Julia Gray-Ling
Arreton Manor,
Main Road,
Newport,
Isle of Wight PO30 3AA
Tel   +44 (0)1983 522604
Email   julia@arretonmanor.co.uk
Web   www.arretonmanor.co.uk

Arreton Manor Yurt

Stroll through the Jacobean manor's impressive grounds, through the parterre to a small private garden, then follow the stone path to your yurt... Soft fabrics in gentle shades, big, squashy cushions and a wrought-iron bedstead make this a delightful, relaxing place to be; with a gas stove for chilly nights. Ten yards away, a wooden cabin houses a flushing loo, shower, porcelain kitchen sink and gas cooker, all sheltered and lit by solar power. The island has great coast and countryside, grand houses and pretty villages. A footpath leads to good pubs and Farmer Jack's farm shop – and there's plenty to see at Arreton.

Minimum stay: 2 nights. Book through Sawday's Canopy & Stars online or by phone.

Rooms	Yurt for 2: £100.
Meals	Breakfast can be ordered on request at an additional charge.
Closed	October–May.

Sawday's Canopy & Stars
Arreton Manor Yurt,
Arreton Manor,
Main Road, Arreton,
Isle of Wight PO30 3AA

Tel	+44 (0)117 204 7830
Email	enquiries@canopyandstars.co.uk
Web	www.canopyandstars.co.uk/arreton

Entry 253   Map 4

Priory Bay Yurts

Listen to the sound of the surf from the decked terrace of these glorious yurts. They sit in the grounds of the Priory Bay Hotel and its two fabulous restaurants; you'll eat well here. Artfully but softly decorated with a lovely fresh feel, the yurts come with sofas and big double beds, elegant claw-foot tubs and flushing loos, and a view of woodland or sea. Out on the deck, through French doors, the private beach waits invitingly below. You have full use of the hotel pool and tennis courts, you can stroll the coastal paths and – for a special occasion – charter the hotel yacht and cruise the bay.

Book through Sawday's Canopy & Stars online or by phone.

Rooms	Yurts for 2: £200–£250. Child bed £40 per night, travel cot £20 per night.
Meals	Complimentary breakfast served in hotel.
Closed	November–March.

Sawday's Canopy & Stars
Priory Bay Yurts,
Priory Road, Seaview,
Priory Bay,
Isle of Wight

Tel	+44 (0)117 204 7830
Email	enquiries@canopyandstars.co.uk
Web	www.canopyandstars.co.uk/priorybay

Entry 254   Map 4

Sergeant Troy

Escape London and be here in an hour, with the delightful added attraction of a field full of llamas! Your cosy hut — Sergeant Troy — has a double bed at one end and roll top bath through saloon doors at the other. The water comes piping hot from the gas boiler, and the loo, steps away, is plumbed in. The woodland is stunning, with bluebells in spring; the décor is elegant: a vintage bureau, a stack of beautiful china. Michelle can furnish you with freshly-baked croissants to warm on the wood-burner. Tempt your woolly neighbours nearer with breakfast of their own — there's a jar-full of goat food in the hut.

Minimum stay: 2 nights with changeovers on Mon, Wed & Fri in peak season (Jul & Aug). Book through Sawday's Canopy & Stars online or by phone.

Dadmans

Once the dower house to Lynsted Park, Dadmans sits in parkland with nearby orchards and grazing cattle and sheep. Your breakfast eggs are laid by rare-breed hens and Amanda sources fantastic local produce for dinner, served in the dining room on gleaming mahogany or in the Aga-warmed kitchen. There's an elegant drawing room to enjoy, and lovely bedrooms have indulgent beds, flowers, views and good bathrooms. Pretty outside too with ancient trees, walled areas, a nuttery and box-edged herb garden, and plenty of castles and cathedrals to visit nearby. A special retreat where you feel part of the family.

Children over 4 welcome.

Rooms	Shepherd's hut for 2: £95–£100.
Meals	Continental breakfast from £10 for 2.
Closed	November–April.

Rooms	1 twin, 1 double with separate bath: £85–£90. Singles by arrangement.
Meals	Dinner, 4 courses, £35. Supper from £15. Pubs/restaurants nearby.
Closed	Rarely.

Sawday's Canopy & Stars
Sergeant Troy,
Little Brookstreet Llamas,
Hartfield Rd, Edenbridge,
Kent TN8 5NH
Tel +44 (0)117 204 7830
Email enquiries@canopyandstars.co.uk
Web www.canopyandstars.co.uk/sergeanttroy

Amanda Strevens
Dadmans,
Lynsted,
Sittingbourne,
Kent ME9 0JJ
Tel +44 (0)1795 521293
Mobile +44 (0)7931 153253
Email amanda.strevens@btopenworld.com
Web www.dadmans.co.uk

Kent

Huntingfield House

A sleepy setting... a long drive through parkland brings you to this Georgian-fronted manor house and delightful host Emma. It's a friendly family home with chickens, ponies and two stable cats who like to go for walks with the basset hounds. Classic country-house bedrooms have garden views, flowers and tea trays. Hop down for breakfast in the sunny elegant dining room: home-reared bacon and sausages, homemade bread and marmalade. Lots of treats nearby will keep you happy: Leeds Castle, Sissinghurst, shopping in Canterbury... Emma is a keen cook – so you might return to a tasty informal supper (or three-course spread) too.

Minimum stay: 2 nights in high season.

Kent

The Linen Shed

A weatherboard house with a winding footpath to the front door and a pot-covered veranda out the back: sit here and nibble something delicious and homemade while you contemplate the pretty garden with its gypsy caravan. Vickie, wreathed in smiles, has created a 'vintage' interior: find wooden flooring, reclaimed architectural pieces, big old roll tops, a mahogany loo seat. Bedrooms (two up, one down) are painted in the softest colours, firm mattresses are covered in fine cotton or linen, dressing gowns hang in the smart bathrooms. Food is seriously good here, and adventurous – try a seaside picnic hamper!

Rooms	1 double, 1 twin: £90–£100. Singles £60–£70. Dinner, B&B £110–£140 per person. Extra bed/sofabed available £30 per person per night.
Meals	Supper, 2 courses, £15. Dinner, 3 courses, £30. Pubs/restaurants 2 miles.
Closed	Rarely.

Rooms	2 doubles with separate bath/shower, 1 double with separate bath (occasionally sharing with family): £85–£110. Singles from £75.
Meals	Picnic hamper from £20. Pub/restaurant 300 yds.
Closed	Rarely.

	Emma Norwood Huntingfield House, Stalisfield Road, Eastling, Faversham, Kent ME13 0HT
Tel	+44 (0)1795 892138
Email	emma@huntingfieldhouse.co.uk
Web	www.huntingfieldhouse.co.uk

	Vickie Hassan The Linen Shed, 104 The Street, Boughton-under-Blean, Faversham, Kent ME13 9AP
Tel	+44 (0)1227 752271
Mobile	+44 (0)7714 646469
Email	bookings@thelinenshed.com
Web	www.thelinenshed.com

Entry 257   Map 5

Entry 258   Map 5

Kent

7 Longport

A delightful, unexpected hideaway bang opposite the site of St Augustine's Abbey and a five-minute walk to the cathedral. You pass through Ursula and Christopher's elegant Georgian house to emerge in a pretty courtyard, with fig tree and rambling rose, to find your self-contained cottage. Downstairs is a cosy sitting room with pale walls, tiled floors and plenty of books, and a clever, compact wet room with mosaic tiles. Then up steep stairs to a swish bedroom with crisp cotton sheets on a handmade bed and views of magnolia and ancient wisteria. You breakfast in the main house or in the courtyard on sunny days. Perfect.

Kent

14 Westgate Grove

Slap bang in the city, overlooking the river Stour and within strolling distance of the cathedral... step inside to find a surprising, cool contemporary feel. Pippa is an interior designer, her husband an architect, and fresh bedrooms have good lighting, smart fabrics and pretty flowers. Bathrooms come with the fluffiest towels; the one for the cosy smaller double has a rain shower and Brazilian black slate. On warm days you breakfast in the walled garden with ancient vines, olives, lemons, mimosa; for cooler evenings there is an outdoor fireplace. Pippa is welcoming and friendly; a great place to stay for exploring Canterbury.

Rooms	Cottage – 1 double with sitting room: £90. Singles £60.
Meals	Restaurants 5-minute walk.
Closed	Rarely.

Rooms	1 double; 1 double with separate bath: £80–£110.
Meals	Pub/restaurant 50 yds.
Closed	Rarely.

	Ursula & Christopher Wacher 7 Longport, Canterbury, Kent CT1 1PE
Tel	+44 (0)1227 455367
Email	info@7longport.co.uk
Web	www.7longport.co.uk

	Pippa Clague 14 Westgate Grove, Canterbury, Kent CT2 8AA
Tel	+44 (0)1227 769624
Mobile	+44 (0)7815 107032
Email	pippaclague@me.com

Entry 259 Map 5

Entry 260 Map 5

Kent

Park Gate

Peter and Mary are a generous team and their conversation is informed and easy. Behind the wisteria-clad façade are two sitting rooms with inglenook fireplaces, ancient beams and polished wood. Fresh comfortable bedrooms have TVs, gorgeous views over the garden to the fields beyond and gleaming bathrooms. Meals are delicious! More magic outside: croquet, tennis and thatched pavilions, wildlife and roses and a sprinkling of sheep to mow the paddock. The house dates back to 1460 and has a noble history: Sir Anthony Eden lived here and Churchill visited during the war. Great value, and convenient for Channel Tunnel and ferries.

Rooms	2 twin/doubles: £85.
	1 single with separate shower: £45.
Meals	Occasional dinner, 3 courses, £30.
	Simple supper £17.50.
	Pubs/restaurants 1 mile.
Closed	Christmas, New Year & January.

Peter & Mary Morgan
Park Gate,
Elham, Canterbury,
Kent CT4 6NE
Tel   +44 (0)1303 840304
Email   marylmorgan@hotmail.co.uk

🐕 🐾 🦌 🗡

Entry 261   Map 5

Kent

Orchard Barn

Alison knows how to spoil (big beds, bread from the mill, home-grown soft fruit, homemade jams), David knows the wildlife, and they both love doing B&B. The big beautiful barn has been sympathetically restored, its middle section left open to create a stunning covered courtyard: find soaring beams, a comfortable leather sofa, fresh flowers. You get two snug, carpeted bedrooms up in the eaves – pale beams, bright colours, and a sweet bath (or shower) room. A delightful village, the ancient port of Sandwich nearby and egrets, kingfishers, swallows and squirrels a walk away. Superb.

Minimum stay: 2 nights at weekends & in high season. Children over 7 welcome.

Rooms	1 double, 1 twin/double: £80-£90.
	Singles £65.
Meals	Pubs/restaurants within 1.5 miles.
Closed	Rarely.

David & Alison Ross
Orchard Barn,
Felderland Lane, Worth,
Kent CT14 0BT
Tel   +44 (0)1304 615045
Mobile   +44 (0)7950 599304
Email   orchardbarnworth@gmail.com
Web   www.orchardbarn-worth.co.uk

🐕 📶 🚂 🗡

Entry 262   Map 5

Kent

Coast House

Across the coast road from this striking
Regency house is the beach. Inside, a homely,
country-house feel with comfy places to sit,
books, family photos, fine china and flowers.
Bedrooms are in a separate wing: seaside
elegance, smart linen, striped curtains,
brownies or flapjacks on a tray… wake to
views of the sun rising over the sea. Joanna's
breakfast will set you up for a day of happy
exploring: local treats, homemade muesli
and marmalade. Admire gorgeous borders
from the hammock, walk (or hop on your
bike) to Walmer and Deal Castles – both can
easily be reached along the traffic-free path
beside the beach.

Kent

Kingsdown Place

Wow. A huge white villa set in terraced
gardens running down to the sea; on clear
days you can see France! Tan has renovated
house and garden with panache: modern
art festoons the walls, statues lurk and all
is light and contemporary. Upstairs are
superb bedrooms: one four-poster with
garden views, and, up a spiral staircase in
the loft, a very private suite with a sitting
room and terrace. All have Conran
mattresses and white linen. Breakfast on
scrambled eggs and smoked salmon or the
full works, out on the terrace in good
weather. Seaside chic and a mere hop from
Deal, Dover, Walmer and Sandwich.

Rooms	1 double, 1 twin sharing bath & sitting room: £80-£100. Singles £60-£85.
Meals	Pubs/restaurants within walking distance.
Closed	Occasionally.

Rooms	1 four-poster, 1 double, each with separate bath & sitting room: £95-£100. 1 suite for 2 with sitting room & terrace: £120-£130. Singles from £75.
Meals	Packed lunch £10. Dinner £25. Restaurant 500 yds. Pub 0.5 miles.
Closed	Christmas & New Year.

Joanna & Bernie Thomson
Coast House,
32 The Beach, Walmer, Deal,
Kent CT14 7HN
Tel +44 (0)1304 366975
Email dealbedandbreakfast@gmail.com
Web www.dealbedandbreakfast.com

Tan Harrington
Kingsdown Place,
Upper Street,
Kingsdown,
Kent CT14 8EU
Tel +44 (0)1304 380510
Email tan@tanharrington.com

Entry 263   Map 5

Entry 264   Map 5

Kent

Farthingales

Deep in rural Kent (yet 15 minutes from Canterbury and Dover) is a village hall-house of great character with a Victorian draper's shop addition. Overlooking Nonington Church and fields beyond, inside all is warm and inviting. The twin in the main house has colourful rugs on wooden floors, and a big bathroom with freestanding blue tub; the bedrooms in the 'old shop' wing have comfy beds and headphones for the TV; sitting rooms are delightful with pretty sofas and cosy wood-burner. Ex-radio presenter Peter brings a fine breakfast to your table overlooking beautiful gardens and orchard; you can breakfast outside on balmy days.

Cots & highchairs available.

Rooms	Main house – 1 twin; 'old shop' wing – 1 double, 2 twins: £75–£95. Singles £65.
Meals	Pub 0.5 miles (discounted meals for Farthingales guests).
Closed	Rarely.

Peter Deeley
Farthingales,
Old Court Hill, Nonington, Dover,
Kent CT15 4LQ
Tel   +44 (0)1304 840174
Email   farthingalesbandb@yahoo.co.uk
Web   www.farthingales.co.uk

Entry 265   Map 5

Kent

Stowting Hill House

A classic manor house in an idyllic setting, close to Canterbury and the North Downs Way. This warm, civilised home mixes Tudor beams with Georgian proportions, there's a huge conservatory full of greenery, a guest sitting room with sofas and log fire, and breakfasts fresh from the Aga. Traditional bedrooms are carpeted and cosily furnished. Your charming, country-loving hosts welcome you with tea and flowers from the garden – a perfect summer spot with its lawns, tree-lined avenue and stone obelisk. You are ten minutes from the Chunnel but this is worth more than one night.

Rooms	1 twin/double, 1 twin: £95–£100. Singles from £60.
Meals	Dinner from £30. Pub 1 mile.
Closed	Christmas & New Year.

Richard & Virginia Latham
Stowting Hill House,
Stowting, Ashford,
Kent TN25 6BE
Tel   +44 (0)1303 862881
Email   lathamvj@gmail.com
Web   www.stowtinghillhouse.co.uk

Entry 266   Map 5

Kent

The Old Rectory

On a really good day (about once every five years) you can see France. But you'll be more than happy to settle for the superb views over Romney Marsh, the Channel in the distance. The big, friendly house, built in 1850, has impeccable, elegant bedrooms and good bathrooms; the large, many-windowed sitting room is full of books, pictures and flowers from the south-facing garden. Marion and David are both charming and can organise transport to Ashford International for you. It's remarkably peaceful — perfect for walking (right on the Saxon Shore path), cycling and birdwatching.

Children over 10 welcome.

Rooms	1 twin; 1 twin with separate bath/shower: £80–£90. Singles £60.
Meals	Pubs within 4 miles.
Closed	Christmas & New Year.

Marion & David Hanbury
The Old Rectory,
Ruckinge, Ashford,
Kent TN26 2PE

Tel	+44 (0)1233 732328
Email	oldrectory@hotmail.com
Web	www.oldrectoryruckinge.co.uk

Entry 267   Map 5

Kent

Snoadhill Cottage

You'll feel at home the moment you arrive at Yvette and Philip's friendly cottage. Once a medieval 'hall house', it's awash with huge oak beams. Up steep stairs and past shelves of books find fresh, sunny bedrooms with lovely views. Enjoy a flagstone terrace for summery breakfasts or a fireside spot in the dining room; expect eggs from the hens, homemade jams, kippers perhaps or a full English. You're surrounded by glorious open countryside, walks and cycle rides start from the door and it's just 25 minutes from the Channel Tunnel. Dip in the swimming pond, chat to Rocky the labrador… and wander the blooming gardens.

Rooms	1 double, 1 twin, each with separate bath/shower: £80–£85. Singles £65.
Meals	Pub 1 mile.
Closed	Rarely.

Yvette James
Snoadhill Cottage,
Snoadhill, Bethersden, Ashford,
Kent TN26 3DY

Tel	+44 (0)1233 822377
Email	enquiries@snoadhillcottage.co.uk
Web	www.snoadhillcottage.co.uk

Entry 268   Map 5

Kent

Romden

Guarded by tall trees and songbirds, lording it over meadows and lanes, this rambling 'castle' with its 16th-century tower has a charmingly lived-in feel. Lovely laid-back Miranda and Dominic make you feel at home, help yourself to cereals while they drum up your bacon and eggs, play croquet or use their pool and tennis court (by arrangement). Bedrooms, sitting room and hall are decked out with pretty wallpapers, antiques, paintings, rugs and throws; log fires keep things toasty; kids can gambol with the dogs on a flower-filled terrace and lawn. And if you're hankering after a real castle, Sissinghurst and Leeds are down the road.

Rooms	1 double, 1 twin; 1 twin with separate bath: £70-£90. Singles £55-£75.
Meals	Pubs/restaurants 1.5 miles.
Closed	Rarely.

Miranda Kelly
Romden,
Smarden, Ashford,
Kent TN27 8RA
Tel +44 (0)1233 770687
Email miranda_kelly@hotmail.com
Web www.romdencastle.co.uk

Entry 269 Map 5

Kent

Hereford Oast

Jack the Jack Russell will meet you, swiftly followed by Suzy who'll bring you tea and cake in the garden: sheer heaven in summer. The 1876 oast house, set back from a country road and gazing on lush fields, has become the loveliest B&B. Downstairs is the dining room, as unique as it is round. Upstairs is the guest room, sunny, fresh and bright, with a blue and white theme and a rural view. As for the village – white-clapboard cottages, pubs, fine church – it's the prettiest in Kent. Sausages from Pluckley and homemade soda bread set you up for cultured jaunts: Leeds Castle, Sissinghurst, Great Dixter... all marvellously close.

Rooms	1 twin/double: £85-£90. Singles £50-£55.
Meals	Pubs 1 mile.
Closed	Rarely.

Suzy Hill
Hereford Oast,
Smarden Bell Road, Smarden,
Ashford, Kent TN27 8PA
Tel +44 (0)1233 770541
Email suzy@herefordoast.fsnet.co.uk
Web www.herefordoast.co.uk

Entry 270 Map 5

Kent

Merzie Meadows

You get your own suite in this lovely ranch-style house with huge windows, pergolas groaning with climbers, and a Mediterranean-style swimming pool in the twittering garden. Pamela is just as light and bright: she keeps horses and hens and gives you locally sourced breakfasts. Your bedroom has a contemporary, uncluttered feel and is beautifully dressed in pale colours with pretty fabrics and a super bed, your own sitting room looks onto the garden and the bathroom is sleek with Italian marble and plump towels. All is peaceful; garden and nature lovers will adore it here.

Minimum stay: 2 nights at weekends April-September.

Rooms	1 suite for 2-3: £98-£110. Singles £98. Extra bed/sofabed available £50 per person per night.
Meals	Pub 2.5 miles.
Closed	Mid-December to February.

	Pamela Mumford
	Merzie Meadows,
	Hunton Road, Marden, Maidstone,
	Kent TN12 9SL
Tel	+44 (0)1622 820500
Mobile	+44 (0)7762 713077
Email	merziemeadows@me.com
Web	www.merziemeadows.co.uk

Entry 271   Map 5

Kent

Reason Hill

Brian and Antonia's 200-acre fruit farm is perched on the edge of the Weald of Kent, with stunning views over orchards and oast houses. The farmhouse has 17th-century origins (low ceilings, wonky floors, stone flags) and a conservatory for sunny breakfasts; colours are soft, antiques gleam, the mood is relaxed. A roomy twin has a bay window and armchairs, the pretty double looks over the garden. Come in spring for the blossom, summer for the fresh fruit and veg from the garden and anytime for a break. The Greensand Way runs along the bottom of the farm, you are close to Sissinghurst Castle and 45 minutes from the Channel Tunnel.

Rooms	1 double, 2 twins: £85-£90. 1 single sharing shower with double (let to same party only): £50.
Meals	Pubs within 1 mile.
Closed	Christmas & New Year.

	Brian & Antonia Allfrey
	Reason Hill,
	Linton, Maidstone,
	Kent ME17 4BT
Tel	+44 (0)1622 743679
Mobile	+44 (0)7775 745580
Email	antonia@allfrey.net
Web	www.reasonhill.co.uk

Entry 272   Map 5

Kent

Kent

The Nut Plat

Splendid isolation: a deck chair on the river bank, ancient woods, not an intrusive sound. A shaded path leads to Ransoms, a lovingly preserved piece of industrial heritage with wood-burner, stained-glass, purpose built kitchen and bathroom hut. And, very separately, also with companion wagon, reclaimed glass and stove – Bomford – a restored late 1800s living van with a cool cream interior and floral linen. Duncan and Rachel welcome help at The Nut Plat; pitch in on the veg patch or borrow the traps and gather up some of the river's abundant crayfish. A beautifully rural spot, close to Canterbury, an hour from London.

Minimum stay: 2 nights. Book through Sawday's Canopy & Stars online or by phone.

Eggpie B&B at Pond Cottage

Afternoon tea and cake is offered on arrival – in the sunken garden in summer. Hard to believe that this stunning house in the middle of Eggpie Lane is just minutes from the A21. It started life in 1580 as a gamekeeper's cottage; now it is listed and loved, by delightful hosts Graham and Mandy. Settle in amongst low beams, standing timbers, ancient slabs, and a charming medley of armchairs and sofas around the inglenook. Three lovely bedrooms are decorated in keeping with the country cottage feel, and an inspired Kentish breakfast is served in the oldest part of the house. Visit Chartwell, Knole, Hever, Penshurst Place.

Rooms	2 wagons for 2: £85-£100.
Meals	Breakfast hampers from £20 for 2.
Closed	November-March.

Rooms	1 double; 2 doubles sharing bath (let to same party only): £90-£135.
Meals	Restaurant 1 mile.
Closed	Rarely.

	Sawday's Canopy & Stars
	The Nut Plat,
	Stone Cottage,
	Tonbridge,
	Kent TN11 9SH
Tel	+44 (0)117 204 7830
Email	enquiries@canopyandstars.co.uk
Web	www.canopyandstars.co.uk/nutplat

	Amanda Webb
	Eggpie B&B at Pond Cottage,
	Eggpie Lane, Weald,
	Sevenoaks,
	Kent TN14 6NP
Mobile	+44 (0)7768 820281
Email	enquiries@eggpiebandb.com
Web	www.eggpiebandb.com

Entry 273   Map 5

Entry 274   Map 5

Kent

Ightham

Lord it through electric oak gates to find B&B in your own modern barn. Gardening enthusiast Caroline's house is close but not hugely visible: you're wonderfully independent. Bedrooms on the ground floor are eclectic and appealing, with pine floors, dazzling white walls and slatted wooden blinds for a moody light; the bathroom is big and contemporary with a walk-in shower. Upstairs: an enormous family space for sitting, eating, playing, and glass doors on to a terrace for outdoor fun. Breakfast is delivered: eggs from the hens, pancakes, French toast. Great walks start from the door; return for supper – Caroline loves to cook.

Kent

Charcott Farmhouse

The 1750s farmhouse is rustic and family orientated, and if you don't come expecting an immaculate environment you will enjoy it here. In the old bake house there's a small sitting room with original beams and bread oven, TV and WiFi; relax in here on cooler days, with cats and a dog to keep you company. On sunny days tea is served in the garden. Bedrooms are pretty and comfortable with oriental rugs, antique furniture and simple bathrooms. Nicholas – a tad eccentric for some – is half French and cooks amazing breakfasts on the Aga, while Ginny's great grandfather (Arnold Hills) founded West Ham football team. Come and go as you please.

Price varies according to season.

Rooms	Barn – 1 double, 1 twin (let to same party only): £115.
Meals	Dinner, 3 courses, £25. Pub/restaurant 5-minute walk.
Closed	Rarely.

Rooms	2 twins; 1 twin with separate bath: £75–£90. Singles from £55.
Meals	Pub 5-minute walk.
Closed	Rarely.

	Caroline Standish
	Ightham,
	Hope Farm, Sandy Lane,
	Ightham, Sevenoaks,
	Kent TN15 9BA
Tel	+44 (0)1732 884359
Email	clstandish@gmail.com
Web	www.ighthambedandbreakfast.co.uk

	Nicholas & Ginny Morris
	Charcott Farmhouse,
	Charcott, Leigh, Tonbridge,
	Kent TN11 8LG
Tel	+44 (0)1892 870024
Mobile	+44 (0)7734 009292
Email	charcottfarmhouse@btinternet.com
Web	www.charcottfarmhouse.com

Entry 275 Map 5

Entry 276 Map 5

22 Lansdowne Road

Built in 1861, the house in leafy Tunbridge Wells "has never been as Victorian as it is now". So says Harold, whose devotion to Victoriana knows no bounds. Deep colours, rich velvets, marble tables, authentic wallpapers, tasselled lamps, portraits of Queen Victoria, tea and scones by the fire… be prepared to take a serious step back in time. Bedrooms are simple in comparison: ruched chintz in the ground-floor double, damask in a twin – and a door to the conservatory. Bathrooms have large mirrors and brand new fittings, breakfast is a locally sourced spread. Those in search of heritage will marvel.

Ramsden Farm

A truly interesting and comfortable house, with south-facing views across the Wealds; charming Sally has renovated these former farm buildings with flair. Unhurried, very good breakfasts are eaten in the huge kitchen with a lemon-coloured Aga and floor to ceiling glass doors opening on to a wooden deck; spill outside on warm days. After a hearty walk you can doze in front of a tree-devouring inglenook; find lovely sunny bedrooms too, with more of that view from each, tip-top mattresses and the crispest white linen. Fantastic bathrooms have travertine marble and underfloor heating. Spoiling and completely peaceful.

Rooms	1 double, 2 twin/doubles: £100–£120. Singles £80.
Meals	Dinner, 3 courses, £35. Pubs/restaurants 5-minute walk.
Closed	Rarely.

Rooms	1 double, 1 twin; 1 double with separate bath: £90–£110.
Meals	Pub 1 mile.
Closed	Rarely.

	Harold Brown
	22 Lansdowne Road,
	Tunbridge Wells,
	Kent TN1 2NJ
Tel	+44 (0)1892 533633
Mobile	+44 (0)7714 264489
Email	info@thevictorianbandb.com
Web	www.thevictorianbandb.com

	Sally Harrington
	Ramsden Farm,
	Dingleden Lane,
	Benenden,
	Kent TN17 4JT
Tel	+44 (0)1580 240203
Email	sally@ramsdenfarmhouse.co.uk
Web	www.ramsdenfarmhouse.co.uk

Entry 277   Map 5

Entry 278   Map 5

Kent

Pullington Barn

Up a private drive and straight in to a vast, beamed expanse of bright light, warm colours, beautiful art and a cheery welcome from Gavin and Anne in their converted barn. There are endless books to choose: settle in the comfy drawing room with its grand piano, or sit in the pretty south-facing garden on a fine day. On the other side, views from the orchard spread over oast houses and church spires. Big bedrooms (one on the ground floor) have good mattresses, coordinated bed linen and feather pillows. You breakfast well on local and homemade produce, served at the travertine table in the dining hall. Lovely walks from the door.

Children over 9 welcome, younger ones by arrangement.

Rooms	1 double, 1 twin: £85-£100. Singles £60-£80.
Meals	Pub/restaurant 0.5 miles.
Closed	Christmas.

Gavin & Anne Wetton
Pullington Barn,
Benenden,
Kent TN17 4EH

Tel	+44 (0)1580 240246
Mobile	+44 (0)7849 759929
Email	anne@wetton.info
Web	www.wetton.info/bandb

Entry 279   Map 5

Kent

Lamberden Cottage

Down a farm track find two 1780 cottages knocked into one, with flagstone floors, a cheery wood-burner in the guest sitting room and welcoming Beverley and Branton. There's a traditional country-cottage feel with pale walls, thick oak beams, soft carpeting and very comfortable bedrooms (the twin has an adjoining bedroom); views from all are across the Weald of Kent. Wander the lovely gardens to find your own private spot, sip a sundowner on the terrace, eat a hearty breakfast in the family dining room; home-grown fresh fruits, homemade marmalades and yogurts. Near to Sissinghurst, Great Dixter and many historic places.

Rooms	1 double, 1 twin with adjoining twin room: £75-£100. Singles from £65. One nighters £80
Meals	Pub 1 mile.
Closed	Christmas & New Year.

Beverley & Branton Screeton
Lamberden Cottage,
Rye Road, Sandhurst, Cranbrook,
Kent TN18 5PH

Tel	+44 (0)1580 850743
Mobile	+44 (0)7768 462070
Email	thewalledgarden@lamberdencottage.co.uk
Web	www.lamberdencottage.co.uk

Entry 280   Map 5

Lancashire

Challan Hall

The wind in the trees, the boom of a bittern and birdsong, that's as noisy as it gets. On the edge of the village, delightful Charlotte's former farmhouse overlooks woods and Lake Haweswater; deer, squirrels and Leighton Moss Nature Reserve are your neighbours. The Cassons are well-travelled and the house, filled with a colourful mish-mash of mementos, is happily and comfortably traditional. Expect a sofa-strewn sitting room, a smart red and polished-wood dining room and two freshly floral bedrooms. Morecambe Bay and the Lakes are on the doorstep – come home to lovely views and stunning sunsets.

Rooms	1 twin/double; 1 twin/double with separate bath: £75. Singles from £45.
Meals	Dinner, 2 courses, £25. Packed lunch available. Pubs 1 mile.
Closed	Rarely.

	Charlotte Casson
	Challan Hall,
	Silverdale,
	Lancashire LA5 0UH
Tel	+44 (0)1524 701054
Mobile	+44 (0)7790 360776
Email	cassons@btopenworld.com
Web	www.challanhall.co.uk

Entry 281   Map 11

Lancashire

Sagar Fold House

In a spectacular setting, a 17th-century dairy and two perfect studios, one up, one down. Private entrances lead to big beamed spaces that marry immaculate efficiency with unusual beauty – very here and now. A gorgeous Indian doorframe serves as a bedhead upstairs, soft colours and contemporary touches lift the spirit, plentiful books and DVDs entertain you and a continental breakfast is supplied – homemade and organic whenever possible. Now gaze over the Italian knot garden, which ties in lines of a lovely landscape. Take walks in deeply peaceful countryside; top-notch places to eat are an easy drive.

Rooms	2 studios for 2, each with kitchenette: £85-£90.
Meals	Continental breakfast in fridge. Pubs/restaurants 1-2 miles.
Closed	Rarely.

	Helen & John Cook
	Sagar Fold House,
	Higher Hodder, Clitheroe,
	Lancashire BB7 3LW
Tel	+44 (0)1254 826844
Mobile	+44 (0)7850 750709
Email	helencook14@gmail.com
Web	www.sagarfoldhouse.co.uk

Entry 282   Map 12

Leicestershire

Breedon Hall

Through high brick walls find a listed Georgian manor house in an acre of garden, and friendly Charlotte and Charles. Make yourselves at home in the fire-warmed drawing room full of fine furniture and pictures; carpets and curtains are in the richest, warmest reds and golds. Charlotte is a smashing cook and gives you homemade granola, jams and marmalade with local eggs, bacon and sausages; you'd kick yourself if you didn't book dinner. Bedrooms are painted in soft colours, fabrics are thick, beds covered in goose down; bathrooms are immaculate. Borrow a bike and discover the glorious countryside right on the cusp of two counties.

Minimum stay: 2 nights at weekends.

Leicestershire

Curtain Cottage

A pretty village setting for this cottage on the main street, next door to Sarah's interior design shop. You have your own entrance by the side and through a large garden, which backs onto fields with horses and the National Forest beyond. A conservatory is your sitting room: wicker armchairs, wooden floors, a contemporary take on the country look. Bedrooms are light and fresh: linen from The White Company on sumptuous beds, slate-tiled bathrooms, stunning fabrics. Breakfast is full English with eggs from the hens or fresh fruit and croissants from the local shop – all is delivered to you. Perfect privacy.

Rooms	2 doubles: £95–£110. Singles £85.	Rooms	1 double, 1 twin: £85. Singles £60–£70.
Meals	Dinner, 3 courses, £35. Pub/restaurant 1-minute walk.	Meals	Pubs/restaurants 150 yds.
Closed	Rarely.	Closed	Rarely.

2014/15
Sawday's
BED & BREAKFAST

One of a kind

	Charlotte Meynell Breedon Hall, Main Street, Breedon-on-the-Hill, Derby, Leicestershire DE73 8AN		**Sarah Barker** Curtain Cottage, 92–94 Main Street, Woodhouse Eaves, Leicestershire LE12 8RZ
		Tel	+44 (0)1509 891361
Mobile	+44 (0)7973 105467	Mobile	+44 (0)7906 830088
Email	charlottemeynell@btinternet.com	Email	sarah@curtaincottage.co.uk
Web	www.breedonhall.co.uk	Web	www.curtaincottage.co.uk

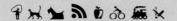

Entry 283   Map 8   Entry 284   Map 8

Leicestershire

Kicklewell House

The last house in the village overlooks miles of fields and the garden includes paddocks and stables. Fiona, easy, hospitable, great fun, loves horses, dogs and fine art; her cream walls glow with artwork, much of which she frames and sells. The house is warm, inviting and a visual delight: big deep sofas, bright ethnic rugs, a trusty Aga, heaps of books. After a scrumptious local breakfast, stride off to the lovely Foxton Canal, or visit one of the big local houses and gardens like Cottesbrooke Hall and Holdenby. Bedrooms are as peaceful and as charming as can be; good dogs are welcomed with open arms.

Rooms	1 double, 1 twin: £90. Singles £50.
Meals	Dinner, 3 courses, £25. Packed lunch £7.50. Pubs 2 miles.
Closed	Christmas & Easter.

Fiona Shann
Kicklewell House,
Laughton,
Lutterworth,
Leicestershire LE17 6QF
Tel   +44 (0)1162 404173
Email fonishann@hotmail.co.uk

Entry 285   Map 8

Leicestershire

The Grange

Behind the mellow brick exterior (Queen Anne in front, Georgian at the back) is a warm family home. Log fires brighten chilly days and you are greeted with kindness and generosity by Mary and Shaun and their sweet dog. Big, beautifully quiet bedrooms, one an atmospheric beamed room in the attic, are hung with strikingly unusual wallpapers and furnished with excellent beds and pretty antiques; bathrooms are simple yet impeccable. Wake to breakfast in the big, flagstoned hall: homemade bread, local bacon and award-winning sausages. The newly designed garden has a treehouse and is large enough to roam.

Rooms	1 double, 1 twin: £80. Singles £50.
Meals	Pubs/restaurants 0.5-1.5 miles.
Closed	Christmas & New Year.

Shaun & Mary Mackaness
The Grange,
Kimcote,
Leicestershire LE17 5RU
Tel   +44 (0)1455 203155
Mobile +44 (0)7808 242530
Email   shaunandmarymac@hotmail.com
Web   www.thegrangekimcote.co.uk

Entry 286   Map 8

Leicestershire

The Gorse House

Passing cars are less frequent than passing horses – this is a peaceful spot in a pretty village. Lyn and Richard's 17th-century cottage has a feeling of lightness and space; there's a fine collection of paintings and furniture, and oak doors lead from dining room to guest sitting room. Country style bedrooms have green views and are simply done. The garden layout was designed by Bunny Guinness, you can bring your horse (there's plenty of stabling) and it's a stroll to a good pub dinner. The house is filled with laughter, breakfasts with home-grown fruits are tasty and the Cowdells are terrific hosts who love having guests to stay.

Lincolnshire

The Barn

Simon and Jane – the nicest people – have farmed for 30 years and love having guests to stay. Breakfasts and suppers are entirely local or home-grown, and delicious; there are endless extras and nothing is too much trouble. In this light-filled barn conversion find old beams, new walls and good antiques; a brick-flanked fireplace glows and heated floors keep toes warm. Above the high-raftered main living/dining room is a comfy, good-sized double; in the adjoining stables, two further rooms, a crisp feel, sparkling showers, restful privacy. Views are to sheep-dotted fields and the village is on a 25-mile cycle trail.

Rooms	1 double: £70. 1 family room for 4: £85-£120. Stable – 1 triple & kitchenette: £70-£105. Singles £40.
Meals	Packed lunch £5. Pub 75 yds (closed on Sun eves).
Closed	Rarely.

Rooms	1 twin/double: £65-£80. Singles £50. Stables – 1 family room for 3: £80. Stables – 1 single with separate bath/shower: £55-£65.
Meals	Supper, 2 courses, £17.50. Dinner, 3 courses, £25. BYO. Pubs in village & 2 miles.
Closed	Rarely.

Lyn & Richard Cowdell
The Gorse House,
33 Main Street, Grimston,
Melton Mowbray,
Leicestershire LE14 3BZ

Tel	+44 (0)1664 813537
Mobile	+44 (0)7780 600792
Email	cowdell@gorsehouse.co.uk
Web	www.gorsehouse.co.uk

Simon & Jane Wright
The Barn,
Spring Lane, Folkingham,
Sleaford,
Lincolnshire NG34 0SJ

Tel	+44 (0)1529 497199
Mobile	+44 (0)7876 363292
Email	sjwright@farming.co.uk
Web	www.thebarnspringlane.co.uk

Entry 287   Map 9

Entry 288   Map 9

Lincolnshire

Baumber Park

Lincoln red cows and Longwool sheep surround this attractive rosy-brick farmhouse – once a stud that bred a Derby winner. The old watering pond is now a haven for frogs, newts and toads; birds sing lustily. Maran hens conjure delicious eggs, and charming Clare, a botanist, is hugely knowledgeable about the area. Bedrooms are light and traditional with mahogany furniture; two have heart-stopping views. Guests have their own wisteria-covered entrance, sitting room with an open fire, dining room with local books and the lovely garden to roam. This is good walking, riding and cycling country; seals and rare birds on the coast.

Usually minimum stay: 2 nights at weekends in high season.

Rooms	2 doubles; 1 twin with separate shower: £65–£75. Singles £35–£60.
Meals	Pubs 1.5 miles.
Closed	Christmas & New Year.

Clare Harrison
Baumber Park,
Baumber,
Horncastle,
Lincolnshire LN9 5NE

Tel	+44 (0)1507 578235
Mobile	+44 (0)7977 722776
Email	mail@baumberpark.com
Web	www.baumberpark.com

Entry 289   Map 9

Lincolnshire

The Grange

Wide open farmland and an award-winning farm on the edge of the Lincolnshire Wolds. This immaculately kept farm has been in the family for generations; Sarah and Jonathan are delightful and make you feel instantly at home. Find acres of farmland and a two-mile farm trail to explore, a trout lake to picnic by and an open fire to warm you in an elegant drawing room with Georgian windows. Sarah gives you delicious homemade cake on arrival and huge Aga breakfasts with home-laid eggs and local produce. Comfortable bedrooms have TVs, tea trays and gleaming bathrooms. Fabulous views stretch to Lincoln Cathedral and the walks are superb.

Rooms	2 doubles: £70–£78. Singles £48–£50.
Meals	Supper from £18. Dinner, 2 courses, from £25. BYO. (No meals during harvest.) Pub/restaurant 1 mile.
Closed	Christmas & New Year.

Sarah & Jonathan Stamp
The Grange,
Torrington Lane,
East Barkwith,
Lincolnshire LN8 5RY

Tel	+44 (0)1673 858670
Mobile	+44 (0)7951 079474
Email	sarahstamp@farmersweekly.net
Web	www.thegrange-lincolnshire.co.uk

Entry 290   Map 9

Lincolnshire

Lincolnshire

The Manor House

One guest's summing up reads: "Absolutely perfect – hostess, house, garden and marmalade." Delightful Ann – interested in horses, food, photography, people – makes you feel immediately at home. You have the run of downstairs: all family antiques, fresh flowers and space. Chintzy, carpeted bedrooms have dreamy views of the lovely sweeping gardens and duck-dabbled lake; dinners are delicious: game casserole, sticky toffee pudding with homemade ice cream... Perfect stillness at the base of the Wolds and a pretty one-mile walk along the route of the old railway that starts from the front door. Very special, and great value.

The Manor House

At the end of a neatly raked gravel drive, a new manor house with wide views and stunning sunsets over the peaceful Trent valley. The Days have farmed in the village since 1898 and look after you with rich warm comfort and friendly ease. Rooms have opulent curtains with chintzy roses, period furniture and rural art. Beautiful gardens are awash with summer roses, ducks on the pond, horses in the paddock, sunny patios – one in front of the annexe is for guests' exclusive use. You can fish for carp in the lake, shooting can be arranged and there are music and art festivals, antique fairs and walks in abundance.

Rooms	1 double, 1 twin: £70–£75. Singles £50.
Meals	Dinner from £20. BYO. Pub/restaurant 2 miles.
Closed	Christmas.

Rooms	1 double; annexe – 1 twin/double with kitchenette: £70. Singles £45.
Meals	Pub/restaurant 3.5 miles.
Closed	Christmas & New Year.

STOP PRESS
NO LONGER DOING B&B

Judy Day
The Manor House,
Manton, Kirton Lindsey,
Gainsborough,
Lincolnshire DN21 4JT
Tel   +44 (0)1652 649508
Mobile +44 (0)7712 766347
Email   enquiries@manorhousebedandbreakfast.co.uk
Web   www.manorhousebedandbreakfast.co.uk

Entry 291   Map 9

Entry 292   Map 13

London

90 Old Church Street

In a quiet street facing the Chelsea Arts Club is an enticing, contemporary haven. Softly spoken Nina is passionate about the arts, knows Chelsea inside out and takes real pleasure in looking after her guests. Antique shop spoils stand alongside more modern delights, the attention to detail is amazing and there are plentiful bunches of flowers. A lush carpet takes you up to the second floor and your super-private, surprisingly peaceful and deliciously designed bedroom and bathroom. Breakfast – fruit platters, yogurt and croissants – is shared with Nina in the kitchen. We love No. 90 – and the little black poodles!

Minimum stay: 2 nights on weekdays, 3 nights at weekends, 4 nights in high season.

Rooms	1 double: £120–£180. Singles £120–£160.
Meals	Continental breakfast £10. Restaurants nearby.
Closed	Occasionally.

Nina Holland
90 Old Church Street,
Chelsea, London SW3 6EP

Tel	+44 (0)20 7352 4758
Mobile	+44 (0)7831 689167
Email	ninastcharles@gmail.com
Web	www.chelseabedbreakfast.com

Entry 293   Map 22

London

37 Trevor Square

A three-minute walk from Hyde Park or Harrods – a fabulous find. The square is peaceful, private, exquisite, so find a pretty corner and enjoy. Margaret ran an interior design company – rather successfully, by the look of things – and serves a superb full English breakfast in the kitchen/diner; there's also a small conservatory you are welcome to use. Bedrooms (one downstairs has an enormous bed and a little patio) have goose down pillows, cashmere duvets, electric blankets and a mini fridge; slip on your robe, listen to some music or watch a DVD – it's all here. Blissful luxury in the middle of Knightsbridge.

Tube: Knightsbridge. Nearest car park £25 for 24 hrs (closed overnight).

Rooms	1 twin/double: £200. 1 double sharing shower with single (let to same party only): £200. 1 single sharing shower with double (let to same party only): £185. Singles £120.
Meals	Restaurants 200 yds.
Closed	Occasionally.

Margaret & Holly Palmer
37 Trevor Square,
Knightsbridge,
London SW7 1DY

Tel	+44 (0)20 7823 8186
Email	margaret@37trevorsquare.co.uk
Web	www.37trevorsquare.co.uk

Entry 294   Map 22

London

6 Oakfield Street

This district dates from the mid-1660s and local historian Simon has maps to prove it; their road is the second smallest in London. Hospitable Margaret and Simon, language, art and Egypt lovers, live in a stylish 1860s house with a beautiful roof mural (hers), a marble-topped table in the dining room and a collection of Egyptian prints. There's an open-plan feel to the kitchen, and a roof terrace where you can sit in summer. Bedrooms are at the top of the house: the twin is little but, being at the back, is silent at night; the double has a big wooden bed and an antique armoire. Stroll to restaurants on Hollywood Road.

Minimum stay: 2 nights at weekends.

Rooms	1 double (extra bed available); 1 twin: £95–£135. Singles £95.
Meals	Restaurants nearby.
Closed	Occasionally.

Margaret & Simon de Maré
6 Oakfield Street,
Little Chelsea,
London SW10 9JB

Tel	+44 (0)20 7352 2970
Mobile	+44 (0)7990 844008
Email	margaretdemare@googlemail.com
Web	www.athomeinnchelsea.com

Entry 295 Map 22

London

15 Delaford Street

A pretty Victorian, terraced Fulham home, inside all charming and spacious. In a tiny, sun-trapping courtyard you can have continental breakfast in good weather – tropical fruits are a favourite and the coffee is very good; a second miniature garden bursts with life at the back. The bedroom, up a spiral staircase, looks down on it all. Expect perfectly ironed sheets on a comfy bed, a quilted throw, books in the alcove, a sunny bathroom and fluffy white towels. The tennis at Queen's is in June and on your doorstep. Tim and Margot – she's from Melbourne – are fun, charming and happy to pick you up from the nearest tube.

Tube: West Brompton. Parking free eves & weekends; otherwise pay & display. 74 bus to West End nearby.

Rooms	1 double: £100–£105. Singles £80.
Meals	Restaurants nearby.
Closed	Occasionally.

Margot & Tim Woods
15 Delaford Street,
Fulham,
London SW6 7LT

Tel	+44 (0)20 7385 9671
Email	woodsmargot@hotmail.co.uk

Entry 296 Map 22

London

London

35 Burnthwaite Road

Near Queen's Club and Wimbledon for tennis and Fulham Broadway's tube, a sweet terraced house on the sunny side of the street. A fresh aqua carpet ushers you up to a bright bedroom on the second floor, and a spotless white bathroom squeezed under the eaves. It's as peaceful as can be. No sitting room but a rather smart dining table for breakfast – croissants, cereals, fresh fruit salad. A traditional and civilised feel prevails, thanks to lovely family pieces, fine china, touches of chintz – and friendly Diana who helps you plan your day. Buses to Piccadilly and Westminster, a stroll to the Thames, all of London at your feet.

Tube: Fulham Broadway, 6-minute walk. Parking pay & display. Bus 211, 414, 14.

21 Barclay Road

A great city find. All is swish here: polished oak floors, a sunny roof terrace and beautifully done bedrooms with decanters of sherry and luxuriously dressed beds (one a splendid king); bathrooms are smart, sparkling Philippe Starck. There's a grand piano and delightful Charlotte and Adrian occasionally host lively social music evenings. Help yourself to good espresso and a light breakfast tray in your room before setting off to tour London. Charlotte, who does something unspeakably high-powered by day, will happily advise you on the best restaurants and places to visit.

Tube: Fulham Broadway, 2-minute walk. Parking free 8pm-9am & all Sunday. 9am-8pm pay & display. Boris Bike stand on road.

Rooms	1 twin/double: £95–£120. Singles from £80.	Rooms	2 doubles: £125–£140.
Meals	Pubs/restaurants within walking distance.	Meals	Food & music evenings occasionally. Pubs/restaurants 2-minute walk.
Closed	Rarely.	Closed	Occasionally.

Diana FitzGeorge-Balfour
35 Burnthwaite Road,
Fulham,
London SW6 5BQ
Tel   +44 (0)20 7385 8081
Mobile +44 (0)7831 571449
Email   diana@dianabalfour.co.uk
Web   www.dianabalfour.co.uk

Charlotte Dexter
21 Barclay Road,
Fulham,
London SW6 1EJ
Tel   +44 (0)20 7384 3390
Mobile +44 (0)7767 420943
Email   info@barclayhouselondon.com
Web   www.barclayhouselondon.com

Entry 297   Map 22

Entry 298   Map 22

8 Parthenia Road

Caroline, an interior designer, mixes the sophistication of the city with the feel of the countryside and her handsome big kitchen is the engine-room of the house. It leads through to a light breakfast room with doors onto a pretty brick garden with chairs and table — hope for fine days. The house is long and thin, Fulham style, and reaches up to a big sloping-ceilinged bedroom in the eaves, cosy, sunny and bright. A remarkably quiet place to stay in an accessible part of town, near the King's Road with all its antique and designer shops, and Chelsea Football ground.

Tube: Parsons Green, 4-minute walk. Parking £17.60 per day in street (9am-5pm), free on Sunday. Bus 22, 2-minute walk.

22 Marville Road

Smart railings help a pink rose climb, orange lilies add a touch of colour, and breakfast is in the pretty back garden on sunny days. Ben the springer and Tizzie the cocker spaniel, and Christine — music lover, traveller, rower — make you feel at home. Your big light-filled bedroom is high up in the eaves and comes in elegant French grey with comfortable beds, crisp linen, pretty lamps, a smart bathroom and a chaise longue for lounging and reading. The house is friendly with treasures from Christine's travels and gentle music at breakfast; there's a baby grand to play too. Restaurants and shops are a stroll away and the Boat Race down the river.

Min stay: 2 nights. At Fulham Rd junc. with Parson's Green Lane, down Kelvedon Rd. Cross Brishop Rd into Homestead Rd; 1st left. Tube: Parsons Green.

Rooms	1 twin/double: £100-£140. Singles from £85.
Meals	Continental breakfast. Restaurants nearby.
Closed	Rarely.

Rooms	1 twin/double: £95-£110. Singles £85.
Meals	Continental breakfast. Pubs/restaurants nearby.
Closed	Rarely.

	Caroline & George Docker 8 Parthenia Road, Fulham, London SW6 4BD
Tel	+44 (0)20 7384 1165
Email	dockercaroline@gmail.com

	Christine Drake 22 Marville Road, Fulham, London SW6 7BD
Tel	+44 (0)20 7381 3205
Email	chris@christine-drake.com
Web	www.londonguestsathome.com

London

31 Rowan Road

Terrific value for money in leafy Brook Green. The two studios are fantastic spaces: one under the eaves (a big comfy bed and armchairs, a deep cast-iron bath from which you can gaze at the birds), the other larger and more contemporary in style, on the lower ground floor, with its own wisteria-clad entrance. All independent with a continental breakfast popped in your fridge. Or join in with family life and stay in the little pink bedroom with books and hats, and take breakfast in the pretty conservatory with Vicky and Edmund. A friendly home with flowers, art, photos and a relaxed vibe – Tiger the terrier and a blossoming garden too.

Tube: Hammersmith. Off-street parking £20 a day.

London

101 Abbotsbury Road

The area is one of London's most desirable and Sunny's family home is opposite the borough's loveliest park, with open-air opera in summer. The top floor is for visitors. Warm, homely bedrooms are in gentle beiges and greens, with pale carpets, white duvets, pelmeted windows and a pretty dressing table for the double. The bathroom, marble-tiled and sky-lit, shines. You are well placed for Kensington High Street, Olympia, Notting Hill, Portobello Market, Kensington Gardens, the Albert Hall, Knightsbridge and Piccadilly! Relax, unwind, feel free to come and go.

Children over 6 welcome. Tube: Holland Park, 7-min walk. Off-street parking sometimes available.

Rooms	1 double with separate bath/shower; 2 twin/doubles with kitchenette. Extra bed available: £65–£120. Singles £65–£100. Extra person £15.
Meals	Continental breakfast. Pubs/restaurants 2 minutes.
Closed	Occasionally.

Rooms	1 double sharing bath with single: £110. 1 single sharing bath with double: £60–£65.
Meals	Continental breakfast. Pubs/restaurants 5-minute walk.
Closed	Occasionally.

	Vicky & Edmund Sixsmith
	31 Rowan Road,
	Brook Green, Hammersmith,
	London W6 7DT
Tel	+44 (0)20 8748 0930
Mobile	+44 (0)7966 829359
Email	vickysixsmith@me.com
Web	www.abetterwaytostay.co.uk

	Sunny Murray
	101 Abbotsbury Road,
	Holland Park,
	London W14 8EP
Tel	+44 (0)20 7602 0179
Mobile	+44 (0)7768 362562
Email	sunny.murray@googlemail.com

Entry 301   Map 22

Entry 302   Map 22

London

1 Peel Street

Pretty, gabled and surprisingly quiet with central London on your doorstep. Fascinating old maps, photos from Susie and Trevor's world travels and objets d'art all create an unusual and elegant feel. The top floor is all yours: the bedroom is full of character, framed by the slanting angles of the roof and soothingly decorated in neutral shades; the shelf above the snug-looking bed is crammed with interesting reads. Breakfast is at a table overlooking the patio: organic bread, pastries, fruit and excellent coffee. Just a stroll to good tapas, wine bars, Hyde Park and Notting Hill. Hop on a bus or tube to explore further.

Rooms	1 double with separate bath/shower: £120. Singles £95.
Meals	Continental breakfast. Pubs/restaurants 2-minute walk.
Closed	Occasionally.

Susan & Trevor Laws
1 Peel Street,
Kensington,
London W8 7PA
Tel   +44 (0)20 7792 8361
Mobile +44 (0)7776 140060
Email   susan@susielaws.co.uk

Entry 303   Map 22

London

The Roost

The immaculate pale blue-painted front door sets the tone for this large and lofty Victorian home. This is boutique B&B and you get smart hotel-standard rooms at a fraction of the price. The furniture is excellent: fine family pieces and clever Liz's handsome finds. There is a conservatory for continental breakfast, a delightful Parson Russell dog and art everywhere. Liz, a former fashion pattern cutter and dancer, is a natural and lovely hostess. The Roost is brilliantly positioned for whizzing into town, yet here you have a lovely park, an irresistible bakery, great restaurants and a farmers' market on Sundays. Marvellous.

Minimum stay: 2 nights at weekends. Free parking weekends. Tube and overground within walking distance.

Rooms	3 doubles (2 with bath/shower; 1 with shower): £110–£125. Singles £90–£110.
Meals	Pubs/restaurants 5-minute walk.
Closed	Rarely.

Liz Crosland
The Roost,
37 Lynton Road, Queen's Park,
London NW6 6BE
Tel   +44 (0)20 7625 6770
Mobile +44 (0)7967 354477
Email   liz@boutiquebandblondon.com
Web   www.boutiquebandblondon.com

Entry 304   Map 22

London

Camellia Cottage

"We'd always built our own houses so I couldn't believe our luck when I spotted this just ready to hop into," chirrups beady-eyed owner Jenny who happens to be a famous singer — you may have heard her on Radio 4's Tweet of the Day recently. Empty nest syndrome inspired her to open it as a B&B, albeit a spartan one — it's the feeling of being in tune with nature rather than creature comforts that attracts guests so don't expect a bed, curtains, four walls or a bathroom. Breakfast, served at the crack of dawn after Jenny's choir practice, is perhaps an acquired taste — unless you like worms rammed down your throat. Gorgeous!

Directions: straighten up and fly right.

Rooms	1 bedroom with bird bath.
Meals	Just basic grubs.
Closed	Open to the elements.

Jenny Wren
Camellia Cottage,
Tweety Pie Lane, Upper Neston,
London GR8 T1T

Tel	282 8200
Email	Twitter only
Web	www.birdsofafeatherstaytogether.co.uk

Entry 305   Map 88

London

66 Camden Square

A modern, architect designed house made of African teak, brick and glass. Climb wooden stairs under a glazed pyramid to light-filled, Japanese-style bedrooms with low platform beds, modern chairs and private sitting room/study. Sue and Rodger have travelled widely so there are pictures, photographs and ethnic pieces everywhere — and a burst of colour from Peckam the parrot. Share their lovely open-plan dining space overlooking a verdant bird-filled courtyard at breakfast — a delicious start to the day. Cool Camden's bustling market is close, along with theatres, restaurants, bars and zoo.

Minimum stay: 2 nights at w/ends. Children over 8 welcome. Tube: Camden Town or Kentish Town. Parking free at weekends; meters during week. Ten mins by taxi or 20-min walk from St Pancras.

Rooms	1 double: £100–£110.
	1 single sharing bath with double (let to same party only): from £60.
Meals	Pubs/restaurants nearby.
Closed	Occasionally.

Sue & Rodger Davis
66 Camden Square,
Camden Town,
London NW1 9XD

Tel	+44 (0)20 7485 4622
Email	rodgerdavis@btopenworld.com

Entry 306   Map 22

Arlington Avenue

This 1848 townhouse is a real find – from here you can follow the canal up to Islington. Inside you find a world of books and art; immaculate bedrooms (the double very spacious) are colourful and filled with pictures, etchings and pretty furniture, with views over several gardens to the back. The grey marble shared guest bathroom is two flights down, but if you don't mind that, you've struck gold. Shop locally, eat picnic suppers in the red and gold dining room, chill drinks in the fridge. You help yourself to breakfast in a lemon coloured country style kitchen; this is laissez-faire B&B and fantastic value.

Tube: Angel & Old Street (15-minute walk). Buses: 5 minutes to stops for City, St Paul's, Tate Modern. Limited parking (by arrangement).

Rooms	1 double sharing bath with single: £55–£70. 1 single sharing bath with double: £45–£65.
Meals	Pubs/restaurants 100 yds.
Closed	Rarely.

Thomas Blaikie
Arlington Avenue,
Islington,
London N1 7AX
Mobile +44 (0)7711 265183
Email thomas@arlingtonavenue.co.uk
Web www.arlingtonavenue.co.uk

Entry 307   Map 22

Russell's

Be in the thick of edgy, vibrant, multi-cultural London in this pink Victorian terraced house bang on the high street. Lovely Annette gives you imaginative breakfasts: try mushrooms cooked in truffle oil. You enjoy a funky guest sitting room with vintage furniture, a friendly whippet called Reggie, interesting book shelves and an easy-going feel. Lovely uncluttered bedrooms (those overlooking the garden are quieter) have good art and great 60s and 70s pieces. Sparkling bathrooms have powerful showers. Very good cafés on the doorstep, a 20-minute walk to the Olympic Stadium, and near Hackney Marshes, with grazing cows!

Rooms	2 doubles, 1 twin/double (all en suite); 1 double, 1 twin/double sharing bath: £75–£115. 1 single: £90. Singles from £75.
Meals	Pubs/restaurants 5-minute walk.
Closed	Rarely.

Annette Russell
Russell's,
123 Chatsworth Road, Clapton,
London E5 0LA
Mobile +44 (0)7976 669906
Email annette@russellsofclapton.com
Web www.russellsofclapton.com

Entry 308   Map 4

London

Fleet River Bakery Rooms

Meet real Londoners, not tides of tourists, in the streets of this vibrant, historic, very central part of town. Your handsome, city-sharp studio is above the bustling bakery/café: nip downstairs for delicious complimentary breakfast and coffee. You have an ample kitchen-cum-living area with a shiny wooden floor, a sofa, and a seriously comfortable bed – all good-looking in a refreshingly frill-free way, and surprisingly quiet. People-watch through the tall windows, cook up some local market produce or head out for a bundle of good restaurants – Covent Garden, Bloomsbury and the West End are all an easy walk.

Availability & booking on owner's website. Tube: Holborn; left from main exit, down Kingsway, 2nd lane on left (Twyford Pl). At end on corner Twyford Pl & Gate St

Rooms	3 doubles, 1 twin, each with kitchenette: £120. Singles £88. Extra bed/sofabed available £15 per person per night.
Meals	Lunch in café downstairs, from £6.50. Packed lunch £7.50.
Closed	Rarely.

Lucy Clapp
Fleet River Bakery Rooms,
71 Lincoln's Inn Fields, Holborn,
London WC2A 3JF

Tel	+44 (0)20 7691 1457
Mobile	+44 (0)7966 267401
Web	www.fleetriverbakery.com

Entry 309   Map 22

London

26 Montefiore Street

Step off a quiet street into a hall of rich golds and a charming, elegant and comfortable bolthole. There's a little bird-filled garden where you can breakfast in summer: an organic spread with homemade jams and bread. This house is brimful of books – your bedroom too. Find white linen on a generous-sized handmade bed, dressing gowns and, down steps, a fresh chic bathroom with fluffy towels and bath oils. No sitting room but there are wicker chairs in a corner of the library/dining room facing the pretty garden. Walk to Battersea Arts Centre and Battersea Park with its festivals and art fairs; not far from Chelsea Flower Show too.

Pets by arrangement. Parking available for £7 per day at weekdays, free at weekends.

Rooms	1 double with separate bath/shower; 1 single in attached study (suitable for a child): £110–£115. Singles £80. Study £50. Single night supplement £5. Dogs £5 per night (discretionally).
Meals	Restaurants 300 yds.
Closed	Occasionally.

D Porter
26 Montefiore Street,
Battersea,
London SW8 3TL

Tel	+44 (0)20 7720 0939
Email	bedandbreakfast.london.sw8@gmail.com

Entry 310   Map 22

20 St Philip Street

Come to retreat from the frenzy of city life. In the 1890 Victorian cottage all is peaceful and calm and Barbara looks after you beautifully. The dining room, with the odd oriental piece from past travels, is where you have your full English breakfast – unusual for London – and across the hall is the elegant sitting room, with gilt-framed mirrors, sumptuous curtains, and a piano. Upstairs is a bright and restful bedroom with pretty linen and a cloud of goose down. The large, sparkling bathroom next door is all yours – fabulous. Nothing has been overlooked and the tiny courtyard garden is a summer oasis.

Train: 6-min Waterloo, 3-min Victoria. Bus: 137, 452 (Sloane Square) & 156 (Vauxhall). Tube: 10 mins. Parking: £2.40 per hour or £10 day, 9.30am-5.30pm (free at weekends).

The Glebe House

Surely one of London's most village-y spots? Find a pretty Georgian house snuggling up to the Church, a community pottery and beehives and allotments in a walled garden. Alix writes for interiors magazines and has weaved her magic into every corner of her home. The sitting room, with velvet and linen sofas on toasty stone floors, was once an archway for horses and carriages; now it's a lofty space with huge doors onto a courtyard. Your bed is antique, your room deeply peaceful, the bathroom bright with white Metro brick tiles. Help yourself to a continental breakfast of cereal, fruit, and artisan breads in the funky kitchen. Alix, son and puppy are a delight.

Rooms	1 double with separate bath & shower: £110. Singles £80. Supplement for one-night stay £5.
Meals	Pubs/restaurants 200 yds.
Closed	Occasionally.

Rooms	3 doubles sharing bath (let to same party only). Extra futon available: £110. Singles £80.
Meals	Continental breakfast. Pubs/restaurants 0.2 miles.
Closed	Rarely.

	Barbara Graham 20 St Philip Street, Battersea, London SW8 3SL
Tel	+44 (0)20 7622 5547
Email	batterseabedandbreakfast@gmail.com
Web	www.batterseabandb.co.uk

	Alix Bateman The Glebe House, Clapham Old Town, London SW4 0DZ
Tel	+44 (0)20 7720 3844
Email	talixjones@hotmail.com
Web	www.theglebehouselondon.com

London

28 Old Devonshire Road

In a quiet part of Balham – close to leafy common, tube and train – are Georgina's lovely home and award-winning garden. Enjoy breakfast under the pear tree, or at the long wooden table in the dining room, with a marble fireplace and a friend's watercolours. You have the top floor to yourself: a sunny, cosy bedroom, with city views, a TV, lots of books; a big bathroom too, with a fab shower and comforting waffle robes to pad about in. Georgina lays on a special breakfast and all sorts of thoughtful extras. She loves to chat (speaks French and Italian too) really knows her London and will help plan your stay.

Rooms	1 double: £100–£105.
	Singles £80–£85.
Meals	Pubs/restaurants 500 yds.
Closed	Rarely.

Georgina Ivor
28 Old Devonshire Road,
Balham, London SW12 9RB

Tel	+44 (0)20 8673 7179
Mobile	+44 (0)7941 960199
Email	georgina@balhambandb.co.uk
Web	www.balhambandb.co.uk

Entry 313   Map 22

London

108 Streathbourne Road

It's a handsome house in a conservation area that manages to be both elegant and cosy. The cream-coloured double bedroom has an armchair, a writing desk, pretty curtains and a big comfy walnut bed; the twin is light and airy. The dining room overlooks a secluded terrace and garden and there are newspapers at breakfast. You can eat in – David, who works in the wine trade, always puts a bottle on the table – or out, at one of the trendy new restaurants in Balham. A friendly city base on a quiet, tree-lined street – maximum comfort, delicious food and good value for London. Delightful.

Minimum stay: 2 nights. Tube: Tooting Bec, 7-minute walk. Bus: 319 from Sloane Square. Free parking weekends, otherwise meters or £7 daily permit.

Rooms	1 double, 1 twin: £90–£100.
	Singles £80–£85.
Meals	Dinner £35.
	Restaurants 5-minute walk.
Closed	Occasionally.

Mary & David Hodges
108 Streathbourne Road,
Balham,
London SW17 8QY

Tel	+44 (0)20 8767 6931
Email	davidandmaryhodges@gmail.com
Web	www.southwestlondonbandb.co.uk

Entry 314   Map 22

London

The Coach House

A rare privacy: you have your own coach house, separated from the Notts' home by a stylish terracotta-potted courtyard with Indian sandstone paving and various fruit trees (peach, pear, nectarine). Breakfast in your own sunny kitchen, or let Meena treat you to a full English in hers (she makes great porridge, too). The lovely big attic bedroom has beams, cream curtains, rugs on polished wood floors; the brick-walled ground-floor twin is pleasant and airy; both look over the peaceful garden. Urban but bucolic – just perfect as a romantic retreat, or a family getaway.

Minimum stay: 3 nights; 2 nights January & February. Tube: Balham Station to Leicester Square & Oxford Street or train to Victoria.

Rooms	Coach House – 1 family room for 2-3; 1 twin with separate shower (let to same party only): £110. £190 for whole Coach House.
Meals	Pub/restaurant 200 yds.
Closed	Occasionally.

	Meena & Harley Nott
	The Coach House,
	2 Tunley Road, Balham,
	London SW17 7QJ
Tel	+44 (0)20 8772 1939
Email	coachhouse@chslondon.com
Web	www.coachhouse.chslondon.com

Entry 315   Map 22

London

38 Killieser Avenue

On a quiet leafy street, the Haworths have brought country-house chic to South London. Philip and Winkle have filled their elegant Victorian townhouse with stunning fabrics, sunny colours and treasures from far-flung travels. The house glows, the garden is ravishing, breakfasts are delicious (so are the scones – book a cream tea course!) and bedrooms are spacious: fine linen, lambswool throws, waffle robes, the scent of roses. Few people do things with as much natural good humour as Winkle, whose passions are cooking, gardening and garden history (tours can be arranged). Transport is close and you can be in Victoria in 15 minutes.

Minimum stay: 2 nights at weekends. Balham tube 15-min walk.

Rooms	1 twin: £110-£115.
	1 single with separate bath: £85-£90.
	£5 supplement for one-night stay.
Meals	Dinner £30-£35.
Closed	Occasionally.

	Winkle Haworth
	38 Killieser Avenue,
	Streatham Hill,
	London SW2 4NT
Tel	+44 (0)20 8671 4196
Email	winklehaworth@hotmail.com
Web	www.thegardenbedandbreakfast.com

Entry 316   Map 22

London

113 Pepys Road

This Victorian terraced house overlooks the first landscaped park of its kind in south-east London; the pretty garden, designed by David's father, is graced with majestic magnolias. Find a quirky mix of classic British furniture and oriental antiques. Picking up from his Chinese mother Anne, David has now taken on the B&B (helped by his housekeeper) and breakfast can be English or oriental. It's a convivial, lived-in home full of family portraits, batiks and books; the Chinese 'Peony' room downstairs has a huge bed, bamboo blinds, kimonos for the bathroom. A short walk to buses and tubes… and blissfully quiet for London.

London

16 St Alfege Passage

The peaceful approach is along the passage between the Hawksmoor church and its graveyard, away from Greenwich hubbub. At the end of the lane is a 'cottage' set about with greenery, lamp posts and benches; inside, a cup of tea and flapjack await you in the eccentrically furnished (stuffed cat on dentist chair, huge parasol) sitting room. Bedrooms are cosy and colourful, with double beds (not huge) that positively encourage intimacy. Breakfast – delicious – is in the basement, another engagingly furnished room awash with character. Robert, an actor, is easy, funny, chatty – and has created an unusual and attractive place.

3-min walk from Greenwich train & Docklands Light Railway station or Cutty Sark DLR station. Parking free from 5pm (6pm Sundays) to 9am.

Rooms	1 double, 1 twin/double; 1 twin with separate bath: £110. Singles £85.	Rooms	1 double, 1 four-poster: £90–£125. 1 single: £80.
Meals	Restaurant 0.5 miles.	Meals	Pubs/restaurants 2-minute walk.
Closed	Rarely.	Closed	Rarely.

	David Marten 113 Pepys Road, New Cross, London SE14 5SE		**Nicholas Mesure & Robert Gray** 16 St Alfege Passage, Greenwich, London SE10 9JS
Tel	+44 (0)20 7639 1060	Tel	+44 (0)20 8853 4337
Email	davidmarten@pepysroad.com	Email	info@st-alfeges.co.uk
Web	www.pepysroad.com	Web	www.st-alfeges.co.uk

Entry 317   Map 22

Entry 318   Map 22

London

24 Fox Hill

This part of London is full of sky, trees and wildlife; Pissarro captured on canvas the view up the hill in 1870 (the painting is in the National Gallery). There's good stuff everywhere – things hang off walls and peep over the tops of dressers; bedrooms are stunning, with antiques, textiles, paintings and big, firm beds. Sue, a graduate from Chelsea Art College, employs humour and intelligence to put guests at ease and has created a special garden too. Tim often helps with breakfasts: eggs to order, good coffee. Owls hoot at night, woodpeckers wake you in the morning, in this lofty, peaceful retreat.

Train: Crystal Palace. Underground: East London line. Collection possible. Good buses to West End & Westminster. Victoria 20 minutes by train.

Norfolk

The Old Rectory

A stately place indeed: a venerable English rectory replete with period furniture, art, history, well-bred hosts (he shoots, she rides) and, in the expansive grounds, a ruined chapel, lake, croquet lawn and pool. Breakfast is served on the terrace in summer. You dine by candlelight on local game and the kitchen garden's offerings, then settle in the Georgian drawing room by the rocking horse. Sleep in the Coach House where plush beds have beautiful linen, warm throws and beaded cushions; dogs can stay in the stables. A rare chance to experience the best of British country life.

Use of swimming pool, by arrangement.

Rooms	1 twin/double; 1 double, 1 twin sharing shower: £90-£120. Singles £60. Dinner, B&B £100 per person. Extra bed/sofabed available £30 per person per night.
Meals	Dinner £35. Pubs/restaurants 5-minute walk.
Closed	Rarely.

Rooms	Coach House - 1 double, 1 twin/double, 1 twin: £85-£105. Singles £65-£85.
Meals	Dinner, 2 courses, £25; 3 courses, £35. Pub 1 mile. Restaurant 1-5 miles.
Closed	Rarely.

	Sue & Tim Haigh 24 Fox Hill, Crystal Palace, London SE19 2XE
Tel	+44 (0)20 8768 0059
Email	suehaigh@hotmail.co.uk
Web	www.foxhill-bandb.co.uk

	Veronica de Lotbiniere The Old Rectory, Ferry Road, King's Lynn, Oxborough, Norfolk PE33 9PT
Tel	+44 (0)1366 328962
Mobile	+44 (0)7769 687599
Email	onky.del@btinternet.com
Web	www.oldrectoryoxboroughbandb.co.uk

Entry 319 Map 4

Entry 320 Map 9

Norfolk

Holland House

Oak-smoked kippers from Cley, meat from Walsingham, eggs from the hens, veg from the garden... prepare yourself for some glorious pampering. Once the dower house to Docking Hall, this red-brick, roadside, 1750s house is deceptively large inside. Find fabric pelmets, shining wood floors, interesting curios and pictures. Melanie and Steve, cooks, gardeners and homemakers, have created three bedrooms for guests, all on the first floor, fabulously comfortable and rather grand. Enjoy a sherry by the drawing room fire, linger by the lavender, and splash out on the Holkham suite – the bathroom is delectable.

Minimum stay: 2 nights.

Norfolk

Tudor Lodgings

A treasured family home on the site of Castle Acre's medieval defences, with dogs, ducks and views of the lovely Nar valley. A cosy guest sitting room leads to the ancient, dark-beamed dining room hung with portraits, where you breakfast on good things homemade and local; do try a Swaffham Sizzler. Cottagey bedrooms are cream-carpeted and have coordinated fabrics, attractive wildlife prints and small shower rooms. Julia is passionate about garden history, Gus is a keen fisherman; both know their history and horses. Peddars Way runs close by and you're not far from the coast – or the village pub!

Rooms	1 suite; 1 double, 1 twin/double, both with separate bath: £105–£170.
Meals	Dinner from £15. Pubs/restaurants 8-minute walk.
Closed	Occasionally.

Rooms	2 twins: £80. Singles £60.
Meals	Pub within walking distance.
Closed	Rarely.

Steve Lewis
Holland House,
Chequers Street, Docking,
King's Lynn, Norfolk PE31 8LH
Tel   +44 (0)1485 518295
Mobile   +44 (0)7976 910272
Email   stevelewisart917@gmail.com
Web   www.hollandhousebandb.co.uk

Julia Stafford-Allen
Tudor Lodgings,
Castle Acre,
King's Lynn,
Norfolk PE32 2AN
Tel   +44 (0)1760 755334
Email   jstaffordallen@btinternet.com
Web   www.tudorlodgings.co.uk

Norfolk

Litcham Hall

For the whole of the 19th century this was Litcham's doctor's house; the Hall is still at the centre of the community. The big-windowed guest bedrooms look onto stunning gardens with yew hedges, a lily pond and herbaceous borders. This is a thoroughly English home with elegant proportions – the hall, drawing room and dining room are gracious and beautifully furnished, and there's a large sitting room for guests. The garden fills the breakfast table with soft fruit in season and John and Hermione are friendly and most helpful. Close to Fakenham, and only 30 minutes from Burnham Market and the coast.

Children & pets by arrangement. Outside pool heated in high summer; use by arrangement.

Rooms	2 doubles; 1 twin with separate bath: £75-£95. Singles by arrangement.
Meals	Pub in village & 5 miles.
Closed	Christmas.

John & Hermione Birkbeck
Litcham Hall,
Litcham,
King's Lynn,
Norfolk PE32 2QQ

Tel	+44 (0)1328 701389
Email	hermionebirkbeck@hotmail.com
Web	www.litchamhall.co.uk

Entry 323　Map 10

Norfolk

Meadow House

Handmade oak banisters, period furniture: this new-build is beautifully traditional. Breakfast is served in the lovely large drawing room, where you find a warm, sociable atmosphere with squashy sofas and comfy chairs for anytime use. One bedroom is cosy and chintzy, the other is larger and more neutral; brand-new bathrooms gleam. Amanda knows B&B and does it well; she's lived in Norfolk most of her life and is delighted to advise. There are footpaths from the door and plenty to see, starting with Walpole's Houghton Hall, a short walk. A bucolic setting for a profoundly comfortable stay, perfect for country enthusiasts.

Rooms	2 twin/doubles: £70-£80. Singles £45.
Meals	Packed lunch £5-£7. Pub 9-minute walk.
Closed	Rarely.

Amanda Case
Meadow House,
Harpley,
King's Lynn,
Norfolk PE31 6TU

Tel	+44 (0)1485 520240
Mobile	+44 (0)7890 037134
Email	amandacase@amandacase.plus.com
Web	www.meadowhousebandb.co.uk

Entry 324　Map 10

Norfolk

Bagthorpe Hall

Ten minutes from Burnham Market, yet here you are immersed in peaceful countryside. Tid is a pioneer of organic farming and the stunning 700 acres include a woodland snowdrop walk. Gina's passions are music, dance and gardens and she organises open days and concerts for charity. Theirs is a large, elegant house with a fascinating hall mural chronicling their family life; bedrooms – one with a tiny en suite shower room – have big comfy beds and lovely views. Breakfasts are delicious with local sausages and bacon, homemade jams and raspberries from the garden. Birdwatching, cycling and walking are all around.

The Merchants House

The oak four-poster – a beauty – came with the house. Part of the building (1400) is the oldest in Wells; in those days, the merchant could bring his boats up to the door. Liz and Dennis know the history, and happily share it. Inside is friendly and inviting: the mahogany shines, bathrooms sparkle, there are books to borrow and pretty sash windows overlook salt marshes. Breakfasts are a treat: homemade bread and jams, local produce and flowers on the table. As for Wells, it's on the famous Coastal Path, has a quay bustling with boats and 16 miles of sands. Birdwatch by day, dine out at night – easy when you're in the centre.

Minimum stay: 2 nights in July & August.

Rooms	1 double; 1 twin/double with separate shower: £90. Singles £50.
Meals	Pubs/restaurants 2 miles.
Closed	Rarely.

Rooms	1 double; 1 four-poster with separate bath/shower: £85-£95. Singles £65.
Meals	Pubs/restaurants 300 yds.
Closed	Rarely.

	Gina & Tid Morton Bagthorpe Hall, Bagthorpe, Bircham, King's Lynn, Norfolk PE31 6QY
Tel	+44 (0)1485 578528
Mobile	+44 (0)7979 746591
Email	dgmorton@hotmail.com
Web	www.bagthorpehall.co.uk

	Elizabeth & Dennis Woods The Merchants House, 47 Freeman Street, Wells-next-the-Sea, Norfolk NR23 1BQ
Tel	+44 (0)1328 711877
Mobile	+44 (0)7816 632742
Email	denniswoods@talktalk.net
Web	www.the-merchants-house.co.uk

Entry 325   Map 10

Entry 326   Map 10

Norfolk

1 Leicester Meadows

Up among 13 acres of wild meadow and woodland – not another building in sight. It's all so relaxed and unhurried: barn owls roosting in the outhouse, hens strutting, geese pottering up from the pond. The 19th-century cottages have been imaginatively restored; Bob was an architect, Sara an art teacher, and both are immensely friendly and helpful. Polished wood and old brick are topped with bright rugs; paintings and ceramics engage the eye; bedrooms have flowers and colourful covers. Hop downstairs for a superb breakfast at the big convivial table: rare-breed bacon, homemade jams and bread, fruits from the kitchen garden.

Minimum stay: 2 nights.

Rooms	1 double with sitting room, 1 twin/double: £80-£95. Singles £65.
Meals	Supper by arrangement from £20. Pub 1 mile.
Closed	Rarely.

Bob & Sara Freakley
1 Leicester Meadows,
South Creake,
Fakenham,
Norfolk NR21 9NZ
Tel   +44 (0)1328 823533
Email   rf@freakley.com
Web   www.leicestermeadows.com

Entry 327   Map 10

Norfolk

Green Farm House

This traditional Norfolk farmhouse has been restored with a natural modern slant. Choose to stay in the 'Garden Room' wing, or upstairs in the main house – both well-dressed bedrooms have smart bathrooms (one with a shower, one with a bath). Sun streams in through the French windows of the chic garden room; find books, DVDs, rugs on slate floors, art, pots of flowers and comfy sofa by the wood-burner. The 'Guest Room' has field views and morning sun. Breakfast is in the conservatory: local sausages, bacon and eggs, homemade marmalade and muesli. Friendly Lucy can arrange sailing; heaven for walkers, cyclists and birdwatchers too.

Cyclists welcome; secure bike shed available.

Rooms	Garden Room - 1 double; Guest Room in house - 1 double : £75-£120. Singles £80.
Meals	Pub within 2 miles.
Closed	Rarely.

Lucy Jupe
Green Farm House,
Balls Lane, Thursford, Fakenham,
Norfolk NR21 0BX
Tel   +44 (0)1328 878507
Mobile   +44 (0)7768 542645
Email   ljupe@nnv.org.uk
Web   www.nnv.org.uk

Entry 328   Map 10

Norfolk

Holly Lodge

The whole place radiates a lavish attention to detail, from the spoilingly comfortable beds to the complimentary bottle of wine. It's perfect for those who love their privacy: these three snug guest 'cottages' have their own entrances as well as smart bedsteads and rugs on stone tiles, neat little shower rooms and tapestry-seat chairs, and books, music and TVs. Enjoy the Mediterranean garden, the handsome conservatory and the utter peace; Holt and historic Little Walsingham are nearby. Your hosts are delightful: ex-restaurateur Jeremy who cooks enthusiastically, ethically and with panache, and Canadian-raised Gill.

Rooms	3 cottages for 2: £90–£120. Singles £70–£100
Meals	Dinner, 2-3 courses with wine, £16–£19.50. Pubs/restaurants 1 mile.
Closed	Rarely.

Jeremy Bolam
Holly Lodge,
Thursford Green,
Norfolk NR21 0AS
Tel   +44 (0)1328 878465
Email   info@hollylodgeguesthouse.co.uk
Web   www.hollylodgeguesthouse.co.uk

Entry 329   Map 10

Norfolk

Burgh Parva Hall

Sunlight bathes the Norfolk longhouse on sunny afternoons; the welcome from the Heals is as warm. The listed house is all that remains of the old village of Burgh Parva, deserted after the Great Plague. It's an inviting, handsome home... old furniture, rugs, books, pictures and Magnet the terrier-dachshund. Large guest bedrooms face the sunsets and the garden flat makes a delightful hideaway, especially in summer. Breakfast eggs come from the garden hens, vegetables and fruits are home-grown, fresh fish is locally sourced and the game may have been shot by William: settle down by the fire and tuck in!

Dogs welcome in the garden-flat twin, but not in the main house.

Rooms	1 twin with separate bath; garden flat - 1 double, 1 twin (self-catering option): £70–£90. Singles £45–£55.
Meals	Dinner £24. BYO. Pub/restaurant 4 miles.
Closed	Rarely.

Judy & William Heal
Burgh Parva Hall,
Melton Constable,
Norfolk NR24 2PU
Tel   +44 (0)1263 862569
Email   judyheal@dsl.pipex.com

Entry 330   Map 10

Norfolk

Cleat House

A fantastic welcome in a peaceful street, a short walk from town and beach. This attractive late-Victorian seaside villa, built for a London merchant, has been sumptuously renovated inside. Bedrooms have original fireplaces and sash windows, upbeat fabrics and original art, and a warm inviting mix of antique and traditional. The guest sitting room comes with an honesty bar, games, books, DVDs and guides – set off for Holkham or Sandringham! Rob and Linda greet you with homemade treats and serve a tasty breakfast at separate tables: very good coffee, kippers, smoked salmon and lots more. You're beautifully cared for here.

Minimum stay: 2 nights at weekends.

Rooms	2 suites for 2; 1 suite for 2 with separate bath: £90–£120. Singles £70–£100.
Meals	Pubs/restaurants within 0.5 miles.
Closed	Occasionally.

Rob & Linda Ownsworth
Cleat House,
7 Montague Road, Sheringham,
Norfolk NR26 8LN

Tel	+44 (0)1263 822765
Mobile	+44 (0)7557 356952
Email	roblinda@cleathouse.co.uk
Web	www.cleathouse.co.uk

Entry 331   Map 10

Norfolk

Plumstead Hall Farmhouse

Percy and Emma's large farmhouse has a gently bustling family feel, and you are made to feel at home as soon as you step onto the lovely old Norfolk pamments in the hall. The bedrooms, up higgledy-piggledy stairs, have feather duvets and pretty covers, green views and a huge bathroom; the second room with a sloping ceiling is simpler. Breakfast is a relaxed, do-it-yourself affair on the mini stove: eggs, bacon, cereals, breads and jams, all locally sourced and eaten in the guest dining room. The north Norfolk beaches are close and there are historic homes to visit. Birdwatchers, walkers and cyclists will be happy as Larry.

Minimum stay: 2 nights.

Rooms	2 doubles sharing bath (let to same party only): £85–£95. Singles £80–£100.
Meals	Pub/restaurant 5 miles.
Closed	Christmas & New Year.

Percy & Emma Stilwell
Plumstead Hall Farmhouse,
Northfield Lane,
Plumstead, Norwich,
Norfolk NR11 7PT

Tel	+44 (0)1263 577660
Email	plumsteadhall@gmail.com
Web	www.plumsteadhallfarmhouse.co.uk

Entry 332   Map 10

Norfolk

Stable Cottage

Sarah's home is set in the grounds of Heydon, one of Norfolk's finest Elizabethan houses. In the Dutch-gabled stable block, fronted by Cromwell's Oak, is her cottage – fresh, sunny and enchanting. Each room is touched by her warm personality and love of beautiful things: seagrass floors, crisp linen and pretty china; the cosy sitting room is set with tea and biscuits for your arrival. Bedrooms are cottagey and immaculate; bathrooms have baskets of treats. Sarah serves a delicious breakfast with golden eggs from her hens, homemade marmalade and garden fruit. Thursford is close and you're 20 minutes from the coast.

For stays of 2 nights or more: £90 per night. Minimum stay: 2 nights at weekends.

Rooms	2 twin/doubles: £100. Singles from £50.
Meals	Pub 1 mile.
Closed	Christmas.

Sarah Bulwer-Long
Stable Cottage,
Heydon Hall, Heydon,
Norwich,
Norfolk NR11 6RE

Tel	+44 (0)1263 587343
Mobile	+44 (0)7780 998742
Web	www.heydon-bb.co.uk

Entry 333   Map 10

Norfolk

Tuttington Hall

A sweeping drive brings you to this grand yet homely 16th-century house. The wide hall feels welcoming, with rugs on polished wood and a beautiful rocking horse; scones or cakes wait by the drawing room fire. Gardens brim with borders, fruit trees and an impressive vegetable patch. David and Andra are keen cooks: dinner is a convivial affair, served in the garden room or in the candlelit period dining room. Breakfast includes homemade bread and jams, eggs from the hens, home-grown tomatoes. Traditional bedrooms have luxurious beds, tea trays and books. Visit Norwich for theatre, galleries, cathedral; the coast is close.

Rooms	1 twin/double: £105–£125. Family wing – 1 family room for 2-4: £105–£157. 1 single: £52.
Meals	Dinner, 3 courses, £32.50. Pubs/restaurants 3 miles.
Closed	Rarely.

Andra & David Papworth
Tuttington Hall,
Tuttington,
Norwich,
Norfolk NR11 6TL

Tel	+44 (0)1263 733417
Email	david@tuttingtonhall.co.uk
Web	www.tuttingtonhall.co.uk

Entry 334   Map 10

Norfolk

The Buttery

Down a farm track, a treasure: your own thatch-and-flint octagonal dairy house perfectly restored by local craftsmen and as snug as can be. You get a jacuzzi bath, a little kitchen and a fridge stocked with delicious bacon and ground coffee so you can breakfast when you want; take it to the sun terrace in good weather. The sitting room is terracotta-tiled and has a music system, a warming fire and a sofabed for those who don't want to tackle the steep wooden stair to the cosy bedroom on the mezzanine. You can play a game of tennis, and walk from the door into peaceful parkland and woods. Lovely!

Minimum stay: 2 nights at weekends.

Rooms	1 double with sitting room & small kitchen: £90–£110.
Meals	Pub 10-minute walk.
Closed	Rarely.

Deborah Meynell
The Buttery,
Berry Hall, Honingham,
Norwich,
Norfolk NR9 5AX

Tel	+44 (0)1603 880541
Email	thebuttery@paston.co.uk
Web	www.thebuttery.biz

Entry 335   Map 10

Norfolk

Church Farm Barns

Fields and peace wrap around this imaginative barn conversion. A pleasing old and modern feel greets you: oak beams and vaulted ceilings combine with sea grass floors, painted furniture, seascapes and photos. Bedrooms, 'Bluebell' and 'Camellia', have pots of flowers, home-baked cookies and views. Expect a delicious and varied choice at breakfast, perhaps Michael's own special kedgeree, local spiced black pudding, proper poached eggs... with homemade bread and jams. Historic Norwich is a 15-minute drive, and cycle rides are good; a family dinner – often with an Italian or North African slant – is sometimes available on your return.

Travel cot available.

Rooms	2 doubles: £75–£85.
Meals	Dinner, 3 courses, £20. BYO. Pub 0.5 miles.
Closed	Rarely.

Felicity & Michael Walmsley
Church Farm Barns,
Rectory Lane, Little Melton,
Norwich, Norfolk NR9 3PF

Tel	+44 (0)1603 811520
Mobile	+44 (0)7710 557246
Email	churchfarmbarns3@gmail.com
Web	www.churchfarmbarns3.co.uk

Entry 336   Map 10

Norfolk

175 Newmarket Road

This Edwardian villa is rather grandly set back from the road in its large garden with mature shrubs and trees. The airy dining room has pretty lamps, art on the walls and a large round table in the bay window overlooking the garden. The comfy seating area at the other end of the room has lots of books and magazines. Charming Dawn gives you extremely elegant, well-dressed bedrooms with an interesting mix of modern and antique furniture, sumptuous linen and leafy views; bathrooms are large, warm and well lit. Wake for a generous and convivial breakfast; then find lots to explore on the doorstep – you can walk to the centre of town.

Minimum stay: 2 nights at weekends.

Rooms	3 doubles: £65–£75.
	Singles £40–£50.
Meals	Pubs 0.25 miles.
Closed	Rarely.

	Dawn & Peter Thompson
	175 Newmarket Road,
	Norwich,
	Norfolk NR4 6AP
Tel	+44 (0)1603 506160
Email	enquiries@bedandbreakfastinnorwich.co.uk
Web	www.bedandbreakfastinnorwich.co.uk

Entry 337   Map 10

Norfolk

Washingford House

Tall octagonal chimney stacks and a Georgian façade give the house a stately air. In fact, it's the friendliest of places to stay and Paris gives you a delicious, locally sourced breakfast including plenty of fresh fruit. The house, originally Tudor, is a delightful mix of old and new. Large light-filled bedrooms have loads of good books and views over the four-acre garden, a favourite haunt for local birds. Bergh Apton is a conservation village seven miles from Norwich and you are in the heart of it; perfect for cycling, boat trips on the Norfolk Broads and the twelve Wherryman's Way circular walks.

Rooms	1 twin/double: £65 £85.
	1 single with separate bath: £35–£50.
Meals	Pubs/restaurants 4–6 miles.
Closed	Christmas.

	Paris & Nigel Back
	Washingford House,
	Cookes Road, Bergh Apton,
	Norwich, Norfolk NR15 1AA
Tel	+44 (0)1508 550924
Mobile	+44 (0)7900 683617
Email	parisb@waitrose.com
Web	www.washingford.com

Entry 338   Map 10

Norfolk

Gothic House

Silver tea and coffee pots and Portmeirion china, pictures and prints from far-flung places, and an unexpected peace in the centre of the city – welcome to Gothic House. The building is listed and Regency and your host, enthusiastic, charming, knows the history. As for breakfast, it is fresh, lavish and locally sourced; in short, a treat. Bedrooms are stylish and spacious with a strong period feel, the double and the two bathrooms on the first floor, and the twin above. Norwich is blessed with culture, character and pubs, and a cathedral with the second tallest spire in England. Fabulous!

Parking space available.

Rooms	1 double with separate bath; 1 twin with separate bath & wc: £95. Singles £65.
Meals	Pubs/restaurants 5-minute walk.
Closed	Rarely.

Clive Harvey
Gothic House,
King's Head Yard,
42 Magdalen Street, Norwich,
Norfolk NR3 1JE
Tel   +44 (0)1603 631879
Email   charvey649@aol.com
Web   www.gothic-house-norwich.com

Entry 339   Map 10

Norfolk

Hoveton Hall

A Regency house snoozing in beautiful parkland and gardens. Formal and grand, yet comfortably friendly, Harry and Rachel's home brims with wonderful woodwork, decorated ceilings, art old and new. Their children are keen to play with visiting young ones, there's a lovely collection of hare sculptures up the stairs and the views over the 620 acres are stunning. Airy bedrooms have well-dressed beds, tea trays, biscuits and flowers. Morning sun lights up the panelled library/sitting room where you have breakfast, shelves are crammed with books and there's a large fire to sit by. Explore the estate, head off for beaches and The Broads.

Rooms	1 double: £120. 1 family room for 4: £140.
Meals	Pubs/restaurants 1 mile.
Closed	Rarely.

Rachel Buxton
Hoveton Hall,
Hoveton Hall Estate,
Hoveton, Norwich,
Norfolk NR12 8RJ
Tel   +44 (0)1603 784 297
Email   rachel@hovetonhallestate.co.uk
Web   www.hovetonhallestate.co.uk

Entry 340   Map 10

Norfolk

Sloley Hall

A grand and gracious yellow-brick Georgian house with formal gardens, tree-studded parkland and glorious views from every window. It has also been beautifully renovated, with flagstoned floors, Persian rugs, gleaming circular tables and vases of garden-grown flowers. Your hosts are delightful – Barbara and Simon were married here and are easy-going and helpful. A huge light-flooded dining room is perfect for breakfast; the drawing room is comfy and uncluttered with a marble fireplace and long views. Bedrooms are large and elegant with sumptuous bed linen; generous bathrooms glow with warmth.

Minimum stay: 2 nights at bank holidays.

Rooms	1 suite for 2; 1 double with separate bath, 1 double with separate shower: £80-£90. Singles from £50. Child bed available.
Meals	Pubs/restaurants 2-4 miles.
Closed	Rarely.

	Barbara Gorton
	Sloley Hall,
	Sloley, Norwich,
	Norfolk NR12 8HA
Tel	+44 (0)1692 538582
Mobile	+44 (0)7748 152079
Email	babsgorton@hotmail.com
Web	www.sloleyhall.com

Entry 341   Map 10

Norfolk

Sutton Hall

Sweep up the gravel drive to a red-brick Victorian country house, in quiet parkland near the Norfolk Broads and coast. Sue serves delicious breakfasts on the terrace, or in a chandelier'd dining room with bay windows to the morning sun. Enjoy local produce, tomatoes from the kitchen garden, and knobbly apples from an orchard where deer and ducks roam free... Rooms are in keeping with the home's comfortable elegance – tall sash windows, a four-poster, fireplace, power showers, an extra bed for children; a Chinese screen adorns the high-ceilinged sitting room. Spend the day on the Broads with the binoculars.

Rooms	2 doubles (extra child bed & cot): £90-£120. Singles £70-£90.
Meals	Pubs/restaurant 1.5 miles.
Closed	Rarely.

	Sue Berry
	Sutton Hall,
	Hall Road, Sutton, Norwich,
	Norfolk NR12 9RX
Tel	+44 (0)1692 584888
Mobile	+44 (0)7977 575788
Email	enquiries@suttonhallnorfolk.co.uk
Web	www.suttonhallnorfolk.co.uk

Entry 342   Map 10

Norfolk

The Old Rectory

Conservation farmland all around; acres of wild heathland busy with woodpeckers and owls; the coast two miles away. Relax in the spacious drawing room of this handsome 17th-century rectory and friendly family home, set in lovely mature gardens (NGS) full of trees and unusual planting. Fiona loves to cook and bakes her bread daily, food is delicious, seasonal and locally sourced, jams are homemade. Comfortable bedrooms have *objets* from diplomatic postings and the spacious suite comes with mahogany furniture and armchairs so you can settle in with a book. Super views, friendly dogs, tennis in the garden and masses of space.

Rooms	1 suite for 2; 1 double with kitchenette, separate bath & shower: £70–£85. Singles £40.
Meals	Dinner from £25. Pubs 2 miles.
Closed	Rarely.

Peter & Fiona Black
The Old Rectory,
Ridlington,
Norfolk NR28 9NZ
Tel   +44 (0)1692 650247
Mobile   +44 (0)7774 599911
Email   ridlingtonoldrectory@gmail.com
Web   www.oldrectorynorthnorfolk.co.uk

Entry 343   Map 10

Norfolk

Norfolk Courtyard

Walk straight in through French windows to your own, underfloor-heated room in the courtyard; independence from the main house where friendly Simon and Catherine live. The rooms are decorated in soft colours, mattresses are perfect, cotton sheets are smooth and your handsome bathroom has limestone tiles – all rather luxurious; there's a welcome tea tray and a fridge to cool a bottle too. Continental breakfast is next door in the old, beamed barn – help yourself to croissants, crumpets, homemade jams, compotes and muesli – and home-laid eggs that you cook in an easy egg steamer: very popular! Stunning walks await on the coast.

Minimum stay: 2 nights (peak season weekends).

Rooms	3 doubles, 1 twin/double: £105–£110. Singles £60. Extra bed/sofabed available £10 per person per night.
Meals	Pub/restaurant 0.5 miles.
Closed	Rarely.

Simon & Catherine Davis
Norfolk Courtyard, Westfield Farm,
Foxley Road, Foulsham, Dereham,
Norfolk NR20 5RH
Tel   +44 (0)1362 683333
Mobile   +44 (0)7969 611510
Email   info@norfolkcourtyard.co.uk
Web   www.norfolkcourtyard.co.uk

Entry 344   Map 10

Norfolk

Norfolk

Carrick's at Castle Farm

This warm-bricked farmhouse is up a long drive and surrounded by 720 acres; John's family have lived here since the 1920s. He and Jean are passionate about conservation and the protection of wildlife, and here you have absolute quiet – for birdwatching, fishing or walking. Return to the drawing room with its open fire, books, and decanter of sherry. Your friendly hosts give you coffee and cake, or wine, when you arrive, and bedrooms are light and luxurious with pretty fabrics and homemade biscuits. Breakfasts and candlelit dinners are delicious, and the garden leads to a footpath alongside the river.

College Farm

Katharine is a natural at making guests feel like friends. Her beautiful farmhouse tucks itself away on the edge of the village and the big friendly kitchen is filled with delicious smells of home baking. Meals are served by the large wood-burner in the grand Jacobean dining room, filled with good antiques, period furnishings and cosy places to sit; food is home-grown, seasonal and local. Sleep well in charming bedrooms with smooth linen, pretty furniture and garden views; bathrooms are small and simple. A fascinating area teeming with pingos, wildlife, old churches... and glorious antique shops.

Children over 12 welcome. Garden available for weddings.

Rooms	1 double, 2 twin/doubles; 1 double with separate bath: £95. Singles £65.
Meals	Dinner, 3 courses, £30. BYO. Pub 0.5 miles.
Closed	Rarely.

Rooms	3 twin/doubles: £90–£100. Singles £45–£50. Dinner, B&B £65–£70 per person. Extra bed/sofabed available £25–£35 per person per night.
Meals	Dinner from £20. Pub 1 mile.
Closed	Rarely.

	Jean Wright Carrick's at Castle Farm, Castle Farm, Swanton Morley, Dereham, Norfolk NR20 4JT
Tel	+44 (0)1362 638302
Email	jean@castlefarm-swanton.co.uk
Web	www.carricksatcastlefarm.co.uk

	Katharine Wolstenholme College Farm, Thompson, Thetford, Norfolk IP24 1QG
Tel	+44 (0)1953 483318
Email	info@collegefarmnorfolk.co.uk
Web	www.collegefarmnorfolk.co.uk

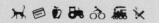

Entry 345   Map 10

Entry 346   Map 10

Norfolk

The Little House

This is a pretty little converted outbuilding with wooden beams, exposed brick, fresh flowers, leather armchairs and your very own, very sweet courtyard with a paddock and garden to explore. Stroll to the pub for some great grub, or laze on Britain's largest common. Karena, a kind mother hen with some beautiful chickens, will look after you then let you get on. Breakfast can be cooked and eaten in the big farmhouse kitchen of the main house or at leisure in your retreat. Norwich Cathedral and the Broads are an easy drive. Good value with an independent feel and the bonus of a hearty breakfast to energise adventures.

Short breaks available.

Rooms	1 annexe for 2: £70–£85. Singles £60.
Meals	Pub within 1 mile.
Closed	Rarely

Karena Taylor
The Little House, College Farm,
New Buckenham Road,
Old Buckenham,
Attleborough,
Norfolk NR17 1PW
Tel +44 (0)1953 861282
Email thelittlehousebandb@gmail.com
Web www.littlehousebandb.com

Entry 347　Map 10

Northamptonshire

Bridge Cottage

A truly peaceful place, yet only a few miles from Peterborough. Sip a glass of wine on the decking down by the Willowbrook; beautiful countryside envelops you, the cattle doze, kingfishers flash by and you may see a red kite (borrow some binoculars). Inside find pretty bedrooms with sloping ceilings, the purest cotton sheets and proper blankets; bathrooms are thickly towelled and full of lovely lotions and bubbles. Breakfast is local and scrumptious and served in the friendliest kitchen facing that heavenly view. There's a tranquil conservatory for a quiet read, and Judy and Rod are brilliant hosts. A hidden gem.

Rooms	1 double, 1 twin; 1 double with separate bath: £80–£86. Singles £47.50–£60.
Meals	Pub/restaurant 500 yds.
Closed	Christmas.

Judy Young
Bridge Cottage,
Oundle Road, Woodnewton,
Peterborough,
Northamptonshire PE8 5EG
Tel +44 (0)1780 470860
Mobile +44 (0)7979 644864
Email enquiries@bridgecottage.net
Web www.bridgecottage.net

Entry 348　Map 9

Northamptonshire

The Old House

Northamptonshire is the county of spires and squires. And here, on the through-road of this fascinating medieval town, is a listed squire's house – once home to a merchant who traded in the marketplace opposite. Enter the heavy oak door and step back 400 years. William, courteous, hospitable and renovating with aplomb, is full of plans. Facing the courtyard at the back (furnished for summery breakfasts and aperitifs) are the quietest rooms; all have sumptuous fabrics and wallpapers, dramatic touches and divine beds. Delightfully quirky, spanking new bathrooms with roll top tubs are as special as all the rest.

Northamptonshire

The Old Rectory

An utterly charming house. This classic English country home has a warm family feel and is brimming with china, lamps, art, antiques, open fires and books; a stuffed crocodile in the downstairs loo makes you smile. The huge garden bedroom, sumptuous and welcoming, has a charming bathroom with a roll top; the other two, comfy and sweet, have pond views. Hop downstairs for breakfast at a long table with pretty blue-checked chairs. The garden leads into meadows; the pool is sheltered by beech hedge and pleached limes. Silverstone and Stratford are close, Northampton a hidden gem – lovely villages, ironstone houses, ancient churches…

Rooms	3 doubles, 1 twin/double: £70. Singles £55.
Meals	Pubs/restaurants 150 yds.
Closed	Rarely.

Rooms	1 double; 1 double, 1 twin sharing bath: £80-£85. Singles £70.
Meals	Pub 2 miles.
Closed	Rarely.

	William Evans
	The Old House,
	5 Market Square,
	Higham Ferrers,
	Rushden,
	Northamptonshire NN10 8BP
Tel	+44 (0)1933 314006
Email	theoldhousehighamferrers@gmail.com
Web	www.theoldhousehighamferrers.co.uk

	Sarah Aldous
	The Old Rectory,
	Maidford,
	Towcester,
	Northamptonshire NN12 8HT
Tel	+44 (0)1327 860203
Mobile	+44 (0)7803 296702
Email	sarahaldous1@me.com

Entry 349   Map 9

Entry 350   Map 8

The Coach House

Sunlight and garden flowers fill this unusual, and welcoming, rosy-brick home. The former coach house and stables have become two luxurious light-filled rooms wrapped round a grassed and paved courtyard: an enchanting spot for breakfast in summer. Sarah's eye for colour shows in the design of her gardens, and her furnishings – an appealing mix of modern and traditional. She gives you a big welcome, and a memorable breakfast too. Perfect for tennis – there's a court in the garden – a nd visits to Silverstone, Stowe, Bletchley Park and Warwick Castle... if you can bear to leave!

Rooms	1 double, 1 twin: £90. £120 during Grand Prix & Motor Sport weekends. Singles £65.
Meals	Packed lunch on request. Pub/restaurant within 5 miles.
Closed	Rarely.

Sarah Baker Baker
The Coach House,
Duncote, Towcester,
Northamptonshire NN12 8AQ
Tel   +44 (0)1327 352855
Mobile   +44 (0)7875 215705
Email   sarahbb54@gmail.com
Web   www.thecoachhouseduncote.co.uk

Entry 351   Map 8

The Vyne

Weighed down by wisteria, this 16th-century cottage rests in a honey-hued conservation village on the cusp of Oxfordshire. Beams and wonky lines abound; rooms are filled with good antiques and eclectic art. The twin overlooking the garden is enchanting, tucked under the rafters, its beds decorated in willow-pattern chintz, its walls glinting with gilded frames; the double has a Georgian four-poster and a sampler-decorated bathroom that's a quick flit next door. Warm and charming, Imogen not only works in publishing but is a contented gardener and Cordon Bleu cook – enjoy supper in her sunny secluded garden.

Babies welcome.

Rooms	1 twin; 1 four-poster with separate bath: £80. Singles from £45.
Meals	Supper £20. Dinner £30. BYO. Pub 2-minute walk.
Closed	Rarely.

Imogen Butler
The Vyne,
High Street, Eydon,
Daventry,
Northamptonshire NN11 3PP
Tel   +44 (0)1327 264886
Mobile   +44 (0)7974 801475
Email   imogen@ibutler2.wanadoo.co.uk

Entry 352   Map 8

Northamptonshire

The Clock Tower

Tumble into a valley with a redbrick clock tower jutting high in the distance. Before you know it, you're outside the front door, in the lovely company of David and Lizzie. There's a drawing room just for you: artistic, charming, with contemporary oils; fling yourself into a deep sofa. Then a conservatory and a garden running to fields. At the top of the house, a huge private suite with sofa and wood-burner, cream carpet and cashmere throw, Shaker hooks for hangers, a bathroom with mood lighting… fling open the window and soak up the view. Breakfasts suit the bright, warm mood: Lizzie cooks what you most enjoy.

Pets by arrangement.

Colledges House

Huge attention to comfort here, and a house full of laughter. Liz clearly derives pleasure from sharing her 300-year-old stone thatched cottage, immaculate garden, conservatory and converted barn with guests. Sumptuous bedrooms have deep mattresses with fine linen, sparkling bathrooms are a good size. The house is full of interesting things: a Jacobean trunk, a Bechstein piano, mirrors and pictures, pretty china, bright fabrics, a beautiful bureau. Cordon Bleu dinners are elegant affairs - and great fun. Stroll around the conservation village of Staverton – delightful.

Children over 8 & babes in arms welcome.

Rooms	1 double with private sitting room downstairs: £85-£95. Singles £60-£65.
Meals	Pubs/restaurants 10-minute drive.
Closed	Christmas & New Year.

Rooms	1 double with separate bath: £95-£99. 1 single: from £68. Cottage - 1 double, 1 twin: £95-£99.
Meals	Dinner, 3 courses, £35. Pub 4-minute walk.
Closed	Rarely.

	David & Lizzie Bland The Clock Tower, Lower Catesby, Daventry, Northamptonshire NN11 6LF
Tel	+44 (0)1327 706987
Mobile	+44 (0)7775 641170
Email	lizziebland@btinternet.com
Web	www.catesbyclocktower.co.uk

	Liz Jarrett Colledges House, Oakham Lane, Staverton, Daventry, Northamptonshire NN11 6JQ
Tel	+44 (0)1327 702737
Mobile	+44 (0)7710 794112
Email	liz@colledgeshouse.co.uk
Web	www.colledgeshouse.co.uk

Entry 353   Map 8

Entry 354   Map 8

Northamptonshire

Staverton Hall

Through impressive iron gates to a grand house in a spectacular setting. Find masses of room, and friendly owners who have young children of their own; they love having families to stay. Relaxed breakfasts (and dinner) at flexible times are served at one table; all is local and delicious. Large, light bedrooms and super-modern bathrooms are upstairs, have good views and feel private. Relax in the huge, creamy-yellow guest sitting room with sash windows, log fire, board games and comfy sofas; there's also a heated pool, a play area, acres of garden, and the pub a walk away. Family heaven.

Pets by arrangement.

Rooms	2 doubles, each with separate bath: £90. 2 singles, each with separate bath: £60. Extra bed/sofabed available.
Meals	Dinner, 3 courses, £30 (min. 4 people). Pub 3-minute walk.
Closed	Rarely.

	Serena Frost
	Staverton Hall,
	Manor Road, Staverton, Daventry,
	Northamptonshire NN11 6JD
Tel	+44 (0)1327 878296
Email	serena@stavertonhall.co.uk
Web	www.stavertonhall.co.uk

Entry 355   Map 8

Northumberland

Matfen High House

Bring the wellies – and jumpers! You are 25 miles from the border and the walking is a joy. Struan and Jenny are good company, love sporting pursuits and will advise on where to eat locally (and drive you there if needed). The sturdy stone house of 1735 is a lived-in, happily shabby-chic kind of place: the en suite bedrooms have fine fabrics and pictures, bathrooms are well-kept and the drawing room promises books and choice pieces. Enjoy local bacon and sausages at breakfast, with Struan's marmalade and bread warm from the oven. The countryside is stunning, Hadrian's Wall and the great castles (Alnwick, Bamburgh) beckon.

Rooms	1 double, 1 twin; 1 double, 1 twin sharing bath: £60-£80. Singles £45.
Meals	Packed lunch £4.50. Restaurant 2 miles.
Closed	Rarely.

	Struan & Jenny Wilson
	Matfen High House,
	Matfen, Corbridge,
	Northumberland NE20 0RG
Tel	+44 (0)1661 886592
Email	struan@struan.enterprise-plc.com
Web	www.matfenhighhouse.co.uk

Entry 356   Map 12

Northumberland

The Hermitage

A magical setting, three miles from Hadrian's wall, in a house of friendship and comfort. Through ancient woodland, up the drive, over the burn and there it is: big, beautiful and Georgian. Interiors are comfortable country-house, full of warmth and charm; bedrooms, carpeted, spacious and delightful, are furnished with antiques, paintings and superb beds; bathrooms have roll top baths. Outside are lovely lawns, a walled garden, wildlife, and breakfasts on the terrace in summer. Katie – who was born in this house – looks after you brilliantly.

Children over 7 & babes in arms welcome.

Northumberland

New Entry

The Grange

You're only seven miles away from Newcastle city centre but this couldn't be more peaceful. Kind owners let you wind down in their elegant Georgian house on the private Blagdon Estate, surrounded by mature trees and lovely gardens. Nod off in cosy, airy bedrooms with pale carpets (quiet at night), wake to eat like a lord at separate tables with Blagdon bacon, award-winning sausages and all the trimmings. There's a gentle woodland walk on the doorstep, rugged countryside and the nearby coast to explore. Newcastle airport is only four miles away (owners can arrange drop off and collection) and you can return to a roaring log fire.

Rooms	1 double, 1 twin; 1 twin with separate bath: £85–£90. Singles from £55.	Rooms	3 doubles: £90–£130. Extra bed/sofabed available £20–£40 per person per night.
Meals	Pub 2 miles.	Meals	Pubs/restaurants 1 mile.
Closed	October–February.	Closed	Never.

	Simon & Katie Stewart		Paul Wappat & Penny Dane
	The Hermitage,		The Grange,
	Swinburne, Hexham,		Great North Road, Seaton Burn,
	Northumberland NE48 4DG		Newcastle upon Tyne,
Tel	+44 (0)1434 681248		Northumberland NE13 6DF
Mobile	+44 (0)7708 016297	Tel	+44 (0)1670 789666
Email	katie.stewart@themeet.co.uk	Email	info@thegrangebandb.co.uk
		Web	www.thegrangebandb.co.uk

Entry 357   Map 16

Entry 358   Map 16

Northumberland

Shieldhall

The converted 18th-century farm buildings are charming. Step in through your own entrance off the central courtyard to cosy bedrooms, flowers and homemade biscuits. Family run and friendly, it's a treat to stay. Stephen and his sons make bespoke and restore antique furniture, and the rooms are named after the different woods they use. Daughter Sarah and her husband John are great hosts; you pop over to the main house for meals. Delicious Aga cooked breakfasts include homemade bread and eggs from the hens; Celia helps with the dinners – have a glass of wine in the beautiful library beforehand: the views over garden and parkland are stunning.

Rooms	Courtyard buildings - 1 double, 1 twin, 1 four-poster: £80. Singles £60.
Meals	Dinner, 4 courses, £28. Pub 7 miles.
Closed	Rarely.

Celia & Stephen Robinson-Gay
Shieldhall,
Wallington,
Morpeth,
Northumberland NE61 4AQ
Tel   +44 (0)1830 540387
Email   stay@shieldhallguesthouse.co.uk
Web   www.shieldhallguesthouse.co.uk

Entry 359   Map 16

Northumberland

Thistleyhaugh

The family thrives on hard work and humour, and if Enid's not the perfect B&B hostess, she's a close contender. Her passions are pictures, cooking and people, and certainly you eat well – local farm eggs at breakfast and their beef at dinner. Choose any of the five large, lovely bedrooms and stay the week; they are awash with old paintings, silk fabrics and crisp linen. Wake refreshed and nip downstairs, past the log fire, to a laden and sociable table, head off afterwards to find 720 acres of organic farmland and a few million more of the Cheviots beyond. Wonderful hosts, a glorious region, a happy house.

Rooms	3 doubles, 1 twin: £100. 1 single: £60-£85.
Meals	Dinner, 3 courses, £25. Pub/restaurant 2 miles.
Closed	Christmas, New Year & January.

Henry & Enid Nelless
Thistleyhaugh,
Longhorsley,
Morpeth,
Northumberland NE65 8RG
Tel   +44 (0)1665 570629
Email   thistleyhaugh@hotmail.com
Web   www.thistleyhaugh.co.uk

Entry 360   Map 16

Northumberland

Bilton Barns

A solidly good farmhouse B&B whose lifeblood is still farming. The Jacksons know every inch of the countryside and coast that surrounds their 1715 home; it's a pretty spot. They farm 400 acres of mixed arable land that sweeps down to the coast yet always have time for guests. Dorothy creates an easy and sociable atmosphere with welcoming pots of tea and convivial breakfasts – all delicious and locally sourced. Comfortable, smartly done bedrooms are traditional with a contemporary feel, the conservatory is huge and filled with sofas and chairs and there's an airy guests' sitting room with an open fire and views to the sea.

Rooms	1 double, 1 four-poster, 1 twin: £80–£88. Singles £40–£65.
Meals	Packed lunch £4–£6. Pub/restaurant 2 miles.
Closed	Christmas & New Year.

Brian & Dorothy Jackson
Bilton Barns,
Alnmouth, Alnwick,
Northumberland NE66 2TB

Tel	+44 (0)1665 830427
Mobile	+44 (0)7939 262028
Email	dorothy@biltonbarns.com
Web	www.biltonbarns.com

Entry 361   Map 16

Northumberland

Redfoot Lea

Prepare to be thoroughly spoiled. This fine renovation of an old farmsteading lies just off the A1 up a quiet lane – perfect for touring the county or a great stopover. Amiable Philippa gives you a super south-facing sitting room and ground-floor bedrooms with comfortable beds, crisp linen, fluffy bathrobes and heated floors; bathrooms are smart and spotless. You breakfast at a large table in the magnificent open-plan hall, scented with glorious flower arrangements; enjoy freshly squeezed orange juice, homemade compotes, local produce, excellent coffee. A short hop from Alnwick Castle and gardens, and stunning beaches.

Rooms	1 double; 1 suite for 2: £90–£100. Singles £65.
Meals	Pubs/restaurants 0.25 miles.
Closed	Rarely.

Philippa Bell
Redfoot Lea,
Greensfield Moor Farm, Alnwick,
Northumberland NE66 2HH

Tel	+44 (0)1665 603891
Mobile	+44 (0)7870 586214
Email	info@redfootlea.co.uk
Web	www.redfootlea.co.uk

Entry 362   Map 16

Northumberland

Courtyard Garden

In the county town of Northumberland, with its grand castle and innovative gardens, step directly off the pavement and enter a courtyard surrounded by shrubs and pretty pots; sit out here on sunny days and sip a glass of something cool. Bedrooms (one overlooking the church, the other the garden) are traditional and immaculate; bathrooms, one with a roll top bath, have original wooden floors, thick towels. Friendly Maureen gives you breakfast in the comfortable sitting room at a round Georgian table underneath the window. Explore the town on foot, stride along white beaches, discover more castles; history is all around you.

Rooms	1 double, 1 twin/double: £80–£90. Singles £65.
Meals	Pub/restaurant within 300 yds.
Closed	Rarely.

Maureen Mason
Courtyard Garden,
10 Prudhoe Street,
Alnwick,
Northumberland NE66 1UW

Tel	+44 (0)1665 603393
Email	maureenpeter10@btinternet.com
Web	www.courtyardgarden-alnwick.com

Entry 363   Map 16

Northumberland

Old Rectory Howick

Christine and David's house on the edge of the village is surrounded by fields and woods, and is only minutes from the beautiful Northumberland coast, a designated AONB. Breakfasts are hearty: Craster kippers from down the road, eggs from Erica, Sylvia and Ella. Scamper about with wide beaches, stunning castles, rugged walks, golf courses and Holy Island, return to a cosy sitting room with a wood-burner. Sleep well in large, airy bedrooms with good bouncy mattresses, chintzy fabrics, top-of-the-range cotton sheets, warm showers and white towels. Wander the peaceful garden – there's a tree house and a croquet lawn.

Minimum stay: 2 nights.

Rooms	2 doubles; 1 twin with separate bath: £75–£95. 1 suite for 4 with separate bath: £140–£160. Singles £65–£75.
Meals	Pubs/restaurants 1 mile.
Closed	December/January.

Christine & David Jackson
Old Rectory Howick,
Howick, Alnwick,
Northumberland NE66 3LE

Tel	+44 (0)1665 577590
Mobile	+44 (0)7879 681753
Email	stay@oldrectoryhowick.co.uk
Web	www.oldrectoryhowick.co.uk

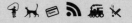

Entry 364   Map 16

Tuggal Hall

Once owned by Lord Beveridge... a lovely stone hall surrounded by fields of horses. Your host is charming and very happy for guests to feel at home. Relax by the log fire in the guest sitting room, cosy with books and magazines, antiques and paintings. Bedrooms are comfortably traditional (with garden views and simple bathrooms) – and you can enjoy a full English, black pudding or Craster kippers for breakfast. The grounds are full of mature trees and the productive kitchen garden provides fresh vegetables for dinner. House martins nest under the eaves, the terriers are friendly, the beautiful Northumbrian coast is just down the road.

Over 15s welcome.

Rooms	1 double, 1 twin, each with separate bath: £90-£95. Singles £45-£50.
Meals	Dinner £35. Pubs/restaurants 5 miles.
Closed	November to mid-March.

	Naomi Barrett
	Tuggal Hall,
	Chathill,
	Northumberland NE67 5EW
Tel	+44 (0)1665 589229
Email	naomibarrett23@btinternet.com

Entry 365   Map 16

Broome

In a coastal village with access to miles of sandy beaches, a totally surprising one-storey house, an Aladdin's cave of beautiful things. The garden room is its hub and has a country cottage feel; enjoy breakfasts here of locally smoked kippers, award-winning Bamburgh Bangers and home-cured bacon from the village. There's also a courtyard for breakfast in the sun. Bedrooms, in their own wing, come with fresh flowers and good books, and a cheerful sitting/dining room just for you. Mary, welcoming and amusing, greets you with delicious homemade cake. Make the most of her knowledge: she knows the area inside out.

Rooms	1 double, 1 twin sharing bath/shower (let to same party only): £100-£110. Singles £70.
Meals	Pubs/restaurants 2-minute walk.
Closed	November-March.

STOP PRESS
NO LONGER DOING B&B

Entry 366   Map 16

Northumberland

Laundry Cottage

History lovers, peace seekers and observers of nature will mellow further in this glorious spot overlooking the Cheviot hills. On arrival enjoy cake and tea with the evening sun – in the sun room, or in the garden on warm days. Douse yourself in one of Ginia's hiker's breakfasts, stride through iron age forts and the remains of Saxon palaces or visit long white beaches; return to Welsh slate floors, wood-burners, good home cooking, feather and down on deep comfy mattresses and fluffy towels. The feel is light and airy, Peter and Ginia are amiable hosts and the super garden is filled with roses in summer.

Rooms	1 double, 1 twin: £70–£75. Singles £50–£70.
Meals	Dinner £18–£22, coffee included. Pub/restaurant 5 miles.
Closed	December–March.

Peter & Ginia Gadsdon
Laundry Cottage,
East Horton,
Wooler,
Northumberland NE71 6EZ
Tel +44 (0)1668 215383
Email peter@gadsdon.me.uk
Web www.laundry-cottage-bnb.co.uk

Entry 367 Map 16

Northumberland

Kilham House, The West Wing

In the Northumberland National Park, a deliciously comfortable and elegant house. Family home to Kathryn and Hugh, who are happy to cook for parties and share their knowledge of this stunning area: inspiring walks (Pennine Way, St Cuthbert's Way), deserted beaches (Holy Island, Bamburgh) as well as castles and gardens galore. Through the private entrance to the West Wing, up winding stairs, find four large bedrooms and a charming guest sitting room warmed by the wood-burner. A continental breakfast is left for you in the upstairs kitchen; if you prefer the full Monty, join your hosts downstairs. The walled garden has views to the Cheviots.

Dogs welcome to stay in downstairs dog room (check availability).

Rooms	1 twin/double (en suite); 2 twin/doubles with separate bath; 1 twin/double sharing bath with an unlisted bedroom (let to same party only): £90–£95. Singles £70.
Meals	Dinner £28. BYO. Pubs/restaurants 4 miles.
Closed	Rarely.

Kathryn Watson
Kilham House, The West Wing,
Mindrum,
Cornhill-on-Tweed,
Northumberland TD12 4QS
Tel +44 (0)1890 850667
Email hugh.watson@mac.com
Web www.runandstay.com

Entry 368 Map 16

Northumberland

Chain Bridge House

Overlooking an idyllic stretch of the river Tweed is the last house in England – Scotland is 100 yards away across the magnificent Union Chain Bridge. In the sitting room: a log fire and books galore. In the bedrooms: goose down duvets and a fresh, airy feel. Livvy, a professional cook, is an active supporter of the Slow Food movement and local producers. Visit the neighbouring honey farm, glorious Bamburgh, Holy Island, the Farnes, or the unspoilt borders beyond: return to a revolving summerhouse in the garden for tea. Children and dogs get a generous welcome in this delightful family home.

Children over 2 welcome.

Rooms	1 double, 1 twin: £90-£95. Singles £60-£65.
Meals	Dinner £30. Supper £15. Packed lunch from £7.50. Pubs/restaurants 5-7 miles.
Closed	Rarely.

Livvy Cawthorn
Chain Bridge House,
Horncliffe,
Berwick-upon-Tweed,
Northumberland TD15 2XT

Tel	+44 (0)1289 382541
Email	info@chainbridgehouse.co.uk
Web	www.chainbridgehouse.co.uk

Entry 369   Map 16

Northumberland

West Coates

Slip through the gates of this Victorian townhouse and you're in the country. Two acres of leafy gardens, with pretty spots to relax, belie the closeness of Berwick's centre. From the lofty ceilings and sash windows to the soft colours, paintings and gleaming furniture, the house has a calm, ordered elegance. Bedrooms have antiques and garden views; one has a roll top bath; fruit, homemade cakes, flowers welcome you. Warm, friendly Karen is a stunning cook, inventively using local produce and spoiling you – she runs a cookery school here too. The coastline is stunning and there are castles and country houses galore to visit.

Minimum stay: 2 nights at weekends, & in high season.

Rooms	2 twin/doubles: £90-£120. Singles £70.
Meals	Pub/restaurant 15-minute walk.
Closed	December/January.

Karen Brown
West Coates,
30 Castle Terrace,
Berwick-upon-Tweed,
Northumberland TD15 1NZ

Tel	+44 (0)1289 309666
Mobile	+44 (0)7814 281973
Email	westcoatesbandb@gmail.com
Web	www.westcoates.co.uk

Entry 370   Map 16

Nottinghamshire

Willoughby House

Past the village pub, through a gate, this three-storey brick farmhouse reflects its owners' skilful interior design. The house brims with tokens of its 18th-century past, like meat hooks in the scullery-turned-sitting room, but feels ever so smart. Bedrooms are large and comfortable: climb up to Harry's room with its brass bed and toy soldiers over the fireplace; Edward's and George's share raftered loft space and a swish bathroom. Sarah rustles up delicious breakfasts in a dining room embraced by poppy red walls and shutters. Stroll round the little village; Georgian towns Southwell and Newark are close.

Rooms	3 twin/doubles, 1 suite for 4; 1 double with separate bath/shower: £85–£105. Singles £65–£75.
Meals	Dinner for special occasions. Packed lunch £7.50. Pub 3-minute walk.
Closed	Rarely.

Andrew & Sarah Nesbitt
Willoughby House,
Main Street, Norwell, Newark,
Nottinghamshire NG23 6JN
Tel   +44 (0)1636 636266
Mobile +44 (0)7789 965352
Email   willoughbybandb@aol.com
Web   www.willoughbyhousebandb.co.uk

Entry 371   Map 9

Nottinghamshire

Compton House

Two minutes from Newark's antique shops and old market, seek out this terraced Georgian townhouse where the mayor once lived. Naturally elegant, and overlooking Fountain Gardens, the sunny drawing room has an open fire. Lisa has filled the place with lovely personal touches and rooms are named after friends, from plush red-gold Judy's room to Harry's bijou single; the best is Cooper's, with a four-poster bed, a roll top bath through a draped archway and a wall hand-painted by a local artist. Pad down to the sunny basement for Lisa's feast of a breakfast. Hotel comforts but a truly homely feel.

Dogs by arrangement.

Rooms	2 doubles, 1 twin/double, 2 twins, 1 four-poster: £95–£130. 1 single with separate shower: from £50.
Meals	Packed lunch £5. Dinner, 3 courses, from £25. Pub/restaurant 0.5 miles.
Closed	Christmas.

Lisa Holloway
Compton House,
117 Baldertongate, Newark,
Nottinghamshire NG24 1RY
Tel   +44 (0)1636 708670
Mobile +44 (0)7817 446485
Email   info@comptonhousenewark.com
Web   www.comptonhousenewark.com

Entry 372   Map 9

Oxfordshire

Uplands House

Come to be spoiled at this handsome house, built in 1875 for the Earl of Jersey's farm manager. All is elegant and lavishly furnished; expect large light bedrooms, crisp linen, thick towels and vases of flowers. There are long views from the orangery, where you can have tea and cake; relax here with a book as the scents of the pretty garden waft by. Chat to Poppy while she creates delicious dinner – a convivial occasion enjoyed with your hosts. Breakfast is Graham's domain – try smoked salmon with scrambled eggs and red caviar. You're well placed for exploring – Moreton-in-Marsh and Stratford are close, Oxford just under an hour.

Rooms	1 double, 1 twin/double, 1 four-poster: £100–£180. Singles £65–£95.
Meals	Dinner, 2-4 courses, £20–£30. Pub 1.25 miles.
Closed	Rarely.

Poppy Cooksey & Graham Paul
Uplands House,
Upton, Banbury,
Oxfordshire OX15 6HJ

Tel	+44 (0)1295 678663
Mobile	+44 (0)7836 535538
Email	poppy@cotswolds-uplands.co.uk
Web	www.cotswolds-uplands.co.uk

Entry 373   Map 8

Oxfordshire

Buttslade House

Choose between a gorgeous ground-floor retreat across the courtyard, or a very pretty twin in the 17th-century farmhouse with barns and stables. The guest sitting room is a clever melody of ancient and contemporary styles: Spanish art, antique sofas, velvet cushions. Beds have seriously good mattresses, feather and down pillows and crisp white linen; bathrooms are smart and sparkling – one with a Victorian roll top. Diana is lovely and will pamper you or leave you, there's a blissful garden to stroll through, breakfast is a feast of fruits and homemade bread and it's a hop to the village pub. A fun and stylish treat.

Rooms	1 double; 1 twin with separate bath: £80–£90. Singles £50.
Meals	Dinner, 3 courses, £25. Lunch £7. Pub 100 yds.
Closed	Rarely.

Diana Thompson
Buttslade House,
Temple Mill Road,
Sibford Gower, Banbury,
Oxfordshire OX15 5RX

Tel	+44 (0)1295 788818
Email	diana@buttsladehouse.co.uk
Web	www.buttsladehouse.co.uk

Entry 374   Map 8

Minehill House

Wind your way up the farm track to the top of a beautiful hill and you arrive at a gorgeous family farmhouse with views for miles and warm, energetic Hester to care for you. Children will have fun on the ping-pong table and trampoline; their parents will enjoy the gleaming old flagstones, vibrant contemporary oils, wood-burning stove and seriously sophisticated food. Rest well in the big double room with its gloriously comfortable bed, verdant leafy wallpaper and stunning views; there's a cubby-hole door to extra twin beds (children love it!) and the bathroom is sparklingly and spacious. Bracing walks start straight from the door.

Home Farmhouse

This 400-year-old house is charming... beams, inglenooks and winding stairs. Rosemary and Nigel have been welcoming guests for 20 years; their gently faded home brims with character, antiques and chintz. Pretty bedrooms have eiderdowns and traditional blankets; bathrooms are small and a little dated. Hop up old stone steps and enjoy independence in the barn room – a simple space with a mixture of family pieces. Breakfast is generous with garden compotes, homemade bread and conserves. The family's travels are evident all over, Samson the wire-haired dachshund is friendly and it's all so laid-back you'll find it hard to leave.

Rooms	1 double with adjoining twin room: £95–£135. Singles from £65. Family £135.
Meals	Dinner, 3 courses, £35. Supper £20. BYO. Packed lunch available. Pubs 1-5 miles.
Closed	Christmas & New Year.

Rooms	1 double, 1 twin/double: £90. Barn – 1 twin/double: £90. Singles £60.
Meals	Dinner £28. Supper £20 (min. 4 people). Pub 100 yds.
Closed	Christmas.

	Hester & Ed Sale Minehill House, Lower Brailes, Banbury, Oxfordshire OX15 5BJ
Tel	+44 (0)1608 685594
Mobile	+44 (0)7890 266441
Email	hester@minehillhouse.co.uk
Web	www.minehillhouse.co.uk

	Rosemary & Nigel Grove-White Home Farmhouse, Charlton, Banbury, Oxfordshire OX17 3DR
Tel	+44 (0)1295 811683
Mobile	+44 (0)7795 207000
Email	grovewhite@lineone.net
Web	www.homefarmhouse.co.uk

Entry 375   Map 8

Entry 376   Map 8

Oxfordshire

The Old Post House

Great natural charm in the 17th-century Old Post House, where shiny flagstones, rich dark wood and mullion windows combine with handsome fabrics and furniture. Bedrooms are big, with antique wardrobes, oak headboards and a comfortably elegant feel. The walled gardens are lovely – with espaliered fruit trees, and a pool for sunny evenings. Christine, a well-travelled ex-pat, has an innate sense of hospitality; breakfasts are delicious (homemade granola, eggs Benedict, blueberry pancakes perhaps). There's village traffic but your sleep should be sound. Deddington is delightful – you will love Harry the friendly terrier too!

Children over 12 welcome.

Rooms	1 twin/double; 1 double with separate bath, 1 four-poster with separate shower: £90. Singles £65.
Meals	Occasional dinner. Pubs/restaurants in village.
Closed	Rarely.

Christine Blenntoft
The Old Post House,
New Street, Deddington,
Oxfordshire OX15 0SP

Tel	+44 (0)1869 338978
Mobile	+44 (0)7713 631092
Email	kblenntoft@aol.com
Web	www.oldposthouse.co.uk

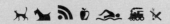

Entry 377   Map 8

Oxfordshire

Manor Farm

An attractive old farmhouse dating from the 17th century with a warm friendly atmosphere. Jeannette and Andrew are generous hosts; Andrew built his own heating system, which runs on pallets and linseed straw – now he's finished a four-seater plane! Elegant, light bedrooms with garden views have pretty lamps and fabrics, sofas and comfortable beds. Wake for a full English served around a big table in an immaculate kitchen: homemade bread, eggs from the hens. There's a wood-burner in the snug sitting room, the garden has a pond and lots of birds, the little village is peaceful and Oxford is a half hour drive.

Rooms	2 doubles, 1 twin: £85-£90. Singles £40-£50.
Meals	Pubs/restaurants 3 miles.
Closed	Rarely.

Andrew & Jeannette Collett
Manor Farm,
Main Street, Poundon, Bicester,
Oxfordshire OX27 9BB

Tel	+44 (0)1869 277212
Mobile	+44 (0)7974 753772
Email	ajcollett@live.co.uk
Web	www.manorfarmpoundon.co.uk

Entry 378   Map 8

Oxfordshire

Heyford House

Old church and handsome house face each other down a village lane – and then the road runs out. In this timeless Oxfordshire valley, the white gate leads into gardens where pathways weave between borders to a kitchen garden and orchards. The house, warm-hearted and well-proportioned, has been in the family for years; your hosts (he a personal trainer, she a chef) live in one wing. Find contemporary art, bright old rugs and open fires – a happy mix of traditional and new. Bedrooms are handsome and comfortable, with excellent bath and shower rooms; Sonja's breakfasts, served by the Aga, are a treat.

Rooms	2 doubles, 2 twin/doubles: £100–£120. Singles £60.
Meals	Supper, 2 courses, £20. Picnic from £10. Additional catering available. Pubs/restaurants 4 miles.
Closed	Rarely.

Leo Brooke-Little
Heyford House,
Church Lane,
Lower Heyford, Bicester,
Oxfordshire OX25 5NZ

Tel   +44 (0)1869 349061
Email   info@stayatheyfordhouse.co.uk
Web   www.stayatheyfordhouse.co.uk

Entry 379   Map 8

Oxfordshire

Rectory Farm

This big country house has a wonderfully settled, tranquil feel – the family have farmed here for three generations. Find large, light bedrooms, floral and pretty, with bold chintz bed covers, draped dressing tables, thick mattresses and tea trays with delicious chocolate shortbread; all have garden views. Sink into comfortable sofas flanking a huge fireplace in the drawing room, breakfast on local bacon and sausage with free-range eggs, stroll the lovely garden, or grab a rod and try your luck on one of the trout lakes. Elizabeth knows her patch well, walkers can borrow maps and lively market town Chipping Norton is close.

Rooms	1 double, 1 twin/double; 1 twin/double with separate bath: £92–£105. Singles £65–£75.
Meals	Pub/restaurant 1.5 miles.
Closed	December–January.

Elizabeth Colston
Rectory Farm,
Salford, Chipping Norton,
Oxfordshire OX7 5YY

Tel   +44 (0)1608 643209
Mobile   +44 (0)7866 834208
Email   enquiries@rectoryfarm.info
Web   www.rectoryfarm.info

Entry 380   Map 8

Oxfordshire

Upper Court Farm

In a quiet, gently hilly spot in the Cotswolds, the super smart Edwardian farmhouse comes with groomed gardens, 30 acres of grassland for Chloë's horses and woodland walks. A dressage rider, she and Tim are interesting hosts and their home is laden with good quality fabrics, country art and family pieces. Charming bedrooms (on the top floor) have madly comfy beds, TVs, drenching showers; there's a cosy sitting room too. Breakfast is generous, locally sourced and delicious with fruit salad, and homemade bread and jams. Relax in the rose garden with a drink or tea and home-baked cakes – two sweet dogs will join you.

Children over 8 welcome.

Rooms	1 double, 1 twin/double; 1 double with separate shower: £85-£120. Singles £70-£100. £10 supplement for one-night stay at weekends March-September.
Meals	Pub 200 yds & 3 miles, café 5-minute walk.
Closed	Rarely.

	Chloë Robson Upper Court Farm, Mill End, Chadlington, Chipping Norton, Oxfordshire OX7 3NY
Tel	+44 (0)1608 676296
Mobile	+44 (0)7717 571792
Email	chloe.uppercourt@gmail.com
Web	www.uppercourtfarm.co.uk

Entry 381   Map 8

Oxfordshire

The Glove House

Handmade chocolates from Turin (Francesco is Italian) and espresso machines in the bedrooms show proper respect for the important things in life. This handsome Georgian house in the heart of Woodstock combines calm contemporary comfort with warm smiles. The sitting room is panelled in golden oak; the suites, overlooking rooftops at the back, are discreet and delicious. Upholstered headboards, best feather duvets, Cotswolds wool throws, books, magazines and small buttoned armchairs... Enjoy a chilled prosecco by the garden's fountain before venturing out for supper; this lovely old town is awash with treats.

Ask about parking. Children over 10 welcome.

Rooms	1 double: £155-£175. 2 suites for 3: £165-£220. Extra bed/sofabed available £55 per person per night.
Meals	Pubs/restaurants nearby.
Closed	Rarely.

	Francesco & Caroline Totta The Glove House, 24 Oxford Street, Woodstock, Oxfordshire OX20 1TS
Tel	+44 (0)1993 813475
Email	info@theglovehouse.co.uk
Web	www.theglovehouse.co.uk

Entry 382   Map 8

Oxfordshire

Manor Farmhouse

This old Cotswold stone farmhouse is tucked down a quiet lane and was once part of the Blenheim estate. Helen and John are good humoured and have been happily welcoming guests for years. Find comfortable, traditional furnishings, lots of water colours and nothing overdone. The two doubles are in a private area of the house. Breakfast is at a polished oak table by the fire – cheerful wading birds from Italy sit at the window, pretty hand-painted Portuguese plates on the dresser. Wander in the lovely garden, have tea in the Victorian-style garden house or under an apple tree. Oxford is an easy drive and it's a stroll to the village pub.

Children over 2 welcome.

Rooms	2 doubles sharing shower (let to same party only): £80–£94. Singles £75.
Meals	Pub within walking distance.
Closed	Christmas.

Helen Stevenson
Manor Farmhouse,
Manor Road, Bladon, Woodstock,
Oxfordshire OX20 1RU
Tel +44 (0)1993 812168
Email helstevenson@hotmail.com
Web www.oxtowns.co.uk/woodstock/
manor-farmhouse/

Entry 383   Map 8

Oxfordshire

Oxford University

Oxford at your fingertips – at a fair price. In the city's ancient heart are Wadham and Keble; in leafy North Oxford is small friendly St Hugh's. Keble's sleeping quarters, functional though a good size, stand in stark contrast to the neo-gothic grandeur of its dining hall – pure Hogwarts! Wadham's hall, medieval, soaring, is yet more glorious – with top breakfasts. Its student-simple bedrooms are reached via crenellated cloisters and lovely walled gardens; ask for a room facing the beautiful quad. At St Hugh's: three residences (one historic), a student bar, romantic gardens and a 15-minute walk into town.

23 colleges in total.

Rooms	52 doubles, 121 twins: £69–£120. 12 family rooms for 3-4: £90–£165. 1052 singles: £35–£85.
Meals	Breakfast included. Keble: occasional supper £22.50. Restaurants 2-15 minutes' walk.
Closed	Mid-January to mid-March; May/June; October/November; Christmas. A few rooms available throughout year.

University Rooms
Oxford University,
Oxford, Oxfordshire
Web www.universityrooms.com/en/
city/oxford/home

Entry 384   Map 8

Oxfordshire

Willow Cottage

You are a short step from a village with an excellent pub (return across fields with a torch). Or treat yourself to dinner at Le Manoir aux Quat'Saisons. Katrina's delicious thatched cottage sits down a quiet lane. Through your own entrance find a guest dining room with armchairs by the old range, interesting prints and paintings, an eclectic mix of antiques and contemporary furniture. Bedrooms are warm, comfortable and stylish with views over the garden; shower rooms (not huge) are brand new and deeply smart. Breakfast, unhurried and bristling with local produce, sets walkers up for the Chiltern Way and the Ridgeway.

Rooms	2 doubles: £90.
	Singles £60.
Meals	Pubs/restaurants 0.5 miles.
Closed	Rarely.

Katrina Sheldon
Willow Cottage,
Denton,
Oxford,
Oxfordshire OX44 9JG
Tel   +44 (0)1865 874728
Email   katrinasheldon@aol.com
Web   www.willowcottage.info

🐈 🛜 🚂 ✕

Entry 385   Map 8

Oxfordshire

Rectory Farm

Come for the happy relaxed vibe, and Mary Anne's welcome with tea and homemade shortbread. There's a wood-burner in the guest sitting room, and bedrooms have beautiful arched mullion windows. The huge twin with ornate plasterwork overlooks the garden and church, the pretty double is cosier and both have good showers and big fluffy towels. Wake for an excellent Aga breakfast with eggs from the hens, garden and hedgerow compotes, home or locally produced bacon and homemade jams. A herd of Red Ruby Devon cattle are Robert's pride and joy; the family have farmed for generations and you can buy the beef. It's a treat to stay.

Minimum stay: 2 nights at weekends & high season.

Rooms	1 double, 1 twin: £86-£88.
	Singles £64.
Meals	Pub 2-minute walk.
Closed	Mid-December to mid-January.

Mary Anne Florey
Rectory Farm,
Northmoor, Witney,
Oxfordshire OX29 5SX
Tel   +44 (0)1865 300207
Mobile   +44 (0)7974 102198
Email   pj.florey@farmline.com
Web   www.oxtowns.co.uk/rectoryfarm

🐈 📧 🛜 🚲 ✕

Entry 386   Map 8

Oxfordshire

Star Cottage

Classic Cotswolds – from the cottagey stone walls to the flower-bright garden – and swathes of open countryside for cyclists and walkers. Step inside to hand-sewn fabrics, cute lampshades, country furniture, fresh flowers and calm, pretty bedrooms: Sally delights in details. She and Peter, a plant biologist, love their winding stone-walled garden with its herbs, climbers and medlar tree; its jelly appears at breakfast, alongside smoked haddock and local sausages. The pub (yards away) offers dinner, Burford market town is a ten-minute walk, Cheltenham and Oxford a half-hour drive. Or kind Peter will fetch from the station.

Rooms	1 double, 1 family room for 2; barn –1 family room for 2 with kitchen: £80–£110. Singles £70–£80.
Meals	Pubs/restaurants within walking distance.
Closed	Rarely.

Peter & Sally Wyatt
Star Cottage,
Meadow Lane, Fulbrook,
Burford,
Oxfordshire OX18 4BW
Tel   +44 (0)1993 822032
Email   wyattpeter@btconnect.com
Web   www.burfordbedandbreakfast.co.uk

Entry 387   Map 8

Oxfordshire

Fox House

In idyllic stonewalled little Holwell is a big stylish house on a corner – the old village school. Welcoming Susan, who is in the antiques business, gives you two super sitting rooms (one with a wood-burner, the other with a barn window and a heated flagstone floor), and three immaculately cosy bedrooms (one double downstairs) and serves delectable breakfasts on pretty blue china with jams and juices from the orchard. The garden is open and leads to pasture and horses, the countryside is delicious in every season and footpaths radiate from the door. The Cotswolds at its finest!

Minimum stay: 2 nights at weekends. Pets by arrangement.

Rooms	1 double; 1 double, 1 twin sharing bath (let to same party only): £100–£125. Singles £80.
Meals	Dinner, 3 courses, £25. Pubs/restaurants 2 miles.
Closed	Occasionally.

Susan Blacker
Fox House,
Holwell,
Burford,
Oxfordshire OX18 4JS
Tel   +44 (0)1993 823409
Email   foxhouse-rooms@btconnect.com
Web   www.foxhouse-rooms.co.uk

Entry 388   Map 8

Oxfordshire

Fyfield Manor

A fabulous house in Oxfordshire (once owned by Simon de Montfort) with vast water gardens, providing a most romantic setting. The Browns have added solar panels too. From the grand wood-panelled hall enter a beamed dining room with high-backed chairs, brass rubbings, wood-burner and pretty 12th-century arch; breakfast on eggs from the hens, garden fruit, organic bacon. Charming bedrooms have views, slippers and comfy sofas. Oxford Park & Ride is nearby, there's walking from the door and delightful Christine has wangled you a free glass of wine in the local pub if you walk or cycle to get there! Superb.

Children over 10 welcome.

Rooms	1 twin/double: £85–£90. 1 family room for 2-4 with sofabed & separate bath (£20 per extra person): £85–£90. Singles £60–£70.
Meals	Pubs within 1 mile.
Closed	Rarely.

Christine Brown
Fyfield Manor,
Benson,
Wallingford,
Oxfordshire OX10 6HA
Tel   +44 (0)1491 835184
Email   chris_fyfield@hotmail.co.uk
Web   www.fyfieldmanor.co.uk

Entry 389   Map 4

Rutland

Old Rectory

Jane Austen fans will swoon. This elegant 1740s village house was used as Mr Collins's 'humble abode' by the BBC: you breakfast in the beautiful dining room that was 'Mr Collins's hall', and you can sleep in 'Miss Bennett's bedroom'. Victoria is wonderful – feisty, fun and gregarious – and looks after you beautifully with White Company linen in chintzy old-fashioned bedrooms, a log fire in the drawing room, fruit from the lovely garden, homemade jams and Aga-cooked local bacon and eggs. Guests love it here. You are near to some pleasant market towns and good walking and riding country. Don't forget the smelling salts!

Rooms	1 double, 1 twin: £85. Singles £45.
Meals	Pubs within 3 miles.
Closed	Rarely.

Victoria Owen
Old Rectory,
Teigh, Oakham,
Rutland LE15 7RT
Tel   +44 (0)1572 787681
Mobile   +44 (0)7717 223678
Email   torowen@btinternet.com
Web   www.teighbedandbreakfast.co.uk

Entry 390   Map 9

Rutland

Old Hall Coach House

A rare and special setting; the grounds of the house meet the edge of Rutland Water, with far-reaching lake and church views. Inside: high ceilings, stone archways, antiques and a conservatory overlooking a stunning garden and croquet lawn. Comfortable bedrooms are traditional (the double has a brand new bathroom, the twin glorious views from both windows). Wake for an Aga-cooked spread of home-laid eggs, sausages and homemade marmalade. Rutland is a mini-Cotswolds of stone villages and gentle hills; Georgian Stamford, Burghley House and Belvoir Castle are all near. Cecilie is a well-travelled, interesting host.

Minimum stay: 2 nights at weekends.

Rooms	1 double; 1 twin with separate bath: £90. Singles from £40.
Meals	Dinner £30. Pub/restaurant 5-minute walk.
Closed	Occasionally.

Cecilie Ingoldby
Old Hall Coach House,
31 Weston Road,
Edith Weston, Oakham,
Rutland LE15 8HQ
Tel   +44 (0)1780 721504
Mobile +44 (0)7767 678267
Email   cecilieingoldby@aol.com
Web   www.oldhallcoachhouse.co.uk

Entry 391   Map 9

Shropshire

Tybroughton Hall

Off a winding country lane, surrounded by 40 acres of grassland, find a pretty white listed farmhouse and a wonderful welcome from Daisy, her family and two dear dogs. Step into the hallway with its polished antique table and bright garden flowers and you know you've made the right choice: this is a house to unwind in. After a day's hiking or biking, bliss to return to bedrooms cosy and comfortable — the traditional double with its country view or the large lovely twin. Breakfasts are worth getting up for: Tim makes the preserves, bees make the honey, hens lay the eggs and the pigs (five beauties!) provide the bacon.

Rooms	1 double; 1 twin with separate bath: £80-£100. Singles £50-£65.
Meals	Dinner £20-£25. Pub 4 miles.
Closed	Rarely.

Daisy Woodhead
Tybroughton Hall,
Tybroughton, Whitchurch,
Shropshire SY13 3BB
Tel   +44 (0)1948 780726
Mobile +44 (0)7850 395885
Email   daisy.woodhead@btinternet.com
Web   www.tybroughtonhall-
           bedandbreakfast.co.uk

Entry 392   Map 7

Shropshire

The Isle

History buffs and nature lovers rejoice. You drive through lion-topped stone pillars to a house built in 1682 (then extended) that stands in 800 acres enfolded by the river Severn. Charming Ros and Edward are down-to-earth and hands-on: eggs, bacon, ham, vegetables, and logs, come from the estate. Flop in front of a huge fire in the drawing room, homely with family antiques, big rug, magazines strewn on large tables. Peaceful bedrooms are large and light with pocket-sprung memory mattresses and snazzy upmarket bathrooms. Walk, fish, ride (there's a livery stable on site) and lap up the views – they're sublime.

Rooms	2 doubles, 1 twin: £75–£95. Singles £50–£60.
Meals	Packed lunch £5. Dinner £20. Pub/restaurant 4.3 miles.
Closed	Rarely.

	Ros & Edward Tate
	The Isle,
	Bicton,
	Shrewsbury,
	Shropshire SY3 8EE
Mobile	+44 (0)7776 257286
Email	ros@isleestate.co.uk
Web	www.the-isle-estate.co.uk

Entry 393   Map 7

Shropshire

Hardwick House

On a quiet street in the heart of Shrewsbury, this fine Georgian house has been in Lucy's family for generations. The dining room (oak panelling, a huge fireplace) is a lovely space to breakfast on locally sourced produce and homemade bread; vases of garden flowers are dotted all around this cheerful family home. Bedrooms are traditional and comfortable with pretty china tea cups; bathrooms are old-fashioned. The walled garden is fabulous; take tea in an 18th-century summerhouse. Birthplace of Darwin, this is a fascinating historic town; walk to the abbey, castle, theatre, festivals and great shops. Lucy is delightful.

Rooms	2 twin/doubles (a twin bedroom adjoining the Acorn room can be made available to form a large suite): £80–£95. Singles £55–£75.
Meals	Pubs/restaurants 150 yds.
Closed	Christmas & New Year.

	Lucy Whitaker
	Hardwick House,
	12 St John's Hill,
	Shrewsbury,
	Shropshire SY1 1JJ
Tel	+44 (0)1743 350165
Email	gilesandlucy@btinternet.com
Web	www.hardwickhouseshrewsbury.co.uk

Entry 394   Map 7

Shropshire

Brimford House

Beautifully tucked under the Breidden Hills, farm and Georgian farmhouse have been in the Dawson family for four generations. Views stretch all the way to the Severn; the simple garden does not try to compete. Bedrooms are spotless and fresh: a half-tester with rope-twist columns and Sanderson fabrics, a twin with Victorian wrought-iron bedsteads, a double with a brass bed, a big bathroom with a roll top bath. Liz serves you farm eggs and homemade preserves at breakfast, and there's a food pub just down the road. Sheep and cattle outdoors, a lovely black lab in, and wildlife walks from the door. Good value.

Shropshire

Whitton Hall

Down a long private drive with fields on either side is a lovely 18th-century farmhouse, elegant but not intimidating, with a sense of timelessness. A large open hallway with a warming fire is a comfortable, peaceful space for relaxing with a book. You breakfast in the dining room, on local muesli, bread, marmalades and jams, milk from their Jersey cows, soft fruit from their garden, sausages and bacon from down the road. Up a stunning staircase are peaceful, light and large bedrooms, with graceful, country house furniture and long views to glorious gardens. Unwind in the peace.

Children over 12 welcome.

Rooms	2 doubles, 1 twin: £70-£80. Singles £50-£60.
Meals	Packed lunch £4.50. Pub 3-minute walk.
Closed	Rarely.

Rooms	1 double, 1 twin/double, each with separate bath/shower: £85-£90. Singles from £50.
Meals	Supper £10-£20. Packed lunch available. Restaurant 1.5 miles.
Closed	Christmas & New Year.

	Liz Dawson
	Brimford House,
	Criggion,
	Shrewsbury,
	Shropshire SY5 9AU
Tel	+44 (0)1938 570235
Mobile	+44 (0)7801 100848
Email	info@brimford.co.uk
Web	www.brimford.co.uk

	Christopher & Gill Halliday & Kate Boscawen
	Whitton Hall,
	Westbury, Shrewsbury,
	Shropshire SY5 9RD
Tel	+44 (0)1743 884270
Mobile	+44 (0)7974 689629
Email	accommodation@whittonhall.com
Web	www.whittonhall.co.uk

Entry 395   Map 7

Entry 396   Map 7

Shropshire

Shropshire

North Farm

Peaceful green Shropshire and a stunning garden surround this classic white farmhouse. Chickens, ducks and geese are happily dotted about and the veg patch blooms. Tess and family look after you well. Bedrooms have flowery fabrics, tip-top linen, Lloyd Loom chairs and pretty tea trays. Wake for a delicious breakfast served on Portmeirion china: homemade marmalade, compotes, eggs from the hens, bacon and sausages from home-reared pigs. Lots to do close by: historic Shrewsbury, Ironbridge, Ludlow, Powis Castle – and the walks are a treat. Settle by the log-burner on your return: books to browse, a glass of wine... lovely.

Lawley House

A lovely calm sense of the continuity of history and family life emanates from this large, comfortable Victorian home. Jackie and Jim are delightful hosts and great fun. Bedrooms welcome you with flowers, duck down pillows – and stupendous views of the Stretton Hills, even from bed. Tea and cake on arrival in the spectacular conservatory set the scene for a spoiling stay, there are binoculars for bird-watchers and a drawing room with a huge variety of books. Awake to birdsong and a royal breakfast in the elegant dining room; enjoy the lushly planted garden – brimming with scents and seating spots. A charming and friendly place.

Children over 12 welcome.

Rooms	1 double, 1 twin; 1 double with separate bath: £85. Singles £55.
Meals	Pubs/restaurants 4-minute drive.
Closed	Rarely.

Rooms	1 double, 1 twin/double: £70-£80. Singles £55-£65. One-night weekend stay, small extra charge.
Meals	Pub/restaurant 1.5 miles.
Closed	Christmas & New Year.

	Tess Bromley North Farm, Eaton Mascot, Cross Houses, Shrewsbury, Shropshire SY5 6HF
Tel	+44 (0)1743 761031
Email	tessbromley@ymail.com
Web	www.northfarm.co.uk

	Jackie & Jim Scarratt Lawley House, Smethcott, Church Stretton, Shropshire SY6 6NX
Tel	+44 (0)1694 751236
Mobile	+44 (0)7980 331792
Email	jscarratt@onetel.com
Web	www.lawleyhouse.co.uk

Entry 397   Map 7

Entry 398   Map 7

Shropshire

Clun Farm House

A relaxed country feel here, with heavenly hills all around. Friendly hosts Susan and Anthony are enthusiastic collectors of country artefacts and have filled their listed 15th-century farmhouse with eye-catching things; the cowboy's saddle by the old range echoes Susan's roots. Bedrooms have aged and oiled floorboards, fun florals and bold walls; there is space for children in the extra bunk room; bathrooms are small and simple. Walk Offa's Dyke and the Shropshire Way; return to rescue hens wandering the garden, a warm smile and a glass of wine by the cosy wood-burner — before supper at one of the local pubs. Good value.

Horses welcome.

Rooms	1 double (extra bunk bed room); 1 twin/double with separate shower: £80. Singles by arrangement.
Meals	Packed lunch £4. Pubs/restaurants nearby.
Closed	Occasionally.

Anthony & Susan Whitfield
Clun Farm House,
High Street, Clun,
Craven Arms, Shropshire SY7 8JB
Tel   +44 (0)1588 640432
Mobile   +44 (0)7885 261391
Email   anthonyswhitfield0158@btinternet.com
Web   www.clunfarmhouse.co.uk

Entry 399   Map 7

Shropshire

Hopton House

Karen looks after her guests wonderfully and even runs courses on how to do B&B! Unwind in this fresh and uplifting converted granary with old beams, high ceilings and a sun-filled dining/sitting room overlooking the hills. The bedroom above has its own balcony; those in the barn, one up, one down, each with its own entrance, are as enticing: beautifully dressed beds, silent fridges, good lighting, homemade cakes. Bathrooms have deep baths (and showers) — from one you can lie back and gaze at the stars. Karen's breakfasts promise Ludlow sausages, home-laid eggs, fine jams and homemade marmalade.

Minimum stay: 2 nights. Over 16s welcome.

Rooms	1 double; barn - 2 doubles: £110-£120.
Meals	Restaurant 3 miles.
Closed	19-27 December.

Karen Thorne
Hopton House,
Hopton Heath,
Craven Arms,
Shropshire SY7 0QD
Tel   +44 (0)1547 530885
Email   info@shropshirebreakfast.co.uk
Web   www.shropshirebreakfast.co.uk

Entry 400   Map 7

Shropshire

Lower Buckton Country House

You are spoiled here in house-party style; Carolyn – passionate about Slow Food – and Henry, are born entertainers. Kick off with homemade cake in the drawing room with its oil paintings, antique furniture and old rugs; return for delicious nibbles when the lamps and wood-burner are flickering. Dine well at a huge oak table (home-reared pork, local cheeses, dreamy puddings), then nestle into the best linen and the softest pillows; bedrooms feel wonderfully restful. This is laid-back B&B: paddle in the stream, admire the stunning views, find a quiet spot with a good book. Great fun!

Minimum stay: 2 nights at weekends. Pets by arrangement.

Millstream Camp

A homely site in a foodie's paradise, this rustic, ramshackle set-up on the old millstream makes a lovely escape. The shepherd's hut serves as your sleeping quarters and the tipi, decked with old Indian saris, campaign trunks and a lacquered table, is your day space. Take it slow and get back to basics: lower a tin bucket into the water to chill a bottle of white, heat your bathwater over the fire (or use the outdoor gas shower) and don't be put off by the compost loo! Up at the house: breakfasts, dinners and cookery courses. The village of Leintwardine is a lovely half-hour walk away along the riverside; the Sun Inn is a must.

Minimum stay: 2 nights. Book through Sawday's Canopy & Stars online or by phone.

Rooms	2 doubles; 1 twin/double with separate bath: £100. Singles £75-£100. Dinner, B&B £85 per person. Extra bed/sofabed available £25-£45 per person per night.
Meals	Dinner, 4 courses, £35. BYO wine. Pub/restaurant 4 miles.
Closed	Rarely.

Rooms	Camp for 2: £90-£100.
Meals	In house breakfasts £15 per person. Breakfast basket from £10 per person.
Closed	October-March.

Henry & Carolyn Chesshire
Lower Buckton Country House,
Buckton, Leintwardine,
Shropshire SY7 0JU

Tel	+44 (0)1547 540532
Mobile	+44 (0)7960 273865
Email	carolyn@lowerbuckton.co.uk
Web	www.lowerbuckton.co.uk

Sawday's Canopy & Stars
Millstream Camp,
Lower Buckton Country House,
Buckton, Leintwardine,
Shropshire SY7 0JU

Tel	+44 (0)117 204 7830
Email	enquiries@canopyandstars.co.uk
Web	www.canopyandstars.co.uk/millstreamcamp

Walford Court

Come for a break from clock-watching and a spot of fresh air. Large bedrooms delight with the comfiest mattresses on king-size beds, scented candles, antiques, books, games and double-end roll top baths – one under a west facing window. Aga-cooked breakfasts include eggs from 'the ladies of the orchard'; candlelit dinners may be served outside on fine evenings. Wander through apple, plum and pear trees, find a motte and bailey, strike out for a long hike. Craig and Debbie are thoughtful and hugely keen on wildlife (you get binoculars) and this is the perfect place to bring a special person – and a bottle of champagne.

Older children by arrangement.

35 Lower Broad Street

You're almost at the bottom of the town, near the river and the bridge. Elaine's terraced Georgian cottage is spotless and cosy; her office doubles as a sitting area for guests with leather armchairs, TV and a desk space for workaholics. Upstairs are two good-sized doubles with a country crisp feel, king-size beds and a pretty blue and white bathroom. Walkers, shoppers, antique- and book-hunters can fill up on a superb breakfast of homemade potato scones, black pudding, organic eggs and good coffee before striding out to explore. This is excellent value, comfortable B&B and can be enjoyed without a car.

Pets by arrangement.

Rooms	1 double; 2 doubles, each with sitting room: £95. Extra bed/sofabed available £30 per person per night.
Meals	Dinner, 2-3 courses, £25-£31. Cold platters. Packed lunch available. Pubs/restaurants 1-3 miles.
Closed	Christmas & Boxing Day.

Rooms	1 double with sitting room & separate bath; 1 double sharing bath (let to same party only): £75. Singles £45.
Meals	Pubs/restaurants 100 yds.
Closed	Rarely.

Debbie & Craig Fraser
Walford Court,
Walford,
Leintwardine, Ludlow,
Shropshire SY7 0JT
Tel   +44 (0)1547 540570
Email   info@romanticbreak.com
Web   www.romanticbreak.com

Elaine Downs
35 Lower Broad Street,
Ludlow, Shropshire SY8 1PH
Tel   +44 (0)1584 876912
Mobile   +44 (0)7970 151010
Email   a.downs@tesco.net
Web   www.ludlowbedandbreakfast.
          blogspot.com

Entry 403   Map 7

Entry 404   Map 7

Rosecroft

A pretty, quiet, traditional house with charming owners, well-proportioned rooms, an elegant sitting room and not a trace of pomposity. Breakfasts are huge enough to set you up for the day: Pimhill organic muesli, smoked or unsmoked local bacon, black pudding, delicious jams. The garden is a delight to stroll through – in summer you can picnic here – while serious walkers are close to the Welsh borders. Bedrooms and bathrooms are polished to perfection; there are fresh flowers, plenty of interesting books, home-baked cakes when you arrive. The village has a super pub and Ludlow is close by.

Children over 12 welcome.

Rooms	1 double; 1 double with separate bath: £80–£90. Singles £65–£75.
Meals	Packed lunch £4. Pub 200 yds.
Closed	Rarely.

Gail Benson
Rosecroft,
Orleton, Ludlow,
Shropshire SY8 4HN

Tel	+44 (0)1568 780565
Email	gailanddavid@rosecroftorleton.co.uk
Web	www.rosecroftbedand breakfast.co.uk

Entry 405   Map 7

Timberstone Bed & Breakfast

The house is young and engaging – as are Tracey and Alex, new generation B&Bers. Come for charming bedrooms – two snug under the eaves, two in the smart oak-floored extension – roll top baths, pretty fabrics, thick white cotton, beams galore... and reflexology or a sauna in the garden studios; Tracey, once in catering, is a reflexologist. In the warm guest sitting/dining room find art, books, comfortable sofas and glass doors onto the terrace. Breakfasts are special with croissants and local eggs and bacon; suppers are delicious too, or you can head off to Ludlow and its clutch of Michelin stars.

Whole house available for self-catering.

Rooms	2 doubles, 1 double with sofabed: £85–£120. 1 family room for 4: £115–£120. Summerhouse - 1 double (summer only): £85–£120. Singles £50–£90.
Meals	Dinner, 3 courses, £25. Pubs/restaurants 5 miles.
Closed	Rarely.

Tracey Baylis & Alex Read
Timberstone Bed & Breakfast,
Clee Stanton, Ludlow,
Shropshire SY8 3EL

Tel	+44 (0)1584 823519
Mobile	+44 (0)7905 967263
Email	timberstone1@hotmail.com
Web	www.timberstoneludlow.co.uk

Entry 406   Map 7

Shropshire

Somerset

The Old Rectory

With its own spring water, horses, dogs and slow pace this Georgian rectory is comfortable country living at its best. Izzy and Andy are charming and interesting and give you scones and tea by the fire in a drawing room full of family photos, plump sofas and books. Elegant bedrooms have fluffy hot water bottles; smart bathrooms have scented lotions in pretty bottles, robes and slippers. Candlelit dinner will often be fish or game with garden vegetables; breakfast is local and leisurely with homemade granola and jams. There's a bootroom for muddy feet and paws, stabling and seven acres to roam.

Pets welcome, sleeping in bootroom.

Glen Lodge

Come for the food and Meryl and David's open house vibe. Their secluded Victorian home is spacious, comfy and surrounded by high banks of woodland. Enjoy delicious meals with an American slant using local venison, lamb, honey, cheeses and fish; they grow fruit and veg, make jams and serve tea and cakes every day – perfect brownies! Polished oak floors are dotted with oriental rugs and log fires burn. Wander the 21 acres, play croquet, sip a sunset drink on the terrace overlooking the wide bay. Exmoor and popular Porlock are on the doorstep; sandy beaches, harbours, boat trips – and a hot tub with an ice bucket – will keep you happy too.

Rooms	1 double, 1 twin/double; 1 double with separate bath: £80-£120. Singles from £65.	Rooms	3 doubles; 1 double, 1 twin, each with separate bath: £90-£95. Singles £60.
Meals	Dinner, 3 courses, £30. Packed lunch £10. Pubs 1.25-4 miles.	Meals	Dinner, 3 courses, £30. Supper £20. Packed lunch £8. Pub/restaurant 0.5 miles.
Closed	Rarely.	Closed	Rarely.

	Isabel Barnard The Old Rectory, Wheathill, Ludlow, Bridgnorth, Shropshire WV16 6QT		**Meryl Salter** Glen Lodge, Hawkcombe, Porlock, Somerset TA24 8LN
Tel	+44 (0)1746 787209	Tel	+44 (0)1643 863371
		Mobile	+44 (0)7786 118933
Email	enquiries@theoldrectorywheathill.com	Email	glenlodge@gmail.com
Web	www.theoldrectorywheathill.com	Web	www.glenlodge.net

Entry 407　Map 7

Entry 408　Map 2

Somerset

Higher Orchard

A little lane tumbles down to the centre of lovely old Dunster. The village is a two-minute walk, yet here you have open views of fields, sheep and sea. Exmoor footpaths start behind the house and Janet encourages explorers, by bike or on foot: ever helpful and kind, she is a local who knows the patch well. The 1860s house keeps its Victorian features, bedrooms are quiet and simple and the double has a view to Blue Anchor bay and Dunster Castle and church. All is homely, with stripped pine, cream curtains, fresh flowers, garden fruit and home-laid eggs for breakfast.

Rooms	1 double, 2 twin/doubles: £70. Singles from £35.
Meals	Packed lunch from £3.50. Restaurants 2-minute walk.
Closed	Christmas.

Janet Lamacraft
Higher Orchard,
30 St George's Street,
Dunster, Somerset TA24 6RS

Tel	+44 (0)1643 821915
Mobile	+44 (0)7896 464420
Email	lamacraft@higherorchard.fsnet.co.uk
Web	www.higherorchard-dunster.co.uk

Entry 409   Map 2

Somerset

The Old Priory

The 12th-century priory leans against its church, with a rustic gate, an enchanting garden, a tumble of flowers. Both house and hostess are dignified, unpretentious and friendly. Here are old oak tables, flagstones, wood panelling, higgledy-piggledy corridors and large bedrooms filled with family antiques. But an ancient English house in a sweet Somerset village needs a touch of pepper and cosmopolitan Jane adds her own special flair with eccentric touches here and there, and books and Horace the dog for company. Peaceful spots and scents in the garden, Dunster Castle above on the hill and walks from the door.

Rooms	1 twin, 1 four-poster; 1 double with separate shower: £100. Singles by arrangement.
Meals	Pubs/restaurants 5-minute walk.
Closed	Christmas.

Jane Forshaw
The Old Priory,
Priory Green,
Dunster,
Somerset TA24 6RY

Tel	+44 (0)1643 821540
Web	www.theoldpriory-dunster.co.uk

Entry 410   Map 2

Somerset

West Liscombe

Along deep Devon lanes, then down the long driveway to a pretty farmhouse surrounded by 20 acres of beautiful fields and woodland. Heaven! Inside is a comfortable cosy home. The grandfather clock tick-tocks in the sitting room, the silver shines, the log-burner glows, and the inviting guest bedrooms, with books and posies of flowers, are up a private staircase. Sit by the summerhouse and enjoy the glorious views; The Exmoor National Park is 500 yards away, the coast a short drive. Head out for fly and sea fishing, pony trekking, hawk walks, mountain biking, bird-watching – and Dulverton for its award-winning restaurants.

Pets by arrangement. Stabling available: good rides from the house onto Exmoor.

Rooms	1 double; 1 twin with separate bath: £80. Singles £45.
Meals	Dinner £25. Pub 5 miles.
Closed	Rarely.

Robert & Deborah Connell
West Liscombe,
Waddicombe,
Dulverton,
Somerset TA22 9RX
Tel   +44 (0)1398 341282
Email deborahconnell@btinternet.com

Entry 411   Map 2

Somerset

Cider Barn

Set back from the lane is a newly converted and refurbished barn. Elm boards have been removed for heated oak floors, fine old proportions remain, Louise's stunning living quarters spread under the beams and the bedrooms lie privately below on the ground floor. There's a sunny guest sitting room leading onto the garden, and delightful Louise, Cordon Bleu trained, serves breakfast at a long table by the wood-burner. You can walk through fields to the river or the hills, book an Indian head massage, stroll to the pub for supper. Bedrooms, one opening to the courtyard, are airy and peaceful with modern fabrics and cream walls. Lovely.

Pets may be considered.

Rooms	1 double, 1 twin/double: £75-£85. Singles £45-£65.
Meals	Pub 1 mile.
Closed	Rarely.

Louise Bancroft
Cider Barn,
Runnington,
Wellington,
Somerset TA21 0QW
Tel   +44 (0)1823 665533
Email louisegaddon@btinternet.com
Web   www.runningtonciderbarn.co.uk

Entry 412   Map 2

Somerset

Bashfords Farmhouse

A feeling of warmth and happiness pervades this exquisite 17th-century farmhouse in the Quantock Hills. The Ritchies love doing B&B – even after over 20 years! – and interiors have a homely feel with well-framed prints, natural fabrics, comfortable sofas, and a sitting room with inglenook, sofas and books. Bedrooms are pretty, fresh and large and look over the cobbled courtyard or open fields. Charles and Jane couldn't be nicer, know about local walks (the Macmillan Way runs by) and love to cook: local meat and game, tarte tatin, homemade bread and jams. A delightful garden rambles up the hill; the pub is just a minute away.

Somerset

Causeway Cottage

Robert and Lesley are ex-restaurateurs, so guests heap praise on their food, most of which is sourced from a local butcher and fishmonger; charming Lesley is an author, runs cookery courses and once taught at Prue Leith's. This is the perfect, pretty Somerset cottage, with an apple orchard and views to the church across a cottage garden and a field. The bedrooms are light, restful and have a country-style simplicity with their green check bedspreads, white walls and antique pine furniture; guests have their own comfortable sitting room. Easy access to the M5 yet with a rural feel. Very special.

Children over 10 welcome.

Rooms	1 twin/double; 2 twin/doubles, each with separate bath/shower: £75. Singles £45.
Meals	Dinner £27.50. Supper £22.50. Pub 75 yds.
Closed	Rarely.

Old favourite

Rooms	1 double, 2 twins: £78-£85. Singles by arrangement.
Meals	Dinner from £28. Pub/restaurant 0.75 miles.
Closed	Christmas.

Charles & Jane Ritchie
Bashfords Farmhouse,
West Bagborough,
Taunton,
Somerset TA4 3EF
Tel   +44 (0)1823 432015
Email   info@bashfordsfarmhouse.co.uk
Web   www.bashfordsfarmhouse.co.uk

Lesley & Robert Orr
Causeway Cottage,
West Buckland, Taunton,
Somerset TA21 9JZ
Tel   +44 (0)1823 663458
Mobile +44 (0)7703 412827
Email   orrs@causewaycottage.co.uk
Web   www.causewaycottage.co.uk

Somerset

Frog Street Farmhouse

Through a pastoral landscape, past green paddocks and fine thoroughbreds, to a beautiful longhouse set in pretty secluded gardens surrounded by 130 acres. Its heart dates back to 1436 and its renovation is remarkable, highlighting beamed ceilings, Jacobean panelling and open fireplaces. Louise and David, brimful of enthusiasm for both house and guests, give you four exquisite bedrooms in French country style, one with its own sitting room – very romantic. Louise happily does evening meals and hosts small house parties with ease. After a day out, return to great leather sofas and a wood-burning stove. What value!

Somerset

29 Strawberry Bank

Henrietta's eye for design is evident in this beautifully renovated 19th-century cottage. Squashy sofas, ethnic baskets, pictures from her travels and garden views... best enjoyed over local or organic sausages and double yolkers (not guaranteed!). You're close to the centre of a charming market town, yet within minutes of the countryside; see it from your bedroom window. Pour yourself a cup of tea from floral china, pad across golden boards, clamber into a huge bed with a dramatic quilt. Delightful Henrietta is happy for you to share her sitting room with wood-burner, and her sunny secluded garden – perfect for a sundowner.

Rooms	3 doubles: £90-£120.
	1 family room for 4: £120-£160.
	Singles £80-£120.
	Extra bed/sofabed available £15 per person per night.
Meals	Dinner, 3 courses, £27.50 (for parties of 8 or more).
	Pubs within 2.5 miles.
Closed	Christmas.

Rooms	1 double: £85.
Meals	Dinner, 3 courses, £25.
	Pubs/restaurants 5-minute walk.
Closed	Rarely.

	Louise & David Farrance
	Frog Street Farmhouse,
	Hatch Beauchamp, Taunton,
	Somerset TA3 6AF
Tel	+44 (0)1823 481883
Mobile	+44 (0)7811 700789
Email	frogstreet@hotmail.com
Web	www.frogstreet.co.uk

	Henrietta Van den Bergh
	29 Strawberry Bank,
	High Street,
	Ilminster,
	Somerset TA19 9AW
Tel	+44 (0)1460 54394
Mobile	+44 (0)7973 838452
Email	info@hvdbphoto.com

Entry 415   Map 2

Entry 416   Map 2

Somerset

Huntstile Organic Farm

Catapult yourself into country life in the foothills of the Quantocks; make that connection between the rolling green hills, the idyllic munching animals and the delicious, organic food on your plate; here it is understood. Lizzie and John buzz with energy in this gorgeous old house with Jacobean panelling and huge walk-in fireplaces, two sitting rooms, sweet and cosy rustic bedrooms, a café, and a restaurant serving their own meat, eggs and vegetables. House parties, weddings, team building, a stone circle for hand-fasting ceremonies – all come under Lizzie's happy and efficient umbrella. And there are woodlands to roam.

Rooms	7 doubles: £60–£120. Apartment - 1 double, 1 twin with sitting room: £62–£150. 3 family rooms for 4: £85–£150. Singles £55–£60.
Meals	Dinner, 3 courses, £22.50–£27. Packed lunch from £6.50. Pub/restaurant 3 miles.
Closed	Rarely.

Lizzie Myers
Huntstile Organic Farm,
Goathurst,
Bridgwater,
Somerset TA5 2DQ
Tel   +44 (0)1278 662358
Email   huntstile@live.co.uk
Web   www.huntstileorganicfarm.co.uk

Entry 417   Map 2

Somerset

Blackmore Farm

Come for atmosphere and architecture: the Grade I-listed manor farmhouse is remarkable. Medieval stone, soaring beams, ecclesiastical windows, giant logs blazing in the Great Hall. Ann and Ian look after guests and busy dairy farm with equal enthusiasm. Furnishings are comfortable, décor is rich, bedrooms are cavernous and the oak-panelled suite (with secret stairway) takes up an entire floor. The rooms in the stables are simpler with green oak and wide doorways. Breakfast is generous and organic and eaten at the 20-foot polished table in baronial splendour. Visit the calves in the dairy and don't miss the excellent farm shop.

Rooms	1 double, 1 four-poster, 1 suite for 2; Courtyard stables – 1 double, 1 twin: £100. Singles £50.
Meals	Occasional dinner for parties. Pubs/restaurants 5-minute walk.
Closed	Rarely.

Ann Dyer
Blackmore Farm,
Cannington,
Bridgwater,
Somerset TA5 2NE
Tel   +44 (0)1278 653442
Email   dyerfarm@aol.com
Web   www.dyerfarm.co.uk

Entry 418   Map 2

Somerset

Pool House

Step into the generous hall, where a quirky gull made of driftwood greets you. Paul and Tricia's house has a friendly heart and you feel instantly at home. All is gleaming and artistic: bedrooms have gorgeous fabrics, garden posies, the best linen, and a chaise longue or easy chairs; en suite bathrooms are tiny but perfect; the dining room is elegant with a glass-topped table and a regal horse sculpture. Sun yourself in the sweet garden; the pool (tucked between barn and pool house) provides a sheltered spot with a Mediterranean vibe. Head out for walks, music festivals, Glastonbury... then back to a fire-warmed drawing room.

Minimum stay: 2 nights at weekends.

Rooms	2 doubles; 1 double with separate bath/shower: £100-£120. Singles £88-£108.
Meals	Pubs within 5 miles.
Closed	Occasionally.

2014/15
Sawday's
PUB AWARD

Most praised breakfast

Paul & Tricia Canham
Pool House,
4 Higher Road,
Woolavington, Bridgwater,
Somerset TA7 8DY
Tel   +44 (0)1278 683756
Email   enquiries@poolhousewoolavington.co.uk
Web   www.poolhousewoolavington.com

Entry 419   Map 2

Somerset

Parsonage Farm

The Quantock Hills are wonderful for walking and cycling, with the Coleridge Way starting down the lane. In this 17th-century farmhouse relaxed hosts give you easy comfort with quarry floors, books, a cosy log-fired sitting room and spacious bedrooms with tranquil country views. Suki, from Vermont, has turned a stable into a studio — her pots and paintings add charm to the décor. Breakfast by the fire is a feast: homemade bread and jam, eggs from the hens, juice from the orchard, porridge and pancakes with maple syrup. Relax in the beautiful walled kitchen garden; there's an outdoor wood-fired pizza oven too!

Children over 2 welcome.

Rooms	1 double, 1 twin/double, each with extra sofabed; 1 double with separate bath: £65-£85. Singles £50-£70.
Meals	Supper £11. Dinner, 2-3 courses, £20-£25. Pub/restaurant 1 mile.
Closed	Christmas.

Susan Lilienthal
Parsonage Farm,
Over Stowey, Nether Stowey,
Somerset TA5 1HA
Tel   +44 (0)1278 733237
Mobile +44 (0)7928 368836
Email   suki@parsonfarm.co.uk
Web   www.parsonfarm.co.uk

Entry 420   Map 2

Somerset

Somerset

Church House

Feel happy in this warm Georgian rectory with sweeping views over gardens, seaside homes and the dramatic Bristol channel. Tony and Jane are great fun, enormously generous and love what they do. Bedrooms are large, pristine and indulgent with goose down duvets as soft as a cloud, swish modern bathrooms, huge towels and thoughtful extras like fluffy hot water bottles and scrumptious biscuits. Breakfasts are a grand feast of eggs from their hens, organic sausages and homemade preserves, all served on delightful china at a long mahogany table. Take the whole house and be cosseted – great for large gatherings.

Crook's View

Crook's View is on Victoria and Andy's peaceful smallholding, so you can drop off whilst literally counting sheep (and goats). Simple decoration, with enamel mugs hanging from old hooks, sheep wool rugs and a wood-burner make the hut homely and warm all year round – and the comfy double bed folds into a daytime settee. Breakfast is provided and there's a private area just outside with a fire-pit, tripod and everything you need to sit out and cook on the open fire. A modern kitchen and bathroom in the farmhouse annexe is 150 yards away. A good spot for walking with views down to the coast, Steep Holm Island, and Crook Peak.

Minimum stay: 2 nights. Book through Sawday's Canopy & Stars online or by phone.

Rooms	4 doubles, 1 twin: £85. Singles from £65.		Rooms	Shepherd's hut for 2: £80.
Meals	Pubs 400 yds.		Meals	Breakfast included
Closed	Rarely.		Closed	Never.

Jane & Tony Chapman
Church House,
27 Kewstoke Road, Kewstoke,
Weston-super-Mare,
Somerset BS22 9YD
Tel   +44 (0)1934 633185
Email   churchhouse@kewstoke.net
Web   www.churchhousekewstoke.co.uk

Sawday's Canopy & Stars
Crook's View,
Woodspring Farm, Kewstoke,
Weston-super-Mare,
Somerset BS22 9YU
Tel   +44 (0)117 204 7830
Email   enquiries@canopyandstars.co.uk
Web   www.canopyandstars.co.uk/
crooksview

Entry 421   Map 2

Entry 422   Map 2

Somerset

Stonebridge

A country house with scrumptious food, a friendly black labrador and croquet on the lawn. When their daughters flew the nest, Liz and Richard opened an independent wing of their listed house: perfect for families and couples. You have two pretty bedrooms (one up, one down) with country furniture and super bathrooms. In winter, a wood-burner keeps your little sitting room cosy; in summer, laze in a sea of flowers. You feast on local eggs, homemade bread and delicious dinners with garden veg. Just off the village road, it's close to Bristol airport, the M5 and Wells. And with hosts this friendly you can't go wrong.

Rooms	1 double, 1 twin/double: £75-£85. Singles £55-£60.
Meals	Dinner, 2-3 courses, £20-£25. Pub 2 miles.
Closed	Christmas.

Richard & Liz Annesley
Stonebridge,
Wolvershill Road,
Banwell,
Somerset BS29 6DR
Tel   +44 (0)1934 823518
Email   liz.annesley@talktalk.net
Web   www.stonebridgebandb.co.uk

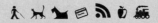

Entry 423   Map 3

Somerset

Burrington Farm

High in the Mendips, Ros and Barry's 15th-century longhouse is blissfully rural, yet Bristol, Bath and Wells are close. Their wonderful house glows: rugs and flagstones, books, burnished beams, paintings and fine old furniture. Guests have a cosy sitting room and bedrooms are charming; you'll need to be nimble to negotiate ancient steps and stairs. For those who prefer a bit more privacy there's a lovely family room in a separate green oak barn — stunningly converted and with views over the enchanting garden. Wake for a locally sourced breakfast round a big table. A friendly, relaxed and special place.

Rooms	1 double; 1 double, 1 twin sharing bath (let to same party only): £85-£120. Barn - 1 family room for 4: £100-£120. Singles £65.
Meals	Pub 10-minute walk.
Closed	Christmas.

Barry & Ros Smith
Burrington Farm,
Burrington,
Somerset BS40 7AD
Tel   +44 (0)1761 462127
Mobile   +44 (0)7825 237144
Email   unwind@burringtonfarm.co.uk
Web   www.unwindatburringtonfarm.co.uk

Entry 424   Map 3

Somerset

Harptree Court

A gorgeous Georgian house that has been in
Charles' family for generations. Inside all is
elegant and grand, but this is very much a
family home; there's a welcoming log fire in
the hall and Charles and Linda are charming
and relaxed. The interior gleams with
flowers, art and polished wood, and the
dining room looks onto the beautiful garden;
warm, sunny bedrooms have delicate fabrics,
china pieces and antiques, and bathrooms
sparkle. An excellent breakfast of garden
fruits, local honey and sausages sets you up
for a walk in the grounds: acres of parkland
with ponds, an ancient bridge, carpets of
spring flowers. A peaceful delight.

Rooms	3 doubles, 1 twin/double: £130. Singles £80.
Meals	Pub 300 yds.
Closed	December/January.

Linda & Charles Hill
Harptree Court,
East Harptree, Bristol,
Somerset BS40 6AA
Tel +44 (0)1761 221729
Mobile +44 (0)7970 165576
Email handb@harptreecourt.co.uk
Web www.harptreecourt.co.uk

Entry 425   Map 3

Somerset

Harptree Court Treehouse & Yurt

The stately grandeur of Harptree Court has
overflowed into a magical treetop escape and
a three-pod yurt in the grounds, packed with
antiques, a roll top bath and more. (What
would a traditional nomad of the Mongolian
Steppes have made of the dishwasher, hot
running water and WiFi?) Star-gaze from
your bed, throw open shutters in the
morning, wander through to the bathroom
pod, relax in the beautiful lounge. Pick the
treehouse and laze on the balcony of your
leafy perch, play chess or conjure a feast in the
kitchen. If you don't fancy cooking, excellent
pub food is a few hundred yards away. Rolling
countryside at your feet, and Bath is nearby.

*Minimum stay: 3 nights. Book through Sawday's
Canopy & Stars online or by phone.*

Rooms	Treehouse for 2: £250-£400. Yurt for 2: £115-£210.
Meals	Breakfast from £12.50 per person.
Closed	Yurt closed October-March, treehouse rarely.

Sawday's Canopy & Stars
Harptree Court Treehouse & Yurt,
Harptree Court, East Harptree,
Bristol, Somerset BS40 6AA
Tel +44 (0)117 204 7830
Email enquiries@canopyandstars.co.uk
Web www.canopyandstars.co.uk/
harptreecourt

Entry 426   Map 3

Somerset

The Post House

Four centuries old, this was Chewton Mendip's post office; now it's a delightful home with a sunny feel. Smiling, stylish Karen loves meeting new people – make the most of her and John's knowledge of Bath, Bristol and Wells. After a day's exploring, return to fresh, lovely bedrooms and bathrooms; the suite, limewashed, pretty and private, has oak floors and a fridge. Huge flagstones cover the oldest part downstairs, there's a big stone fireplace in the Old Bakery Cottage and the odd low beam; pale walls display charming sketches from an artist friend, much of the furniture is French country, and a Gallic-rustic mood prevails.

Rooms	1 double: £80–£120. The Old Bakery Cottage: 1 double: £80–£120. 1 suite for 2 with sitting room: £80–£120.
Meals	Pub 0.5 miles.
Closed	Rarely.

Karen Price
The Post House,
Bath Way,
Chewton Mendip, Wells,
Somerset BA3 4NS
Tel   +44 (0)1761 241704
Email   info@theposthousebandb.co.uk
Web   www.theposthousebandb.co.uk

Entry 427   Map 3

Somerset

Beryl

A historical gem set in 13 acres of beautiful gardens and parkland. This stunning piece of gothic architecture, brimming with fine antiques, offers a wealth of luxury, warmth and welcome. Arrive for tea and cake and feel instantly relaxed in Holly and Mary-Ellen's cherished family home. Each unique bedroom has a talking point – an extravagantly draped four-poster, an original bath clad in mahogany reached by a tiny staircase. Wake to the aroma of locally sourced bacon – Aga-cooked breakfasts are a feast. The rose-filled garden is yours to enjoy; in warmer months dive into the refreshing outdoor pool while children have fun in the play area.

Chair lift to first floor. Byworth & Nowell jewellery boutique in the Coach House.

Rooms	6 doubles, 3 twin/doubles, 1 twin; 1 double with separate shower: £100–£160. 2 family rooms for 3 (one room with single bed, 2 with sofabeds): £160–£220. Singles £80–£100.
Meals	Pubs/restaurants within 1 mile. Kitchenette available.
Closed	Christmas.

Holly & Mary-Ellen Nowell
Beryl,
Hawkers Lane,
Wells,
Somerset BA5 3JP
Tel   +44 (0)1749 678738
Email   stay@beryl-wells.co.uk
Web   www.beryl-wells.co.uk

Entry 428   Map 3

Somerset

Stoberry House

Super swish B&B in this old coach house surrounded by 26 acres of parkland, but within walking distance of Wells; Frances has thought of everything and has oodles of local knowledge. Bedrooms are sumptuous and differently styled; two are in the main house, and there's one little love nest in a richly clad studio. Bathrooms are vamped up and spacious. There is a huge choice at breakfast: fresh fruit, porridge, boiled eggs with soldiers, prunes and berries, ham and salami, pancakes with grilled bacon, whatever you desire. Work it off with a stroll around the gorgeous gardens: the scents, sculptures and views are fantastic.

Rooms	1 double, 1 twin/double: £90–£135. Studio: 1 double & sitting room: £125–£166. Singles £65–£135.
Meals	Supplement for cooked breakfast. Pubs/restaurants 0.5 miles.
Closed	Rarely.

	Frances Young Stoberry House, Stoberry Park, Wells, Somerset BA5 3LD
Tel	+44 (0)1749 672906
Email	stay@stoberry-park.co.uk
Web	www.stoberry-park.co.uk

Entry 429   Map 3

Somerset

Coach House

Take a glass of wine to your private courtyard and absorb the peace; or picnic in the gardens. In the hamlet of Dulcote, a mile from Wells, is your own two-storey, two-bedroom coach house flooded with light, full of character and the latest mod cons. Downstairs, a black and white zebra theme plays; upstairs, white walls, crisp linen, high beams, a glimpse of Wells Cathedral and views that reach to the Mendips. Friendly Chumba the dog greets you and your (well-behaved) waggy friend. Karen leaves eggs from her hens and other goodies in your fridge so you can breakfast in your jim-jams. A delightful B&B for nature lovers and dog-walkers.

Minimum stay: 2 nights. Over 12s welcome.

Rooms	Annexe – 1 double, 1 twin, sharing sitting room, sofabeds & kitchen (let to same party only): £95. Singles £90. Whole house £95 per night for 2 plus £30 per extra person per night.
Meals	Pubs within 2 miles.
Closed	Rarely.

	Karen Smallwood Coach House, Little Fountains, Dulcote, Wells, Somerset BA5 3NU
Tel	+44 (0)1749 678777
Mobile	+44 (0)7789 778880
Email	stay@littlefountains.co.uk
Web	www.littlefountains.co.uk

Entry 430   Map 3

Somerset

Hillview Cottage

Catherine is a wonderful host: warm-spirited, cultured and humorous. She knows the area well, and is happy to show you around Wells Cathedral – she's an official guide. This is a comfy tea-and-cakes family home with rugs on wooden floors and antique quilts. Bedrooms have a French feel, the bathroom an armchair for chatting and there's a friendly sitting room with an open fire. The stunning vaulted breakfast room has huge beams, an old Welsh dresser with hand painted mugs, a cheerful red Aga, a wood-burner to sit by and glorious views; breakfasts are superb. Guests love it here; excellent value too.

Rooms	1 twin/double; 1 twin sharing bath with twin/double (let to same party only): £75-£80. Singles from £55.
Meals	Pubs 5-minute walk.
Closed	Rarely.

	Michael & Catherine Hay
	Hillview Cottage,
	Paradise Lane, Croscombe,
	Wells, Somerset BA5 3RN
Tel	+44 (0)1749 343526
Mobile	+44 (0)7801 666146
Email	cathyhay@yahoo.co.uk
Web	www.hillviewcottage.me.uk

Entry 431   Map 3

Somerset

Upper Crannel Farm Barn

Your views, across sheep and the lush Somerset Levels, reach to both Glastonbury and Wells; birds wing across a vast, silent sky. Phoebe has created a magical place: up you climb to the first floor of the barn, into a huge sitting room with a vast medieval painted fireplace. Each room is a work of art, with stacks of it on the walls – the kitchen is handsome and seductive, the bedroom is generous and richly clad. Breakfast will be left for you to cook when you want, you can walk across fields to climb Glastonbury Tor, and Wells is just five miles. This house is a treat, and Phoebe is too.

Minimum stay: 2 nights.

Rooms	1 double with sitting room & kitchen (extra bedrooms available): £120.
Meals	Pubs/restaurants 2.5 miles.
Closed	Rarely.

	Phoebe Judah
	Upper Crannel Farm Barn,
	Glastonbury,
	Somerset BA6 9AD
Tel	+44 (0)1458 831758
Email	phoebe.judah@btinternet.com

Entry 432   Map 3

Somerset

Westbrook House

David is an interior designer; Keith a garden designer – hence this blend of good taste and style in a revamped 1870s house with acres of beautiful grounds blending seamlessly with open countryside. Wander through a young orchard, spot unusual plants, sit on stone benches or a sunny patio. Inside, every object has a story (your hosts are full of smiles and stories too): tapestries from India, a mirrored cabinet from an officer's mess, ornate brass lanterns. Light floods into the dining room as you breakfast on local treats – all the while absorbing the peace of this tranquil hamlet, where cows amble down the lane.

Rooms	1 double, 1 twin; 1 double with separate bath: £100. Singles £65–£80.
Meals	Dinner £30. Pub/restaurant 4 miles.
Closed	Rarely.

Keith Anderson & David Mendel
Westbrook House,
West Bradley, Glastonbury,
Somerset BA6 8LS
Tel +44 (0)1458 850604
Email mail@westbrook-bed-breakfast.co.uk
Web www.westbrook-bed-breakfast.co.uk

Entry 433   Map 3

Somerset

Studio Farrows

An appealingly quirky studio hidden in the luxuriant garden of artists Paul and Tracey. They live in the main house and are relaxed, helpful hosts. They'll arrange a swim in a friend's walled pool, and all sorts of courses from baking to glass blowing; or you can simply relax in this comfy, peaceful retreat… You have a big living space with giant wood-burner, kitchen, books, eclectic art and furniture (including an Anglia!); bedrooms are colourful, bathrooms sleek. Breakfast is a continental feast: Parma ham, cheese, pastries, garden fruits, granola and more. Sit out on the veranda, light the fire baskets, gaze at the stars. Bliss.

Pets by arrangement. Minimum stay: 2 nights.

Rooms	2 doubles with sitting room & kitchen: £95–£114. Extra bedroom with sofabed £30 per person.
Meals	Dinner may be available on request.
Closed	Rarely.

Tracey Baker
Studio Farrows,
Aller, Langport,
Somerset TA10 0QW
Tel +44 (0)1458 252599
Email tracey@studiofarrows.com
Web www.studiofarrows.com

Entry 434   Map 3

Somerset

The Lynch Country House

Peace and privacy at this immaculate Regency house in a Somerset valley. First-floor bedrooms are traditionally grand, attic rooms are smaller but pretty; those in the coach house have a more modern feel. Rich colours prevail, fabrics are flowery and linen best Irish. You'll feel as warm as toast and beautifully looked after. A stone staircase goes right to the top where the observatory lets in cascading light; the flagged hall, high ceilings, long windows and private tables at breakfast create a country-house hotel feel. The lovely garden has black swans on a lake, hundreds of trees and a terrace from which to drink it all in.

Rooms	1 double, 1 four-poster; 1 double with separate bath & extra single bed; 2 twin/doubles, each with extra single bed: £80-£115. Coach House: 2 doubles, 2 twins/doubles: £90. Singles £70-£95.
Meals	Pubs 5-minute walk.
Closed	Rarely.

Mike McKenzie
The Lynch Country House,
4 Behind Berry,
Somerton,
Somerset TA11 7PD
Tel   +44 (0)1458 272316
Email   enquiries@thelynchcountryhouse.co.uk
Web   www.thelynchcountryhouse.co.uk

Entry 435   Map 3

Somerset

Barwick Farm House

A 17th-century farmhouse sitting in organically managed land dotted with hens, horses and Dorset sheep. Angela is delightful and has worked wonders with gorgeous limewash colours in every room. Step into a beautiful hall to find a house full of ancient elm boards, colourful rugs, open fires, books, china and pots of flowers. Pretty bedrooms have good linen on comfy beds; the downstairs one has its own breakfast room and garden entrance (perfect for the disabled), and a big copper tub; one bathroom is cleverly clad in reclaimed grain store panels. Wake to birdsong and sizzling local bacon; excellent walking and cycling start from the door.

Rooms	2 doubles, 1 twin/double: £80-£90. Singles £50-£60.
Meals	'Early Bird' packed breakfasts also available. Restaurant 100 yds.
Closed	Rarely.

Angela Nicoll
Barwick Farm House,
Barwick, Yeovil,
Somerset BA22 9TD
Tel   +44 (0)1935 410779
Mobile   +44 (0)7967 385307
Email   info@barwickfarmhouse.co.uk
Web   www.barwickfarmhouse.co.uk

Entry 436   Map 3

Somerset

Church Byres

Meander down lanes and tree-lined drive to a courtyard flanked by farm buildings: four solid stone farm byres. One side is your hosts', the other is yours, so you have your own wing; it's great value for a family. Peter and Jenny, attentive and fun, can whip up supper (perhaps lamb cutlets, fish pie, cannelloni), or direct you to some good local country pubs. It's a treat to come home to your own wood-burner and deep sofas, white bathrobes and muted tones: the mood is warmly contemporary. Take a chilled beer from your own fridge to the guest terrace by the front lawn – lovely!

Children under 12 half price.

Rooms	1 twin; 1 double sharing bath (let to same party only): £80-£90. Singles £50.
Meals	Supper £30. Pubs/restaurants 3 miles.
Closed	Christmas.

	Jenny Cox
	Church Byres,
	South Barrow,
	Yeovil,
	Somerset BA22 7LN
Mobile	+44 (0)7765 175058
Email	bookings@somerset-bb.co.uk
Web	www.somerset-bb.co.uk

Entry 437   Map 3

Somerset

Yarlington House

A mellow Georgian manor surrounded by impressive parkland, romantic rose gardens, apple tree pergola and laburnum walk. Your hosts are friendly and flexible artists with an eye for quirky detail; Carolyn's embroideries are everywhere. Something to astound at every turn: fine copies of 18th-century wallpapers, elegant antiques, statues with hats atop and tremendous art. Traditional bedrooms with glorious garden views and proper 50s bathrooms have a faded charm. Enjoy a full English breakfast, grape juice from the glasshouse vines, log fires and lovely local walks. Surprising, unique.

Pets by arrangement.

Rooms	1 double, 1 twin: £140. Singles £70.
Meals	Pubs/restaurants within 0.5 miles.
Closed	25 July - 23 August.

	Carolyn & Charles de Salis
	Yarlington House,
	Yarlington,
	Wincanton,
	Somerset BA9 8DY
Tel	+44 (0)1963 440344
Email	carolyn.desalis@yarlingtonhouse.com
Web	www.yarlingtonhouse.com

Entry 438   Map 3

New Entry

Yarlington Yurt

In the grounds of dignified Yarlington House, the equally refined Yarlington Yurt is tucked behind the walled garden (where there's an honesty box for fruit and veg in season). Decorated in a style described as 'late 18th-century with French influence', with a twin-bedded pod curtained off from the double, it comes decked with rugs, lamps, and paintings, and fairy lights set in the canopy; the compost loo is a dash outside. The wood-burner belts out the heat, while next door's pavilion with kitchen and shower room is fully plumbed-in. Cook here, or head up to the house for breakfast by arrangement.

Bookings start on a Mon or Fri in high season and for a minimum of 2 nights at other times. Book through Sawday's Canopy & Stars online or by phone.

Cary Place

In the heart of town yet sitting in three acres... a honey-stoned gem. Debra's home has an open-house vibe — helped along perfectly by Humphrey the terrier. Step into a generous hall to find an elegant sitting room for guests, polished floors, original art and gorgeous colours in every room. Bedrooms are a delight: sofas at the end of sleigh beds, tip-top linen and pretty fabrics. Hop down for breakfast in the airy dining room, or out on a sunny terrace: fruits from the orchard, croissants, organic sausages and bacon. Come and go as you want — walk to cafés, delis and independent shops; Glastonbury and Stourhead are close.

Extra room available.

Rooms	Yurt for 4: £95–£145.
Meals	Breakfast from £10 per person.
Closed	Never.

Rooms	1 double, 1 twin; 1 double with separate bath: £105.
Meals	Pubs/restaurants within walking distance.
Closed	Rarely.

	Sawday's Canopy & Stars
	Yarlington Yurt,
	Yarlington House, Yarlington,
	Wincanton Somerset BA9 8DY
Tel	+44 (0)117 204 7830
Email	enquiries@canopyandstars.co.uk
Web	www.canopyandstars.co.uk/ yarlingtonyurt

	Debra Henderson
	Cary Place,
	4 Upper High Street,
	Castle Cary,
	Somerset BA7 7AR
Tel	+44 (0)1963 359269
Email	info@caryplace.co.uk
Web	www.caryplace.co.uk

Entry 439   Map 3

Entry 440   Map 3

Somerset

Ansford Park Cottage

An old farmworker's house, modernised and freshly spruced, stands proud in verdant countryside. Long views from the clipped garden drift into the distance; warm Sue (plus cute Jack Russells) greets you. You sleep in the extension to the front of the house; one bedroom has valley views, the other has views over the Mendips. Both have comfy beds, books, homely touches and peacefulness. Breakfast is a leisurely affair of local bacon and eggs. Tramp off on an inspiring walk – Leland trail, Macmillan Way – you're spoilt for choice. Escape London by train (95 minutes) – collection from the station can be arranged.

Pets by arrangement.

Rooms	1 twin/double; 1 twin/double with separate bath: £75.
Meals	Dinner £25. Packed lunch £5. Pub/restaurant 1 mile.
Closed	Christmas & rarely.

Susan Begg
Ansford Park Cottage,
Ansford Park,
Maggs Lane, Castle Cary,
Somerset BA7 7JJ
Tel   +44 (0)1963 351066
Email   beggsusan@tiscali.co.uk
Web   www.ansfordparkcottage.co.uk

Entry 441   Map 3

Somerset

Culverwell House

Cynthia and Barry's friendly old house is tucked down a little track in this sleepy village. Step into your own sitting room, with mezzanine bedroom upstairs: eclectic art, 60s and 70s pieces, huge funky mobile, a comfy bed with pretty Indian cover, pots of flowers on window sills (and snoozing Cortina the cat perhaps). Breakfast where you want: sitting room, pretty dining room next door, vine-clad conservatory or out in the flowery garden in a sunny spot. Delicious choices – garden grapes and figs, bagels with bacon or smoked salmon and cream cheese, organic scrambled eggs. Wells and Glastonbury are a hop, walks start from the door.

Minimum stay: 2 nights. Children over 10 welcome. Pets by arrangement.

Rooms	1 double: £100–£120.
Meals	Dinner £25. Pubs/restaurants 5 miles.
Closed	Rarely.

Cynthia Taylor
Culverwell House,
Top Street,
Pilton, Shepton Mallet,
Somerset BA4 4DF
Tel   +44 (0)1749 890437
Email   cynthiafroufrou@sky.com
Web   www.culverwellhouse.co.uk

Entry 442   Map 3

Somerset

Glyde Cottages

Smell Victoria's just-baked bread as you enter this charmingly restored merchant's house – all 16th-century stone walls and aged oak beams. Relax in the guests' sitting room with its inglenook stuffed with logs, or stroll to the pub; wind your way up a spiral staircase to a beautifully rustic room with a hand-crafted bed and stripped floors. Children may venture up to the attic twin where a rocking horse waits; breakfasts are a home-cooked delight at the long wooden table. Strike out to Alfred's Tower – or opt for a plump slice of cake and croquet on the lawn. Just watch out for errant chickens!

Rooms	1 double with adjoining twin available (let to same party only; £20 per child, £25 per adult): £85.
Meals	Dinner, 2 courses, £18. Pub within walking distance.
Closed	Rarely.

Victoria Savage
Glyde Cottages,
Upton Noble,
Shepton Mallet,
Somerset BA4 6BA

Tel   +44 (0)1749 850230
Email   v.savage@live.com
Web   www.glydecottages.co.uk

Entry 443   Map 3

Somerset

Broadgrove House

Head down the long, private lane and arrive at Sarah's peaceful 17th-century stone house with its pretty walled cottage garden and views to Alfred's Tower and Longleat. Inside is just as special. Beams, flagstones and inglenook fireplaces have been sensitively restored; rugs, pictures, comfy sofas and polished antiques add warmth and serenity. The twin, at the end of the house, has its own sitting room. Breakfast on homemade and farmers' market produce before exploring Stourhead, Wells, Glastonbury. Sarah, engaging, well-travelled and a great cook, looks after you warmly.

Children by arrangement.

Rooms	1 twin with sitting room; 1 double with separate bath: £80-£90. Singles £60.
Meals	Pub/restaurant 1 mile.
Closed	Christmas.

Sarah Voller
Broadgrove House,
Leighton, Frome,
Somerset BA11 4PP

Tel   +44 (0)1373 836296
Mobile +44 (0)7775 918388
Email   broadgrove836@tiscali.co.uk
Web   www.broadgrovehouse.co.uk

Entry 444   Map 3

Somerset

Claveys Farm

For the artistic seeker of inspiration, not those who thrill to standardised luxury. Fleur is a talented artist, Francis works for English Heritage, both have a passion for art, gardening and lively conversation. Rugs are time-worn, panelling and walls are distempered with natural pigment, bedrooms are better than simple, bathrooms old. From the Aga-warm kitchen of this lived-in, historic farmhouse come eggs from the hens, honey from the bees, oak-smoked bacon from Fleur's rare-breed pigs and homemade bread and jams. Fields, footpaths and woodland for walks, and a garden for children to adore. Bring your woolly jumpers!

Rooms	1 double with separate bath, sometimes shared with twin; 1 twin with separate bath, sometimes shared with double or owner: £75. Singles £50.
Meals	Dinner, 3 courses, £25. BYO. Packed lunch £7. Pub in village.
Closed	Rarely.

	Fleur & Francis Kelly
	Claveys Farm,
	Mells, Frome,
	Somerset BA11 3QP
Tel	+44 (0)1373 814651
Mobile	+44 (0)7968 055398
Email	bandb@fleurkelly.com

Entry 445   Map 3

Somerset

Penny's Mill

The old part of Nunney village, with its small pretty streets, has a shop, a café and Rosie's gorgeous old stone millhouse down in the river valley. You are greeted warmly with tea and biscuits at a large wooden table in the kitchen, or in the drawing room upstairs with family photos, paintings and a big window looking over the millpond. Bedrooms are light and bright, painted in gentle blues and greens with a mix of antique and modern furniture; bathrooms have Molton Brown soaps and white fluffy towels. Rosie's fine breakfast sets you up for a short walk to Nunney Castle, or a yomp further afield.

Rooms	1 double, 1 twin/double with own living room: £90. 1 family room for 2 sharing living room & shower room: £150.
Meals	Dinner £25-£35. Pub 300 yds.
Closed	Rarely.

	Rosie Davies
	Penny's Mill,
	Horn Street, Nunney, Frome,
	Somerset BA11 4NP
Tel	+44 (0)1373 836210
Email	stay@pennysmill.com
Web	www.stayatpennysmill.com

Entry 446   Map 3

Somerset

Old Reading Room

Mells is a treasure with its medieval centre and liberal sprinkling of charming cottages; you'll find Vicky and John's attractive house down a track in the quiet wooded valley. It's a home with a friendly feel: books, art, pots of flowers, intriguing finds from family travels, comfy sofas around the wood-burner. Beds are wrapped in fine cotton and colourful quilts; sweet bathrooms have scented candles. Come down for breakfast in the kitchen – homemade bread, eggs from happy hens – delivered by a friend on a pony! Sunny cottage garden, walks from the door, a five-minute drive to Babington House… and entertaining hosts.

Somerset

Swallow Barn

Views sweep over hills from this eco-friendly barn conversion – join the Macmillan Way from the garden. You have your own entrance to a wing of Penny and Paul's home; each warm bedroom has its own sunny spot outside too. Find tip-top linen on big luxurious beds, espresso machines and homemade shortbread, Smart TVs (with Sky) and comfy seating; swish wet rooms (one with a nifty mirror audio system) have huge shower heads and Somerset Lavender soaps. Penny gives you breakfast and cream tea in the stunning wild flower meadow or under the wisteria pergola in summer. Wells, Bath and Frome are all a hop: arty haunts, markets and theatre beckon.

Usually minimum stay: 2 nights (but check availability). Dogs by arrangement.

Rooms	2 doubles: £90. Singles £75.
Meals	Pubs/restaurants 5-minute walk.
Closed	Rarely.

Rooms	2 doubles: £130.
Meals	Pub 5-minute walk.
Closed	Christmas.

Most praised breakfast

Vicky & John Macdonald
Old Reading Room,
Mells,
Frome,
Somerset BA11 3QA
Tel   +44 (0)1373 813487
Email johnmacdonaldm@gmail.com

Penny Reynolds
Swallow Barn,
The Cross,
Buckland Dinham, Frome,
Somerset BA11 2QS
Mobile +44 (0)7967 003261/
        +44 (0)7790 586085
Email   paulpennyreynolds@hotmail.com

Entry 447   Map 3

Entry 448   Map 3

Somerset

Jericho

'Jericho' means in the middle of nowhere and here above lovely Mells you have space around your ears and long views. Babington House and excellent pubs are close, yet sybarites may just want to wallow in the generous bedroom and sitting room with doors to a vine-hung loggia and parterre, French Grey panelling, original art, and a wet room with a drenching shower. Stephen, a product designer, has orchestrated the look, and furniture, rugs and fabrics chime contentedly with the architecture. Find top-notch coffee and tea on your tea tray, hand-pressed apple juice from the orchard, and exquisite vegetarian breakfasts delivered to you.

Rooms	1 suite for 2 with sitting room: £100–£110.
Meals	Pub 3 miles.
Closed	Rarely

2014/15

Sawday's
BED & BREAKFAST

Most praised breakfast

	Stephen Morgan
	Jericho,
	Mells Down,
	Mells, Frome,
	Somerset BA11 2RL
Tel	+44 (0)1373 813242
Email	mail@stayatjericho.co.uk
Web	www.stayatjericho.co.uk

Entry 449   Map 3

Somerset

Flint House

Off a village lane, up a sweeping drive, is an elegant 18th-century home with a private chapel. Smart yet relaxed, it's a perfect mix: a sophisticated sitting room with valley views, a roaring fire in the snug. Modern-classic bedrooms are delightful; there's a cosy twin next door to one – ideal for a family sharing. Breakfast treats await on the summer veranda, from pancakes to poached plums. Take to the tennis court or sit under wisteria, cake in hand, and gaze on the noble garden – Jacquie is loving its restoration. Your easy-going hosts will provide dinner or you can pop to the local. Walks galore – and Bath irresistibly near.

Rooms	1 double; 1 double, 1 twin, sharing shower (let to same party only): £60–£100. Singles £60.
Meals	Dinner, 3 courses, £20–£25. Picnic lunch £8. Afternoon tea £4. Pubs 10-minute walk.
Closed	Rarely.

	Jacquie Hamshaw Thomas
	Flint House,
	Common Lane, Holcombe,
	Radstock, Somerset BA3 5DS
Tel	+44 (0)1761 232419
Mobile	+44 (0)7723 031378
Email	htsuk@btconnect.com
Web	www.flinthousebandb.co.uk

Entry 450   Map 3

Somerset

The Old Vicarage

The vicarage sits at the foot of Jack and Jill's hill in a sleepy Mendip village. Both bedrooms have goose down comfort: one has an antique French bed and limestone wet room; the sunny blue room upstairs has a freestanding roll top. Your hosts are informal and friendly and their home exudes charm: a medieval stone floor in the hall, old flagstones, carpets designed by Lizzy, flowers, wood-burners and a pretty kitchen. Hens potter, carp laze in the canal pond; breakfast when you want on a full English, garden compotes and delicious coffee. National Trust gems and splendid walking on the Colliers Way will keep you busy.

Rooms	1 double with sitting room; 1 four-poster with separate wc: £95-£110.
Meals	Pub 100 yds.
Closed	Never.

Elizabeth Ashard
The Old Vicarage,
Church Street, Kilmersdon,
Radstock,
Somerset BA3 5TA
Tel +44 (0)1761 436926
Email lizzyashard@gmail.com
Web www.theoldvicaragesomerset.co.uk

Entry 451 Map 3

Staffordshire

Manor House Farm

A working rare-breed farm in an area of great beauty, a Jacobean farmhouse with oodles of history. Behind mullioned windows is a glorious interior crammed with curios and family pieces, panelled walls and wonky floors... hurl a log on the fire and watch it roar. Three rooms have four-posters; one bathroom flaunts rich red antique fabrics. Chris and Margaret are passionate hosts who serve perfect breakfasts (eggs from their own hens, sausages and bacon from their pigs and home-grown tomatoes) and give you the run of a garden resplendent with plants, vistas, tennis, croquet, two springer spaniels and one purring cat. Heaven.

Minimum stay: 2 nights at weekends during high season.

Rooms	1 double, 2 four-posters: £68-£80. 1 family room for 4 (four-poster): £80-£100.
Meals	Pub/restaurant 1.5 miles.
Closed	Christmas.

Chris & Margaret Ball
Manor House Farm,
Prestwood, Denstone, Uttoxeter,
Staffordshire ST14 5DD
Tel +44 (0)1889 590415
Mobile +44 (0)7976 767629
Email cmball@manorhousefarm.co.uk
Web www.manorhousefarm.co.uk

Entry 452 Map 8

Suffolk

Pavilion House

A conservation village surrounded by chalk grassland – famous for its flora, fauna and butterflies; marked walks are straight from this 16-year-old red-brick house. Friendly Gretta teaches cooking and you are in for a treat: homemade cake, enormous breakfasts with her own bread and jams, proper dinners or simple suppers. Sleep peacefully in traditional, comfortable bedrooms (all downstairs) with crisp linen and TVs. There's a guest sitting room too: English comfort with an oriental feel, parquet floors, antiques, original drawings, a cosy logburner. Wander the superb garden. Newmarket and Cambridge are close.

Suffolk

The Old Vicarage

Up the avenue of fine horse chestnut trees to find just what you'd expect from an old vicarage: a Pembroke table in the flagstoned hall, a refectory table sporting copies of *The Field*, a piano, silver pheasants, a log fire that warms the sitting room and homemade cake on arrival. The house is magnificent, with huge rooms and passageways. Comfy mattresses are dressed in old-fashioned counterpanes, and the double has hill views. Weave your way through the branches of the huge copper beech to the garden that Jane loves; she grows her own vegetables, keeps hens and cooks a fine breakfast.

Children over 7 welcome.

Rooms	1 double; 1 double, 1 twin/double, each with separate bath/shower: £85–£125. Singles £55–£60. Child bed available.
Meals	Lunch from £10. Dinner from £25. Supper from £15. BYO. Pub 1.5 miles.
Closed	Christmas.

Rooms	1 double with extra single room off double (let to same party only); 1 twin with separate bath: £80–£90. Singles £50.
Meals	Dinner £20. BYO. Packed lunch £6. Pub 1 mile.
Closed	Christmas.

	Gretta & David Bredin Pavilion House, 133 Station Road, Dullingham, Newmarket, Suffolk CB8 9UT
Tel	+44 (0)1638 508005
Mobile	+44 (0)7776 197709
Email	gretta@thereliablesauce.co.uk
Web	www.pavilionhousebandb.co.uk

	Jane Sheppard The Old Vicarage, Great Thurlow, Newmarket, Suffolk CB9 7LE
Tel	+44 (0)1440 783209
Mobile	+44 (0)7887 717429
Email	s.j.sheppard@hotmail.co.uk
Web	www.thurlowvicarage.co.uk

Entry 453   Map 9

Entry 454   Map 9

Suffolk

The Lucy Redman Garden and B&B

Off a country lane, through an estate village, hides this immaculate, thatched, 1930s house – a gem. Lucy and Dominic are full of life and fun. Lucy is an artistic garden designer so all glows with texture and colour, and the garden is a stunner. Family antiques blend with multi-cultural pieces, there are books, paintings and pets. Choose between the cosy, ochre-walled 'Indian' room upstairs and the 'Moroccan' down, with aqua walls and vibrant Mexican tiles. Wake to eggs from the hens, plum jams from the trees, and lovely homemade marmalade. Views swoop over garden, grazing horses and miles of Suffolk countryside. A happy place!

Suffolk

The Old Manse Barn

A large, lush loft apartment in sleepy Suffolk; this uncluttered living space of blond wood, white walls and big windows has an urban feel yet overlooks glorious countryside. Secluded from the main house, in a timber-clad barn, all is fabulous and spacious: leather sofas, glass dining table, stainless steel kitchenette. Floor lights dance off the walls, surround-sound creates mood and you can watch the stars from your bed. Homemade granola, fruits, cold meats, cheeses and fresh pastries are popped in the fridge – bliss. There's peace for romance, solitude for work, a garden to sit in and lovely Sue to suggest the best pubs.

Rooms	1 double, 1 twin/double: £80-£90. Singles £70.
Meals	Pubs/restaurants 2 miles.
Closed	Rarely.

Rooms	Apartment - 1 double & kitchenette: £80-£85.
Meals	Pubs within walking distance.
Closed	Rarely.

	Lucy & Dominic Watts
	The Lucy Redman Garden and B&B,
	6 The Village, Rushbrooke,
	Bury St Edmunds, Suffolk IP30 0ER
Tel	+44 (0)1284 386250
Mobile	+44 (0)7503 633671
Email	lucyredman7@gmail.com
Web	www.lucyredman.co.uk

	Sue & Ian Jones
	The Old Manse Barn,
	Chapel Road, Cockfield,
	Bury St Edmunds, Suffolk IP30 0HE
Tel	+44 (0)1284 828120
Mobile	+44 (0)7931 753996
Email	bookings@theoldmansebarn.co.uk
Web	www.theoldmansebarn.co.uk

Entry 455 Map 10

Entry 456 Map 10

Suffolk

16 Bolton Street

The house, part medieval, part Tudor, rests on a quiet street within striking distance of lovely, bustling Lavenham: this is one of England's showpiece towns. Heavy beams, low doorways, books, magazines, fresh flowers and gentle hosts create a warm happy feel; steep oak stairs lead to fresh, cosy bedrooms where patchwork quilts, colourful cushions and handmade curtains abound. Gillian likes nothing better than to spoil her guests with breakfasts of local sausages and bacon, potato cakes, her special mushroom recipe, yogurt and fresh fruit. A delightful, relaxed, generous place to stay.

Minimum stay: 2 nights at weekends.

Rooms	1 double, 1 twin/double: £75–£90.
Meals	Pubs/restaurants within walking distance.
Closed	Rarely.

Gillian de Lucy
16 Bolton Street,
Lavenham,
Suffolk CO10 9RG

Tel	+44 (0)1787 249046
Mobile	+44 (0)7747 621096
Email	gdelucy@aol.com
Web	www.guineahouse.co.uk

Entry 457   Map 10

Suffolk

The Old Rectory Country House

In a hamlet of thatched cottages by the Church of St Lawrence sits a handsome rectory, quietly steeped in ancient history. Find elegant proportions, family antiques and owner Frank who asks only that you feel at home. The drawing room has an honesty bar and walking maps, the garden is a delight and you can use the pool. Feel spoiled in big smart bedrooms with pretty fabrics, smooth linen and lovely views; the Stables are charming with books, a garden suite and comfy sofas. Be lazy and have continental breakfast in your room, or rouse yourself for local sausages and bacon by a log fire in the magnificent dining room. A treat.

Rooms	2 doubles, 1 twin/double, each with extra child's bed/cot: £85–£199. Stables – 3 doubles, extra single in 2, sharing sitting/dining room & kitchen (self-catering also): £75–£189. Singles £65–£85. Sun to Thurs only.
Meals	Meals by arrangement for guests booking the whole house only. Pub 1 mile.
Closed	Rarely.

Frank Lawrenson
The Old Rectory Country House,
Rectory Road, Great Waldingfield,
Lavenham, Sudbury,
Suffolk CO10 0TL

Tel	+44 (0)1787 372428
Email	info@theoldrectorycountryhouse.co.uk
Web	www.theoldrectorycountryhouse.co.uk

Entry 458   Map 10

Suffolk

Stone Farm

This wonderful modern house has glorious views over the Brett valley and a wildflower meadow on the roof. Walls of curved glass pull the landscape in, there are decked terraces for lounging and the garden and woodland are full of birds and wildlife. Your bedroom is a beauty: a huge bed with a nifty mattress (one half firm, the other medium!), a wow of a bathroom and panoramic views. Janey is delightful and her local homemade breakfasts are a flexible feast – left for you to cook at a time to suit, or made for you and served on your own terrace (or in her kitchen). A rare treat… you're beautifully looked after here.

Rooms	1 double: £125-£150. Singles £100.
Meals	Occasional supper.
	Pubs/restaurants 0.8 miles.
Closed	Rarely.

Janey Auchincloss
Stone Farm,
Brent Eleigh Road, Lavenham,
Sudbury, Suffolk CO10 9PE
Tel   +44 (0)1787 247880
Email   janey.auchincloss@btinternet.com
Web   www.stonefarmlavenham.co.uk

Entry 459   Map 10

Suffolk

Shilling Grange

In the heart of medieval Lavenham, this impressive timbered wool merchant's home has been snoozing quietly here for nearly 600 years. Sheila loves welcoming guests to her fascinating house, which brims with beams, diamond leaded windows and huge old inglenook – *Twinkle Twinkle Little Star* was written here too! Generous bedrooms have excellent beds, sofas, TVs and welcome trays. You have breakfast in the sunny dining room: high ceilings, original 1425 wall paintings and separate tables with pots of flowers. Sit in the walled garden under a magnificent magnolia, visit nearby Sudbury and Bury St Edmunds, stroll out for supper. Perfect.

Rooms	3 doubles: £105-£146.
Meals	Pubs/restaurants 5-minute walk.
Closed	Rarely.

Sheila Lane
Shilling Grange,
Shilling Street, Lavenham,
Sudbury, Suffolk CO10 9RH
Tel   +44 (0)1787 249423
Email   info@shillinggrange.com
Web   www.shillinggrange.com

Entry 460   Map 10

Suffolk

Copinger Hall

A stunning bay-windowed house which has been in the family since the 16th century, yet is anything but ancient in feel. At the end of a sweeping gravel drive, past the church which adjoins the garden, it is 'country smart', deeply comfortable and very much a home – complete with two noisily amiable dogs. Lisa is someone to whom throwing open the doors to guests brings immeasurable pleasure, a gifted and generous host. Breakfasts (superb breakfast menu!) are in the elegant dining room, and guests have the use of the drawing room, garden and tennis court. Head out for Aldeburgh, Lavenham and the music at Snape Maltings.

Rooms	1 double, 1 twin/double; 1 double with separate bath/shower: £100–£120. Singles £85.
Meals	Pub & restaurant within 1 mile.
Closed	Occasionally.

	Lisa & Stephen Minoprio
	Copinger Hall,
	Brettenham Road, Buxhall,
	Stowmarket, Suffolk IP14 3DJ
Tel	+44 (0)1449 736000
Mobile	+44 (0)7775 621715
Email	lisa@copingerhall.com

Entry 461   Map 10

Suffolk

Haughley House

A timber-framed medieval manor in three acres of garden overlooking farmland. The attractive village is in a conservation area, and your hosts, the Lord of the Manor and his wife, are accomplished cooks and passionate about organic food; they produce their own beef, game, eggs, vegetables and soft fruits. Breakfast is an Aga-cooked feast of homemade bread, Suffolk cured bacon and black pudding, fresh juices and compote; delicious dinners are served in an elegant, silk-lined dining room. You'll find genuine country-house style here with tea and homemade cake on arrival, pretty wallpapers, flowers and a welcoming fire in the hall.

Rooms	2 doubles, 1 twin: £100–£120. Singles £65–£75.
Meals	Dinner, 3 courses, £28. Restaurants 12 miles.
Closed	Rarely.

	Jeffrey & Caroline Bowden
	Haughley House,
	Haughley, Suffolk IP14 3NS
Tel	+44 (0)1449 673398
Mobile	+44 (0)7860 284722
Email	bowden@keme.co.uk
Web	www.haughleyhouse.co.uk

Entry 462   Map 10

Suffolk

Holbecks House

Up the drive through parkland studded with ancient trees and step into the flagstoned hall of this 18th–century house. Find gracious rooms, soft colours, Persian rugs, antiques, hunting prints and books to browse. Perry is delightful and looks after you well; settle into big peaceful bedrooms with good beds, chocolates and long rural views. Just beyond the market town of Hadleigh, the house snoozes on a hill with acres of garden, orchard, croquet lawn, rose walk and pond. Explore Constable Country, visit Munnings Museum in Dedham, the Gainsborough Museum in Sudbury and the cathedral city of Bury St Edmunds.

Minimum stay: 2 nights at weekends.

Rooms	1 double, 1 twin/double; 1 double with separate bath: £90–£130. Extra bed/sofabed available £20 per person per night.
Meals	Supper £20. BYO. Pubs/restaurants 0.5 miles.
Closed	Rarely.

Perry Coysh
Holbecks House,
Holbecks Lane, Hadleigh, Ipswich,
Suffolk IP7 5PE

Tel	+44 (0)1473 823211
Mobile	+44 (0)7875 167771
Email	info@holbecks.com
Web	www.holbecks.com

Entry 463   Map 10

Suffolk

Poplar Farm House

Only a few miles from Ipswich but down a green lane, this rambling farmhouse has a pretty, whitewashed porch and higgledy-piggledy roof. All light, elegant and spacious with wonderful flowers, art, sumptuous soft furnishings (made by Sally) and quirky sculptures; expect comfy beds, laundered linen and smart bathrooms. Sally is relaxed and friendly and will give you eggs from her handsome hens, homemade bread, veg from the garden on an artistically laid table. Play tennis, swim, steam in the sauna or book one of Sally's arts and crafts courses, then wander in the woods beyond with beautiful dogs Shale and Rune. Great value.

Rooms	1 twin, 2 doubles sharing 2 bath/shower rooms: £65. Yurt - 1 double (in summer): £65. Singles £45.
Meals	Dinner, 3 courses, £15–£25. Packed lunch £7. Pub 1 mile.
Closed	Rarely.

Sally Sparrow
Poplar Farm House,
Poplar Lane, Sproughton, Ipswich,
Suffolk IP8 3HL

Tel	+44 (0)1473 601211
Mobile	+44 (0)7950 767226
Email	sparrowsally@aol.com
Web	www.poplarfarmhousesuffolkbb.eu

Entry 464   Map 10

Suffolk

The Old Rectory

Through the front door to a generously proportioned and flagstoned hall and a smiling welcome from Christopher. Archways lead down the corridor to the library (cosy with maps, books and open fire) and a tall elegant staircase leads to spacious bedrooms, one with delightful bow windows and a view of the sea. There are sash windows and shutters, pelmets and antiques, heaps of good books. Outside: 20 acres of woodlands, meadows, paddocks, croquet lawn and vegetable garden (walled and wonderful). Walks galore on the Deben Peninsula, music at Snape Maltings; it's Suffolk at its best and peace reigns supreme.

Whole house available for weekly and weekend lets, please enquire with owner for price.

Rooms	2 doubles, 1 twin: £90–£120. Singles £60–£90. Extra bed/sofabed available £30 per person per night.
Meals	Dinner, 3 courses, £30. Pub 5-minute walk.
Closed	Occasionally.

Christopher Langley
The Old Rectory,
Alderton,
Woodbridge,
Suffolk IP12 3DE

Tel	+44 (0)1394 410003
Email	clangley@keme.co.uk
Web	www.oldrectoryaldertonbandb.co.uk

Entry 465   Map 10

Suffolk

Melton Hall

There's more than a touch of theatre to this beautiful listed house. The dining room is opulent red; the drawing room, with its delicately carved mantelpiece and comfortable sofas, has French windows to the terrace. There's a four-poster in one bedroom, an antique French bed in another and masses of fresh flowers and books. The garden includes an orchid and wildflower meadow: a designated County Wildlife Site. River walks, the coast and the Saxon burial site Sutton Hoo are close. Generous Cindy, her delightful children, little dog Poppy and cats Bea and Bubbles, all give a great welcome.

Rooms	1 double: £105–£130. 1 double, sharing bath with 1 single: £105–£130. 1 single, sharing bath with 1 double: £60.
Meals	Dinner, 1–3 courses, £19–£38. BYO. Pubs/restaurants nearby.
Closed	Rarely.

Lucinda de la Rue
Melton Hall,
Woodbridge,
Suffolk IP12 1PF

Tel	+44 (0)1394 388138
Mobile	+44 (0)7775 797075
Email	cindy@meltonhall.co.uk
Web	www.meltonhall.co.uk

Entry 466   Map 10

Suffolk

Church House

A short hop from riverside Woodbridge and musical Snape Maltings, between a conservation churchyard and a history-rich field, is something different and unusual: a customised house of gentle colours and textures, home to an architect and a designer. From the hand-carved, oak porch to the lovely wildlife garden, there's a feeling of warmth and delight. Under the eaves: two jewel-bright and comfortable bedrooms full of books and fresh flowers. In the kitchen: a big farmhouse table laid for beautiful breakfasts. And, a short walk away, an excellent village pub.

Children over 8 welcome.

Rooms	1 twin/double; 1 twin with separate bath/shower: £80-£85. Singles £65-£75.
Meals	Pub 1 mile.
Closed	Rarely.

Sally & Richard Pirkis
Church House,
Clopton,
Woodbridge,
Suffolk IP13 6QB
Tel   +44 (0)1473 735350
Email   sallypirkis@gmail.com
Web   www.churchhousebandbsuffolk.co.uk

Entry 467   Map 10

Suffolk

Willow Tree Cottage

Seductively near RSPB Minsmere, medieval castles, fabulous walks and the glorious coast; and Edwardian Southwold with its pier and sandy beach. The evening sun pours into the back of this contemporary cottage with butter yellow walls; you are on the edge of the village but all is quiet with an orchard behind and a bird-filled garden for tea. No sitting room, but easy chairs in your pretty bedroom face views. Caroline is a good cook and breakfast is large (try her kedgeree). Snape Maltings, for music lovers, is just four miles away; Aldeburgh with its shingle beach, fishing boats, fun shops and good places to eat is a short drive too.

Minimum stay: 2 nights at weekends.

Rooms	1 double: £70-£75. Singles £50-£60.
Meals	Pub/restaurant 1.5 miles.
Closed	Rarely.

Caroline Youngson
Willow Tree Cottage,
3 Belvedere Close, Kelsale,
Saxmundham, Suffolk IP17 2RS
Tel   +44 (0)1728 602161
Mobile +44 (0)7747 624139
Email   cy@willowtreecottage.me.uk
Web   www.willowtreecottage.me.uk

Entry 468   Map 10

Suffolk

Church Farmhouse

This Elizabethan farmhouse is by the ancient thatched church in a little hamlet close to Southwold. Minsmere RSPB bird sanctuary, Snape Maltings and the coast are nearby for lovely days out. Sarah, characterful, well-travelled and entertaining, is also an excellent cook, so breakfast will be a treat with bowls of fruit, Suffolk bacon and free-range eggs; occasional candle-lit dinners are worth staying in for, too. Bedrooms have supremely comfy beds well-dressed in pure cotton. Although there is no sitting room, you can enjoy tea and cake and linger in the garden, there are flowers in every room and books galore.

Minimum stay: 2 nights at weekends.

Rooms	1 double, 1 twin/double; 1 double with separate bath: £90–£110. Singles £60–£75.
Meals	Dinner £28. Pubs/restaurants within 4 miles.
Closed	Christmas.

Sarah Lentaigne
Church Farmhouse,
Uggeshall, Southwold,
Suffolk NR34 8BD

Tel	+44 (0)1502 578532
Mobile	+44 (0)7748 801418
Email	sarahlentaigne@btinternet.com
Web	www.churchfarmhousesuffolk.co.uk

Entry 469 Map 10

Suffolk

Valley Farm

Soaps and sweeties in baskets, walking and cycle route maps on tap, DVDs to borrow: some of the personal touches you'll find at this delightfully unpretentious B&B. The soft brick farmhouse in a lovely corner of Suffolk sits in two acres of new landscaped garden, with a play area for children, a field for kite flying and a wonderful indoor solar-heated pool, shared with the self-catering guests. You get jams from their fruits for breakfast – Jackie and Andrew have a passion for real food – and two friendly and comfortable carpeted bedrooms, each with a spotless shower room.

Minimum stay: 2 nights at weekends.

Rooms	1 double: £80–£100. 1 family room for 3-4: £80–£120.
Meals	Pub 0.4 miles.
Closed	Rarely.

Jackie Circus
Valley Farm,
Bungay Road,
Holton, Halesworth,
Suffolk IP19 8LY

Tel	+44 (0)1986 874521
Email	mail@valleyfarmholton.co.uk
Web	www.valleyfarmholton.co.uk

Entry 470 Map 10

Suffolk

Bulls Hall

Half a mile from the village of Occold – a B&B of character and peace. The house is 16th-century and listed, the lovely grounds – lawns, meadow, summerhouse and ponds – teem with wildlife. Warm, friendly Angela welcomes you to a cosy, traditional, unspoiled home: low doorways, a big inglenook, a deep new mattress on a vintage iron bed, books, guides, games and delightfully uneven brick floors. There's a long parquet'd double off the dining room, a staircase to a lofty family suite, and a beautiful breakfast to wake up to: Suffolk black bacon, homemade jams, eggs from the hens. Visit the Broads, stroll to the pub.

Minimum stay: 2 nights on bank holidays.

Rooms	1 double: £70–£80.
	1 family suite for 4 (2 doubles) with separate shared bath (let to same party only): £100–£140. Singles £50.
Meals	Pub/restaurant 0.5 miles.
Closed	Never.

	Angela Hall
	Bulls Hall,
	Bulls Hall Road,
	Occold, Eye,
	Suffolk IP23 7PH
Tel	+44 (0)1379 678683
Email	angela.hall53@gmail.com

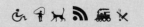

Entry 471   Map 10

Suffolk

Camomile Cottage

Aly and Tim's 16th-century longhouse is a feast of old beams, kilims, antiques and art. They give you homemade cake on arrival; relax in the garden or the guest lounge, kick off your shoes and enjoy a glass of wine by the log fire. Beamed bedrooms have period furnishings, goose down duvets, luxury linen, flowers and handmade chocolates; bathrooms have Molton Brown toiletries. Aly will also bring you tea in bed! Breakfast is in the garden room: cornbread toast, eggs from the hens, croissants and all sorts of cooked choices. Eye is an attractive old market town; Southwold, Bury St Edmunds and Snape Maltings are all close.

Minimum stay: 2 nights at weekends.

Rooms	2 doubles: £99–£110.
	Singles £85.
Meals	Pubs/restaurants 0.5 miles.
Closed	Rarely.

	Aly Kahane
	Camomile Cottage,
	Brome Avenue, Eye,
	Suffolk IP23 7HW
Tel	+44 (0)1379 873528
Email	aly@camomilecottage.co.uk
Web	www.camomilecottage.co.uk

Entry 472   Map 10

Surrey

Swallow Barn

A squash court, coach house and stables, once belonging to next-door's manor, have become a home of old-fashioned charm. Full of family memories, and run very well by Joan, this B&B is excellently placed for Windsor, Wisley, Brooklands and Hampton Court; close to both airports too. Lovely trees in the garden, fields and woods beyond, a paddock and a swimming pool... total tranquillity, and you can walk to the pub. None of the bedrooms is huge but the beds are firm, the garden views are pretty and the downstairs double has its own sitting room. Breakfasts are both generous and scrumptious.

Children over 8 welcome.

Rooms	1 double with sitting room; 1 twin with separate shower: £80–£90. Apple Store - 1 twin: £80–£90. Singles from £45.
Meals	Pub/restaurant 0.75 miles.
Closed	Rarely.

Joan Carey
Swallow Barn,
Milford Green, Chobham,
Woking, Surrey GU24 8AU

Tel	+44 (0)1276 856030
Mobile	+44 (0)7768 972904
Email	info@swallow-barn.co.uk
Web	www.swallow-barn.co.uk

Entry 473   Map 4

Surrey

Broadway Barn

If you love art, gardening and good food, you'll love Mindi and her brilliant conversion of a pretty brick Regency barn on Ripley High Street. You sleep in comfortable bedrooms styled with creativity: a painting from a Parisian laundrette, ceramic lamps with bird motifs, leather chests as tables. You relax in a long, light, mirrored conservatory with glazed terrace doors, and are free to wander around the newly planted walled garden. You breakfast deliciously on local eggs and home-baked treats... Minutes from Guildford and Wisley's RHS garden, the village has a Michelin-starred restaurant, cafés and pubs.

Rooms	4 doubles: £95. Singles £95.
Meals	Restaurant next door.
Closed	Rarely.

Mindi McLean
Broadway Barn,
High Street,
Ripley,
Woking, Surrey GU23 6AQ

Tel	+44 (0)1483 223200
Email	mindi@broadwaybarn.com
Web	www.broadwaybarn.com

Entry 474   Map 4

Surrey

South Lodge

The beautiful Surrey Hills surround this smart home overlooking the village green. Paul and Joanna's house gets the sun all day and has a country chic feel. They look after you well, and give you tea and cake on arrival, three cosy, pretty bedrooms in the eaves and locally sourced and homemade treats at breakfast. Joanna's catering business is run from the house so there are always people coming and going – this is a fun place to stay with a lovely friendly feel. Hop next door for a tasty supper at The Grumpy Mole (popular so you need to book). Handy for Gatwick, too – it's a 15-minute drive.

Rooms	2 doubles; 1 twin with separate bath: £95. Singles £85. Surcharge for one night stay at weekend.
Meals	Evening meal by arrangement. Pub next door.
Closed	Christmas.

Joanna Rowlands
South Lodge,
Brockham Green,
Brockham, Betchworth,
Surrey RH3 7JS

Tel	+44 (0)1737 843883
Email	bookings@brockhambandb.com
Web	www.brockhambandb.com

Entry 475   Map 4

Surrey

Blackbrook House

A large Victorian house sitting in lawns and garden and with a wide gravel drive; this has a rural feel but you are less than two miles from the centre of Dorking. Emma and Rae, both easy-going, give you a super little sitting room with a hidden TV and space to make a cup of tea; both bedrooms are spacious, smart and feminine with floral fabrics, deep pocket sprung mattresses and good linen, bathrooms are tip-top. Breakfast is beautifully presented with cereals and fruit or the full Monty. Walk it off over lawns, shrubs and woods – or strike out further over National Trust land.

Rooms	1 double: £90-£100. 1 suite for 2: £95-£115. Singles from £60.
Meals	Pub 0.5 miles.
Closed	Christmas & New Year.

Emma & Rae Burdon
Blackbrook House,
Blackbrook, Dorking,
Surrey RH5 4DS

Tel	+44 (0)1306 888898
Mobile	+44 (0)7880 723512
Email	blackbrookbb@btinternet.com
Web	www.surreybandb.co.uk

Entry 476   Map 4

Surrey

Hambledon House

Through an old ornate iron gate, up a sweeping drive in rolling parkland and... enter another world. With an Elizabethan core and Victorian additions, Vanessa's house is a unique celebration of the Arts and Crafts movement. It's been in her family for generations and the restoration, with a marvellous Italian slant, is well underway. Find rooms of pure opulence with regal beds and bags of character, fabulous bathrooms, art, antiques, vast fireplaces, stunning stained glass, an orangery for breakfasts and a wonderful garden with a long reflecting pond. Vanessa is great fun and you're free to wander everywhere. Magical.

Surrey

The Dovecote at Greenaway

An enchanting cottage in an idyllic corner of Chiddingfold. People return time and again – for the house (1545), the garden with dovecote, vegetables, flowers and hens, the glowing interiors, and Sheila and John. The sitting room is inviting with rich colours and textures, and the turning oak staircase leads to bedrooms that are cosy and sumptuous at the same time. Bathrooms are bliss, with deep roll top tubs. Come for gorgeous countryside and walks on the Greensand Way... who would guess London and the airports were so close? Delightful B&B; guests are full of praise.

Rooms	3 doubles: £110–£130. Singles £75. Extra beds available for children £40 per night.
Meals	Dinner, 3 courses, £30. Catering for house parties. Pubs/restaurants 10-minute walk.
Closed	Rarely.

Rooms	1 double; 1 double, 1 twin sharing bath: £95–£115. Singles £75.
Meals	Pubs 300 yds.
Closed	Rarely.

	Vanessa Rhode
	Hambledon House,
	Vann Lane, Hambledon,
	Godalming, Surrey GU8 4HW
Tel	+44 (0)1428 683815
Mobile	+44 (0)7768 645500
Email	vanessaswarbreck@yahoo.co.uk
Web	www.hambledonhouse.com

	Sheila & John Marsh
	The Dovecote at Greenaway,
	Pickhurst Road,
	Chiddingfold,
	Surrey GU8 4TS
Tel	+44 (0)1428 682920
Email	info@bedandbreakfastchiddingfold.co.uk
Web	www.bedandbreakfastchiddingfold.co.uk

Entry 477   Map 4

Entry 478   Map 4

Surrey

Colliers Farm

Acres of grounds and a restored 17th-century farmhouse with all the trimmings will make you want to stay longer. Step into a hallway with a welcoming wood-burner; Marina rustles up tea and cake (delicious brownies!) on flowery china — served outside with the roses and roaming hens in summer. Pastel walls blend with soaring beams, stained glass and vases of flowers. Luxurious bedrooms come with TVs, DVDs, iPod docks and tip-top bathrooms; one is downstairs, all have comfy armchairs. Breakfast in the elegant dining room is a local spread with homemade compotes, bread and marmalade. Trips to Goodwood, Guildford and Chichester are easy.

Sussex

Lordington House

Croquet on the lawn in summer, big log fires and woolly jumpers in winter, brilliant food all year round. On a sunny slope of the Ems valley, life ticks by peacefully as it has always done... The house is vast and impressive, a lime avenue links the much-loved garden with the AONB beyond and friendly guard dog Shep looks on. The 17th-century staircase is a glory, the décor is engagingly old-fashioned: Edwardian beds with firm mattresses and floral covers, carpeted Sixties-style bathrooms, toile wallpaper on wardrobe doors. A privilege to stay in a house of this age and character!

Children over 5 welcome. Pets by arrangement.

Rooms	2 doubles, 1 twin: £110–£160. Singles from £75.
Meals	Pubs/restaurants 0.25 miles.
Closed	Rarely.

Rooms	1 double (en suite); 1 twin/double with separate bath/shower; 1 double sharing bath/shower with single: £100–£130. 1 single sharing bath/shower with double: £50–£65.
Meals	Packed lunch from £6. Pub 1 mile.
Closed	Rarely.

	Marina Shellard
	Colliers Farm,
	Midhurst Road, Fernhurst,
	Haslemere, Surrey GU27 3EX
Tel	+44 (0)1428 652265
Email	info@colliersfarm.co.uk
Web	www.colliersfarm.co.uk

	Mr & Mrs Hamilton
	Lordington House,
	Lordington,
	Chichester,
	Sussex PO18 9DX
Tel	+44 (0)1243 375862
Email	hamiltonjanda@btinternet.com

Entry 479   Map 4

Entry 480   Map 4

Sussex

Crows Hall Farm

The Renwicks are tremendous hosts. Their wonderful flagstone-halled farmhouse in the South Downs National Park is great for walking and cycling and close to Goodwood. Amanda's style is simple and cottagey, but never twee. She's gone for pale moss green walls, open brickwork and a classically dressed, big handmade bed in the main room. The other has a brass bed and fantastic views of the walled garden and beyond: a sea of green. In between, the beamed bathroom is fab and fun, with flamingos, freestanding bath and shower. Breakfasts are fresh, local, flexible feasts on the terrace or in the quirky rustic kitchen. Marvellous!

Rooms	1 double with separate bath; 1 double sharing bath (let to same party only): £110–£150.
Meals	Pubs 2.5 miles.
Closed	Rarely.

Amanda Renwick
Crows Hall Farm,
Chilgrove Road,
Lavant, Chichester,
Sussex PO18 9HP
Tel   +44 (0)1243 527855
Email   B&B@crowshall.com

Entry 481   Map 4

Sussex

Seabeach House

Sitting sleepily behind its white gate this pretty stone cottage is surrounded by the Sussex Downs National Park. Throughout Francesca's friendly home her love of folk art, rich oils, antiques and hand-painted pieces adds zest. Comfy cottagey bedrooms are on the ground floor; wake to local sausages and eggs, garden tomatoes, homemade jams with croissants and brioche. Francesca loves cooking, and dinner, with home-grown veg, is good too. Explore garden and fields, admire wide views from a pretty terrace and chat to Popeye the dog. There's art, theatre and sailing in Chichester, the castle in Arundel, and events galore at Goodwood.

Rooms	Annexe 1 double, 1 twin sharing bath (let to same party only): £85–£150. Singles £75.
Meals	Dinner, 3 courses, £25. BYO. Pub 1 mile.
Closed	Rarely.

Francesca Emmet
Seabeach House,
Selhurst Park, Halnaker, Chichester,
Sussex PO18 0LX
Tel   +44 (0)1243 537944
Email   francescaemmet@hotmail.co.uk
Web   www.bandbatseabeachhouse.co.uk

Entry 482   Map 4

The Old Manor House

Wild flowers in jugs, old wooden floors and beams, pretty cottagey curtains: Judy's manor house near Chichester has bags of character and she is friendly and kind. Originally constructed round a big central fireplace, the rooms are all refreshingly simple allowing features to shine. Sweet bedrooms up steep stairs have seagrass floors, limed furniture, gentle colours and warm bathrooms. Enjoy delicious breakfasts by the wood-burner in the dining room: fresh fruit smoothies and an organic full English. Great for horse racing, castle visiting, sailing, theatre and festivals; fantastic walks on the South Downs, too. Lovely.

Rooms	2 doubles: £95.
Meals	Pub/restaurant 500 yds.
Closed	Christmas.

Judy Wolstenholme
The Old Manor House,
Westergate Street,
Westergate, Chichester,
Sussex PO20 3QZ
Tel +44 (0)1243 544489
Email judy@veryoldmanorhouse.com
Web veryoldmanorhouse.com

Entry 483   Map 4

Itchenor Park House

The Duke of Richmond reportedly built Itchenor Park for his French mistress in 1783; it's a listed Georgian house in beautiful formal gardens on a 700-acre farmed estate. It is remote and utterly peaceful, and a path across the fields brings you to Chichester harbour for boat trips and sailing bustle. There are great walks to the beach, too, and around the village. You stay in a cosy self-contained apartment in the wing with your own sitting room, kitchenette and wood-burner. And you may enjoy the lovely little walled garden, sheltered from the winds. Susie leaves you breakfast to have at your leisure.

Rooms	1 double, with sitting room, sofabed & kitchenette: £100. Singles from £80.
Meals	Breakfast in fridge. Pub 5-minute walk.
Closed	Rarely.

Susie Green
Itchenor Park House,
Itchenor, Chichester,
Sussex PO20 7DN
Tel +44 (0)1243 512221
Mobile +44 (0)7718 902768
Email susiedgreen@gmail.com
Web www.itchenorpark.co.uk

Entry 484   Map 4

Stream Cottage

One of Sussex's prettiest villages, an endearing 1587 thatched cottage, the cheeriest hosts and a breakfast menu including blueberry pancakes, smoked salmon, homemade plum compote and, for the very hungry, 'The Famous Amberley Monty'! Through a private door and up a narrow staircase find your own sweet sitting room with comfy sofa and chair, lots of books and a charming bedroom with plenty of space and dual aspect low windows overlooking the garden. Your sparkling bathroom is downstairs (robes are provided) with big bottles of Cowshed potions and a sleek bath for resting weary limbs. Arundel and the South Downs await.

The Shepherd's Return

A simple, magical space – a prettily decorated shepherd's hut only an hour from London. In her peaceful West Sussex cottage garden with countryside all around, Lizzie has created something especially enchanting for her guests. She uses local and organic wherever possible, from the sheepskin hot water bottle to all the natural wool, bed linen and the breakfast hamper that arrives for you every morning. Light and heat are solar; bath and shower are in Lizzie's nearby cottage, the loo in the next door mini shepherd's hut. If you're not too busy unwinding, the beautiful South Downs should definitely be explored.

Minimum stay: 2 nights. Book through Sawday's Canopy & Stars online or by phone.

Rooms	1 double with separate bath & living room: £80–£100. Singles £80.
Meals	Pubs in village.
Closed	Christmas & occasionally.

Rooms	Shepherd's hut for 2: £120–£125. There will be a £5 charge for logs on arrival.
Meals	Breakfast included (summer & winter menu). Pubs 10 miles.
Closed	Never.

	Mike & Janet Wright
	Stream Cottage,
	The Square,
	Amberley, Arundel,
	Sussex BN18 9SR
Tel	+44 (0)1798 831266
Email	janet@streamcottage.co.uk
Web	www.streamcottage.co.uk

	Sawday's Canopy & Stars
	The Shepherd's Return,
	The Hollow, Sutton End,
	Pulborough, Sussex RH20 1PY
Tel	+44 (0)117 204 7830
Email	enquiries@canopyandstars.co.uk
Web	www.canopyandstars.co.uk/ shepherdsreturn

Entry 485   Map 4

Entry 486   Map 4

Sussex

Sussex

The Hyde Granary

A 1,000-acre estate, where roe deer roam and the odd buzzard circles above. The granary stands at the end of a one-mile drive, alongside a coach house and clock tower, in the shadow of the big house. Airy interiors are just the ticket: timber frames, exposed walls, beams in the dining room and a drying room for walkers. Bedrooms are uncluttered and have a country feel: one has a claw-foot bath, the other is in the eaves. Margot, a homeopath, can realign your back after a long journey, and does super breakfasts. There's a small garden for sundowners in summer, you can walk to the village and Gatwick is close.

Chyngton House South

A gracious 18th-century Grade II manor house set on the edge of the South Downs National Park. Step into a delightfully light and welcoming hall/living room; settle by the fire with tea and cake served on bone china. Alison and Andrew's home has medieval origins and is full of fascinating historic photos and original art; bedrooms have large well-dressed beds, elegant colours and views of the downs. Breakfast, at separate tables, is in the cosy wood-panelled library: muesli, fruits, homemade bread and all the cooked trimmings. The Seven Sisters cliffs are a 20-minute walk, and pretty Alfriston has great places to eat.

Rooms	1 double; 1 double with separate bath/shower: £80. Singles £60.	Rooms	2 doubles, 1 twin/double: £110–£120. Singles £85.
Meals	Pub 1.7 miles.	Meals	Pubs/restaurants 3 miles.
Closed	Christmas & New Year.	Closed	Rarely.

	Margot Barton		**Alison & Andrew Burrell**
	The Hyde Granary,		Chyngton House South,
	The Hyde, London Road, Handcross,		Hamsey Lane, Seaford,
	Haywards Heath, Sussex RH17 6EZ		Sussex BN25 4DW
Tel	+44 (0)1444 401930	Tel	+44 (0)1323 899773
Email	margot@thehydegranary.com	Email	chyngtonhouse@btconnect.com
Web	www.thehydegranary.com	Web	www.chyngtonhouse.com

Entry 487   Map 4

Entry 488   Map

Sussex

Ocklynge Manor

On top of a peaceful hill, a short stroll from Eastbourne, find tip-top B&B in an 18th-century house with an interesting history – ask Wendy! Now it is her home, and you will be treated to home-baked bread, delicious tea time cakes and scrummy jams – on fine days you can take it outside. Creamy carpeted, bright and sunny bedrooms, all with views over the lovely walled garden, create a mood of relaxed indulgence and are full of thoughtful touches: dressing gowns, DVDs, your own fridge. Breakfasts are superb: this is a very spoiling, nurturing place.

Please see owner's website for availability.

Rooms	1 twin; 1 double with separate shower: £100–£110. 1 suite for 3: £110–£120. Singles from £50.
Meals	Pub 5-minute walk.
Closed	Rarely.

Wendy Dugdill
Ocklynge Manor,
Mill Road, Eastbourne,
Sussex BN21 2PG

Tel   +44 (0)1323 734121
Mobile   +44 (0)7979 627172
Email   ocklyngemanor@hotmail.com
Web   www.ocklyngemanor.co.uk/availability_22.html

Entry 489   Map 5

Sussex

Hailsham Grange

Come for elegance and ease. Noel looks after you very well in his lovely Queen 'Mary Anne' home. No standing on ceremony here, despite the décor: classic English touched with chinoiserie in perfect keeping with the house; all is luxurious and special. Busts on pillars, delicious fabrics, books galore and bedrooms a treat: a sunny double, a romantic four-poster, smart suites. Summery breakfasts are served on the flagged terrace, marmalades and jams on a silver salver. The town garden, with its box parterre and gothic summerhouse, is an equal joy. Close by are gardens to visit, Glyndebourne, the sea and South Downs National Park.

Minimum stay: 2 nights bank holidays. Enquire with owners for special low season prices.

Rooms	1 four-poster, 1 double: £110–£150. Coach House, 2 suites for 2: £110–£120. Singles £70–£85.
Meals	Pub/restaurant 300 yds.
Closed	Rarely.

Noel Thompson
Hailsham Grange,
Hailsham,
Sussex BN27 1BL

Tel   +44 (0)1323 844248
Email   noel@hgrange.co.uk
Web   www.hailshamgrange.co.uk

Entry 490   Map 5

Sussex

Globe Place

A listed 17th-century house beside the church in a tiny village, ten minutes from Glyndebourne. Alison – a former chef to the Beatles – is a great cook and can provide you with a delicious and generous hamper, and tables and chairs too. Willie is a former rackets champion who gives tennis coaching; there's a court in the large, pretty garden, and a pool. Relax by the inglenook fire in the drawing room after a walk on the Cuckoo Trail or the South Downs, then settle down to a great supper – local fish, maybe, with home-grown vegetables. An easy-going, fun and informal household.

Children over 12 welcome.

Sussex

Netherwood Lodge

The scent of fresh flowers and a smattering of chintz over calm uncluttered interiors will please you. Engaging Margaret is a mine of local knowledge and offers you peaceful, cosy, ground-floor bedrooms beautifully dressed with wool carpets, designer interlined curtains, luxurious bed linens and gloriously comfortable beds. Enjoy an award-winning breakfast overlooking the garden (it's stunning); all is homemade or locally sourced. Then set off to discover this beautiful corner of East Sussex – ideal for walking, visiting National Trust houses and gardens and, of course, Glyndebourne.

Rooms	2 doubles, 1 twin, each with separate bath: £90. 2 singles sharing bath (let to same party only): £55. Cottage - 1 twin/double: £110. Singles £55.
Meals	Dinner £30. BYO wine. Hamper £35. Pub 10-minute drive.
Closed	Christmas.

Rooms	1 twin; 1 double with separate bath: £100-£120. Singles from £80.
Meals	Pub/restaurant 0.75 miles.
Closed	Rarely.

Alison & Willie Boone
Globe Place,
Hellingly,
Sussex BN27 4EY
Tel +44 (0)1323 844276
Mobile +44 (0)7870 957608
Email stay@globeplace.co.uk
Web www.globeplace.co.uk

Margaret Clarke
Netherwood Lodge,
Muddles Green,
Chiddingly, Lewes,
Sussex BN8 6HS
Tel +44 (0)1825 872512
Email netherwoodlodge@hotmail.com
Web www.netherwoodlodge.co.uk

Sussex

Old Whyly

Breakfast in a light-filled, chinoiserie dining room – there's an effortless elegance to this manor house, once home to one of King Charles's Cavaliers. Bedrooms are atmospheric, one in French style. The treats continue outside with a beautiful flower garden annually replenished with 5,000 tulips, a lake and orchard, a swimming pool and a tennis court – fabulous. Dine under the pergola in summer: food is a passion and Sarah's menus are adventurous with a modern slant. Glyndebourne is close so make a party of it and take a divine 'pink' hamper, with blankets or a table and chairs included. Sheer bliss.

Sussex

Thimbles

Enter the characterful hallway of this higgledy-piggledy house and fall under the spell of its charm. Imagine family antiques, pictures, plates, just-picked flowers and duvets as soft as a cloud: a timeless elegance, a fresh country style. Feast your eyes on the garden, six gentle acres that rise to fantastic views… a hammock, 89 varieties of roses, humming honey bees, a lake with an island (for barbecues!), a long lazy swing. Breakfasts and suppers are a dream: eggs from the hens, bacon from the pigs, jams from a jewel of a kitchen garden. Vicki, her family and Lottie the Irish terrier are the icing on the cake.

Minimum stay: 2 nights over bank holiday weekends.

Rooms	2 twin/doubles; 1 double, 1 twin/double, each with separate bath: £00–£110. Singles by arrangement.
Meals	Dinner, 3 courses, £35. Hampers £38. Pub/restaurant 0.5 miles.
Closed	Rarely.

Rooms	1 suite for 2: £80–£90. 1 single sharing bath with family (extra bed available): £45–£55. Singles £45–£75. Extra bed £30.
Meals	Dinner, 1-3 courses, £12.50–£21.50. Lunch £12.50. Pub 1 mile.
Closed	Rarely.

	Sarah Burgoyne Old Whyly, London Road, East Hoathly, Sussex BN8 6EL
Tel	+44 (0)1825 840216
Email	stay@oldwhyly.co.uk
Web	www.oldwhyly.co.uk

	Vicki Wood Thimbles, New Pond Hill, Cross in Hand, Heathfield, Sussex TN21 0NB
Tel	+44 (0)1435 860745
Mobile	+44 (0)7960 588447
Email	vicki.simonwood@btinternet.com
Web	www.thimblesbedandbreakfast.co.uk

Entry 493   Map 5

Entry 494   Map 5

Longbourn

Through the gates and down the drive to a big Victorian house in 12 lovingly nurtured acres. Longbourn is a smallholding with conservation flocks of sheep, pigs and fowl, and a farm shop on site – hence the exceptional breakfasts! (Fresh croissants too.) As for the house, it is large, light, immaculate and a perfect showcase for a fascinating collection of military lithographs. Big bedrooms, one opening to veranda and garden, have deep carpets and elegant wallpapers; the guests' drawing room is equally impressive. Roland and Jane, she an ex-costume designer, are completely charming and love to share their home.

Minimum stay: 2 nights in high season.

Rooms	1 double; 1 double with separate bath: £90–£140. Singles £70–£105.
Meals	Pubs/restaurants within 5 miles.
Closed	Rarely.

Jane Horton
Longbourn,
Burwash Road, Broad Oak,
Heathfield,
Sussex TN21 8XG

Tel	+44 (0)1435 882070
Email	jane@overthestile.com
Web	www.longbourn1895.co.uk

Entry 495   Map 5

King John's Lodge

Deep in the High Weald, down a maze of country lanes, is an enchanting 1650s house in eight acres of heaven: Jill's pride and joy. Inside: oak beams, stone fireplaces, big sofas, and a Jacobean dining room with leaded glass windows, fine setting for a perfect English breakfast. Wing chairs, floral fabrics, dressers with china bowls: the country-house feel extends to the comfortable, carpeted bedrooms. Discover Sissinghurst, Great Dixter, Rye… return to sweeping lawns, wild gardens, ancient apple trees, a woodland walk (spot Titania and Oberon) and a delightful nursery and tea room run by Jill's son.

Minimum stay: 2 nights at weekends & in high season.

Rooms	2 doubles, 1 twin: £95. 1 family room for 3: £130–£150. Singles from £65.
Meals	Dinner, 3 courses, £30 (min. 4). Pubs/restaurants 2.5 miles.
Closed	Rarely.

Jill Cunningham
King John's Lodge,
Sheepstreet Lane,
Etchingham,
Sussex TN19 7AZ

Tel	+44 (0)1580 819232
Email	kingjohnslodge@aol.com
Web	www.kingjohnslodge.com

Entry 496   Map 5

Sussex

Pelham Hall

A 14th-century hall house with a unique touch. Matthew and Chris have worked a stunning refurbishment here with antiques, gorgeous fabrics and hip style. Delightful bedrooms are filled with personality; the ground floor bedroom has French doors overlooking the charming garden; inventively designed bathrooms have plush robes and lotions. Breakfast by the wood-burner, or on the rooftop terrace in summer (glorious views across the Weald); tuck into homemade granola, compote, croissants, delicious cooked choices. Set out for Rudyard Kipling's Batemans, garden gems Sissinghurst and Great Dixter; adorable Carlito the dog welcomes you home.

Rooms	2 twin/doubles; 1 suite for 2 with private sitting room: £90-£120.
Meals	Pubs/restaurants 8 miles.
Closed	Rarely.

Matthew Fox
Pelham Hall,
High Street, Burwash,
Etchingham,
Sussex TN19 7ES

Tel	+44 (0)1435 882335
Email	bookings@pelhamhall.co.uk
Web	pelhamhall.co.uk

Entry 497   Map

Sussex

The Cloudesley

One mile from the sea, a remarkable house full of beautiful things. Shahriar – photographer, holistic therapist, Chelsea gold-medal winner – has created an artistic bolthole: books, African masks, an honesty bar, chic bedrooms and two sitting rooms that double as art galleries. You are looked after with great kindness. Shahriar has a couple of treatment rooms where, in cahoots with local therapists, he offers massage, shiatsu and reiki. You breakfast on exotic fruits, Armagnac omelettes, or the full cooked works; in summer on a bamboo terrace. Don't miss Derek Jarman's cottage at Dungeness or St Clement's for great food.

Minimum stay: 2 nights at weekends. Whole house available. Children over 6 welcome.

Rooms	4 doubles, 1 twin: £75-£135. Extra bed £25.
Meals	Pubs/restaurants 5-minute drive.
Closed	Rarely.

Shahriar Mazandi
The Cloudesley,
7 Cloudesley Road,
St Leonards-on-Sea,
Sussex TN37 6JN

Mobile	+44 (0)7507 000148
Email	info@thecloudesley.co.uk
Web	www.thecloudesley.co.uk

Entry 498   Map 5

Glottenham Castle

History-steeped Glottenham, in Rob and Emma's eco-capable hands, has four brilliantly contrasting spaces sharing outdoor showers and compost loos – all off-grid. Rossetti's full of Victorian eccentricity: peacock feathers, oriental carpet, antique bed, embroidered quilts. Bodichon is pure shabby chic, full of vintage finds: French linen sheets, floral bedspreads, an old luggage trunk. Of the two geodomes de Glottyngham is rustic-quirky with handmade furniture, sheepskin rugs, hand-loomed linen. De Etchyngham is the most remote and idiosyncratic: classic 20th-century fabrics and retro pieces (Ercol, G-Plan). Unconventional.

Bookings start on a Monday or Friday. Book through Sawday's Canopy & Stars online or by phone.

Appletree Cottage

An enviable position facing south for this old hung-tile farmer's house, covered in roses, jasmine and wisteria; views are over farmland towards the coast at Fairlight Glen. Jane will treat you to tea and cake when you arrive – either before a warming fire in the drawing room, or in the garden in summer. Bedrooms are sunny, spacious, quiet and traditional, with gorgeous garden views. Breakfast well on apple juice from their own apples, homemade jams and marmalade, local bacon and sausages. Perfect for walkers with a footpath at the front gate; birdwatchers will be happy too, and you are near the steam railway at Bodiam.

Minimum stay: 2 nights at weekends May-Sept. Children over 8 welcome.

Rooms	2 geodomes for 2-4: £95-£132
	1 yurt for 3: £81-£109
	1 tent for 4: £69-£92.
Meals	Breakfast hampers from £20 for 2.
Closed	September-April.

Rooms	1 twin/double; 2 doubles sharing
	bath (let to same party only): £90.
	1 single with separate bath: £60.
Meals	Pub/restaurant 0.5 miles.
Closed	Rarely.

Sawday's Canopy & Stars
Glottenham Castle,
Glottenham Farm, Bishops Lane,
Robertsbridge, Sussex TN32 5EB
Tel +44 (0)117 204 7830
Email enquiries@canopyandstars.co.uk
Web www.canopyandstars.co.uk/glottenham

Jane & Hugh Willing
Appletree Cottage,
Beacon Lane, Staplecross,
Robertsbridge, Sussex TN32 5QP
Tel +44 (0)1580 831724
Mobile +44 (0)7914 658861
Email appletree.cottage@hotmail.co.uk
Web www.appletreecottage.co

Entry 499   Map

Entry 500   Map 5

Sussex

Swan House

Effortless style drifts through the beamed rooms of this boutiquey B&B in a 1490s bakery, from a roaring inglenook fireplace to an honesty bar in a mock bookcase – all run by relaxed creative hosts Brendan and Lionel. Bedrooms hold surprises: Elizabethan frescoes, an old pulley for bags of flour, a window seat, seashell mosaics and handmade soaps. Step out into lively Old Hastings, wander down to see fishing boats tucked in for the night or find an antiques bargain. Seagulls herald the new day: pick a morning paper; breakfast like kings on organic croissants and local kippers (dinners also on request). Unique.

Warwickshire

Park Farm House

Fronted by a circular drive, the warm red-brick farmhouse is listed and old – it dates from 1655. Linda is friendly and welcoming, a genuine B&B pro, giving you an immaculate guest sitting room filled with pretty family pieces. The bedrooms sport comfortable mattresses, mahogany or brass beds, blankets on request, bathrobes, flowers and magazines; bathrooms are traditional but spotless. A haven of rest from the motorway (morning hum only) this is in the heart of a working farm yet hugely convenient for Birmingham, Warwick, Stratford and Coventry. You may get their own beef at dinner and the vegetables are home-grown.

Rooms	3 doubles: £120-£150. 1 suite for 4: £115-£145. Singles £80-£120.
Meals	Restaurants 2-minute walk.
Closed	Christmas.

Rooms	1 double, 1 twin: £79-£82. Singles from £48.
Meals	Dinner, 3 courses, from £25. Supper £19. Pub/restaurant 1.5 miles.
Closed	Rarely.

	Brendan McDonagh Swan House, 1 Hill Street, Hastings, Sussex TN34 3HU
Tel	+44 (0)1424 430014
Email	res@swanhousehastings.co.uk
Web	www.swanhousehastings.co.uk

	Linda Grindal Park Farm House, Spring Road, Barnacle, Shilton, Coventry, Warwickshire CV7 9LG
Tel	+44 (0)2476 612628
Web	www.parkfarmguesthouse.co.uk

Entry 501   Map 5

Entry 502   Map 8

Warwickshire

Mows Hill Farm

This late-Victorian farmhouse is a working farm of 1,300 acres that has been in the family for generations. Cattle gaze at you from their stalls and all is peaceful. Lynda and Edward's richly furnished home has an elegant, comfortable sitting room with field views, loads of books and magazines, family portraits and an open fire. Beamed bedrooms have cotton sheets, cosy bathrobes, fresh flowers and armchairs for flopping. Wake for a breakfast of homemade bread and jams, fruit salad, home-reared bacon, just-laid eggs – in the oak-floored dining room or in the sunny conservatory. A warm, family home.

Children over 10 welcome.

Rooms	1 twin/double; 1 double with separate bath: £80-£90. Singles £65. Extra bed/sofabed available £15-£30 per person per night.
Meals	Pub/restaurant 3 miles.
Closed	Rarely.

	Lynda Muntz
	Mows Hill Farm,
	Mows Hill Road, Kemps Green,
	Tanworth in Arden,
	Warwickshire B94 5PP
Tel	+44 (0)1564 784312
Mobile	+44 (0)7919 542501
Email	mowshill@farmline.com
Web	www.b-and-bmowshill.co.uk

Entry 503   Map 8

Warwickshire

Shrewley Pools Farm

A charming, eccentric home and fabulous for families, with space to play and animals to see: sheep, bantams and pigs. A fragrant, romantic garden with a blossoming orchard and a fascinating house (1640), all low ceilings, aged floors and steep stairs. Timbered passages lead to large, pretty, sunny bedrooms (all with electric blankets) with leaded windows and polished wooden floors and a family room with everything needed for a baby. In a farmhouse dining room Cathy serves sausages, bacon, and eggs from the farm, can do gluten-free breakfasts and is happy to do teas for children. Buy a day ticket and fish in the lake.

Rooms	1 twin: £65. 1 family room for 4 (cot available): £110. Singles from £50.
Meals	Packed lunch £5. Child's high tea £5. Pub/restaurant 1.5 miles.
Closed	Christmas.

	Cathy Dodd
	Shrewley Pools Farm,
	Five Ways Road,
	Haseley, Warwick,
	Warwickshire CV35 7HB
Tel	+44 (0)1926 484315
Mobile	+44 (0)7818 280681
Email	cathydodd@hotmail.co.uk
Web	www.shrewleypoolsfarm.co.uk

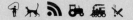

Entry 504   Map 8

Warwickshire

Warwickshire

Austons Down

A fine modern country house with splendid views of the rural Vale of Arden. Your hosts are generous and chatty and look after you well. Their comfortable and relaxed family home has an elegant, light-filled sitting room complete with antiques, fabulous marquetry and open fire; bedrooms are fresh and traditional, bathrooms immaculate. Breakfast on homemade bread, compotes, a continental spread or full English. Admire Jacob sheep on the farm, relax in the terraced gardens. Plenty to visit nearby too: Warwick Castle, Stratford, National Trust properties, classic car museums... and the Monarch's Way is on the doorstep.

Sequoia House

A riverside stroll along the old tramway path brings you to the centre of Stratford. Step into the handsome hallway of this impeccable Victorian house to find high ceilings, deep bays, generous landings and a homely sitting room. The Evanses downsized from the hotel they used to run here, and are happy to treat just a few guests: trouser presses (yes!) and piles of towels mingle with fine old furniture in immaculate bedrooms; two have Swan Theatre views. Hotel touches, a lovely warm welcome, Jean's cake on arrival and homemade preserves at breakfast. Park off road – or leave the car at home.

Rooms	1 double, 2 twin/doubles: £90-£120. Singles £65 (Mon-Thurs).	Rooms	4 doubles: £125. Singles £85.
Meals	Supper from £15. Dinner from £30. Pubs/restaurants 1 mile.	Meals	Pub/restaurant 100 yds.
Closed	Rarely.	Closed	Christmas & New Year.

	Lucy Horner		**Jean & Philip Evans**
	Austons Down,		Sequoia House,
	Saddlebow Lane,		51 Shipston Road,
	Claverdon,		Stratford-upon-Avon,
	Warwickshire CV35 8PQ		Warwickshire CV37 7LN
Tel	+44 (0)1926 842068	Tel	+44 (0)1789 268852
Mobile	+44 (0)7767 657352	Mobile	+44 (0)7833 727914
Email	lmh@austonsdown.com	Email	info@sequoia-house.co.uk
Web	www.austonsdown.com	Web	www.sequoia-house.co.uk

Entry 505   Map 8

Entry 506   Map 8

Warwickshire

Cross o' th' Hill Farm

Stratford is a 12-minute walk by footpath across a field, and from the veranda you can see the church where Shakespeare is buried. The farm predates medieval Stratford with later additions to the house in 1860, though it has an earlier Georgian feel. All is chic, spacious and full of light with deco chandeliers, floor to ceiling sash windows, large uncluttered bedrooms and contemporary bathrooms. Wake to bird song, play the baby grand piano, enjoy croquet on the lawn and picnic in the gardens and orchards. Decima grew up here; she and David are charming hosts and passionate about art and architecture.

Minimum stay: 2 nights at weekends.

Rooms	2 doubles; 1 double with separate bath/shower: £96. Singles from £68.
Meals	Pubs/restaurants 15-minute walk.
Closed	15 December - 28 February.

	Decima Noble
	Cross o' th' Hill Farm,
	Clifford Lane, Stratford-upon-Avon,
	Warwickshire CV37 8HP
Tel	+44 (0)1789 204738
Mobile	+44 (0)7973 971067
Email	decimanoble@hotmail.com
Web	www.cross-o-th-hill-farm.com

Entry 507   Map 8

Warwickshire

Stamford Hall

Soft hills and lines of poplars bring you to the high, pretty red-brick Georgian house with a smart hornbeam hedge. James, whose art decorates the walls, and Alice look after you impeccably but without fuss. You have a generous sitting room overlooking the garden, with gleaming furniture, early estate and garden etchings, and pastel blue sofas. Peaceful bedrooms are on the second floor and both have charm: soft wool tartan rugs on comfy beds, calming colours, attractive fabrics, restful outlooks. Wake to home-baked soda bread and Alice's full English; walk it off in open countryside or head for Stratford.

Rooms	1 double, 1 twin: £85. Singles £60.
Meals	Pub 1 mile.
Closed	Christmas & occasionally.

	James & Alice Kerr
	Stamford Hall,
	Fosse Way, Ettington,
	Stratford-upon-Avon,
	Warwickshire CV37 7PA
Tel	+44 (0)1789 740239
Email	stamfordhall@gmail.com
Web	www.stamfordhall.co.uk

Entry 508   Map 8

Warwickshire

Marston House

A generous feel pervades this lovely family home; Kim's big friendly kitchen is the hub of the house. She and John are easy-going and kind and there's no standing on ceremony. Feel welcomed with tea on arrival, delicious breakfasts, oodles of interesting facts about what to do in the area. The house, with solar electricity, is big and sunny; old rugs cover parquet floors, soft sofas tumble with cushions, sash windows look onto the smart garden packed with birds and borders. Bedrooms are roomy, traditional and supremely comfortable. A special, peaceful place with a big heart, great walks from the door and Silverstone a short hop.

Rooms	2 twin/doubles, each with separate bath/shower: £95–£110. Singles £75.
Meals	Supper, 3 courses, £30. Dinner £35 (min. 4). Pub 5-minute walk.
Closed	Occasionally in winter.

Kim & John Mahon
Marston House,
Byfield Road, Priors Marston,
Southam, Warwickshire CV47 7RP

Tel	+44 (0)1327 260297
Mobile	+44 (0)7813 831028
Email	kim@mahonand.co.uk
Web	www.ivabestbandb.co.uk

Entry 509   Map 8

Warwickshire

The Old Manor House

An attractive 16th-century manor house with beautiful landscaped gardens sweeping down to the river Stour. The beamed double has oak furniture and a big bathroom; the fresh twin rooms (one in a private wing) are simply lovely. There is a large and elegant drawing and dining room for visitors to share, with antiques, contemporary art and an open fire. Jane prepares first-class breakfasts, and in warm weather you can have tea on the terrace: pots of tulips in spring, old scented roses in summer, meadow land beyond. A comfortable, lived-in family house with Stratford and the theatre close by.

Children over 7 welcome.

Rooms	1 double, 2 twin/doubles, each with separate bath: £90–£110. Singles £50–£65.
Meals	Supper £20. Dinner, 3 courses, from £25. Restaurants nearby.
Closed	Rarely.

Jane Pusey
The Old Manor House,
Halford, Shipston-on-Stour,
Warwickshire CV36 5BT

Tel	+44 (0)1789 740264
Mobile	+44 (0)7786 467916
Email	info@oldmanor-halford.fsnet.co.uk
Web	www.oldmanor-halford.co.uk

Entry 510   Map 8

Warwickshire

Salford Farm House

Beautiful within, handsome without. Thanks to subtle colours, oak beams and lovely old pieces, Jane has achieved a seductive combination of comfort and style. A flagstoned hallway and an old rocking horse, ticking clocks, beeswax, fresh flowers: this house is well-loved. Jane was a ballet dancer, Richard has green fingers and runs a fruit farm and farm shop nearby – you may expect meat and game from the Ragley Estate and delicious fruits in season. Bedrooms have a soft, warm elegance and flat-screen TVs, bathrooms are spotless and welcoming, views are to garden or fields. Wholly delightful.

Rooms	2 twin/doubles: £95. Singles £70.
Meals	Dinner £28. Restaurant 2.5 miles.
Closed	Rarely.

	Jane & Richard Beach
	Salford Farm House,
	Salford Priors,
	Evesham,
	Warwickshire WR11 8XN
Tel	+44 (0)1386 870000
Email	salfordfarmhouse@aol.com
Web	www.salfordfarmhouse.co.uk

Entry 511   Map 8

Wiltshire

Brook House

The minute you pull up in the drive you know you're in for a treat. Henry Lamb lived in this Georgian house, Evelyn Waugh came to visit, now it's the home of delightful Kate who gives you local sausages and homemade bread at breakfast. You'll love her farmhouse kitchen with its long cheerful table, the guest sitting room with its open log fire, and the beautiful, luxurious bedrooms, one with a balcony for the view. Gaze on with a glass of wine: the garden with its gorgeous planting and river running through, the visiting ducks, resident hens, the water meadows beyond. The village is charming, Salisbury is close.

Rooms	1 double, 1 twin/double: £85-£95. Singles £55.
Meals	Pub 3-minute walk.
Closed	Rarely.

	Kate Seal
	Brook House,
	Homington Road, Coombe Bissell,
	Salisbury, Wiltshire SP5 4LR
Tel	+44 (0)1722 718242
Mobile	+44 (0)7595 509937
Email	info@brookhousesalisbury.com
Web	www.brookhousesalisbury.com

Entry 512   Map 3

Wiltshire

The Garden Cottage

You'll love the Woodford Valley and this thatched cottage at the edge of the village. It has long views, stacks of character and traditionally decorated rooms: a ground floor twin with roll top bathroom and two cosy doubles upstairs that share a bathroom. Fabrics are flowered, headboards upholstered, mattresses top quality. Breakfast in the handsome, stone-floored country kitchen, or in the pretty garden, on good things local and homemade – like Annie's soda bread. An ancient mulberry reigns supreme in the front garden; roses, honeysuckle and herbaceousness are yours to sit amongst. Then off to Avebury, or Stonehenge?

Cash or cheque accepted.

Rooms	2 doubles sharing bath (let to same party only); 1 twin with separate bath: £70.
Meals	Pub 0.5 miles.
Closed	Rarely.

Annie Arkwright
The Garden Cottage,
Upper Woodford,
Salisbury,
Wiltshire SP4 6PA
Tel   +44 (0)1722 782447
Email annie747@btinternet.com

Entry 513   Map

Wiltshire

The Mill House

In a tranquil village next to the river is a house surrounded by water meadows and wilderness garden. Roses ramble, marsh orchids bloom and butterflies shimmer. This 12-acre labour of love is the creation of ever-charming Diana and her son Michael. Their home, the time-worn 18th-century miller's house, is packed with country clutter – porcelain, foxes' brushes, ancestral photographs above the fire – while bedrooms are quaint and flowery, with firm comfy beds. Locally sourced breakfasts are served at small tables in the pretty dining room. Diana has lived here for many many years, and has been doing B&B for at least 28 of them!

Children over 6 welcome.

Rooms	3 doubles, 1 family room for 4; 1 twin with separate bath: £100. Singles from £65.
Meals	Pub 5-minute walk.
Closed	Rarely.

Diana Gifford Mead & Michael Mertens
The Mill House,
Berwick St James, Salisbury,
Wiltshire SP3 4TS
Tel   +44 (0)1722 790331
Web   www.millhouse.org.uk

Entry 514   Map 3

Wiltshire

Dowtys

A beautifully converted Victorian dairy farm with fabulous views over the Nadder valley. Peaceful, private, stylish bedrooms, one on the ground floor, have original beams, antiques and supremely comfy Vi-Spring beds; bathrooms are perfect. The sunny guest sitting room has a contemporary feel too, with its wood-burner and sliding doors to the well-tended garden. Enjoy a delicious breakfast in the old milking parlour, now the dining room, or on the terrace, sit beneath the espaliered limes in the lovely garden, dip into the National Trust woods. Footpaths start from the gate and your charming hosts will help you with all your plans.

Rooms	1 double (ground floor) with sitting room; 1 twin, 1 double, each with separate bath/shower (second triple bedroom only available as a family suite sharing bath): £78-£95. Singles from £60.
Meals	Packed lunch on request. Pub 0.25 miles.
Closed	Rarely.

Di & Willi Verdon-Smith
Dowtys,
Dowtys Lane,
Dinton, Salisbury,
Wiltshire SP3 5ES
Tel +44 (0)1722 716886
Email dowtys.bb@gmail.com
Web www.dowtysbedandbreakfast.co.uk

Entry 515   Map 3

Wiltshire

The Duck Yard

Independence with your own terrace, entrance and sitting room. Peace too, at the end of the lane; find a charming and colourful cottage garden, a summerhouse and free-ranging ducks and hens. Harriet makes wedding cakes, looks after guests well and cheerfully rustles up fine meals at short notice; breakfasts feature delicious homemade bread. Your carpeted bedroom and aquamarine bathroom are tucked under the eaves; below is the sitting room, cosy with wood-burner, books and old squashy sofas, leading to a sunny terrace. Good for walkers: maps are supplied and you may even borrow a dog.

Rooms	1 twin/double with sitting room: £70-£80. Singles £55.
Meals	Dinner, 3 courses, £25. Packed lunch £7. Pub 2 miles.
Closed	Christmas & New Year.

Harriet & Peter Combes
The Duck Yard,
Sandhills Road,
Dinton, Salisbury,
Wiltshire SP3 5ER
Tel +44 (0)1722 716495
Mobile +44 (0)7729 777436
Email harriet.combes@googlemail.com

Entry 516   Map 3

Wiltshire

Deverill End

Colourful gardens surround this comfortable house, and fantastic views of the Wiltshire downs and Wylye valley, fields of horses and tall steeple stretch as far as the eye can see. Sim and Joy are well-travelled and friendly; their sunny sitting room, warmed by a wood-burner, is full of books, art and African treasures. Comfortable bedrooms are all downstairs: soft colours, posies of flowers and little shower rooms. Have breakfast in the kitchen or dining room; feast on eggs and fruits from the garden, homemade jams and home-grown tomatoes in season – they used to grow 300 acres of them in Africa! Bath and Salisbury are an easy hop.

Children over 10 welcome.

Wiltshire

Oaklands

A comfortable townhouse, a south-facing garden, two dear dogs and a lovely old Silver Cross pram sitting under the stairs. It was the first house in Warminster to have a bathroom; these have multiplied since and the interiors have had a makeover – no wonder this delightful, spacious 1880s house has been in the family forever. Andrew and Carolyn, relaxed and charming, serve delicious breakfasts in the lovely, light-suffused conservatory at the drawing room end. Bedrooms, desirable and welcoming, overlook churchyard, lawns and trees; find soft colours, cosy bathrooms, family antiques. Restaurants are a stroll.

Rooms	2 doubles, 1 twin: £75. Singles £65–£75.
Meals	Pub 0.4 miles.
Closed	Rarely.

Rooms	1 double (en suite); 1 double, 1 twin/double sharing bath (let to same party only): £70–£85. Singles from £55.
Meals	Occasional dinner (min. 4 guests). Pub/restaurant 0.5 miles.
Closed	Christmas & rarely.

	Joy Greathead Deverill End, Deverill Road, Sutton Veny, Warminster, Wiltshire BA12 7BY
Tel	+44 (0)1985 840356
Email	deverillend@gmail.com
Web	www.deverillend.co.uk

	Carolyn & Andrew Lewis Oaklands, 88 Boreham Road, Warminster, Wiltshire BA12 9JW
Tel	+44 (0)1985 215532
Mobile	+44 (0)7702 587533
Email	apl1944@yahoo.co.uk
Web	www.stayatoaklands.co.uk

Entry 517 Map 3

Entry 518 Map 3

Wiltshire

Rushall Manor

A gorgeous country house – and Caroline is a treat of a host. The dining room shines with glass, antiques and family portraits; a particularly impressive admiral gazes benignly down as you tuck into breakfast: local eggs and sausages, and jams from the orchard. The harmonious sitting room has comfy sofas, books and games; pretty bedrooms have perfect mattresses and linen (and, from one, fantastic views up to Salisbury Plain); bathrooms come with cast-iron baths, scented soaps and lashings of hot water. Stonehenge and Salisbury are nearby, walks are good, and Caroline holds the village fête in her delightful garden.

Rooms	1 twin (en suite); 1 double, 1 twin, each with separate bath: £100. Singles £60.
Meals	Dinner £30. Pubs 1 mile.
Closed	Rarely.

Caroline Larken
Rushall Manor,
Rushall, Pewsey,
Wiltshire SN9 6EG

Tel   +44 (0)1980 630301
Email   bandb@rushallmanor.com
Web   www.rushallmanor.com

Entry 519   Map 3

Wiltshire

Westcourt Farm

A medieval, Grade II* cruck truss hall house... beautifully restored by Rozzie and Jonny and snoozing amid wildflower meadows, hedgerows, ponds and geese. Delightful people, they love to cook and can spoil you rotten. Rooms are well decorated, crisp yet traditional, the country furniture is charming and the architecture fascinating. Bedrooms have comfortable beds and fine linen, bathrooms are spot-on; there's a lovely light drawing room and a barn for meetings and parties too. Encircled by footpaths and fields, Westcourt is the oldest house in a perfect village, two minutes from a rather good pub.

Rooms	1 double, 1 twin: £85. Singles £50.
Meals	Pub/restaurant in village.
Closed	Rarely.

Jonny & Rozzie Buxton
Westcourt Farm,
Shalbourne, Marlborough,
Wiltshire SN8 3QE

Tel   +44 (0)1672 871399
Email   rozzieb@btinternet.com
Web   www.westcourtfarm.com

Entry 520   Map 3

Wiltshire

Dorchester House

Down a lane with leafy views to the castle and gorgeous garden… yet this house is in the middle of the lively market town. Inside all is immaculate and sumptuous. Find silk curtains, sink-into sofas, a grand piano and shelves laden with tea cups, figurines and antique porcelain; the dining room gleams with colour and candlelight. Sunny bedrooms are pretty in chintz, with flowers, art and delicious linen. Deborah is a Leith's chef and breakfast is good too with baked eggs under a herb crust, croissants and all sorts of homemade treats. Theatre and museum are an amble, there's a summer festival, and Bath is a 40-minute drive.

Minimum stay: 2 nights at weekends. Pets by arrangement.

Rooms	1 double; 1 twin sharing bath with single: £50–£100. 1 single sharing bath with twin: £50. Dinner, B&B £65–£75 per person.
Meals	Dinner, 3 courses with wine, £20–£30. Pubs/restaurants 5-minute walk.
Closed	Rarely.

	Deborah Dobson Dorchester House, Castle Grounds, Devizes, Wiltshire SN10 1HH
Tel	+44 (0)1380 722123
Email	dobsondesignassociates@gmail.com
Web	www.dorchester-house.co.uk

Entry 521   Map

Wiltshire

Granby House

This grand country house has a delicious boutique hotel feel. The sweeping drive leads you through beautifully landscaped gardens and you arrive to tea by the fire. Nothing is too much trouble for Maddie and Hud – you will be welcomed as one of the family. Lose yourself for hours in the garden: gazebo, terraces with balustrades, a wisteria walk and wandering guinea fowl. Sink into luxuriously comfortable bedrooms named after the trees; two lead onto a shared balcony; all have rich fabrics and a welcoming sherry. Pretty Bradford-on-Avon has independent shops and cafés, and you can take the train to Bath. A special place.

Young people over 16 welcome.

Rooms	3 doubles, 3 twins: £90–£175. Extra bed/sofabed available £40.
Meals	Pubs/restaurants 1 mile.
Closed	Rarely.

	Madeline Cooper Granby House, Elms Cross, Bradford-on-Avon, Wiltshire BA15 2AL
Tel	+44 (0)1225 868000
Email	info@granbyhousebandb.co.uk
Web	www.granbyhousebandb.co.uk

Entry 522   Map

Wiltshire

The Limes

Through the electric gates, past the gravelled car park and the pretty, box-edged front garden and you arrive at the middle part of a 1620 house divided into three. The beams, stone mullions and leaded windows are charming, and Ellodie is an exceptional hostess. Immaculate, comfortable bedrooms have pretty curtains and fresh flowers, smart bathrooms have good soaps and thick towels, logs glow in the grate, and breakfasts promise delicious Wiltshire bacon, prunes soaked in orange juice and organic bread. You are on the main road leading out of Melksham – catch the bus to Bath from right outside the door.

Rooms	2 twin/doubles: £88-£92.
	1 single: £58-£62.
Meals	Pub 1.5 miles.
Closed	January 2015 to early March.

Ellodie van der Wulp
The Limes,
Shurnhold House, Shurnhold,
Melksham,
Wiltshire SN12 8DG

Tel	+44 (0)1225 790627
Mobile	+44 (0)7974 366892
Email	eevanderwulp@gmail.com

Entry 523   Map 3

Wiltshire

Glebe House

The rogues' gallery of photographs up the stairs says it all: Glebe House is quirky and fun. Friendly Ginny spoils you rotten with pressed linen and sociable dinners. Charming, cosy and comfortable are the bedrooms, one with an Indian theme; delightful is the drawing room with its landscape oils and a large rug from Jaipur; settle into the sofa and roast away by the fire. Breads and jams are homemade – Ginny's marmalade won Gold at the Dalemain World's Original Marmalade competition! Beautiful woodland fills the valley, the cottage garden, alive with birds, wraps around the house and Mr Biggles – the grey parrot – chats by the Aga.

Rooms	1 double, 1 twin: £80-£85.
	Singles £50-£60.
Meals	Dinner, 3 courses, from £25 (BYO).
	Pub 4 miles.
Closed	Christmas.

Ginny Scrope
Glebe House,
Chittoe, Chippenham,
Wiltshire SN15 2EL

Tel	+44 (0)1380 850864
Mobile	+44 (0)7767 608841
Email	ginnyscrope@gmail.com
Web	www.glebehouse-chittoe.co.uk

Entry 524   Map 3

Wiltshire

Mays Farm

Come to be refreshed… a lovely old Cotswold stone farmhouse with a vast 17th-century inglenook and a relaxed feel. Kim and Penelope's home is charming, with art collected on their travels, shelves of books, striped sofas, wood fires and beautiful wide elm boards. Bedrooms are pretty, fresh and comfy. Breakfast is a moveable feast: at the big kitchen table, in the library/dining room, out on the sunny patio – or even a continental in bed; tuck into homemade bread, Aga porridge, jams made by a friend. The walled garden has a little wildflower meadow, espaliered apple trees – and an old privy with double seats inside… very friendly!

Minimum stay: 2 nights at weekends.

Rooms	2 doubles, 2 twins: £90–£120. 1 single: £65–£95. Extra bed/sofabed available £10–£20 per person per night.
Meals	Pubs/restaurants 2 miles.
Closed	Rarely.

Penelope & Kim Swithinbank
Mays Farm,
25 The Street,
Hullavington,
Chippenham,
Wiltshire SN14 6DP
Tel +44 (0)1666 838332
Email kimss@mac.com

Entry 525   Map

Wiltshire

Manor Farm

Farmyard heaven in the Cotswolds. A 17th-century manor farmhouse in 550 arable acres; horses in the paddock, dozing dogs in the yard, tumbling blooms outside the door and a perfectly tended village, with duck pond, a short walk. Beautiful bedrooms are softly lit, with muted colours, plump goose down pillows and the crispest linen. Breakfast in front of the fire is a banquet of delights, tea among the roses is a treat, thanks to charming, welcoming Victoria; she will arrange a table for dinner at the pub too. This is the postcard England of dreams, with Castle Combe, Lacock, grand walking and gardens to visit.

Children over 12 welcome.

Rooms	2 doubles; 1 twin with separate bath: £84. Singles from £46.
Meals	Pub nearby.
Closed	Rarely.

Victoria Lippiatt-Onslow
Manor Farm,
Alderton, Chippenham,
Wiltshire SN14 6NL
Tel +44 (0)1666 840271
Mobile +44 (0)7721 415824
Email victoria.lippiatt@btinternet.com
Web www.themanorfarm.co.uk

Entry 526   Map 3

Wiltshire

Manor Farm

The road through the sleepy Wiltshire village brings you to a charming Queen Anne house with a *petit château* feel, enfolded by a beautiful walled garden with wildflower meadow, hens and ducks, orchard and groomed lawns. Inside is as lovely. The eclectically furnished drawing room, shared among guests, has a real fire and a lived-in, family feel. Bedrooms are comfortable and elegant with Queen Anne panelling, feather pillows on comfortable beds, good art and garden views. Wake for scrumptious, all-organic breakfasts, served in the dining room or kitchen. Clare is an artist and runs a gallery and courses in the studio.

Children over 4 welcome.

Rooms	2 doubles: £100. Singles £65.
Meals	Pub 3-minute walk.
Closed	Christmas & New Year.

	Clare Inskip
	Manor Farm,
	Little Somerford, Malmesbury,
	Chippenham, Wiltshire SN15 5JW
Tel	+44 (0)1666 822140
Mobile	+44 (0)7970 892344
Email	clareinskip@gmail.com

Entry 527   Map 3

Wiltshire

Dauntsey Park House

Be awed by history here. Parts of the house – like the grand dining room where you breakfast – date from Elizabethan times; the stunning summer drawing room is Edwardian. Both rooms are yours to use. Emma and her Italian husband have four young children and a flair for matching new with old: a striking glass chandelier sets off the sturdy oak table beneath; a turbine keeps the house in hot water. Up a wide staircase, two wallpapered bedrooms with views to the river are huge and comfortable with a self-indulgent feel (one has a thunderbox loo!). St James the Great church with its 14th-century doom board is in the garden. Lovely.

Rooms	1 double, 1 twin: £120. Singles £75.
Meals	Pubs/restaurants in village.
Closed	Occasionally.

	Emma Amati
	Dauntsey Park House,
	Dauntsey, Chippenham,
	Wiltshire SN15 4HT
Tel	+44 (0)1249 721777
Email	enquiries@dauntseyparkhouse.co.uk
Web	www.dauntseyparkhouse.co.uk

Entry 528   Map 3

Wiltshire

Wiltshire

Bullocks Horn Cottage

Up a country lane is this hidden-away house which the delightful Legges have turned into a haven of peace. Liz loves fabrics and flowers and mixes them with flair, Colin has painted a mural for the conservatory, bright with plants and wicker sofa. Super bedrooms, both twins, have lovely views; the sitting room has a log fire, fine antiques, big comfy sofas, and the garden is so special it's appeared in magazines. Home-grown organic veg and herbs and local seasonal food make an appearance at dinner which, on balmy nights, you may eat under the arbour, covered in climbing roses and jasmine.

Children over 10 welcome.

Carriers Farm

The stylishly converted dairies behind the main house are surrounded by acres of peaceful, organic pasture. Old milk churns act as planters, and you step in to delightful bedrooms 'Hare', 'Pheasant' or 'Fox'. Find restful whites with oak floors, pretty pine pieces, feather pillows and tip-top linen. Wake for delicious breakfast choices served in the sunny garden room: smoked salmon and cream cheese, homemade breads and jams, local ham and sausages, eggs from the hens. Fiona is friendly and helpful, and it's a treat to stay. Westonbirt Arboretum and Highgrove are close, and you can walk over the fields to supper at the pub.

Rooms	1 twin; 1 twin/double with separate shower: £95. Singles supplement £15
Meals	Dinner £25–£30. BYO. Pub 1.5 miles.
Closed	Christmas.

Rooms	3 doubles: £80. Singles from £65.
Meals	Pubs within walking distance.
Closed	Rarely.

Colin & Liz Legge
Bullocks Horn Cottage,
Charlton, Malmesbury,
Wiltshire SN16 9DZ

Tel	+44 (0)1666 577600
Email	bullockshorn@clara.co.uk
Web	www.bullockshorn.co.uk

Fiona Butterfield
Carriers Farm,
Luckington Road, Sherston,
Malmesbury, Wiltshire SN16 0QA

Tel	+44 (0)1666 841445
Email	carriersfarm@btinternet.com
Web	www.carriersfarm.co.uk

Entry 529   Map 3

Entry 530   Map

Wiltshire

Bridges Court

You're in the heart of the village with its small shop, friendly pub and the Melvilles' lovely 18th-century farmhouse. They haven't lived here long but it's so homely you'd never tell. Dogs wander, horses whinny, there's a beautiful garden with a Kiftsgate rose and a swimming pool for sunny days. On the second floor, off a corridor filled with paintings, are three florally inspired bedrooms: comfortable, bright and spacious with views to the village green. Breakfast leisurely on all things local at the long table in a dining room filled with silver and china. And there's a pleasant guests' sitting room to relax in.

Worcestershire

Huntlands Farm

Deep in the rural shires Lucy and Stephen run delightful B&B on a working farm (sheep, cattle, pigs). They've lovingly coaxed this 15th-century house back to life: huge rooms, two with four-posters, are deeply comfortable with patterned rugs on wide floorboards, reclaimed wardrobes and views over the orchard or farm. You get roll top tubs to wallow in, fluffy towels and local soaps. Breakfast in the convivial dining room on eggs from the hens, sausages from the pigs and homemade preserves. There's dinner too, roasts and stews or traditional Caribbean fare. The Malvern showground is nearby.

Minimum stay: 2 nights. Children over 10 welcome.

Rooms	1 double, 1 twin; 1 double with separate bath: £80–£90. Singles £60. (Discount for 3 nights or more, excluding Badminton w/e.)
Meals	Pub in village.
Closed	Rarely.

Rooms	2 doubles: £90–£100. 1 suite for 2: £95–£100.
Meals	Dinner, 3 courses, £24.50. Pubs/restaurants 0.5 miles.
Closed	Rarely.

	Fiona Melville
	Bridges Court,
	Luckington,
	Wiltshire SN14 6NT
Tel	+44 (0)1666 840215
Mobile	+44 (0)7711 816839
Email	fionamelville2003@yahoo.co.uk
Web	www.bridgescourt.co.uk

	Lucy Brodie
	Huntlands Farm,
	Gaines Road, Whitbourne,
	Worcester,
	Worcestershire WR6 5RD
Tel	+44 (0)1886 821955
Mobile	+44 (0)7828 286360
Email	lucy@huntlandsfarm.co.uk
Web	www.huntlandsfarm.co.uk

Entry 531   Map 3

Entry 532   Map 8

The Old Rectory

The listed 18th-century rectory has taken on a new lease of life, thanks to welcoming Claire (and John and two spaniels) whose ethos is flexibility and whose generosity spreads far. Relax in the library, the breakfast room, the garden full of birds, the grand red drawing room that overlooks Elgar country. Beautiful bedrooms are sumptuously furnished with old and new pieces, fluffy bathrobes and feather duvets, artisan biscuits and Malvern spring water. Claire is an inspired cook: breakfasts, beautifully sourced, are a treat, and candlelit dinners are amazing. Bliss for walkers, foodies, romantics, and all who love the Malverns.

Old Country Farm & The Lighthouse

Ella's passion for this tranquil place — and conservation of its wildlife — is infectious. She's keen on home-grown and local food too so breakfast is delicious. Dating from the 1400s, the farm is a delightful rambling medley: russet stone and colour-washed brick, huge convivial round table by the Aga, rugs on polished floors. The sitting room has wood-burner, piano and books, and you sleep soundly in pretty, cottagey bedrooms: lovely linen, garden flowers. In winter you stay in The Lighthouse, down the lane: an inspired green-oak retreat with soaring beams, snug library, comfy downstairs bedrooms and roses in the garden. Magical.

Rooms	3 doubles, 1 twin/double: £130–£150. Singles £100.
Meals	Dinner £37.50. Pubs/restaurants 1 mile.
Closed	Never.

Rooms	1 double; 2 doubles, each with separate bath/shower: £65–£90. Singles £35–£55.
Meals	Pubs/restaurants 3 miles.
Closed	Rarely.

One of a kind

Claire Dawkins
The Old Rectory,
Rectory Lane,
Cradley, Malvern,
Worcestershire WR13 5LQ

Tel   +44 (0)1886 880109
Mobile +44 (0)7920 801701
Email oldrectorycradley@btinternet.com
Web   www.oldrectorycradley.com

Ella Grace Quincy
Old Country Farm & The Lighthouse,
Mathon,
Malvern,
Worcestershire WR13 5PS

Tel   +44 (0)1886 880867
Email ella@oldcountryhouse.co.uk
Web   www.oldcountryhouse.co.uk

Entry 533   Map 8

Entry 534   Map 8

Worcestershire

Bidders Croft

Completely rebuilt in 1995 from 200-year-old bricks, this solid house has oak-framed loggias and an enormous conservatory where you eat overlooking the garden, orchard, vineyard and the Malvern Hills. Traditional bedrooms with mirror-fronted wardrobes and dressing tables are warm and comfortable; bathrooms shine. Bill and Charlotte give you a log fire, books and magazines in the drawing room and an Aga-cooked breakfast with home-produced eggs and fruits. There is a large terrace overlooking lawns and an ornamental pond; the hills beckon walkers, the views soar and the Malvern theatres are a short drive.

Minimum stay: 2 nights. Children over 12 welcome.

Rooms	1 double; 1 twin with separate bath: £90-£95. Singles £55.
Meals	Pub/restaurant 250 yards.
Closed	Christmas & New Year.

Bill & Charlotte Carver
Bidders Croft,
Welland,
Malvern,
Worcestershire WR13 6LN
Tel   +44 (0)1684 592179
Email carvers@bidderscroft.com
Web   www.bidderscroft.com

Entry 535   Map 8

Worcestershire

The Birches

Thoughtful Katharine is attentive; Edward puts you at ease humming a jolly tune. Come and go as you please from this self-contained annexe, spotless and contemporary. French windows lead to a pretty terrace, then to a charming garden opening to fields and views of the Malverns. Though the house is easily accessible, the tranquillity is sublime; plenty of spots to sit and ponder the view back to the timber-framed house. Hens pottering on the lawn lay eggs for breakfast, served — in your room — with local bacon and sausages, and bread from Ledbury's baker. Wander further for abundant leafy walks and lovely Regency Malvern.

Rooms	Annexe - 1 double: £80. Singles £60.
Meals	Pub/restaurant 0.3 miles.
Closed	Rarely.

Katharine Litchfield
The Birches,
Birts Street, Birtsmorton, Malvern,
Worcestershire WR13 6AW
Tel   +44 (0)1684 833821
Mobile +44 (0)7875 458441
Email   katharine-thebirches@hotmail.co.uk
Web   www.the-birchesbedandbreakfast.co.uk

Entry 536   Map 8

Worcestershire

South House Alpacas

If it's the good life you're after then look no further. This handsome Georgian house looks out over not only a beautiful walled garden complete with ancient mulberry tree but rows of neat vegetables, trellised vines and an orchard with a growing herd of alpacas. Guests stay on the first floor of the old coach house and the softly carpeted, beamed rooms are light and spacious with wooden furniture and gorgeous beds; shower with organic soap whilst gazing out on your Andean neighbours! Your charming hosts are passionate about their animals and their little slice of England: this is the most civilised self-sufficiency project imaginable.

Rooms	2 doubles: £110–£120.
Meals	Supper £15.
	Dinner, 2-3 courses, £25–£35.
	Pub 1 mile.
Closed	Rarely.

Amanda Dartnell
South House Alpacas,
Main Street,
South Littleton, Evesham,
Worcestershire WR11 8TJ

Tel	+44 (0)1386 830848
Email	amandadartnell@icloud.com
Web	www.southhousealpacas.com

Entry 537   Map 8

Yorkshire

Broomhead

High in the ancient county of Hallamshire, amid curlews and skylarks and 6,000 acres of National Park, is the renovated stable block of Broomhead Hall. This warm, light, contemporary conversion is home to a lovely young family, passionate about the land and their responsibility for it. After a day of trout fishing or picnicking beside Ewden Beck, bliss to come home to cosy soothing bedrooms with beds heaped with pillows and breathtaking views. A fire-warmed snug rammed with books, a huge oil painting of the grouse moor up high, eggs from their hens and home-baked bread at breakfast: it's fabulous.

Rooms	2 twin/doubles: £100.
	Singles £80.
Meals	Packed lunch £8.
	Pub/restaurant 2.5 miles.
Closed	Rarely.

Catherine Rimington Wilson
Broomhead,
Bolsterstone,
Sheffield, Yorkshire S36 4ZA

Tel	+44 (0)1142 882161
Mobile	+44 (0)7706 483346
Email	catherine_heaton@yahoo.co.uk
Web	www.broomheadestate.co.uk

Entry 538   Map 12

Yorkshire

Sunnybank

A Victorian gentleman's residence just a short walk up the hill from the centre of bustling *Last of the Summer Wine* Holmfirth, still with its working Picturedrome cinema (touring bands too), arts and folk festivals, restaurants and shops. Attentive hosts look after you when the Whites are away. Peaceful bedrooms have a mix of contemporary, Art Nouveau and Art Deco pieces, caramel cream velvets and silks, spoiling bathrooms and lovely valley or garden views. A full choice Yorkshire breakfast will set you up for a lazy stroll round the charming gardens, or a brisk yomp through rural bliss.

Minimum stay: 2 nights at weekends. Children over 12 welcome.

Rooms	2 doubles, 1 twin/double with extra single bed: £68–£115. Singles £58–£105.
Meals	Afternoon tea, with sandwiches, on request. Packed lunch £12. Pubs/restaurants 500 yds.
Closed	Rarely.

Mike & Sue Ardley
Sunnybank,
78 Upperthong Lane,
Holmfirth,
Yorkshire HD9 3BQ

Tel +44 (0)1484 684065
Email info@sunnybankguesthouse.co.uk
Web www.sunnybankguesthouse.co.uk

Entry 539   Map 12

Yorkshire

Thurst House Farm

This solid Pennine farmhouse, its stone mullion windows denoting 17th-century origins, is English to the core. Your warm, gracious hosts give guests a cosy and carpeted sitting room with an open fire in winter; bedrooms are equally generous, with inviting brass beds, lovely antique linen and fresh flowers. Outside: clucking hens, two friendly sheep and a hammock in a garden with beautiful views. Tuck into homemade bread, marmalade and jams at breakfast, and good traditional English dinners, too – just the thing for walkers who've trekked the Calderdale or the Pennine Way.

Children over 8 welcome.

Rooms	1 double; 1 family room for 4: £80. Singles by arrangement.
Meals	Dinner, 4 courses, £25 (BYO). Packed lunch £5. Restaurants within 0.5 miles.
Closed	Christmas & New Year.

David & Judith Marriott
Thurst House Farm,
Soyland, Ripponden, Sowerby
Bridge, Yorkshire HX6 4NN

Tel +44 (0)1422 822820
Mobile +44 (0)7759 619043
Email judith@thursthousefarm.co.uk
Web www.thursthousefarm.co.uk

Entry 540   Map 12

Yorkshire

Field House

You drive over bridge and beck to this listed, 1713 farmhouse – expect comfort, homeliness and open fires. Pat and Geoff love showing guests their hens, horses, goats and lambs, and will tell you about the 14 circular walks or lend you a torch so you can find the pub across the fields! Ramblers and dog walkers will be in heaven – step out of the front door, past the lovely walled garden and you're in rolling, Brontë countryside. Good big bedrooms are in farmhouse style, one bathroom has a roll top bath. Geoff's breakfasts are generous in the finest Yorkshire manner.

Yorkshire

Ponden House

Bump your way up the farm track to Brenda's sturdy house, high on the Pennine Way. The spring water makes wonderful tea, the ginger scones are delicious and the house hums with interest and artistic touches. Comfy sofas are jollied up with throws, there are homespun rugs and hangings, paintings, plants and a piano. Feed the hens, plonk your boots by the Aga, chat with your lovely leisurely hostess as she turns out fab home cooking; food is a passion. Bedrooms are exuberant, comfortable and cosy, it's great for walkers and there's a hot tub under the stars (bookable by groups in advance). Good value with a relaxed, homely feel.

Rooms	1 twin/double, 1 double with extra single bed: £70-£80. 1 family room for 4 with separate bath/shower: £70-£80. Singles £39-£46. Children £20. Cot & highchair available.
Meals	Packed lunch available. Pub/restaurant 200 yds.
Closed	Rarely.

Rooms	2 doubles; 1 twin with separate bath (occasionally sharing bath with family): £75-£80. Singles from £45.
Meals	Dinner, 3 courses, £18. BYO. Packed lunch £6. Pub/restaurant 1 mile.
Closed	Rarely.

	Pat & Geoff Horrocks-Taylor Field House, Staups Lane, Stump Cross, Halifax, Yorkshire HX3 6XX
Tel	+44 (0)1422 355457
Mobile	+44 (0)7729 996482
Email	stayatfieldhouse@yahoo.co.uk
Web	www.fieldhouse-bb.co.uk

	Brenda Taylor Ponden House, Stanbury, Haworth, Yorkshire BD22 0HR
Tel	+44 (0)1535 644154
Email	brenda.taylor@pondenhouse.co.uk
Web	www.pondenhouse.co.uk

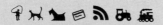

Entry 541   Map 12

Entry 542   Map 12

Yorkshire

No 3 at Settle

Freshly baked Aga scones set the scene for a pampering stay. Judith is a keen cook, and she and Martin are friendly hosts. No 3 is at the end of a terrace of handsome 19th-century houses, near the centre of this bustling Yorkshire Dales market town. Elegant bedrooms (quiet at night) have supremely comfortable beds, TVs, tea trays with jars of homemade treats, and luxurious bathrooms. Breakfast is in the attractive kitchen at a long oak table by French windows – eat out on the terrace on sunny days. Your hosts can help plan outings: National Park walks, Way of the Roses cycle route, local theatre... return for a tasty supper.

Children over 7 welcome.

Rooms	3 doubles: £95–£130. Singles £85–£120. Extra bed/sofabed available at no charge.
Meals	Dinner, 3 courses, £25–£35 (min. 6). Picnic £10–£20. Pubs/restaurants 100 yds.
Closed	Rarely.

Judith King & Martin Perkins
No 3 at Settle,
Duke Street, Settle,
Yorkshire BD24 9AW
Tel   +44 (0)1729 825673
Mobile +44 (0)7717 708906
Email   info@no3atsettle.co.uk
Web   www.no3atsettle.co.uk

Entry 543   Map 12

Yorkshire

Ellerbeck House

Walk from the door of this beautifully restored country house, or head west to the Lakes, east to the Dales, north to Scotland. Period rooms display exquisite antiques and Harriet's artistic touch: sofas and curtains in dark pink and cream, Persian rugs on shiny oak floors, marble fireplaces, stained glass in the stairwell, huge sash windows overlooking the lawn. One window holds the breakfast table – full Cumbrian, at flexible times. Outside, a courtyard for sitting out with the birds and the breeze. It's all so pretty, as is this bucolic – yet accessible – spot near Kirkby Lonsdale, Settle, and Kendal of Mint Cake fame.

Rooms	1 double: £90. Singles £45–£55.
Meals	Pubs/restaurants 2 miles.
Closed	Rarely.

Harriet Sharp
Ellerbeck House,
Westhouse, Ingleton,
Carnforth,
Yorkshire LA6 3NH
Tel   +44 (0)15242 41872
Email   harrietnsharp@gmail.com
Web   www.ellerbeckhouse.co.uk

Entry 544   Map 12

Yorkshire

Yorkshire

Low Mill

Off the village green this handsome historic mill in the Dales keeps many of its original features. The huge beamed guest sitting room has a roaring fire, and the old waterwheel is working! Friendly relaxed Neil and Jane have restored their home, then filled it with interesting art, quirky sculpture, flowers and vintage gems. Bedrooms have tip-top linen and luxurious throws; bathrooms are fabulous. Eat well at separate tables on all things local and home grown, bacon, pancakes, homemade bread; and for dinner, perhaps Yorkshire ham or herby lamb. The pretty riverside garden is perfect for chilling with a glass of wine.

Waterford House

Middleham Castle — northern stronghold of Richard III — stands around the corner from this attractive Georgian house. Martin and Anne are great hosts and their house is full of beautiful things: clocks everywhere, polished chests, vintage luggage, interesting art. There's an open fire in the sitting room, claret walls in the dining room — and delicious breakfasts from Anne. Pretty bedrooms (one up steep stairs) have bags of comfort: four-posters, decanters of sherry, homemade cakes. Middleham is a racing village with 14 stable yards — horses clop by in the morning on their way to the gallops. Bring hiking boots and unravel the Dales.

Rooms	2 doubles: £105–£170. 1 suite for 2: £90–£160. 25% discount for singles.	Rooms	2 doubles, 1 four-poster, 1 four-poster with extra single: £98–£135.
Meals	Dinner, 2-3 courses, £17.50–£22.50. Pubs 5-minute drive.	Meals	Singles from £85. Restaurants within 200 yds.
Closed	Rarely.	Closed	Christmas & January.

Neil McNair
Low Mill,
Bainbridge,
Leyburn,
Yorkshire DL8 3EF
Tel +44 (0)1969 650553
Email lowmillguesthouse@gmail.com
Web www.lowmillguesthouse.co.uk

Martin Cade & Anne Parkinson
Cade
Waterford House,
Kirkgate, Middleham, Leyburn,
Yorkshire DL8 4PG
Tel +44 (0)1969 622090
Email info@waterfordhousehotel.co.uk
Web www.waterfordhousehotel.co.uk

Entry 545   Map 12

Entry 546   Map 12

Yorkshire

The Grange

Through glorious Dales to the pretty village green, where you have a wing of this attractive, old stone house to yourselves. Step into an airy space with original oak beams, comfy sofa, Persian rug and books. Antique and contemporary pieces blend, the bed is clad in pure cotton, the simple shower room has fluffy towels, and there's a kitchen area for rustling up snacks. Your hosts are delightful: Sam has his cabinet making business in the outbuildings; Georgina (professional cook) brings over locally sourced breakfasts and hearty suppers: eggs from the hens, homemade marmalade, smoked salmon… lasagne, crumbles. A friendly place.

Minimum stay: 2 nights at weekends.

Rooms	1 double with sitting & kitchen area: £80. Singles £60–£75. Dinner, B&B £100–£120 per person.
Meals	Dinner, 3-courses £40, 2-courses £30, light supper £15. Restaurant 75 yds.
Closed	Never.

Georgina Anderson
The Grange,
East Witton, Leyburn,
Yorkshire DL8 4SL
Mobile +44 (0)7957 144467
Email georgina@thegrangebedandbreakfast.co.uk
Web www.thegrangebedandbreakfast.co.uk

Entry 547   Map 12

Yorkshire

Manor House

It's the handsomest house in the village. Annie – warm, intelligent, fun – invites you in to spacious interiors elegantly painted and artfully cluttered. Tall shuttered windows and a big open fire, candles in glass sconces and heaps of flowers, soft wool carpets and charming fabrics: a genuinely relaxing family home. Bedrooms are a treat, one with green views on two sides and a bathroom with a French country feel; fittings are vintage but spotless. Stride the Dales or discover Georgian Richmond, a hop away; return to a simple delicious supper, with veg from the garden and eggs from the hens.

Rooms	1 double; 1 twin/double with separate bath: £95. Singles £80.
Meals	Supper, 2 courses, £25. BYO. Pubs 1 mile.
Closed	Christmas.

Annabel Burchnall
Manor House,
Middle Street,
Gayles, Richmond,
Yorkshire DL11 7JF
Tel +44 (0)1833 621578
Email annieburchnall@hotmail.com

Entry 548   Map 12

Lovesome Hill Farm

Who could resist home-reared lamb followed by apple crumble cake? This is a working farm and the Pearsons the warmest people imaginable; even in the mayhem of the lambing season they greet you with delicious homemade biscuits and Yorkshire tea. Their farmhouse is as unpretentious as they are: chequered tablecloths, cosy bedrooms (four in the old granary, one in the cottage) with garden and hill views, and a Victorian-style sitting room. Wake to award winning breakfasts of their own bacon and sausages, home-laid eggs and homemade bread and jams. Easy access to A167 and brilliantly placed for Moors and Dales. Good for walkers, families, business people.

Mill Close

Country-house B&B in a tranquil spot among fields and woodland; spacious, luxurious and with your own entrance through a flower-filled conservatory. Beds are large and comfortable, there's a grand four-poster with a spa bath, lovely linen and sconces for flickering candle light. Be spoiled by handmade chocolates, fluffy robes, even your own 'quiet' fridge. An elegant, pretty blue and cream sitting room has an open fire – but you are between the National Park and the Dales so walks are a must. Start with one of Patricia's famous breakfasts: bacon and sausages from the farm, smoked haddock or salmon, homemade jams. Bliss.

Rooms	1 double, 1 twin: £72-£80. 1 family room for 4: £80-£110. 1 single. £42-£45. Gate Cottage - 1 double: £84-£90.
Meals	Dinner, 2 courses, £18-£25. BYO. Packed lunch £5. Pub 4 miles.
Closed	Rarely.

Rooms	1 four-poster, 2 twin/doubles: £80-£95. Singles £45-£65.
Meals	Pubs/restaurants 2 miles.
Closed	Christmas & New Year.

John & Mary Pearson
Lovesome Hill Farm,
Lovesome Hill, Northallerton,
Yorkshire DL6 2PB
Tel +44 (0)1609 772311
Email lovesomehillfarm@btinternet.com
Web www.lovesomehillfarm.co.uk

Patricia Knox
Mill Close,
Patrick Brompton, Bedale,
Yorkshire DL8 1JY
Tel +44 (0)1677 450257
Email pat@millclose.co.uk
Web www.millclose.co.uk

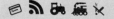

Entry 549   Map 12

Entry 550   Map 12

Yorkshire

Low Sutton

Judi's biscuits are a sweet welcome, Steve has a twinkle in his eye: they're B&B pros. Wood fires in the vast dining/sitting room and cosy snug burn fuel from their own copse; good insulation and underfloor heating keep the homely rooms comfy. Curl up in a soft white robe with a book, or wallow in the sparkling bathrooms – one is solar-heated (more greenie points!). There are six acres to explore with ponies, sheep, dogs and chickens; taste the fruit keen cook Judi jams up for breakfast and expect good dinners with veggies from the garden. Country delights from abbeys to markets are in easy reach.

Rooms	2 doubles: £75. Singles £50.
Meals	Packed lunch £5. Dinner £25. Pub/restaurant 1.5 miles.
Closed	Rarely.

	Judi Smith
	Low Sutton,
	Masham, Ripon, Yorkshire HG4 4PB
Tel	+44 (0)1765 688565
Mobile	+44 (0)7821 600521
Email	info@lowsutton.co.uk
Web	www.lowsutton.co.uk

Entry 551   Map 12

Yorkshire

Firs Farm

The landscape is rural and rolling, the lanes are narrow and quiet, and Healey is pretty-as-a-picture: mellow York stone, smart gardens and immaculate paintwork on every house. Richard and Sarah, relaxed and genial, offer homemade cakes and coffee when you arrive and the cosy feel of their home makes you feel instantly at ease. Enjoy a sitting room with an open fire and fabulous fabrics, fresh and cottagey bedrooms with spotted upholstered windows seats, and vases of flowers in every corner. There are great views from the lovely walled garden, acres to roam, wonderful walking, and tip-top towns to visit all around.

Children over 10 welcome.

Rooms	1 double; 1 twin/double with separate bath/shower: £75–£90. Singles £65.
Meals	Packed lunch £7. Pubs/restaurants 1 mile.
Closed	Christmas & New Year.

	Richard & Sarah Townsend
	Firs Farm,
	Healey, Ripon,
	Yorkshire HG4 4LH
Tel	+44 (0)1765 688910
Email	sarah@firsfarmbandb.co.uk
Web	www.firsfarmbandb.co.uk

Entry 552   Map 12

Yorkshire

Laverton Hall

The hall is a beauty, even on a dull day, and the village is a dream. Half an hour from Harrogate find space, beauty, history (it's 400 years old), three walled gardens and comfort in great measure: beloved antiques, a rocking horse in the hall, feather pillows, thick white towels, and sumptuous breakfasts followed by delightful Rachel's Cordon Bleu dinner (delicious rack of lamb a favourite). The sunny guest sitting room is elegant and charming, the cream and white twin and the snug little single have long views to the river. The area is rich with abbeys and great houses, and then there are the glorious Dales to be explored.

Rooms	1 twin/double: £95.
	1 single: £60.
Meals	Supper, 3 courses, £30.
	Pubs/restaurants 2 miles.
Closed	Christmas.

Rachel Wilson
Laverton Hall,
Laverton, Ripon, Yorkshire HG4 3SX

Tel	+44 (0)1765 650274
Mobile	+44 (0)7711 086385
Email	rachel.k.wilson@hotmail.co.uk
Web	www.lavertonhall.co.uk

Entry 553   Map 12

Yorkshire

Mallard Grange

Perfect farmhouse B&B. Hens, cats, sheepdogs wander the garden, an ancient apple tree leans against the wall, guests unwind and feel part of the family. Enter the rambling, deep-shuttered 16th-century farmhouse, cosy with well-loved family pieces, and feel at peace with the world. Breakfast is generous – homemade muffins, poached pears with cinnamon, a sizzling full Monty. A winding steep stair leads to big, friendly bedrooms, two cheerful others await in the converted 18th-century smithy, and Maggie's enthusiasm for this glorious area is as genuine as her love of doing B&B. It's a gem!

Minimum stay: 2 nights at weekends.

Rooms	2 twin/doubles: £85–£105.
	Old Blacksmith's Shop & Carthouse
	– 2 twin/doubles: £85–£105.
	Singles from £70.
Meals	Pubs/restaurants 10-minute drive.
Closed	Christmas & New Year.

Maggie Johnson
Mallard Grange,
Aldfield, Ripon, Yorkshire HG4 3BE

Tel	+44 (0)1765 620242
Mobile	+44 (0)7720 295918
Email	maggie@mallardgrange.co.uk
Web	www.mallardgrange.co.uk

Entry 554   Map 12

Copper Beech Glade

A timeless, bucolic setting and a trio of well-travelled gypsy wagons gathered around a fire-pit, circled by copper beeches. Bella has pastel florals, horse brasses and a decorative wood-burner; vibrant red Carmen comes with an intricate red and gold fabric ceiling; Rosita, the baby one, is for children. The log cabin has a modern kitchen and space for more guests, there's a compost loo, shower and a games lawn for badminton and croquet. A brimming welcome hamper and lots of breakfast choices will keep you happy too. Paddle in the trout beck, head out for nearby Harrogate, Thirsk, York and the wild moors of Brontë country. Bring the whole family!

Minimum stay: 2 nights. Book through Sawday's Canopy & Stars online or by phone.

Carlton House

Quietly tucked into a corner of the sedate green, a short stride from the pub, lies a stylishly renovated 18th-century farmhouse. The old wash house, tractor shed and stable have become airy, chic, characterful rooms with beams and fabulous bathrooms. In summer, pull up a chair in a pretty yard with hanging baskets or find a tranquil spot in the charmingly secret garden. The dining room with open fire is a delight, so linger over a breakfast of delicious local produce, then set off for market towns, dales and moors. There's a big-hearted family feel here – Denise's oat and raisin crunchies and soda bread are to die for! Lovely.

Rooms	1 camp for 6 (1 double in Bella, 1 double in Carmen, 1 double sofabed in cabin): £165-£195.	Rooms	Outbuildings - 2 doubles, 1 twin/double: £68-£85. Singles from £50.
Meals	Welcome hamper provided. Breakfast available to order.	Meals	Pub/restaurant 2-minute walk.
Closed	December-March.	Closed	Rarely.

Sawday's Canopy & Stars
Copper Beech Glade,
Markington Hall, Markington,
Harrogate, Yorkshire HG3 3PQ
Tel   +44 (0)117 204 7830
Email   enquiries@canopyandstars.co.uk
Web   www.canopyandstars.co.uk/
          copperbeechglade

Denise & David Mason
Carlton House,
Sandhutton,
Thirsk,
Yorkshire YO7 4RW
Tel   +44 (0)1845 587381
Email   info@carltonbarns.co.uk
Web   www.carltonbarns.co.uk

Entry 555   Map 12

Entry 556   Map 12

Yorkshire

The Old Rectory

Once the residence of the Bishops of Whitby this elegant rectory has a comfortable lived-in air. Both Turner and Ruskin stayed here and probably enjoyed as much good conversation and comfort as you will. Bedrooms are pretty, traditional and with grand views; the drawing room is classic country house with a fine Venetian window and enticing window-seat, gleaming antiques and flowers. The graceful, deep pink dining room looks over a large garden of ancient redwood and walnut trees. Caroline and Tim are charming, breakfasts are generous; wander at will to find an orchard, tennis court and croquet lawn.

Children over 3 welcome.

Rooms	1 double with separate bath & dressing room, 1 twin/double with separate bath & shower: £70–£74. Singles from £45.
Meals	Pub/restaurant opposite.
Closed	Rarely.

Tim & Caroline O'Connor-Fenton
The Old Rectory,
South Kilvington, Thirsk,
Yorkshire YO7 2NL

Tel +44 (0)1845 526153
Mobile +44 (0)7981 329764
Email ocfenton@talktalk.net
Web www.oldrectorythirsk.co.uk

Entry 557 Map 12

Yorkshire

Shallowdale House

Phillip and Anton have a true affection for their guests so you will be treated royally. Sumptuous bedrooms dazzle in yellows, blues and limes, acres of curtains frame wide views over the Howardian Hills, bathrooms are immaculate. You breakfast on the absolute best: fresh fruit compotes, dry-cured bacon, homemade bread. Admire the amazing garden, then walk off in any direction straight from the house. Return to a cosily elegant drawing room with a fire in winter, and an enticing library. Dinner is a real treat – coffee and chocolates before you crawl up to bed? Bliss.

Children over 12 welcome. Minimum stay: 2 nights at weekends.

Rooms	2 twin/doubles; 1 double with separate bath/shower: £110–£135. Singles £90–£105.
Meals	Dinner, 4 courses, £39.50. Pub 0.5 miles.
Closed	Christmas & New Year.

Anton van der Horst & Phillip Gill
Shallowdale House,
West End,
Ampleforth,
Yorkshire YO62 4DY

Tel +44 (0)1439 788325
Email stay@shallowdalehouse.co.uk
Web www.shallowdalehouse.co.uk

Entry 558 Map 12

Yorkshire

Cundall Lodge Farm

Ancient chestnuts, crunchy drive, sheep grazing, hens free-ranging. This four-square Georgian farmhouse could be straight out of Central Casting. Smart, traditional rooms have damask sofas, comfy armchairs, bright wallpapers and views to Sutton Bank's White Horse or the river Swale – and tea and oven-fresh cakes welcome you. Spotless bedrooms are inviting: pretty fabrics, antiques, flowers, Roberts radios. This is a working farm and the breakfast table groans with eggs from the hens, homemade jams and local bacon. The garden and river walks guarantee peace, and David and Caroline are generous and delightful.

Over 14s welcome.

Rooms	2 doubles, 1 twin/double: £80-£95.
Meals	Packed lunch £7.
	Pubs/restaurants 2 miles.
Closed	Christmas & January.

Caroline Barker
Cundall Lodge Farm,
Cundall, York,
Yorkshire YO61 2RN

Tel	+44 (0)1423 360203
Mobile	+44 (0)7773 494260
Email	enquiries@cundall-lodgefarm.co.uk
Web	www.cundall-lodgefarm.co.uk

Entry 559   Map 12

Yorkshire

Poppleton House

Down a driveway off Main Street, through restored gates, to a wonderful red-brick Georgian house and a big welcome from Kathleen. Inside is graceful, stately, spacious and light: elegant breakfasts at a mahogany table and flowers in every room – Kathleen arranges flowers professionally. Luxuriate in pale wool carpeting and heritage colours, cornicing, pelmets and chandeliers, silver-framed photos and a grand piano. Everything feels relaxed in this peaceful grown-up place, and that includes the bedrooms. Behind: an acre of garden, with secret corners and pathways. Beyond: York, its river walks and its Minster, a bus ride away.

Minimum stay: 2 nights at weekends.

Rooms	2 doubles; 1 double with separate bath/shower: £90-£125.
Meals	Pubs/restaurants in village & in York, 4 miles.
Closed	Christmas & New Year.

Kathleen Doggett
Poppleton House,
3 Main Street,
Nether Poppleton, York,
Yorkshire YO26 6HS

Tel	+44 (0)1904 781160
Email	info@poppletonhouse.co.uk
Web	www.bbyork.co.uk

Entry 560   Map 12

The Chantry

A listed house in a village setting, with warm, humorous and engaging owners, Diana and Nigel. A member of the York Slow Food movement, and half Lebanese by birth, Diana reflects her culture in her delicious cooking; the big ramshackle kitchen is the heart of the house and she relishes the chance to produce her legendary Lebanese banquet. Spacious bedrooms have high ceilings and an old-fashioned décor while bathrooms are swisher; the mood is comfy, warm, authentic and ever so gently eccentric. Pull yourself away from the suntrap terrace and sally forth into town: York, history-rich, is a sturdy walk (or a 20-minute bike ride) away.

Rooms	1 double, 1 twin: £90. Singles £70. Dinner, B&B £75–£100 per person. Extra bed/sofabed available £25 per person per night.
Meals	Dinner, aperitif, 3 courses & petit fours, £30. Pubs 200 yards, restaurant 0.5 miles.
Closed	Rarely.

	Diana Naish
	The Chantry,
	Chantry Lane, Bishopthorpe, York,
	Yorkshire YO23 2QF
Tel	+44 (0)1904 709767
Mobile	+44 (0)7850 912203
Email	diananaish@athomecatering.
	freeserve.co.uk

Entry 561 Map 12

Corner Farm

Tea and home-baked cakes on arrival: you get a lovely welcome here! This peaceful farmhouse is so well insulated it's snug and warm even on the coldest day. With York so close and stunning estates nearby, this is a cosy nest from which to explore the area – or just the village pub. Bathrooms are swish and bedrooms are light, fresh and comfortable: cast-iron beds, fine sheets, cute satin cushions. Much-loved Dexters graze on six acres. Tim and Sharon are aiming for self-sufficiency – and apples from the orchard are pressed for your breakfast, flexibly served and with lots of choice, including home-laid eggs.

Rooms	1 double, 1 twin: £80. Singles £55.
Meals	Packed lunch £4. Pub 100 yds.
Closed	Rarely.

	Sharon Stevens
	Corner Farm,
	Low Catton, York,
	Yorkshire YO41 1EA
Tel	+44 (0)1759 373911
Mobile	+44 (0)7711 440796
Email	cornerfarmyork@gmail.com
Web	www.cornerfarmyork.co.uk

Entry 562 Map 13

Yorkshire

Yorkshire

The Mount House

A dollop of stylish fun in the rolling Howardian Hills (an AONB), Kathryn and Nick's redesigned village house is light, airy and filled with gorgeous things — from good antiques to splashy modern art and fresh flowers. The ground-floor twin with white cast-iron beds has its own cosy book-filled sitting room; the sunny upstairs double has views across the roof tops to open countryside. Kathryn, an excellent cook, will spoil you at breakfast — supper too, if you wish — sometimes in the pretty garden. Discover Castle Howard, Nunnington Hall, old market towns and great walking; only 20 minutes from York too. Super.

Helmsley Garden Cottage

Your own stone cottage with hydrangeas at the door — perfect! Tucked behind Louise's house and antique shop, it looks on to a sunny patch of garden and is filled with gorgeous furniture and fabrics, old beams and warm charm. The dining room is cosy with comfy armchairs, tea-making things and homemade treats; there's a little table for tasty meals too — Louise brings it all to you. Up the stairs to find your snug, pretty bedroom under the eaves. It's a short walk to cafés, shops and Helmsley Castle; return and settle with a book on one of the elegant antique sofas — one cloudy blue, the other rich red — and feel completely at home.

Rooms	1 double, 1 twin with sitting room; 1 double with separate bath: £80–£130. Singles from £60.
Meals	Dinner, 2–4 courses, £25–£35. BYO. Pub/restaurant 200 yds.
Closed	Rarely.

Rooms	1 double with dining & sitting room: £100–£150. Singles £80.
Meals	Dinner from £10 per person. Pubs/restaurants 1-minute walk.
Closed	Rarely.

	Kathryn Hill
	The Mount House,
	Terrington, York,
	Yorkshire YO60 6QB
Tel	+44 (0)1653 648206
Mobile	+44 (0)7780 536937
Email	mount.house@clayfox.co.uk
Web	www.howardianhillsbandb.co.uk

	Louise Craig
	Helmsley Garden Cottage,
	1 Bondgate,
	Helmsley, York,
	Yorkshire YO62 5BW
Tel	+44 (0)1439 771864
Email	louise.craig@aol.co.uk

Entry 563 Map 13

Entry 564 Map 13

Yorkshire

Hunters Hill

The moors lie behind this elegant farmhouse, and it's just yards from the National Park. Farmland, woods and great views... the position is marvellous and you can walk from the door. The house is full of light and flowers; bedrooms are pretty but not overly grand, and look onto valley or church. The lovely lived-in drawing room displays comfortable old sofas, paintings and fine furniture; rich colours, hunting prints and candles at dinner create a warm and cosy feel. The family has poured affection and life into this interesting house and the result is a home that's charming and remarkably easy to relax in... Wonderful.

Rooms	1 double; 1 twin/double with separate bath: £90–£110. Singles £55.
Meals	Dinner, 3 courses, £35. Pub/restaurant 10-minute walk.
Closed	Rarely.

	Jane Otter Hunters Hill, Sinnington, York, Yorkshire YO62 6SF
Tel	+44 (0)1751 431196
Email	ejorr@tiscali.co.uk

Entry 565   Map 13

Yorkshire

Habton House Farm

Mellow stone, smart painted windows and a warm relaxed greeting from Lucy and James: a good start! You breakfast well here too, on home-produced sausages, bacon, eggs and jams, all delicious, at a big table in an elegant dining room. There are two cosy sitting rooms with wood fires to choose from, and the smartly done bedrooms have a pleasing medley of modern and vintage pieces, views of hill and river and immaculate bathrooms. Visit the pigs, fish for brown trout in the river, hire a bike; further afield are the North Yorks Moors and the coast. A tasty supper at the local pub is an added bonus.

Children over 8 welcome.

Rooms	3 doubles, 1 twin/double: £85–£110. Singles £60–£90.
Meals	Pub 0.5 miles.
Closed	Christmas & New Year.

	Lucy Haxton Habton House Farm, Little Habton, Malton, Yorkshire YO17 6UA
Tel	+44 (0)1653 669707
Mobile	+44 (0)7876 433351
Email	habtonhouse@gmail.com
Web	www.habtonhouse.co.uk

Entry 566   Map 13

Yorkshire

Brickfields Farm

Down a long peaceful track, but a stone's throw from bustling Kirkbymoorside, is this walker's paradise. Friendly Janet sends you off to the North Yorks Moors with maps and information, and a tasty breakfast, served at separate tables in the conservatory overlooking guinea fowl and sheep. Bedrooms, one in the house and others in the barn or converted cow shed, are lovely: a French vintage four-poster, antiques, heavy curtains, sprung mattresses, flowers, a hidden fridge. All have stunning views over the fields. Bathrooms have big open showers, thick towels and plenty of lotions. Come to be pampered.

Rooms	1 twin: £100–£130.
	Barn - 4 suites for 2: £100–£130.
	Cow Shed - 1 four-poster suite for 2, 1 suite for 2: £100–£130.
Meals	Pub/restaurant 1 mile.
Closed	Rarely.

	Sheila Trousdale Ward & Neil Ward
	Brickfields Farm,
	Kirkby Mills,
	Kirkbymoorside,
	Yorkshire YO62 6NS
Tel	+44 (0)1751 433074
Email	bookings@brickfieldsfarm.co.uk
Web	www.brickfieldsfarm.co.uk

Entry 567   Map 13

Yorkshire

Low Farm

The first thing you see is the amazing view – it's a jaw-dropper! This handsome old farmhouse in the heart of the North Yorks Moors National Park will relax you from the moment you step in – a warm home where Linda welcomes with tea and homemade cake. Fresh comfortable bedrooms have far-reaching views and immaculate en suite bathrooms. In the morning, feast on freshly squeezed juice and homemade jam, Whitby kippers or the full works, all sourced locally; the polished table in the cosy dining room is set with pretty china and flowers. Castle Howard is a hop, the walks are fabulous and you can stroll to the village bistro.

Rooms	1 double, 1 twin: £90–£110.
Meals	Packed lunch available.
	Pub 0.25 miles.
Closed	Rarely.

	Linda & Andrew Dagg
	Low Farm,
	Rosedale Abbey,
	Pickering,
	Yorkshire YO18 8SE
Tel	+44 (0)1751 417003
Email	adagg@moorsweb.co.uk
Web	www.lowfarmrosedale.co.uk

Entry 568   Map 13

Yorkshire

Rectory Farmhouse

Walk from the door onto the North Yorkshire Moors; it's a brisk 30-minute stride across fields to the steam railway. Michael and Heather have been here since 1997, and their thriving smallholding has a flock of rare-breed sheep and hens, along with dogs and horses. Cosy old-fashioned bedrooms have pine furniture, fluffy robes and flowery fabrics. Relax in front of the log fire, or enjoy home-baked cakes and tea or sherry in the guest lounge. Tuck into a hearty breakfast in the dining room. homemade jams, bread and sausages; it's a stroll across the green to the pub for supper. Good value – and superb for walking, biking and riding.

Minimum stay: 2 nights. Children over 8 welcome.

Rooms	1 double, 1 twin: £70–£80. Apartment – 1 double, 1 twin sharing bath (let to same party only): £70–£80. Singles from £50.
Meals	Dinner, 2 courses, £15. BYO. Pub in village.
Closed	Christmas & New Year.

Michael & Heather Holt
Rectory Farmhouse,
Levisham, Pickering,
Yorkshire YO18 7NL

Tel	+44 (0)1751 460304
Mobile	+44 (0)7971 625898
Email	info@rectoryfarmlevisham.co.uk
Web	www.rectoryfarmlevisham.co.uk

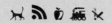

Entry 569   Map

Yorkshire

Union Place

A listed Adam Georgian townhouse – elegance epitomised. Lofty well-proportioned rooms with polished floors and cornices and fireplaces intact are delightfully dotted with sophisticated, quirky *objets*: bead-and-embroidery lampshades and chandeliers, bone china, a small mirrored Indian ceramic child's dress – and your urbane host Richard's accomplished paintings. Bedrooms, one painted duck egg blue, one green with floral wallpaper, are beautiful, with lots of lace and fine linen; the claw-foot roll top in the shared bathroom cuts a dash. Breakfast is unbeatable… then it's off to explore the North Yorkshire Moors. Superb.

Rooms	2 doubles sharing bath: £70–£75.
Meals	Pubs/restaurants within walking distance.
Closed	Christmas.

Richard & Jane Pottas
Union Place,
9 Upgang Lane,
Whitby,
Yorkshire YO21 3DT

Tel	+44 (0)1947 605501
Email	pottas1@btinternet.com
Web	www.unionplacewhitby.co.uk

Entry 570   Map 13

Yorkshire

20 St Hilda's Terrace

Little back lanes, an old gate, a secret walled garden and a large bay-windowed Georgian house. You're bang in the heart of Whitby yet the feel is very peaceful with light and airy rooms, fresh flowers, botanical fabrics, elegant antiques and original art. Your pretty bedroom is reached up a graceful staircase; find high ceilings, a plump bed, antique furniture and views through sash windows. Your breakfast is continental and you can have it in the drawing room, the garden on fine days, or in bed if you're feeling lazy. Stroll to the beach for wild walks, romp on the Yorkshire Moors, explore the shops in town – returning will be a pleasure.

Rooms	1 double with separate bath/shower: £60-£70.
Meals	Pubs/restaurants 0.3 miles.
Closed	Rarely.

Pip Baines
20 St Hilda's Terrace,
Whitby,
Yorkshire YO21 3AE
Tel   +44 (0)1947 602435
Email   marylouisa@talktalk.net

Entry 571   Map 13

Yorkshire

Thorpe Hall

Arrive and listen: nothing, bar the wind in the trees and the odd seagull. The eye gathers glimmering sea and mighty headland, the final edge of the moors... are there still smugglers? This old listed house smells of polish and flowers, the drawing room breathes history. Angelique is a delight and has furnished it all, including TV-free bedrooms (one downstairs), with an eclectic mix of old and new; wonky walls and creaky floors add to the atmospheric feel. She's hung contemporary art on ancient walls and made a veg patch with young Phoebe. David helps out with simple breakfast when he's not globetrotting. The very opposite of stuffy.

Rooms	3 doubles, 1 twin; 3 doubles sharing separate bath & shower rooms: £70-£90. Singles £70-£80. Extra bed/sofabed available £15 per person per night.
Meals	Pub within 0.25 miles.
Closed	Usually Christmas & January.

Angelique Russell
Thorpe Hall,
Middlewood Lane, Fylingthorpe,
Whitby, Yorkshire YO22 4TT
Tel   +44 (0)1947 880667
Email   thorpehall@gmail.com
Web   www.thorpe-hall.co.uk

Entry 572   Map 13

Yorkshire

Dale Farm

Huge skies as you drive along the open road to Dale Farm… the sea is just over the brow. Nifty inside too: bedrooms and bathrooms sparkle in whites and beach blues; mattresses are luxurious and handmade (the double is snugly in the attic); lots of books in the sitting room. Paul is a keen cook so breakfast is a varied feast: home-grown tomatoes, salmon from a local smokehouse, full English and more; hearty suppers too! Peaceful woodland surrounds you; the logs fuel the biomass boiler and fires. Ramble and find Paul's metal sculptures and a fire-pit in the woods, croquet on the lawn, a beach down the road with a café… lovely.

Rooms	1 double, 1 twin; 1 triple with separate bath: £80. 3 cabins for 2 (bath & wc in house 50yds): £350. Short breaks available at £50 per night. Singles £60. Extra bed/sofabed available £20 per person per night.
Meals	Dinner, 3 courses, from £15. Pubs/restaurants 2 miles.
Closed	Rarely.

	Elizabeth Halliday
	Dale Farm,
	Bartindale Road, Hunmanby, Filey,
	Yorkshire YO14 0JD
Tel	+44 01723 890175
Mobile	+44 (0)7751 674706
Email	elizabethhalliday1@gmail.com
Web	www.dalefarmholidays.co.uk

Entry 573   Map 13

Yorkshire

The Wold Cottage

Drive through mature trees, and a proper entrance with signs, to a listed Georgian manor house in 300 glorious acres; tea awaits in the guest sitting room. The graceful dining room has heartlifting views across the landscaped gardens, and there are many original features: fan-lights, high ceilings, broad staircases. Bedrooms are sumptuous, traditional, with lots of thoughtful extras: chocolates, biscuits, monogrammed waffle robes. You are warmed by straw bale heating, and the food is local and delicious. An award-winning breakfast sets you up for a day of discovery: visit RSPB Bempton Cliffs, and the Wolds that have inspired David Hockney.

Rooms	2 doubles, 2 twins: £100–£120. Barn - 1 double, 1 family room for 4: £100–£120. Singles £60–£75.
Meals	Supper £25. Wine from £12.95.
Closed	Rarely.

	Derek & Katrina Gray
	The Wold Cottage,
	Wold Newton, Driffield,
	Yorkshire YO25 3HL
Tel	+44 (0)1262 470696
Mobile	+44 (0)7811 203336
Email	katrina@woldcottage.com
Web	www.woldcottage.com

Entry 574   Map 13

Yorkshire

Village Farm

Tucked behind houses and shops, this was once the village farm with land stretching to the coast. Now the one-storey buildings overlooking a courtyard are large bedrooms in gorgeous colours with luxurious touches. Chrysta, who moved from London, is living her dream and looks after you well: baths are deep, beds crisply comfortable, heating is underfoot. Delicious breakfasts are served at wooden tables in a cheerful light room with a contemporary feel; dinner is candlelit and locally sourced. Stride the cliffs, watch birds at Flamborough Head or make for Spurn Point – remote and lovely.

Rooms	1 double, 1 twin/double: £80. 1 family room for 4: £80–£95. Singles £60.
Meals	Dinner, 2-3 courses, £18–£22. Pubs/restaurants within 20 yds.
Closed	Rarely.

Chrysta Newman
Village Farm,
Back Street, Skipsea, Driffield,
Yorkshire YO25 8SW

Tel +44 (0)1262 468479
Email info@villagefarmskipsea.co.uk
Web www.villagefarmskipsea.co.uk

Entry 575 Map 13

Yorkshire

New Entry
INSPECTED & SELECTED
A SPECIAL PLACE

Dowthorpe Hall

Caroline is lovely, cooking is her passion and she trawls the county for the best: fish and seafood from Hornsea, Dexter beef, game from the local shoot; her fruits and veg are home-grown. All is served in a sumptuous Georgian dining room by flickering candlelight, after which you retire to a comfortable drawing room; this is a marvellously elegant, and happy, house. Sleep peacefully on a luxurious mattress, wake to the aroma of bacon, sausages, eggs and home-baked bread. There are acres of gorgeous garden to roam – orchards, pathways, potager and pond – and a trio of historic houses to visit.

Rooms	1 twin/double; 1 double with separate bath: £90–£110. Singles £70.
Meals	Dinner £25. Pubs 0.25-5 miles.
Closed	Rarely.

John & Caroline Holtby
Dowthorpe Hall,
Skirlaugh, Hull,
Yorkshire HU11 5AE

Tel +44 (0)1964 562235
Email john.holtby@farming.co.uk
Web www.dowthorpehall.com

Entry 576 Map 13

Guernsey

Seabreeze

Maggie's house – the most southern on Guernsey – comes with enormous views: Herm and Sark glistening in the water under a vast sky. The breakfast terrace is hard to beat, there are sofas in the conservatory, cliff-top paths for fabulous walks, a beach for picnics in summer. The house started life as HQ for French pilots flying seaplanes in WWI; these days warm, rustic interiors make for a great island base. It's not grand, just very welcoming with rooms that hit the spot: pretty linen, bathrobes, super showers, fresh flowers. You can hire bikes locally, then spin up the lane to a top island restaurant. Brilliant.

Rooms	1 double; 3 twin/doubles with kitchen: £75-£125. Reduction for single occupancy £25 per night.
Meals	Pubs/restaurants 500 yds & 0.5 miles.
Closed	Rarely.

	Maggie Talbot–Cull
	Seabreeze,
	La Moye Lane,
	Route de Jerbourg, St Martin,
	Guernsey GY4 6BN
Tel	+44 (0)1481 237929
Email	seabreeze-guernsey@mail.com
Web	www.guernseybandb.com

Entry 577   Map 4

Aberdeenshire

Lynturk Home Farm

The stunning drawing room, with pier-glass mirror, baby grand and enveloping sofas, is reason enough to come; the food, served in a candlelit, deep-sage dining room, is delicious, with produce from the farm. You're treated as friends here and your hosts are delightful. It's peaceful, too, on the Aberdeenshire Castle Trail. The handsome farmhouse has been in the family since 1762 and you can roam the surrounding, rolling 300 acres. Inside: flowers, polished furniture, Persian rugs, family portraits and supremely comfortable bedrooms. "A blissful haven," says a guest.

Rooms	1 double, 2 twin/doubles: £100. Singles £60. Dinner, B&B £30 per person.
Meals	Dinner, 4 courses, £30. Pub 1 mile.
Closed	Rarely.

John & Veronica Evans-Freke
Lynturk Home Farm,
Alford,
Aberdeenshire AB33 8HU
Tel   +44 (0)1975 562504
Mobile   +44 (0)7773 389793
Email   lynturk@hotmail.com

Entry 580   Map 19

Angus

Newtonmill House

The house and grounds are in perfect order; the owners are warm, charming and discreet. This is a little-known part of Scotland, with glens and gardens to discover; fishing villages, golf courses and deserted beaches, too. Return to a cup of tea in the sitting room or summerhouse, a wander in the lovely walled garden, and a marvellous supper of local produce; Rose grows interesting varieties of potato and her hens' eggs make a great hollandaise! Upstairs are crisp sheets, soft blankets, feather pillows, flowers, homemade fruit cake and warm sparkling bathrooms with thick towels. Let this home envelop you in its warm embrace.

Dogs by arrangement.

Rooms	1 twin; 1 double with separate bath: £100–£120. Singles from £70.
Meals	Dinner, £30–£38. BYO. Packed lunch £10. Pub 3 miles.
Closed	Christmas.

Rose & Stephen Rickman
Newtonmill House,
Brechin, Angus DD9 7PZ
Tel   +44 (0)1356 622533
Mobile   +44 (0)7793 169482
Email   rrickman@srickman.co.uk
Web   www.newtonmillhouse.co.uk

Entry 581   Map 19

Hawthorn Cottage

The most southerly of the Scottish islands, Arran is splendid for nature lovers. When you've worn yourselves out you can flop in Fiona's low, whitewashed cottage. It's up a bumpy track and far from smart but brimming with reality. The cottage is split in two: you get one end with a bedroom (up a rusty spiral stair), a bathroom and a sitting room (downstairs) and a small kitchen area. Find hotchpotch furniture, original old bath, frayed rugs, a piano, a cosy wood-burner to sit by and electric storage heating for chilly days. Fiona leaves your continental breakfast hanging on the door. Will not suit boutique hotel lovers one iota!

Achanduin Cottage

Sara's restoration of this old crofthouse is just right. The feel is restful, comfortable, understated. Everything's well chosen: rustic and reclaimed pieces, interesting art, colourful rugs. The bright east suite has its own sitting room with wood-burner; the west room has a fine mahogany bed, old farmhouse desk and a grand roll top bath in its bookish bathroom. All this set back in yachty Ardfern, sitting pretty on its Highland Loch… Perfect for Highland lovers – Donald's an outdoors guide – for lovers of art, good food and conversation – Sara's an inspired cook; both have a keen sense of place and sustainability.

Rooms	1 twin/double with separate bath & kitchenette: £50.
Meals	Continental breakfast. Pub/restaurant 2 miles.
Closed	Rarely.

Rooms	1 double: £75. 1 suite for 2: £85.
Meals	Pub 200 yds.
Closed	Rarely.

Fiona Mackenzie
Hawthorn Cottage,
Brodick, Isle of Arran,
Argyll & Bute KA27 8DF

Tel	+44 (0)1770 302534
Email	fionamackenzie569@btinternet.com
Web	hawthorn-cottage.eu

Sara Wallace
Achanduin Cottage,
Ardfern, Lochgilphead,
Argyll & Bute PA31 8QN

Tel	+44 (0)1852 500708
Email	sara@achanduincottage.co.uk
Web	www.achanduincottage.com

Entry 582   Map 14

Entry 583   Map 14

Argyll & Bute

Melfort House

A truly seductive combination of a wild landscape of ancient woods and hidden glens with rivers that tumble to a blue sea and a big, beautiful house with views straight down the loch. The whole place glows with polished antiques, oak floors, exquisite fabrics, prints and paintings. And Yvonne and Matthew are brilliant at looking after you – whether you're super-active, or not – their fabulous Scottish food's a treat. Bedrooms have soft plaids, superb views and handmade chocolates; bathrooms have huge towels and locally made soaps. Sally forth with boots or bikes, return to a dram by the log fire. Don't book too short a stay!

Rooms	2 twin/doubles;
	1 suite for 2: £95-£125.
	Singles from £70.
	Sofabed £15.
Meals	Dinner, 3 courses, from £32.
	Packed lunch £10.
	Pub/restaurant 400 yds.
Closed	Rarely.

	Yvonne & Matthew Anderson
	Melfort House,
	Kilmelford, Oban,
	Argyll & Bute PA34 4XD
Tel	+44 (0)1852 200326
Mobile	+44 (0)7795 438106
Email	relax@melforthouse.co.uk
Web	www.melforthouse.co.uk

Entry 584   Map 14

Argyll & Bute

Glenmore

A pleasingly idiosyncratic traditional country house with no need to stand on ceremony. Built in the 1800s but with 1930s additions setting the style, find solid oak doors and floors, red-pine panelling, Art Deco pieces and a unique carved staircase. Alasdair's family has been here for 150 years and many family antiques remain. One of the huge doubles can be arranged as a suite to include a single room and a sofabed; bath and basins are chunky 30s style with chrome plumbing. From the organic garden and the house there are magnificent views of Loch Melfort with its bobbing boats; you're free to come and go as you please.

Rooms	1 double with separate
	bath/shower: £85-£100.
	1 family room for 5: £95-£170.
	Singles £50-£65.
Meals	Pub 0.5 miles, restaurant 1.5 miles.
Closed	Christmas & New Year.

	Melissa & Alasdair Oatts
	Glenmore,
	Kilmelford, Oban,
	Argyll & Bute PA34 4XA
Tel	+44 (0)1852 200314
Mobile	+44 (0)7786 340468
Email	oatts@glenmore22.fsnet.co.uk
Web	www.glenmorecountryhouse.co.uk

Entry 585   Map 17

Argyll & Bute

Greystones

A baronial mansion built for the owner of a diamond mine. He clearly liked a good view – a five-mile sweep across Oban bay lands on the Isle of Mull. Inside, bright white interiors soak up the light, while coolly uncluttered bedrooms have chic bathrooms and well-dressed beds. One has a turret with armchairs looking out to sea, another has a vast walk-in shower, three have the view. You breakfast downstairs on honey-drenched porridge while watching boats come and go on the water. There's a sitting room with smart sofas, a list of local restaurants, a library of DVDs. Castles and gardens wait, as do ferries to far-flung islands.

Minimum stay: 2 nights in bigger rooms.

Rooms	4 doubles: £110–£145.
	1 suite for 2: £160.
	Singles from £80 (singles in low season and late availability only).
Meals	Pubs/restaurants 5-minute walk.
Closed	Rarely.

Mark & Suzanne McPhillips
Greystones,
13 Dalriach Road,
Oban,
Argyll & Bute PA34 5EQ

Tel	+44 (0)1631 358653
Email	stay@greystonesoban.co.uk
Web	www.greystonesoban.co.uk

Entry 586   Map 17

Argyll & Bute

Ardtorna

Come for perfect comfort and uninterrupted views of loch and mountain. These thoughtful, professional hosts are happy to share their new, open-plan, eco-friendly house where contemporary Scandinavian and Art Deco styles are cleverly blended with homely warmth. Sink into a bedroom with a wall of glass for those views; each has a wet room or spa bath with Molton Brown treats. Flowers and jauntily coloured coffee pots decorate the oak table in the stunning dining room, and food is home-baked and delicious. Argyll brims with historic sites and walks; return to watch the sun go down over the Morvern hills. Fabulous.

Rooms	4 twin/doubles: £150–£200.
	Singles from £125.
Meals	Room service supper £10–£20.
	Pub/restaurant 3 miles.
Closed	Rarely.

Karen O'Byrne
Ardtorna,
Mill Farm, Barcaldine, Oban,
Argyll & Bute PA37 1SE

Tel	+44 (0)1631 720125
Mobile	+44 (0)7867 785524
Email	info@ardtorna.co.uk
Web	www.ardtorna.co.uk

Entry 587   Map 17

Argyll & Bute

Meall Mo Chridhe

Caring owners, exquisite food and a welcome sight amid the savage beauty of Britain's most westerly village. The warm ochre walls of this listed Georgian manse peep through wooded gardens across the Sound to Mull. Rooms are beautiful – French antiques, a wood stove, roll top baths – but it's the food that draws most to this far-flung spot. What David magics from his 45-acre smallholding (a bit of everything that grows, grunts, bleats or quacks) Stella transforms into feasts. Dine on spiced mackerel, minted lamb, hazelnut meringue; and duck eggs at breakfast. A gem buried in spectacular, wild walking country.

Ayrshire

Heughmill

Acres of fields and lawn with free-range hens that kindly donate for breakfast and views to the sea. The house is just as good, surrounded by old stone farm buildings, with climbing roses and a small burn tumbling through. Inside, a lovely country home with tapestries in an airy hall, an open fire in the sitting room, a sunny conservatory and a terrace that sits under a vast sky. Country-house bedrooms are stylishly homely; find delightful art, an old armoire, a claw-foot bath; two have the view. Your hosts are relaxed and entertaining – Julia sculpts, Mungo cooks breakfast on the Aga – and rural Ayrshire awaits.

Rooms	3 doubles: £103–£204. Singles £51.50–£102.	Rooms	2 twin/doubles, 1 twin: £65–£80. Singles on request.
Meals	Dinner from £37. Pub 0.25 miles.	Meals	Pubs/restaurants within 2 miles.
Closed	Rarely.	Closed	Christmas & New Year.

	Stella & David Cash Meall Mo Chridhe, Kilchoan, Acharacle, Argyll & Bute PH36 4LH		**Mungo & Julia Tulloch** Heughmill, Craigie, Kilmarnock, Ayrshire KA1 5NQ
Tel	+44 (0)1972 510238		
Mobile	+44 (0)7730 100639	Tel	+44 (0)1563 860389
Email	enquiries@westcoastscotland.co.uk	Email	mungotulloch@hotmail.com
Web	www.westcoastscotland.co.uk	Web	www.stayprestwick.com

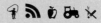

Entry 588   Map 17

Entry 589   Map 14

Ayrshire

Alton Albany Farm

Discover Ayrshire… pine forests, hills and wild beauty. Alasdair and Andrea (sculptor / garden photographer) are generous hosts who love having you to stay – your visit starts with tea, coffee and cake. There's an arty vibe with their work on display; the dining room brims with garden books and games; large bedrooms have cosy lamps and more books. Big breakfasts by a log fire are a treat, perhaps with haggis, garden fruit, homemade bread. Rich in wildlife and orchids the garden has a rambling charm, the salmon-filled river Stinchar runs past and dogs are welcome – resident Clover and Daisy are friendly. Great fish restaurant nearby.

Special group rates for 6 friends or family.

Rooms	1 double: £85.
	1 double, 1 twin sharing bath (let to same party only): £80.
	Singles £50.
Meals	Pubs/restaurants 15-minute drive.
Closed	Rarely.

Andrea & Alasdair Currie
Alton Albany Farm,
Barr, Girvan, Ayrshire KA26 0TL

Tel	+44 (0)1465 861148
Mobile	+44 (0)7881 908764
Email	alasdair@gardenexposures.co.uk
Web	www.altonalbanyfarmbandb. wordpress.com

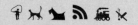

Entry 590   Map 14

Dumfries & Galloway

The Waterside Rooms

Prepare to be given a thorough looking after! Generous spirited Nic and Julie gave up their day jobs, travelled around Europe in a camper van and ended up here, dipping their toes in the Solway Firth. Birdwatchers will swoon, burnt out city folk will find balm, independence seekers will adore their own entrance to a neat-as-a-pin suite: peaceful colours soothe in a comfy sitting room, well-dressed bedroom and sparkling shower room; your own fridge too. Breakfast on a feast of local produce and homemade breads and preserves in the colourful main house, sit in the pretty garden with its watery views, walk, cycle, sail. Blissful.

Rooms	1 suite for 2 with sitting room: £95.
	Extra bed/sofabed available £12 per person per night.
Meals	Pub/restaurant 3 miles.
Closed	Never.

Nic & Julie Pearse
The Waterside Rooms,
Dornock Brow House, Dornock,
Eastriggs, Annan,
Dumfries & Galloway DG12 6SX

Tel	+44 (0)1461 40232
Email	enquiries@thewatersiderooms.co.uk
Web	www.thewatersiderooms.co.uk

Entry 591   Map 11

The House on the Shore

Impossible not to be wowed by this incredible shoreline setting with views across the Solway Firth. The 1,250-acre estate has been in Jamie's family for generations; he and Sheri are excellent hosts and love their dower house with its rich and varied woodland and wildlife, formal gardens and stupendous views. Grand but with a family feel, this is old country house style at its best with rugs on polished floors, paintings, open fires and fresh flowers. The farm produces its own meat, an enormous walled kitchen garden is being restored, and a peach tree fruits abundantly; you'll eat well. Very special.

Rooms	1 double, 1 twin: £90–£100. Singles £65–£80.
Meals	Dinner, 3 courses, £25. BYO. Pub/restaurant 2 miles.
Closed	Rarely.

Jamie & Sheri Blackett
The House on the Shore,
Arbigland,
Kirkbean, Dumfries,
Dumfries & Galloway DG2 8BQ
Tel   +44 (0)1387 880717
Email   sheri@arbigland.com
Web   www.arbiglandestate.co.uk

Entry 592   Map 11

Chipperkyle

This beautiful Scottish-Georgian family home has not a hint of formality, and the sociable Dicksons put you at your ease. Your sitting and dining rooms connect through a large arch; find gloriously comfy sofas, family pictures, rugs on wooden floors, masses of books and a constant log fire. Upstairs: good linen, striped walls, armchairs and windows with views – this wonderful house just gets better and better. There are 200 acres, dogs, cats, donkeys and hens – children can collect the eggs and go on tractor rides. The countryside is magnificent, beaches fabulous and this is a classified dark sky area. A house full of flowers and warmth.

Minimum stay: 2 nights at weekends, & in high season.

Rooms	1 double (cot available); 1 twin with separate bath/shower: £100. Discounts for children.
Meals	Occasional dinner available for groups. Pub 3 miles.
Closed	Rarely.

Willie & Catriona Dickson
Chipperkyle,
Kirkpatrick Durham, Castle Douglas,
Dumfries & Galloway DG7 3EY
Tel   +44 (0)1556 650223
Mobile   +44 (0)7917 730009
Email   cidickson@btinternet.com
Web   www.chipperkyle.co.uk

Entry 593   Map 11

Dumfries & Galloway

Chlenry Farmhouse

Handsome in its glen; a traditional family farmhouse full of old-fashioned comfort with charming, well-travelled owners and friendly dogs. In peaceful bedrooms with leafy views, solid antiques jostle with photos, flowers, bowls of fruit, and magazines on country matters. There are capacious bath tubs, robes – and suppers for walkers: the Southern Upland Way passes nearby. Breakfasts are properly fortifying and evening meals can be simple or elaborate, often with game or fresh salmon. Convenient for ferries to Belfast and Larne; Galloway gardens and golf courses are close too – return to a snug sitting room with an open fire.

Dumfries & Galloway

Three Glens

Getting here is part of the adventure – up a steep track to a stunning green build with views that shoot off in every direction. Emerging from the stone dyke that breaks the hill, the house is surrounded by sheep and wind. Kerri and Andy welcome you in and feed you well: a full Scottish breakfast, a gorgeous dinner, and everything (just about) sourced from the farm. What a place to hole up in when the weather is bad! Sheep horns for hooks, vines in the conservatory, a great biomass wood-burner, a wall of windows that swish open. Luxurious bedrooms await downstairs, one with a private terrace. Feel your heart soar.

Dogs welcome but not in the house.

Rooms	1 twin/double with separate bath; 1 double, 1 twin sharing bath: £90. Singles £50.	Rooms	2 doubles, 2 twin/doubles: £170. Dinner, B&B £135 per person.
Meals	Supper £20. Dinner, 4 courses, £40. Packed lunch £6. Pub 1.5 miles.	Meals	Dinner, 3 courses with wine, £35. Pubs/restaurants 5-minute walk.
Closed	Christmas, New Year, February & occasionally.	Closed	Rarely.

Favourite newcomer

	David & Ginny Wolsley Brinton Chlenry Farmhouse, Castle Kennedy, Stranraer, Dumfries & Galloway DG9 8SL		**Neil & Mary Gourlay** Three Glens, Moniaive, Thornhill, Dumfries & Galloway DG3 4EW
Tel	+44 (0)1776 705316	Tel	+44 (0)1848 200589
Mobile	+44 (0)7704 205003	Mobile	+44 (0)7974 757654
Email	wolseleybrinton@aol.com	Email	info@3glens.com
Web	www.chlenryfarmhouse.com	Web	www.3glens.com

Entry 594   Map 14

Entry 595   Map 15

Dumfries & Galloway

Holmhill Country House

Among the rolling hills of Dumfries and Galloway, by the banks of the Nith, is a hidden gem of a Georgian country house. It was a favourite of philosopher Thomas Carlyle, who had his own pipe-smoking spot in the marvellously colourful garden. There are seven acres to explore, utter tranquillity, stunning views of the Keir Hills and excellent fishing. Rosie and Stewart love sharing their family home with guests, and can treat you to breakfast, and possibly dinner, by the fire in the graceful dining room. Masses of space everywhere, each room deftly combining rustic virtue with modern savoir-faire.

Discounted rate £195 for 2 nights, £280 for 3 nights (singles £140 for 2 nights, £200 for 3 nights).

Rooms	2 twin/doubles: £105. Singles £75.
Meals	Dinner, 3 courses, £30. Pubs/restaurants 0.5 miles.
Closed	Christmas & New Year.

Rosie Lee
Holmhill Country House,
Thornhill,
Dumfries & Galloway DG3 4AB
Tel   +44 (0)1848 332239
Email   booking@holmhill.co.uk
Web   www.holmhill.co.uk

Entry 596   Map 15

Dumfries & Galloway

New Entry

White Hill

Fresh air, huge gardens and stacks of Scottish charm. The aged paint exterior is forgotten once you're inside this treasure-trove of history and heritage. The Bell-Irvings are natural hosts; twenty generations of their family have lived here and worn the floorboards dancing. Throw logs on the fire, ramble round the azalea'd gardens or explore the woods, fish the river, and dine opulently under the gaze of portraits of their 'rellies'. Breakfast is a delightfully hearty affair. A very special chance to share a real ancestral home in the Scottish borders with a kind, funny, lovely couple (and their very friendly springer spaniel).

Rooms	2 twins: £88. Singles £54.
Meals	Dinner £30 (by prior arrangement). Pubs/restaurants 4 miles.
Closed	Rarely.

Robin & Janet Bell-Irving
White Hill,
Ecclefechan, Lockerbie,
Dumfries & Galloway DG11 1AL
Tel   +44 (0)1576 510206
Email   johnbi@talktalk.net
Web   www.aboutscotland.com/south/whitehill.html

Entry 597   Map 15

Dumfries & Galloway

Byreburnfoot House

Tucked away up a gravelled drive overlooking the banks of the salmon-rich Esk, this pretty Victorian forester's house combines traditional charm with modern comforts. Find an elegant and rural decor, with airy rooms, wooden floors and antique pieces – grandfather clock, writing desk, chandeliers. Beds are big, the linen is trimmed and views are sublime. Warm hosts Bill and Lorraine are keenly green-fingered: their 1.5 acres of orchards, flower-fringed lawns and organic kitchen garden are productive – and their cooking is delicious! Bill is happy to arrange salmon and trout fishing. Stay a few days and become part of it all.

Rooms	2 doubles; 1 twin/double with separate bath: £90–£95. Singles £65.
Meals	Dinner, 3 courses, £30. Packed lunch from £7.50. Pub/restaurant 5 miles.
Closed	Rarely.

	Bill & Loraine Frew
	Byreburnfoot House,
	Canonbie,
	Dumfries & Galloway DG14 0XB
Tel	+44 (0)1387 371209
Mobile	+44 (0)7764 194901
Email	enquiries@byreburnfoot.co.uk
Web	www.byreburnfoot.co.uk

Entry 598   Map 15

Edinburgh & the Lothians

2 Cambridge Street

A mischievous humour, tinged with historical and cultural references, alerts you to the specialness of this place, a ground-floor B&B in the lee of Edinburgh Castle, in the heart of theatre land. Find fin-de-siècle Scotland, with darkly striking colours on walls, antiques aplenty, and a captivating attention to detail. There are interactive art installations that sing and play, a line of old theatre seats up on the wall, photos and 'objets' serving startling and original purposes. Erlend and Hélène are delightful and free-spirited; Erlend, a quietly spoken (but don't be fooled) Shetlander, serves a breakfast to remember.

Rooms	2 doubles: £95–£140. Singles £90–£110.
Meals	Pubs/restaurants 1-minute walk.
Closed	Christmas.

	Erlend & Hélène Clouston
	2 Cambridge Street,
	Edinburgh EH1 2DY
Tel	+44 (0)131 478 0005
Email	erlendc@blueyonder.co.uk
Web	www.wwwonderful.net

Entry 599   Map 15

14 Hart Street

The brightly lit Georgian house has a smart front of polished brass and glossy paint. The warm raspberry hall is lined with art, and the graceful dining room is just as inviting: decanters on the sideboard, period furniture, glowing lamps, and a welcoming home-baked something. Fresh bright bedrooms are elegant and comfortable with whisky and wine on a tray and smart, sparkling bathrooms. Wake for breakfast at a beautifully polished table, with plenty of coffee, newspapers and chat; James and Angela are easy to talk to and love having guests to stay. Perfect for a peaceful city break, and Princes Street is a five-minute walk.

24 Saxe Coburg Place

A ten-minute walk from the centre of Edinburgh, this 1827 house stands in a quiet Georgian square with a central communal garden. The three attractive bedrooms are on the garden level and are self-contained with their own entrance; find comfortable beds, good lighting, handsome antiques and a small kitchen for making tea and coffee. Bathrooms are spotless and one has Paris metro tiling in white and green. Excitingly you can nip over the road to the refurbished Victorian Baths for a swim, sauna or workout in the gym; return to a generous continental breakfast served in the little hall – or on the pretty terrace in summer.

Rooms	2 doubles, 1 twin/double: £90-£120.
Meals	Restaurants 10-minute walk.
Closed	Rarely.

Rooms	1 double, 1 twin/double: £100-£150. 1 single: £50-£70.
Meals	Continental breakfast. Restaurants/pubs 5-minute walk.
Closed	Rarely.

James & Angela Wilson
14 Hart Street,
Edinburgh EH1 3RN
Tel +44 (0)131 557 6826
Mobile +44 (0)7795 203414
Email hartst.edin@virgin.net
Web www.14hartst.com

Diana McMicking
24 Saxe Coburg Place,
Edinburgh EH3 5BP
Tel +44 (0)131 315 3263
Mobile +44 (0)7979 351717
Email diana@saxecoburgplace.co.uk
Web www.saxecoburgplace.co.uk

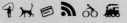

Entry 600   Map 15

Entry 601   Map 15

10 London Street

A Roman X marks this special spot: a beautiful Georgian terraced house in Edinburgh's world heritage New Town, home to descendants of Scots author John Gibson Lockhart. Step into a family home of period elegance and charming informality: accept a dram by the fire in the sash-windowed drawing room (with baby grand piano), relax at the dining table over a leisurely continental breakfast. Sleep undisturbed in 'Beauregard', with its lovely views and paintings, or pick 'Gibson' with its off-courtyard privacy and self-catering option. The best of Edinburgh is a stroll away, good buses zip you further afield, but at night-time all is quiet.

Geraldsplace

Elegant Georgian New Town... so splendid and handsome it's a World Heritage Site. Welcoming, enthusiastic, charming Gerald runs a B&B on one of its finest streets. His patio basement apartment is full of character, comfort and colour. Bedrooms have cosiness, warmth, fine fabrics, excellent art... and special extras: DVDs and a book swop shelf, a laptop with fast broadband, a tea tray, a decanter of single malt whisky; bathrooms are newly done. Breakfast is a feast and mostly organic. There's a private garden opposite, an incredibly convenient location and, of course, Gerald, your brilliantly well-informed, up-to-the-minute host.

Minimum stay: 3 nights.

Rooms	2 doubles (1 with self-catering option): £100-£120.
Meals	Continental breakfast. Pub/restaurant 500 yds.
Closed	Rarely.

Rooms	2 twin/doubles: £89-£129. £69-£99 (additional supplement during festivals).
Meals	Restaurants within 3-minute walk.
Closed	Rarely.

Pippa Lockhart
10 London Street,
Edinburgh EH3 6NA
Tel   +44 (0)131 556 0737
Email   pippa@hjlockhart.co.uk
Web   www.londonstreetaccommodation.co.uk

Gerald Della-Porta
Geraldsplace,
21b Abercromby Place,
Edinburgh EH3 6QE
Tel   +44 (0)131 558 7017
Mobile   +44 (0)7766 016840
Email   gerald11@geraldsplace.com
Web   www.geraldsplace.com

Entry 602   Map 15

Entry 603   Map 15

Number29

You overlook St Mary's Cathedral green from this elegant, Georgian, West End townhouse – a stone's throw from Princes Street. Renovated with style and quirky touches, it feels grand yet friendly; Simon and Corinne welcome you into their home with charm. Ceilings are high, cornices and wooden shutters original and light floods in. The beautiful staircase is crowned by a cupola and lit at night, a wood-burner warms you in the dining room and you sleep in peaceful bedrooms with views, restful with flowers and immaculately dressed beds. Wake for a splendid, locally sourced variety of treats at breakfast. A delicious place.

11 Belford Place

Guests love Sue's modern townhouse, quietly tucked away in a private road above the Water of Leith yet a short distance from the city. From the wooden-floored entrance a picture-lined staircase winds upward. Handsome bedrooms display china cups and floral spreads; dazzling bathrooms have Molton Brown goodies. Wake for Stornoway black pudding, kedgeree, homemade jams and delicious ginger compote at the gleaming table. Owls sometimes hoot in the pretty sloping garden, there's an outside luggage store, parking is free and art galleries and Murrayfield Stadium are nearby.

Minimum stay: 2 nights in August. Children over 12 welcome.

Rooms	1 double: £100–£120.
	2 suites for 2: £110–£170.
	Singles from £100.
Meals	Pubs/restaurants 150 yds.
Closed	Rarely.

Rooms	2 twin/doubles: £70–£120.
Meals	Restaurants 10-minute walk.
Closed	Christmas.

Simon & Corinne Rawlins
Number29,
29 Manor Place,
Edinburgh EH3 7DX
Tel +44 (0)131 225 6385
Mobile +44 (0)7780 527500
Email info@number29edinburgh.co.uk
Web www.number29edinburgh.co.uk

Susan Kinross
11 Belford Place,
Edinburgh EH4 3DH
Tel +44 (0)131 332 9704
Mobile +44 (0)7712 836399
Email suekinross@blueyonder.co.uk

 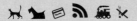

Entry 604 Map 15   Entry 605 Map 15

12 Belford Terrace

Leafy trees, a secluded garden, a stone wall and, beyond, a quiet riverside stroll. On the doorstep of the Modern Art and Dean galleries with Edinburgh's theatres and restaurants just a 15-minute walk, this Victorian end terrace, beside Leith Water, oozes an easy-going elegance, helped by Carolyn's laid-back but competent manner. Garden level bedrooms have their own entrance and are big and creamy with stripy fabrics, antiques, sofas and huge windows. (The single has a Boys Own charm.) Carolyn spoils with crisp linen, books and biscuits and a delicious, full-works breakfast. After a day in town, relax on the sunny terrace.

Millers64

Who could fail to relax here after a busy day? The bedrooms are comfortable and contemporary, the hosts are knowledgeable and friendly, and the breakfasts are stupendous (jam and marmalade courtesy of Louise and Shona's mum), served gourmet style at the big table. This elegant terraced villa is reached via Leith Walk, a wide busy thoroughfare that gets you to Edinburgh's hub in 20 minutes on foot; Leith's waterfront is an easy half mile. Victorian stained glass and cornices mix with a serene eastern theme (note the stylish pewter sinks from Thailand) and the quietest room is at the back.

Children over 10 welcome. Ask about parking.

Rooms	1 double, 1 twin/double: £70–£110. 1 single with separate shower: £40–£55.	Rooms	1 double: £110–£130. 1 suite for 2: £120–£150. Singles from £80.
Meals	Pub/restaurants within 10-minute walk.	Meals	Pubs/restaurants 0.5 miles.
Closed	Christmas.	Closed	24 February – 9 March, 30 April – 10 May.

	Carolyn Crabbie 12 Belford Terrace, Edinburgh EH4 3DQ		Louise Clelland Millers64, 64 Pilrig Street, Edinburgh EH6 5AS
Tel	+44 (0)131 332 2413		
Email	carolyncrabbie@blueyonder.co.uk	Tel	+44 (0)131 454 3666
		Email	louise@millers64.com
		Web	www.millers64.com

Entry 606   Map 15

Entry 607   Map 15

Edinburgh & the Lothians

Edinburgh & the Lothians

Wallace's Arthouse Scotland

The apartment door swings open to a world of white walls, smooth floors, modern art, acoustic jazz, and smiling Wallace with a glass of wine – well worth the three-storey climb up this old Assembly Rooms building. Your host – New York fashion designer and arts enthusiast, Glasgow-born, not shy – has created a bright, minimalist space sprinkled with humour and casual sophistication. Bedrooms capture light and exude his inimitable style; the kitchen's narrow bar is perfect for a light breakfast. Leith is Edinburgh's earthy side with its docks and noisy street life, but fine restaurants abound and the centre is close. Memorable.

Two Hillside Crescent

Leave your worries behind as you enter this exquisitely restored Georgian townhouse. All is peaceful, spacious and light, with an upbeat contemporary feel. Bedrooms are on the first and second floors: imagine sleek modern furniture, big beds, superb mattresses, clouds of goose down, crisp linen, and immaculate bathrooms with organic toiletries and lashings of hot water. Over a superb breakfast your charming hosts will help you get the most out of your stay. Calton Hill is across the road for the best views of the city, and you're a stroll from the start of the Royal Mile. Wonderful.

Rooms	2 doubles: £115. Singles £95.
Meals	Pubs/restaurants 10 yds.
Closed	Christmas Eve & Christmas Day.

Rooms	5 twin/doubles: £125–£165. Singles from £95.
Meals	Pubs/restaurants across the road.
Closed	Rarely.

	Wallace Shaw
	Wallace's Arthouse Scotland,
	41-4 Constitution Street,
	Edinburgh EH6 7BG
Tel	+44 (0)131 538 3320
Mobile	+44 (0)7941 343714
Email	cawallaceshaw@mac.com
Web	www.wallacesarthousescotland.com

	Elaine Adams
	Two Hillside Crescent,
	Edinburgh EH7 5DY
Tel	+44 (0)131 556 4871
Email	info@twohillsidecrescent.com
Web	www.twohillsidecrescent.com

1 Albert Terrace

A warm-hearted home with a lovely garden, an American hostess and a gorgeous Siamese cat. You are 20 minutes by bus from Princes Street yet the guests' sitting room overlooks pear trees and clematis and the rolling Pentland Hills. Cosy up in the winter next to a stylish log-effect wood-burner; in summer, take your morning paper onto the sunny terrace. Books, flowers, interesting art and ceramics and – you are on an old, quiet street – utter, surprising peace. Bedrooms are colourful, spacious and bright, one with an Art Deco bathroom and views over the garden. Clarissa is arty, easy, generous and loves having guests.

Minimum stay: 2 nights in August.

Glebe House

A treasure of a home – and host! A perfect Georgian family house with all the well-proportioned elegance you'd expect, it is resplendent with original features – fireplaces, arched glass, long windows – that have appeared more than once in interiors magazines. Bedrooms are light and airy with pretty fabrics and lovely linen. The beach is a stone's throw away, views are leafy-green, golfers have over 21 courses to choose from. There's also a fascinating sea bird centre close by – and you are 30 minutes from Edinburgh: regular trains bring you to the foot of the castle.

Rooms	1 double; 1 double sharing bath with single: £75-£85. 1 single sharing bath with double: £40.
Meals	Pubs/restaurants nearby.
Closed	Rarely.

Rooms	1 double, 1 four-poster; 1 twin with separate bath: £120-£130. Singles by arrangement.
Meals	Restaurants 2-minute walk.
Closed	Christmas & New Year.

	Clarissa Notley 1 Albert Terrace, Edinburgh EH10 5EA
Tel	+44 (0)131 447 4491
Email	canotley@aol.com

	Gwen & Jake Scott Glebe House, Law Road, North Berwick, Edinburgh EH39 4PL
Tel	+44 (0)1620 892608
Mobile	+44 (0)7973 965814
Email	gwenscott@glebehouse-nb.co.uk
Web	www.glebehouse-nb.co.uk

Entry 610   Map 15

Entry 611   Map 16

Edinburgh & the Lothians

Traprain Cottage

Beneath the big farming skies of East Lothian, martins swoop over the top of Traprain Law, while bees hum and hens potter in the garden of these carefully renovated labourers' cottages. You have independence in the oldest part, with a suite of rooms up in the eaves and a bright comfortable twin next to the cosily private sitting room: just the place to toast one's feet by the fire or hunker down with a book after a day's coastal walking or golfing. Ask Jim and Kirstie where to go over a welcome of afternoon tea, or during a traditional and local breakfast served in the kitchen, or on the terrace if the weather is fine.

Rooms	1 twin with separate shower; 1 double with adjoining twin for children & separate bath: £90; £120 with 2 children under 12. Singles £50.
Meals	Dinner, 2-3 courses, £22.50-£28. Pubs/restaurants 4 miles.
Closed	Christmas & New Year.

Kirstie Shearer
Traprain Cottage,
Standingstone Farm,
Haddington, Edinburgh EH41 4LF

Tel	+44 (0)1620 825375
Email	kirstie.shearer@morham.org
Web	www.trapraincottagebandb.co.uk

Entry 612   Map 16

Fife

Blair Adam

If staying in a place with genuine Adam features is special, how much more so in the Adam family home! They've been in this corner of Fife since 1733: John laid out the walled garden, son William was a prominent politician, Sir Walter Scott used to come and stay... you may be similarly inspired. The house, in a swathe of parkland and forest overlooking the hills and Loch Leven, has big, comfortable light-flooded rooms filled with intriguing contents, and superb walks from the door. The pretty bedroom is on the ground floor and you eat with your friendly hosts in the dining room, with coffee by the fire in the library after dinner.

Rooms	1 twin: £100-£200. Singles £70.
Meals	Dinner, with wine, £25. Restaurants 5 miles.
Closed	December/January.

Keith & Elizabeth Adam
Blair Adam,
Kelty,
Fife KY4 0JF

Tel	+44 (0)1383 831221
Mobile	+44 (0)7986 711099
Email	adamofblairadam@hotmail.com

Entry 613   Map 15

Fife

Fife

Montrave House

Nicholas and Airin's family home is a seamless marriage of Indonesian pieces and Scottish antiques. Sofas are deep, bedrooms have rich colour and comfort, art is striking, there are games and a card table – and one son does magic tricks upon request. Nicholas has designed local eco-builds and used green measures here too: recycled materials, air source heat pumps, wood-burning stoves. Breakfast is just as interesting: apricots from the garden, waffles perhaps, or a traditional Indonesian. Badgers, red squirrels and buzzards can be spotted, the pretty fishing villages of the East Neuk of Fife explored and Edinburgh is an hour.

Pets by arrangement.

Greenlaw House

With superb views towards the Lomond Hills, Debbie's bright, warm converted farm steading will please you the moment you step in. The oak-floored sitting room has Afghan rugs, sofas around a log-burner, a grand piano, and leads to a decked area for summer sun. In all the rooms is a medley of modern and antique, and fascinating art. The ground-floor bedroom has a lovely old chest and books; the more lived-in upstairs one has the view. Debbie loves to cook: smoked salmon and scrambled eggs, porridge with cream, local honey. Falkland Palace, hunting haunt of the Stuart kings, is close; there are wonderful walks and sea eagles soar.

Rooms	1 double; 1 four-poster with separate bath: £75-£90. 1 single: £40-£55.
Meals	Dinner, 2 courses, £25. Pubs/restaurants 3 miles.
Closed	Rarely.

Rooms	1 double; 1 double with separate bath: £80-£90. Singles £40-£50.
Meals	Dinner £25-£30. Restaurants 15-minute drive.
Closed	Christmas & New Year.

	Airin Gilmour Montrave House, Leven, Fife KY8 5NY
Tel	+44 (0)1333 352647
Email	info@montrave.com
Web	www.montrave.com

	Debbie Butler Greenlaw House, Braeside, Collessie, Cupar, Fife KY15 7UX
Tel	+44 (0)1337 810413
Email	butlerjackson@googlemail.com
Web	www.greenlawhouse.com

Entry 614   Map 15

Entry 615   Map 15

Fife

Kinkell

An avenue of beech trees patrolled by guinea fowl, Hebridean sheep and Highland cows leads to the house. If the sea views and salty smack of St Andrews Bay air don't get you, step inside and have your senses tickled. Your hosts are wonderful and offer you a glass of something on arrival; the elegant drawing room has two open fires, rosy sofas, a grand piano – gorgeous. Bedrooms and bathrooms are immaculate and sunny. Sandy and Frippy are great cooks and make full use of local produce. Gaze on the sea from the garden, head down to the beach, walk the wild coast. A friendly, comfortable family home.

Online booking available.

Rooms	3 twin/doubles: £100. Singles £60.
Meals	Dinner £30. Restaurants in St Andrews, 2 miles.
Closed	Rarely.

Sandy & Frippy Fyfe
Kinkell,
St Andrews, Fife KY16 8PN

Tel	+44 (0)1334 472003
Mobile	+44 (0)7836 746043
Email	fyfe@kinkell.com
Web	www.kinkell.com

Entry 616   Map 16+19

Glasgow

64 Partickhill Road

Be greeted by three free-range hens and Gertie the terrier on arrival at this relaxed family home. It's the bustling West End but the road is peaceful and there's a lovely big garden. Caroline and Hugh are lovers of the arts: the house is full of pictures, vintage finds and books. There are wood floors, rugs, a fire in the comfy sitting room and your bedroom is bright and spacious. Tuck into a delicious breakfast, in the conservatory, of good croissants, organic bacon and sausages, homemade bread and jams. Easy for the underground, trendy cafés and delis, museums, theatres and the university. A city treat.

Rooms	1 double with extra twin available: £80-£90.
Meals	Packed lunch available. Pubs/restaurant 0.25 miles.
Closed	Occasionally.

Caroline Anderson
64 Partickhill Road,
Glasgow G11 5NB

Tel	+44 (0)141 339 1946
Mobile	+44 (0)7962 144509
Email	carolineanderson64@gmail.com

Entry 617   Map 15

Highland

The Grange

A Victorian townhouse with its toes in the country: the mountain hovers above, the loch shimmers below and the garden slopes steeply to great banks of rhododendrons. Bedrooms, the one in the turret with a sumptuous bathroom, are large, luscious, warm and inviting: crushed velvet, beautiful blankets, immaculate linen – all ooze panache. Expect decanters of sherry, ornate cornices, a Louis XV bed and a superb suite with contemporary touches. Elegant breakfasts are served at glass-topped tables; Joan's warm vivacity and love of B&B means guests keep coming back. And just a 10-minute walk into town.

Rooms	2 doubles: £130-£140.
	1 suite for 2: £130-£145.
Meals	Restaurants 12-minute walk.
Closed	Mid-November to March.

Joan & John Campbell
The Grange,
Grange Road, Fort William,
Highland PH33 6JF
Tel   +44 (0)1397 705516
Email   info@thegrange-scotland.co.uk
Web   www.thegrange-scotland.co.uk

Entry 618   Map 17

Highland

Arisaig House

Imposing Arisaig – a 19th-century industrialist's highland fantasy – sits in a walkers' paradise; the views to Skye are to die for. In former days it was a hotel; now Sarah, who has known Arisaig all her life, revels in returning house and gardens to their former glory. The sitting room is bright with Sanderson sofas, portraits and paintings and a huge open fire, and bedrooms are spacious and charming, with comfortable furniture and updated bathrooms. Lovely generous Sarah, passionate Slow Food member, serves breakfasts, high teas and dinners at the long oak table: don't miss the Stornoway black pudding!

Rooms	4 twin/doubles;
	6 suites for 2: £145-£165.
	Singles £85.
Meals	Dinner, 3 courses, from £25.
	Pub/restaurant 3 miles.
Closed	Rarely.

Sarah Winnington-Ingram
Arisaig House,
Arisaig,
Highland PH39 4NR
Tel   +44 (0)1687 450730
Email   sarahwi@arisaighouse.co.uk
Web   www.arisaighouse.co.uk

Entry 619   Map 17

Highland

The Berry

Drive through miles of spectacular landscape then bask in the final approach down a winding single-track road to Allt-Na-Subh — just five houses overlooking the loch. Joan, who is friendly and kind, prepares delicious meals in her Rayburn-warmed kitchen — the hub of this character-filled house. Inside is fresh and light with stylish bedrooms — one up, one down; the sitting room has a log fire and stunning views. Eat fish straight from the boats, pop over to Skye, stride the hills and spot golden eagles, red deer and otters. The perfect place for naturalists and artists, or those seeking solace. A hidden gem.

Minimum stay: 2 nights.

Rooms	1 double with separate shower; 1 double sharing bath with owner: £80. Singles from £45.
Meals	Dinner, 3 courses with wine, £30. Packed lunch £10. Pub 3 miles.
Closed	Rarely.

Joan Ashburner
The Berry,
Allt-Na-Subh, Dornie,
Kyle of Lochalsh,
Highland IV40 8DZ
Tel   +44 (0)1599 588259

Entry 620   Map 17

Highland

Aurora

The perfect spot for walkers and climbers (single-track roads, lochs, rivers and mountains) and the perfect B&B for groups: three smart, uncluttered bedrooms have flexible sleeping arrangements and spick and span shower rooms. The guest sitting room is light and airy with binoculars, books to borrow, maps and a small fridge for your wine — stay put for glorious sunsets and views to Harris. Breakfast time is generously bendy; good seasonal food is important here and you eat round a big table. There's a drying room and bike storage, but those wanting to relax will love it here too.

Minimum stay: 2 nights. Children over 12 welcome.

Rooms	2 doubles: £78-£88. 1 triple: £120-£132. Singles £68-£78.
Meals	Packed lunch £6. Pub/restaurant within 0.5 miles.
Closed	November-March.

Ann Barton
Aurora,
Shieldaig, Torridon,
Highland IV54 8XN
Tel   +44 (0)1520 755246
Email   info@aurora-bedandbreakfast.co.uk
Web   www.aurora-bedandbreakfast.co.uk

Entry 621   Map 17

Highland

The Peatcutter's Croft

Some say there's more beauty in a mile on the west coast than in the rest of the world put together – vast skies, soaring mountains, shimmering water, barely a soul in sight. Pauline and Seori left London to give their family the freedom to roam. Now they have a colourful cast of companions: sheep, hens, ducks, rabbits – all live here. In the adjoining byre: country simplicity, a Norwegian wood-burner, colour, texture and style. Sea eagles patrol the skies, porpoises bask in the loch, red deer come to eat the garden. This, coupled with Pauline's home cooking, makes it very hard to leave. Dogs and children are very welcome.

Highland

The Old Ferryman's House

This former ferryman's house is small, homely and lived-in, just yards from the river Spey with its spectacular mountain views. Explore the countryside or relax in the garden with a tray of tea and homemade treats; plants tumble from whisky barrels and pots and you can spot woodpeckers. The sitting room is cosy with a wood-burning stove and brimming with books and magazines (no TV). Generous Elizabeth, a keen traveller who lived in the Sudan, cooks delicious, imaginative meals: herbs and veg from the garden, eggs from her hens, heathery honeycomb, homemade bread and jams. An unmatched spot for explorers, and very good value.

Rooms	1 apartment for 2 with mezzanine for 2 children: £70. £100 for family of 4. Singles from £45.
Meals	Dinner, 3 courses, £30. BYO. Pub/restaurant 30 miles.
Closed	Christmas.

Rooms	1 double, 1 twin/double sharing 1 bath and 2 wcs with single: £70. 1 single sharing 1 bath and 2 wcs with twin/double & double: £35.
Meals	Dinner, 3 courses, £25. BYO. Packed lunch £7.50.
Closed	Occasionally in winter.

	Seori & Pauline Burnett
	The Peatcutter's Croft,
	Croft 12, Badrallach, Dundonnell,
	Garve, Ullapool, Highland IV23 2QP
Tel	+44 (0)1854 633797
Email	info@peatcutterscroft.com
Web	www.peatcutterscroft.com

	Elizabeth Matthews
	The Old Ferryman's House,
	Boat of Garten,
	Highland PH24 3BY
Tel	+44 (0)1479 831370

Entry 622   Map 17

Entry 623   Map 18

Highland

Rehaurie Cottage

You are steeped in history here, surrounded by woodland, castles, cairns and ancient battlefields. This 19th-century woodcutter's cottage is mercifully free of tartan; instead find clean lines, neutral colours and a contemporary feel. Spacious bedrooms are at either side of the house, one in cool greys with its own sitting room, the other in pretty rose-pink and cream with a private feel; both have sparkling, well-designed bathrooms. Sylvia and Chris, lovely people, give you an ample breakfast in the dining room which leads to a veranda; walks from the door are stunning. Discover golf courses, fishing and Highland games in Nairn.

Minimum stay: 2 nights at weekends. Over 16s welcome.

Rooms	2 doubles, each with separate bath/shower: £85–£125. Singles from £65.
Meals	Packed lunch £7.50. Supper from £17.50. Pub 5 miles.
Closed	Rarely.

Sylvia Gabriel
Rehaurie Cottage,
Nairn,
Highland IV12 5JD

Tel	+44 (0)1309 651322
Mobile	+44 (0)7513 974276
Email	rehaurie@hotmail.co.uk
Web	www.rehaurie.co.uk

Entry 624   Map 18

Highland

Craigiewood

The best of both worlds: the remoteness of the Highlands (red kites, wild goats) and Inverness just four miles. The landscape surrounding this elegant cottage exudes a sense of ancient mystery augmented by these six acres — home to woodpeckers, roe deer and glorious roses. Inside, maps, walking sticks, two cats and a lovely, family-home feel — what you'd expect from delightful owners. Bedrooms, old-fashioned and cosy, overlook a garden reclaimed from Black Isle gorse. Gavin runs garden tours and can take you off to Inverewe, Attadale, Cawdor and Dunrobin Castle. Warm, peaceful and special.

Rooms	2 twins: £80–£90. Singles £40–£50.
Meals	Pub 2 miles.
Closed	Christmas & New Year.

Araminta & Gavin Dallmeyer
Craigiewood,
North Kessock, Inverness,
Highland IV1 3XG

Tel	+44 (0)1463 731628
Mobile	+44 (0)7831 733699
Email	2minty@craigiewood.co.uk
Web	www.craigiewood.co.uk

Entry 625   Map 18

Highland

Knockbain House

This is a well-loved farm, its environmental credentials supreme, and David and Denise are warm and interesting. A beautiful setting, too: landscaped gardens, a 700-acre farm (cows, lambs, barley) and rolling countryside stretching to Cromarty Firth. A grandfather clock ticks away time to relax, by floor-to-ceiling windows and a wood-burner in the antiques-filled sitting room; over a breakfast or dinner of home-grown foods; with a drink on the pond-side terrace; in bedrooms with new bathrooms and stunning views. Revel in the birds, walks and your hosts' commitment to this glorious unspoilt nature.

Babes in arms & over 10s welcome.

Rooms	1 double, 1 twin: £70-£95. Singles £40-£45.
Meals	Dinner, on request, 3 courses, £30. Pubs/restaurants 1 mile.
Closed	Christmas & New Year.

David & Denise Lockett
Knockbain House,
Dingwall,
Highland IV15 9TJ
Tel   +44 (0)1349 862476
Mobile   +44 (0)7736 629838
Email   davidlockett@avnet.co.uk
Web   www.knockbainhouse.co.uk

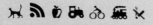

Entry 626   Map 18

Highland

Wemyss House

The peace is palpable, the setting overlooking the Cromarty Firth is stunning. Take an early morning stroll and spot buzzards, pheasants, rabbits and roe deer. The deceptively spacious house with sweeping maple floors is flooded with light and fabulous views, big bedrooms are warmly decorated with Highland rugs and tweeds, there's Christine's grand piano in the living room, Stuart's handcrafted furniture at every turn, and a sweet dog called Bella. Aga breakfasts include homemade bread, preserves and eggs from happy hens. Dinners are delicious; Christine and Stuart are wonderful hosts.

Rooms	2 doubles, 1 twin: £105-£115.
Meals	Dinner £38. Restaurants 15-minute drive.
Closed	Rarely.

Christine Asher & Stuart Clifford
Wemyss House,
Bayfield, Tain,
Highland IV19 1QW
Tel   +44 (0)1862 851212
Mobile   +44 (0)7759 484709
Email   stay@wemysshouse.com
Web   www.wemysshouse.com

Entry 627   Map 18

Highland

St Callan's Manse

Fun, laughter and conversation flow in this warm and happy home. You share it with prints, paintings, antiques, sofas, amazing memorabilia, two dogs, four ducks, 10 hens and 1,200 teddy bears of every size and origin. Snug bedrooms have pretty fabrics, old armoires, flower-patterned sheets and tartan blankets; your sleep will be sound. Caroline cooks majestic breakfasts and dinners; Robert, a fund of knowledgeable anecdotes, can arrange just about anything. All this in incomparable surroundings: 60 acres of land plus glens, forests, buzzards, deer and the odd golden eagle. A gem.

Dogs by arrangement.

Rooms	2 doubles, each with separate bath/shower: £90. Singles £65.
Meals	Dinner, 2-4 courses, £20-£25. BYO. Pub/restaurant in village, 1.5 miles.
Closed	March & occasionally.

Robert & Caroline Mills
St Callan's Manse,
Rogart,
Highland IV28 3XE
Tel +44 (0)1408 641363
Email caroline@rogartsnuff.me.uk

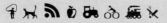

Entry 628   Map 21

Highland

Thrumster House

A Victorian laird's house in an 8,500 acre estate. Drive south a mile to the 5,000-year-old neolithic remains of the Yarrow Archeological Trail for brochs, round houses and long cairns, then back to the big old house, "steamboat gothic" in the words of an American guest. The vaulted hall gives an ecclesiastical feel, with fires burning at both ends and a grand piano on the landing (it gets played wonderfully). Big bedrooms have mahogany dressers, brass beds, floral wallpapers, lots of books. Islay and Catherine look after guests well and conversation flows. There's woodland to walk through and free trout fishing in the lochs too.

Rooms	1 double, 1 twin: £95. Singles £50.
Meals	Dinner, 3 courses with wine, £30. Pub 5-minute walk.
Closed	Rarely.

Islay & Catherine MacLeod
Thrumster House,
Thrumster, Wick,
Highland KW1 5TX
Tel +44 (0)1955 651387
Mobile +44 (0)7840 750407
Email cat.macleod@btinternet.com
Web www.thrumster.co.uk

Entry 629   Map 21

Isle of Skye

Napier Cottage

A beautiful house, filled with light, that floats above the Sound of Sleat with fabulous views across the water. Seals bask on local rocks, herons come in search of supper, the odd pod of minke whales passes through. The house, newly built in traditional style, is delightful: books everywhere, a wood-burner in the sitting room, afternoon tea (on the house) in the conservatory. Big bedrooms have warm colours, pretty fabrics, comfy beds, excellent bathrooms, watery views. Christine cooks tasty breakfasts: fruit salad, good locally sourced produce and homemade marmalade. For dinner, Kinloch Lodge is close if you want to splash out.

Minimum stay: 2 nights in high season.

Rooms	2 doubles: £120–£130.
	Singles £86.
Meals	Pub/restaurant 1 mile.
Closed	November–March.

	Christine Jenkins & Ian Rudd
	Napier Cottage,
	Isleornsay, Sleat,
	Isle of Skye IV43 8QX
Tel	+44 (0)1471 833460
Email	napiercottage@gmail.com
Web	www.napiercottage.co.uk

Entry 630   Map 17

Lanarkshire

The Lint Mill

Rolling hills, fields of sheep and a babbling stream surround this perfectly peaceful converted mill. Deborah and Colin escaped city life to create a smallholding full of flowers, beehives, vegetables, funky sheep, pigs, chickens with fancy houses and horses with a dressage paddock. The light, roomy wing has a separate entrance and private garden, a spiral staircase, its own sitting room and a big wood-burner. Unwind, walk in the countryside, enjoy the fruits (and scones) of their labour, get creative in their artists' studio or pop to excitement in Edinburgh or Glasgow. Foodies will be treated to all manner of local delights.

Rooms	1 double with sitting room &
	conservatory: £80.
	Singles £50. Extra bed £40.
Meals	Dinner, 2–4 courses, £15–25.
	Supper £10.
	Platter for 2, £15.
	Restaurants 2 miles.
Closed	Rarely.

	Colin & Deborah Richardson-Webb
	The Lint Mill,
	Carnwath, Lanark,
	Lanarkshire ML11 8LY
Tel	+44 (0)1555 840042
Email	info@thelintmill.co.uk
Web	www.thelintmill.co.uk

Entry 631   Map 15

Lanarkshire

Cormiston Farm

Wend your way through the soft hills of the Clyde Valley to a Georgian farmhouse in 26 acres of farmland and mature garden. Richard's a keen cook and produce from the walled garden – including delicious eggs from the quails – takes centre stage. Wonderful to retire to quiet, spacious rooms with bucolic views, stunning beds and rich fabrics; characterful Art Deco bathrooms, too. Tuck nippers up in bunks, then slip back for a snifter in front of the log fire in the sitting room. It's home from home, and licensed, too! There's untamed landscape to explore – and the children will love the friendly alpacas.

Rooms	2 doubles, each with separate bath: £86-£108. Singles £65-£81. Extra bunk room available.
Meals	Dinner, 4 courses, £25-£30. Supper, 2 courses, £20. Pub 2 miles.
Closed	Rarely.

Richard Philipps
Cormiston Farm,
Cormiston Road, Biggar, Lanarkshire
ML12 6NS
Tel   +44 (0)1899 221507
Email   info@cormistonfarm.com
Web   www.cormistonfarm.com

Entry 632   Map 15

Moray

Milton Brodie

Peaceful independence in your own wing of Oliver and Abigail's friendly family home. Now with a wisteria-clad Georgian façade, this lovely old house goes back to the 11th century. Your suite has its own sitting room with log fire, books, a table for breakfast (delicious!) and vases of garden flowers; the bedroom is charming with fine linen and feather comfort. Soak in the long blue tub, drift off by the fire with a malt… bliss. There are acres of parkland to explore: ancient trees, woodland paths, banks of bluebells, a walled kitchen garden. Heaps to do beyond too: forts, abbeys, Elgin cathedral, whisky tours and the stunning Moray coast.

Rooms	1 suite for 2 with sitting room: £150.
Meals	Pubs/restaurants 15-minute walk.
Closed	Rarely.

Oliver & Abigail Pilcher
Milton Brodie,
Kinloss, Forres,
Moray IV36 2UA
Tel   +44 (0)1343 850571
Email   oli@oliverpilcher.com
Web   www.miltonbrodie.com

Entry 633   Map 18

Moray

Westfield House

Sweep up the drive to the grand home of an illustrious family: Macleans have lived here since 1862, and there are 500 peaceful acres of farmland. Inside: polished furniture and burnished antiques, a tartan-carpeted hall, an oak stair hung with ancestral oils. Veronica cooks sublimely; dinner is served at a long candelabra'd table, with vegetables from the vegetable garden. A winter fire crackles in the guest sitting room, old-fashioned bedrooms are inviting (plump pillows, fine linen, books, lovely views), the peace is deep. The coast is close and the walking is splendid; a historic house in a perfect setting and Veronica is charming.

Rooms	1 twin; 1 twin with separate bath & shower: £90-£100. 1 single with separate bath: £50.
Meals	Supper, 2 courses, £20. Dinner, 3 courses, £25. Pub 3 miles.
Closed	Rarely.

Veronica Maclean
Westfield House,
Elgin,
Moray IV30 8XL
Tel +44 (0)1343 547308
Email veronica.maclean@yahoo.co.uk
Web www.westfieldhouseelgin.co.uk

Entry 634   Map 18

Perth & Kinross CANOPY&STARS

Pilot Panther

A classic 1950 showman's wagon, built by The Coventry Steel Company, whose journey has been a long and rambling one... It has settled in a fine location with dramatic views of the spectacular, ever-changing loch from every window. Off the rustic living and sleeping area, with the oven and grill, is the double bunk room. The loos and shower are a minute's walk away at the hotel, handily an award-winning point of pilgrimage for Scottish foodies! They have their own fishery, bakery and tea rooms too, which can provide you with takeaway ingredients or eat-in goodies. So: quirky comfort, good food, outstanding walking – great!

Minimum stay: 2 nights. Book through Sawday's Canopy & Stars online or by phone.

Rooms	1 wagon for 4 (1 large double, 2 bunks): £125-£150. £10 per dog.
Meals	Breakfast in hotel.
Closed	December-March.

Sawday's Canopy & Stars
Pilot Panther,
Monachyle Mhor Hotel,
Balquhidder, Lochearnhead,
Perth & Kinross FK19 8PQ
Tel +44 (0)117 204 7830
Email enquiries@canopyandstars.co.uk
Web www.canopyandstars.co.uk/
pilotpanther

Entry 635   Map 18

Perth & Kinross

Beinn Bhracaigh

Excellent views stretch out from this Victorian villa. All the bedrooms are in relaxing creams, with duck-egg blues in throws and subtly patterned cushions propped like toast in a toast rack; TVs and fine Scottish soaps complete the Perthshire picture. Friendly hosts give you a continental breakfast in your room or a full Scottish and good coffee at separate tables in the dining room. Great fun and conviviality can be had in the evening when guests take over the honesty bar with its many wines and more than 50 whiskies. Amble to Pitlochry Theatre; discover an area rich with castles, fishing, white water rafting and walks.

Minimum stay: 2 nights at weekends. Children over 8 welcome.

Rooms	8 doubles, 3 twin/doubles: £69–£103. 1 suite for 2: £89–£129. Singles from £49.
Meals	14 pubs/restaurants within 10-minute walk.
Closed	Rarely.

James & Kirsty Watts
Beinn Bhracaigh,
14 Higher Oakfield,
Pitlochry,
Perth & Kinross PH16 5HT

Tel	+44 (0)1796 470355
Email	info@beinnbhracaigh.com
Web	www.beinnbhracaigh.com

Entry 636   Map 15+18

Perth & Kinross

The Steading

Hens scatter as you approach this house behind the hamlet of Tullicro — a clever fusion of modern Scottish and Scandinavian design. Built of local Aberfeldy stone, Sarah Jane's home has splendid mountain and river views. Breakfast on the loggia (when sunny) or at the picture window, on fine local and organic food (seeded breads, raspberries, smoked salmon…). The upstairs bedroom has a magnificent star-gazey skylight; both rooms have the right balance of comfort and contemporary chic. Fine Scottish woollens, French linens, firm mattresses, thick towels in pristine warm-floored shower rooms. Evenings in front of that wood-burner beckon.

Minimum stay: 2 nights at weekends.

Rooms	1 double, 1 twin/double: £95. Singles £70.
Meals	Pub/restaurant 2 miles.
Closed	Rarely.

Sarah Jane Burton
The Steading,
Tullicro, By Camserney, Aberfeldy,
Perth & Kinross PH15 2JG

Tel	+44 (0)1887 820718
Mobile	+44 (0)7813 066662
Email	enquiries@steadingaberfeldy.co.uk
Web	www.steadingaberfeldy.co.uk

Entry 637   Map 15+18

Perth & Kinross

Essendy House

Down a tree-lined drive blazing with colour, Tess and John's charming country house is surrounded by lochs, castles and serenity. Inside is cosy and comfortable with warm fires, flowers, porcelain, Italianate murals and an unusual collection of family artefacts. Traditionally furnished bedrooms have antiques, good linen, garden views and silk or floral touches. Enjoy hearty breakfasts and suppers in the huge dining room or family kitchen; the terrace is heaven in summer. There's lots to do: visit cathedral and theatre, walk in Macbeth's Birnam Wood, play golf, ski, fish and admire the swooping ospreys.

Perth & Kinross

Mackeanston House

They grow their own organic fruit and vegetables in the walled garden, make their own preserves, bake their own bread. Likeable and energetic – Fiona a wine buff and talented cook, Colin a tri-lingual guide – your hosts are hospitable people whose 1690 farmhouse combines informality and luxury in peaceful, central Scotland. Light-filled bedrooms have pretty fabrics, fine antiques, TVs and homemade cake. Roomy bathrooms have robes and a radio; one has a double shower (with a seat if you wish it). Dine by the log fire in the dining room, or in the conservatory with views to Stirling Castle.

Rooms	1 double, 1 twin: £110. Singles £55. Dinner, B&B £80 per person.	Rooms	1 double, 1 twin/double: £90–£104. Singles £65–£67. Dinner, B&B £79–£85 per person. Extra bed/sofabed available £25 per person per night.
Meals	Packed lunch £5. Supper, 2 courses, £25. Pub/restaurant 2 miles.	Meals	Dinner, 3 courses, £33; 4 courses, £36. Pub 1 mile.
Closed	Christmas & New Year; February/March.	Closed	Rarely.

	John Monteith Essendy House, Blairgowrie, Perth & Kinross PH10 6QY		**Fiona & Colin Graham** Mackeanston House, Doune, Stirling, Perth & Kinross FK16 6AX
Tel	+44 (0)1250 884260	Tel	+44 (0)1786 850213
Mobile	+44 (0)7841 121538	Mobile	+44 (0)7921 143018
Email	johnmonteith@hotmail.com	Email	info@mackeanstonhouse.co.uk
Web	www.essendy.org	Web	www.mackeanstonhouse.co.uk

Entry 638   Map 15+18

Entry 639   Map 15

Perth & Kinross

Old Kippenross

What a setting! Old Kippenross rests in 150 peaceful acres of gorgeous park and woodland overlooking the river Allan – spot red squirrels and deer, herons, dippers and otters. The 15th-century house has a Georgian addition and an air of elegance and great courtesy, with its rustic white-vaulted basement, and dining and sitting rooms strewn with soft sofas and Persian rugs. Sash-windowed bedrooms are deeply comfortable, warm bathrooms are stuffed with towels. Susan and Patrick (an expert on birds of prey) are welcoming, the food is good and there's a croquet lawn in the walled garden.

Children over 10 welcome. Dogs by arrangement only.

Rooms	1 double; 1 twin/double with adjoining single room (let to same party only): £104-£106. Singles £67-£69.
Meals	Dinner £30. BYO. Pub 1.5 miles.
Closed	Rarely.

Susan & Patrick Stirling-Aird
Old Kippenross,
Kippenross, Dunblane,
Perth & Kinross FK15 0LQ
Tel   +44 (0)1786 824048
Email   kippenross@hotmail.com
Web   www.oldkippenross.co.uk

Entry 640   Map 15

Scottish Borders

Skirling House

An intriguing house with 1908 additions, impeccably maintained. The whole lovely place is imbued with the spirit of Scottish Arts & Crafts, augmented with Italianate flourishes. Colourful blankets embellish chairs; runners soften flagged floors; the carvings, wrought-ironwork and rare Florentine ceiling are sheer delight. Upstairs, superb comfort holds sway: carpets and rugs, window seats and wicker, fruit and flowers. Bob cooks the finest local produce, Isobel shares a love of Scottish contemporary art and both look after you beautifully. They've planted some 25,000 trees, and grand woodland walks start from the door.

Rooms	3 doubles, 1 twin/double, 1 twin: £120-£180. Singles £60-£95.
Meals	Dinner £35. Pubs/restaurants 2 miles.
Closed	Christmas & January/February.

Bob & Isobel Hunter
Skirling House,
Skirling, Biggar,
Scottish Borders ML12 6HD
Tel   +44 (0)1899 860274
Email   enquiry@skirlinghouse.com
Web   www.skirlinghouse.com

Entry 641   Map 15

Scottish Borders

Fauhope House

Near to Melrose Abbey and the glorious St Cuthbert's Walk, this solid 1890s house is immersed in bucolic bliss. Views soar to the Eildon Hills through wide windows with squashy seats; all is luxurious, elegant, fire-lit and serene with an eclectic mix of art. Bedrooms are warm with deeply coloured walls, thick chintz, pale tartan blankets and soft carpet; bathrooms are modern and pristine. Breakfast is served with smiles at a flower-laden table and overlooking those purple hills. A short walk through the garden and over a footbridge takes you to the interesting town of Melrose, with shops, restaurants and its own theatre.

Rooms	3 twin/doubles: £100–£110. Singles from £60.
Meals	Pub/restaurant 0.5 miles.
Closed	Rarely.

Ian & Sheila Robson
Fauhope House,
Gattonside, Melrose,
Scottish Borders TD6 9LY

Tel	+44 (0)1896 823184
Mobile	+44 (0)7816 346768
Email	info@fauhopehouse.com
Web	www.fauhopehouse.com

Entry 642   Map 15

Scottish Borders

Whitehouse Country House

A proud avenue of trees leads to Angela and Roger's handsome 19th-century country house in the heart of the Scottish Borders. They have been welcoming guests for over 20 years providing comfort, relaxation and great hospitality. Enjoy log fires and deep armchairs in the elegant dining and drawing rooms, traditional bedrooms with the most comfortable beds and glorious views from every room. Angela's cooking is heavenly and she uses wild salmon, game and the finest in season local produce. Explore historic Border towns, cycle the Tweed Cycleway, walk St Cuthbert's Way – your hosts know the area well and are happy to advise.

Pets by arrangement.

Rooms	1 double, 2 twins: £120–£140. Singles £80–£90. Dinner, B&B £109–£119 per person. Extra bed/sofabed available £25–£35 per person per night.
Meals	Dinner £22–£29. Supper tray £10. Packed lunch £7. Pub 3 miles.
Closed	Rarely.

Angela & Roger Tyrer
Whitehouse Country House,
St Boswells, Melrose,
Scottish Borders TD6 0ED

Tel	+44 (0)1573 460343
Mobile	+44 (0)7877 800582
Email	stay@whitehousecountryhouse.com
Web	www.whitehousecountryhouse.com

Entry 643   Map 16

Scottish Borders

Singdean

Remote, high up and rugged. You have your own entrance to a smart-and-soulful suite in this glorious Border cottage. You'll be toasty warm and comfortable: find an enormous double bed, delicious linen, exposed stonework, reclaimed wood cladding and thick fabrics. Take a deep breath out, light the candles, scent the bath… romantics will be thrilled to bits. Fresh, ski-style breakfasts are brought to you, packed lunches can be sorted and if you don't want to budge, have supper with friendly Christa and Del. They'll even drop you at the pub and pick you up. Walks are awe-inspiring but Hawick has cashmere!

Rooms	1 suite for 2: £125-£138. Singles £115-£124. Extra bed/sofabed available £20 per person per night.
Meals	Packed lunch & supper included by prior arrangement (voluntary contribution to the Landscaping fund). Pub 6 miles.
Closed	Rarely.

Christa & Del Dobson
Singdean,
Newcastleton,
Scottish Borders TD9 0SP

Tel	+44 (0)1450 860622
Email	info@hanselundgretel.com
Web	www.hanselundgretel.com

Entry 644   Map 16

Stirling

Cardross

Dodge the lazy sheep on the long drive to arrive (eventually!) at a sweep of gravel and lovely old Cardross in a gorgeous setting. Bang on the enormous ancient door and either Archie or Nicola (plus labradors and lively Jack Russells) will usher you in. And what a delight it is; come here for a blast of Scottish history! Traditional big bedrooms have airiness, long views, antiques, wooden shutters, towelling robes and good linen; one bathroom has a cast-iron period bath. The drawing room is vast, the house is filled with warm character, the Orr Ewings can tell you all the history.

Young people over 14 welcome.

Rooms	1 twin; 1 twin with separate bath: £110-£120. Singles £70-£75.
Meals	Occasional dinner £35. Pubs/restaurants 3-6 miles.
Closed	Christmas & New Year.

Sir Archie & Lady Orr Ewing
Cardross,
Port of Menteith, Kippen,
Stirling FK8 3JY

Tel	+44 (0)1877 385223
Email	enquiries@cardrossestate.com
Web	www.cardrossestate.com

Entry 645   Map 15

Stirling

Stirling

Powis House

A sprawling 18th-century mansion with the volcanic Ochil Hills as a stunning backdrop and a colourful entrance hall of antlers and stuffed animals. Country style bedrooms invite with polished old floors, tartan throws, garden views and original bathrooms. You have a huge dining room with warming wood-burner, a guest lounge on the first floor, a sunny stone-flagged patio with places to sit and acres of estate with a woodland walk to explore. Colin and Jane are caring and interesting; Colin is a keen cook and has ghost stories galore to share. Historical Stirling is close: castle, university, festival and more.

Bramble Bield

Three fairytale wagons gather at the foot of the Ochil Hills, near historic Stirling and in the grounds of Powis House. Holly (green) and Rowan (red) are gypsy bowtops; Bramley is a potter's wagon that accompanies Rowan to make a twosome perfect for a family. All are traditionally snug and enchanting. You share the central fire-pit by the hawthorn, but get your own outdoor space too. The well-stocked kitchen, shower room (eco toiletries) and compost loo (nothing to fear!) are shared between the three. Book one wagon – or all three for a fun gathering. Friendly Colin and Jane leave breakfast in the Stables: Danish pastries, fresh eggs, coffee.

Bookings start on a Monday, Wednesday or Friday. Book through Sawday's Canopy & Stars online or by phone.

Rooms	2 doubles, 1 twin: £90–£100. Singles £65.
Meals	Dinner, 4 courses with coffee, £25. Pub/restaurant 3 miles.
Closed	Rarely.

Rooms	1 gypsy caravan for 2 (2 child beds available); 1 gypsy caravan camp for 4: £70–£134.
Meals	Continental breakfast included. Full Scottish cooked breakfast available in the main house for a small additional cost.
Closed	November – February.

	Jane & Colin Kilgour
	Powis House,
	Stirling FK9 5PS
Tel	+44 (0)1786 460231
Email	info@powishouse.co.uk
Web	www.powishouse.co.uk

	Sawday's Canopy & Stars
	Bramble Bield,
	Bramble Bield, Powis House,
	Stirling FK9 5PS
Tel	+44 (0)117 204 7830
Email	enquiries@canopyandstars.co.uk
Web	www.canopyandstars.co.uk/ bramblebield

Entry 646   Map 15

Entry 647   Map 15

Stirling

Quarter

This stately 1750s house commands views across Stirling's lush countryside and comes complete with crunching gravel drive and original ceiling dome. It was owned by the same family for generations until the Macleans took over its high ceilings, cornicing features and sash windows. Pad your way upstairs to two comfortable bedrooms and bathrooms, brightened with a pretty floral touch. Breakfast is a grand affair at a long polished table in the dining room (the free-range hens providing the eggs). You are cocooned in extensive grounds, yet have easy access to Stirling, Edinburgh, Perth and Glasgow.

Dogs welcome by arrangement.

Rooms	1 twin/double, 1 twin: £100. Singles £55.
Meals	Pub/restaurant 4 miles.
Closed	Christmas.

	Pippa Maclean
	Quarter,
	Denny,
	Stirling FK6 6QZ
Tel	+44 (0)1324 825817
Email	quarterstirling@hotmail.co.uk
Web	www.quarterstirling.com

Entry 648 Map 15

Western Isles

Pairc an t-Srath

Richard and Lena's lovely home overlooks the beach at Borve – another absurdly beautiful Harris view. Inside, smart simplicity abounds: wooden floors, white walls, a peat fire, colourful art. Airy bedrooms fit the mood perfectly: trim carpets, chunky wood beds, Harris tweed throws, excellent shower rooms (there's a bathroom, too, if you want a soak). Richard crofts, Lena cooks, perhaps homemade soup, venison casserole, wet chocolate cake with raspberries. Views from the dining room tumble down hill, so expect to linger over breakfast. You'll spot otters in the loch, while the standing stones at Callanish are unmissable.

Rooms	2 doubles, 1 twin: £104. 1 single: from £52.
Meals	Dinner, 3 courses, £37. Restaurant 3 miles, pub 7 miles.
Closed	Rarely.

	Lena & Richard MacLennan
	Pairc an t-Srath,
	Borve, Isle of Harris,
	Western Isles HS3 3HT
Tel	+44 (0)1859 550386
Email	info@paircant-srath.co.uk
Web	www.paircant-srath.co.uk

Entry 649 Map 20

Wales

Photo: Rhedyn, Powys,
entry 676

Carmarthenshire

Sarnau Mansion

Listed and Georgian, this handsome house has 16 acres of grounds complete with pond, well-tended walled garden and woodland with nesting red kites. Bedrooms are calm and traditionally furnished with heritage colours, art poster prints and green views; big bathrooms have plenty of hot water. The oak-floored sitting room with leather Chesterfields has French windows leading onto the rhododendron lawn, the guest dining room has separate tables, and there's home cooking from Cynthia. A peaceful place from which to explore beaches, castles and more – 15 minutes from the National Botanic Garden of Wales.

Children over 5 welcome.

Rooms	2 doubles, 1 twin; 1 double with separate bath: £80–£90. Singles £50.
Meals	Dinner, 3 courses, around £25. BYO. Pub 1 mile.
Closed	Rarely.

	Cynthia & David Fernihough
	Sarnau Mansion,
	Llysonnen Road, Bancyfelin,
	Carmarthen,
	Carmarthenshire SA33 5DZ
Tel	+44 (0)1267 211404
Email	d.fernihough@btinternet.com
Web	www.sarnaumansion.co.uk

Entry 650   Map 6

Carmarthenshire

Ty Cefn Tregib

Two characterful Mongolian yurts and the shining 76er – an American Airstream trailer – in the lovely Towy Valley, a stroll from Llandeilo. Each has its own space and style: the comfy, funky 76er a king-size bed, kitchen, table and sofa; the loo and shower separate and next door. The Waterfall Pagoda Yurt – with its waterscape – has Japanese fabric hangings, lacquered furniture and a dragon-guarded 'yurtmobile' kitchen/washroom. Colourful, comfortable Gert's Yurt, furthest from the house, sheltered on the hillside with fine views, has a wood-burner, a big double, and a yurtmobile. That's three holidays in one great spot!

Bookings start on a Monday or Friday. Book through Sawday's Canopy & Stars online or by phone.

Rooms	1 yurt for 2: £64–£90. 1 pagoda yurt for 2: £64–£111. 1 Airstream for 2: £64–£111.
Meals	Continental breakfast basket £8 for 2. Honesty box for the duck eggs, apple juice, plums and homemade jam when available.
Closed	November–April.

	Sawday's Canopy & Stars
	Ty Cefn Tregib,
	Ffairfach,
	Llandeilo,
	Carmarthenshire SA19 6TD
Tel	+44 (0)117 204 7830
Email	enquiries@canopyandstars.co.uk
Web	www.canopyandstars.co.uk/tregib

Entry 651   Map 7

Carmarthenshire

The Glynhir Estate

This fine old house on a Huguenot estate stands on the western edge of the Black Mountain. Outside: a waterfall, a two-acre kitchen garden, a brigade of chickens, and peacocks that patrol the grounds with panache. Inside, the house has spurned the urge to take itself too seriously and remains decidedly lived in. Find William Morris wallpaper in the dining room, lemon trees in the conservatory and old cabinets stuffed with interesting things in the sitting room. Country-house bedrooms fit the mood perfectly: smart and comfortable with excellent bathrooms. You can ride, walk, fish or visit Aberglasney Garden – just ask Katy.

Rooms	5 doubles: £85–£104.
	1 family room for 4 (suitable for 2 adults and 1–2 children under 12): £104–£122.
	Singles £55.
Meals	Dinner from £19.25.
	Pubs/restaurants 2 miles.
Closed	November–March.

	Katy Jenkins
	The Glynhir Estate,
	Glynhir Road, Llandybie,
	Ammanford,
	Carmarthenshire SA18 2TD
Tel	+44 (0)1269 850438
Mobile	+44 (0)7810 864458
Email	enquiries@theglynhirestate.com
Web	www.theglynhirestate.com

Entry 652 Map 7

Ceredigion

Ffynnon Fendigaid

Arrive through rolling countryside – birdsong and breeze the only sound; within moments you will be sprawled on a leather sofa admiring modern art and wondering how a little bit of Milan arrived here along with Huw and homemade cake. A place to come and pootle, with no rush; you can stay all day to stroll the fern-fringed paths through the acres of wild garden to a lake and a grand bench, or opt for hearty walking. Your bed is big, the colours are soft, the bathrooms are spotless and the food is local – try all the Welsh cheeses. Wide beaches are close by, red kites and buzzards soar above you. Pulchritudinous.

Rooms	2 doubles: £77–£79.
	Singles £47–£50.
Meals	Dinner, 2–3 courses, £20–£22.
	Pub 1 mile.
Closed	Rarely.

	Huw Davies
	Ffynnon Fendigaid,
	Rhydlewis,
	Llandysul,
	Ceredigion SA44 5SR
Tel	+44 (0)1239 851361
Mobile	+44 (0)7974 135262
Email	ffynnonf@btinternet.com
Web	www.ffynnonf.co.uk

Entry 653 Map 6

Ceredigion

Broniwan

The Jacobs began farming organically here in the 70s and concentrate now on their kitchen garden – meals celebrate their success. Their cosy ivy-clad home is quietly, colourfully stylish, with books, watercolours and good local art; the attractive guest bedroom has a traditional Welsh bedspread and views to the Preseli Hills. There are acres to roam and the meadow garden's pond brims with life. Carole is passionate about history and literature and can advise on days out: try the Museum of Quilts in Lampeter, or Aberglasney, an hour's drive. Do linger; this is such a rich spot.

Minimum stay: 2 nights.

Rooms	1 double: £80–£90. Singles £45.
Meals	Dinner, on request, £25–£30. BYO. Restaurants 7-8 miles.
Closed	Rarely.

Carole & Allen Jacobs
Broniwan,
Rhydlewis,
Llandysul,
Ceredigion SA44 5PF
Tel   +44 (0)1239 851261
Email   broniwan@btinternet.com
Web   www.broniwan.com

Entry 654   Map 6

Conwy

St Curigs Church

Blessed are those who enter, especially mountain lovers of a gregarious nature. This converted church is a proper family home so be prepared to fit in with all and sundry: Welsh harp may echo in the domed mosaic ceiling, there are marble pillars and stained glass and breakfast is taken at a large table beneath the pine-vaulted apse. Bedrooms are country cosy and in one four-poster a stone pulpit watches over you while underfloor heating keeps it all warm. The views to Snowdon are glorious, walks galore lead from the door and after tackling the sensational Glyder Ridge you can soak in the hot tub. Ecclesiastical bohemia at its best.

Extra rooms available. Bunk room £20 per person including breakfast.

Rooms	2 twins, 2 four-posters: £70–£75. 1 bunk room for 4: £20.
Meals	Pub 300 yds.
Closed	Rarely.

Alice Douglas
St Curigs Church,
Capel Curig,
Betws-y-Coed,
Conwy LL24 0EL
Tel   +44 (0)1690 720469
Email   alice@alicedouglas.com
Web   www.stcurigschurch.com

Entry 655   Map 7

Conwy

Pengwern Country House

The steeply wooded Conwy valley snakes down to this stone and slate property set back from the road in Snowdonia National Park, and the walks are wonderful. Inside has an upbeat traditional feel: a large sitting room with tall bay windows and pictures by the Betws-y-Coed artists who once lived here. Settle with a book by the wood-burner; Gwawr and Ian are naturally friendly and treat guests as friends. Bedrooms have rough plastered walls, colourful fabrics and super bathrooms; one comes with a double-ended roll top tub and views of Lledr Valley. Breakfast on fruits, herb rösti, soda bread – superb.

Minimum stay: 2 nights.

Rooms	1 double, 1 four-poster, 1 twin/double: £72-£84. Singles from £62.
Meals	Packed lunch £5.50. Pubs/restaurants within 1.5 miles.
Closed	Christmas & New Year.

	Gwawr & Ian Mowatt Pengwern Country House, Allt Dinas, Betws-y-Coed, Conwy LL24 0HF
Tel	+44 (0)1690 710480
Email	gwawr.pengwern@btopenworld.com
Web	www.snowdoniaaccommodation.co.uk

Entry 656   Map 7

Denbighshire

Plas Efenechtyd Cottage

Efenechtyd means 'place of the monks' but there's nothing spartan about Dave and Marilyn's handsome brick farmhouse. Breakfasts of local sausages, eggs from their hens, salmon fishcakes with mushrooms and homemade bread are served at a polished table in the dining room with exotic wall hangings from Vietnam and Laos. Light bedrooms have an uncluttered feel, excellent mattresses and good linen; bathrooms are warm as toast. In the pretty cottage garden: a summerhouse and Marilyn's beehive. Motor to Ruthin, with its windy streets and interesting shops, or strike out for Offa's Dyke with a packed lunch; this is stunning countryside.

Rooms	2 doubles, 1 twin: £70. Singles £50.
Meals	Packed lunch £6. Pub 1.6 miles.
Closed	Rarely.

	Dave Jones & Marilyn Jeffery Plas Efenechtyd Cottage, Efenechtyd, Ruthin, Denbighshire LL15 2LP
Tel	+44 (0)1824 704008
Mobile	+44 (0)7540 501009
Email	info@plas-efenechtyd-cottage.co.uk
Web	www.plas-efenechtyd-cottage.co.uk

Entry 657   Map 7

Flintshire

Plas Penucha

Swing back in time with polished parquet, tidy beams, a huge Elizabethan panelled lounge with books, leather sofas and open fire – a cosy spot for Nest's dogs and for tea in winter. Plas Penucha – 'the big house on the highest point in the parish' – has been in the family for 500 years. Airy, old-fashioned bedrooms have long views across the garden to Offa's Dyke and one has a shower in the corner. The L-shaped dining room has a genuine Arts & Crafts interior; outside, rhododendrons and a rock garden flourish. There are views to the Clywdian Hills and beyond is St Asaph, with the smallest medieval cathedral in the country.

Rooms	1 double, 1 twin: £76. Singles £38.
Meals	Dinner £19. Packed lunch £5. Pub/restaurant 2–3 miles.
Closed	Rarely.

Nest Price
Plas Penucha,
Pen y Cefn Road, Caerwys, Mold,
Flintshire CH7 5BH

Tel	+44 (0)1352 720210
Email	nest@plaspenucha.co.uk
Web	www.plaspenucha.co.uk

Entry 658   Map 7

Gwynedd

Caerynwch

Feast your eyes on a mountain framed against brilliant skies from this Georgian home. Come for peace, space, acres of beautiful garden, woodland and burbling streams, and vast trees sheltering rhododendrons and plants collected by Andrew's botanist grandmother. Inside is unpretentious and charming with big comfy country bedrooms and those mesmerising views. Gaze at Cadair Idris from a grand-scale drawing room; cosy up in a sitting room with a wood-burner; breakfast under the gaze of the ancestors. Snowdonia and river walks beckon – and then there's the pub, a short stroll through the grounds.

Pets welcome, sleeping downstairs.

Rooms	1 double; 1 double, 1 twin, each with separate bath/shower: £100. Singles £50.
Meals	Pub within 1 mile.
Closed	Christmas, New Year.

Andrew & Hilary Richards
Caerynwch,
Brithdir, Dolgellau,
Gwynedd LL40 2RF

Tel	+44 (0)1341 422263
Email	richards@torrentwalkcottages.com
Web	www.torrentwalkcottages.com

Entry 659   Map 7

Gwynedd

The Slate Shed at Graig Wen

Sarah and conservationist John spent months travelling in a camper looking for their own special place and found this lovely old Welsh slate cutting mill... captivated by acres of wild woods and stunning views. You'll feel at ease as soon as you step into their eclectic modern home with its reclaimed slate and wood, cosy wood-burners, books, games, snug bedrooms (one downstairs) and superb bathrooms. Breakfast communally on local eggs and sausages, honey from the mountainside, homemade bread and granola. Hike or bike the Mawddach Trail, climb Cadair Idris, wonder at the views... and John's chocolate brownies.

Rooms	4 doubles, 1 twin/double: £75–£130. Singles £65.
Meals	Packed lunch £6.50. Pub 5 miles.
Closed	Rarely.

Sarah Heyworth
The Slate Shed at Graig Wen,
Arthog,
Gwynedd LL39 1BQ

Tel	+44 (0)1341 250482
Email	hello@slateshed.co.uk
Web	www.slateshed.co.uk

Entry 660   Map 7

Gwynedd

Y Goeden Eirin

A little gem tucked between the sea and the mountains, an education in Welsh culture, and a great place to explore wild Snowdonia, the Llyn peninsula and the dramatic Eifl mountains. Inside presents a cosy picture: Welsh-language and English books share the shelves, paintings by contemporary Welsh artists enliven the walls, an arty 70s décor mingles with sturdy Welsh oak in the bedrooms – the one in the house the best – and all bathrooms are super. Wonderful food is served alongside the Bechstein in the beamed dining room – the welcoming, thoughtful Eluned and John have created an unusually delightful space.

Rooms	1 double, 2 twin/doubles: £80–£90. Singles £60–£70. Dinner, B&B £88–£118 per person.
Meals	Dinner, 4 courses, £28. Wine from £14. Packed lunch £12. Pub/restaurant 0.75 miles.
Closed	Christmas, New Year & occasionally.

John & Eluned Rowlands
Y Goeden Eirin,
Dolydd, Caernarfon,
Gwynedd LL54 7EF

Tel	+44 (0)1286 830942
Mobile	+44 (0)7708 491234
Email	john_rowlands@tiscali.co.uk
Web	www.ygoedeneirin.co.uk

Entry 661   Map 6

Monmouthshire

Penpergwm Lodge

On the edge of the Brecon Beacons, a large and lovely Edwardian house. Breakfast round the mahogany table, relax by the fire in the sitting room with books to read and piano to play. The Boyles have been here for years and pour much of their energy into three beautiful acres of parterre and potager, orchard and flowers. Bedrooms are gloriously traditional – ancestral portraits, embroidered bed covers, big windows, good chintz – with garden views; bathrooms are a skip across the landing. A pool and tennis for the sporty, two summerhouses for the dreamy, a good pub you can walk to. Splendid, old-fashioned B&B.

Monmouthshire

Upper Red House

Head down the lane into deepest Monmouthshire and the meadows, orchards and woodland of Teona's organic farm. There are six ponds and miles of bushy hedges; bees, ponies, peafowl and wildlife flourish. The 17th-century house, restored from dereliction, has lovely views, flagstones and oak, limewashed walls and a magical feel. Up steep stairs are rustic bedrooms with beams, lots of books, no TV; the attic rooms get the best views of all. Bathrooms are simple, one has a huge old roll top tub. After a good vegetarian breakfast at the long kitchen table take a farm tour, explore Offa's Dyke or the Wye Valley and revel in the silence.

Children over 8 welcome.

Rooms	2 twins, each with separate bath: £75. Singles £45.
Meals	Pub within walking distance.
Closed	Rarely.

Rooms	1 double; 1 double sharing bath with 2 singles (let to same party only): £80–£95. 2 singles sharing bath with 1 double (let to same party only): £35–£45.
Meals	Vegetarian packed lunch £6. Pubs/restaurants 3.5 miles.
Closed	Rarely.

	Catriona Boyle Penpergwm Lodge, Penpergwm, Abergavenny, Monmouthshire NP7 9AS
Tel	+44 (0)1873 840208
Email	boyle@penpergwm.co.uk
Web	www.penplants.com

	Teona Dorrien-Smith Upper Red House, Llanfihangel-Ystern-Llewern, Monmouth, Monmouthshire NP25 5HL
Tel	+44 (0)1600 780501
Email	upperredhouse@mac.com
Web	www.upperredhouse.co.uk

Entry 662   Map 7

Entry 663   Map 7

Monmouthshire

Myrtle Cottage

The family has found a slice of heaven in Llandogo. You're in the heart of their home and little Elsie, George and Alicia make terrific hosts. Bedrooms have a private balcony or French windows leading to the garden, and lovely wide views across the Wye Valley. Breakfasts in the family kitchen are scrumptious. Tori bakes fabulous breads, cakes and waffles, and you could find yourself lingering all day for the wood-fired pizzas and Ed's microbrewery beers. Hike up and down the river, visit the pub at Brockweir, drop in on the brewery – we recommend Humpty's Fuddle!

Rooms	2 doubles sharing bath with family: £70. Singles £50.
Meals	Supper by arrangement, £12.50–£30. Monthly pizza evenings. Picnics & lunches £7.50–£25. Pubs/restaurants 3 miles.
Closed	Rarely.

	Edward & Tori Biggs
	Myrtle Cottage,
	Llandogo, Monmouth,
	Monmouthshire NP25 4TP
Mobile	+44 (0)7824 663550
Email	shop@meadowfarm.org.uk
Web	www.wye-valley-accommodation.co.uk

Entry 664   Map 7

Pembrokeshire

Cresswell House

On a peaceful and pretty tidal river creek between Narberth and Tenby, this Georgian Quay Master's house is heaven for walkers, bird-watchers and lovers of a good pub – there's one just down the road. Guests have a separate entrance to cosy, modern-rustic style, third-floor rooms: Welsh blankets, good white linen, pristine stone-tiled bathrooms, sofas, DVDs, coffee machines, a shared fridge. Philip and Rhian's love of art is evident (as is their friendly, lively lurcher!); they make jams and bread for relaxed, full-Welsh breakfasts and happily advise on what to do. An easy-going place – great nearby beaches too.

Rooms	1 double, 1 twin/double: £85.
Meals	Pubs/restaurants 5-minute drive.
Closed	Rarely.

	Philip Wight & Rhian Davies
	Cresswell House,
	Cresswell Quay,
	Kilgetty,
	Pembrokeshire SA68 0TE
Tel	+44 (0)1646 651435
Email	rhian@cresswellhouse.co.uk
Web	www.cresswellhouse.co.uk

Entry 665   Map 6

Pembrokeshire

Cresselly House

Imagine staying at the Georgian mansion of an old country friend – that's what it's like to stay at Cresselly. Step into a sunny square hall with a sweeping stair and the ancestors on the walls. Beeswax and lavender scent the air, cosy bedrooms are as grandly traditional as can be, new bathrooms sparkle and views swoop over the park. For breakfast or dinner (if requested) you can seat yourself at the fine Georgian mahogany dining table, gleaming from many decades of polishing. The walking and riding are glorious, and there's impressive stabling for your horse: this is the heartland of the South Pembrokeshire Hunt.

Rooms	2 doubles, 2 twins: £110-£150. Singles £95.
Meals	Supper, 2 courses, £25-£55. Pub 1 mile.
Closed	Rarely.

Hugh Harrison-Allen
Cresselly House,
Cresselly,
Kilgetty,
Pembrokeshire SA68 0SP
Tel +44 (0)1646 651992
Email info@cresselly.com
Web www.cresselly.com

Entry 666   Map 6

Pembrokeshire

Pembrokeshire Farm B&B

Down a beautiful lane flanked by moss-covered walls, two miles from Narberth, is an old fortified longhouse in 25 rolling acres – pristine, peaceful and cosy. Here live three dogs, three donkeys, cats, hens and friendly hosts Rayner and Carol. There's a real fire and books aplenty, equine paintings and fantastic art, and big gorgeous gardens with croquet, a lake and a boat to mess about in. The décor is traditional, the bed linen immaculate, the bathrooms are spanking new and the views to the Preseli Hills gorgeous. Narberth's restaurants are good but Carol's cooking is fabulous.

Rooms	1 double; 1 double with separate bath: £80. Singles £73.
Meals	Dinner, 3 courses, from £25. Pubs/restaurants 2 miles.
Closed	Rarely.

Rayner & Carol Peett
Pembrokeshire Farm B&B,
Caermaenau Fawr, Clynderwen,
Pembrokeshire SA66 7HB
Tel +44 (0)1834 860338
Mobile +44 (0)77966 15332
Email info@pembrokeshirefarmbandb.co.uk
Web www.pembrokeshirefarmbandb.co.uk

Entry 667   Map 6

Pembrokeshire

Knowles Farm

The Cleddau estuary winds its way around this organic farm – its lush grasses feed the cows that produce milk for the renowned Rachel's yogurt. Your hosts love the land, are committed to its conservation and let you come and go as you please; picnic in the garden, wander the bluebell woods, discover a pond; dogs like it too. You have your own entrance to old-fashioned, lived-in pretty bedrooms with comfy beds, simple bathrooms, glorious views and an eclectic selection of books to browse. Breakfast and supper are fully organic or very local: delicious! If Gini is busy with the farm there are terrific river pubs that serve dinner.

Rooms	2 doubles; 1 twin with separate bath: £75-£90. Singles £50.
Meals	Supper from £12. Dinner, 4 courses, £22, (not in school holidays). Packed lunch £6. Pub 1.5 miles, restaurant 3 miles.
Closed	Rarely.

Virginia Lort Phillips
Knowles Farm,
Lawrenny,
Pembrokeshire SA68 0PX
Tel +44 (0)1834 891221
Email ginilp@lawrenny.org.uk
Web www.lawrenny.org.uk

Entry 668 Map 6

Pembrokeshire

Penfro

This is fun – idiosyncratic and a tad theatrical, rather than conventional and uniformly stylish. The Lappins' home is an impressive Georgian affair, formerly a ballet school. Judith is warm and friendly; her taste – she's also a WWI expert – is eclectic verging on the wacky and she minds that guests are comfortable and well-fed. You eat communally at the scrubbed table in the flagged Aga kitchen: tasty dinners, homemade jams and good coffee at breakfast. The garden is big and beautiful so enjoy its conversational terrace. And discuss which of the three very characterful bedrooms will suit you best, plumbing and all!

Minimum stay: 2 nights at weekends in the summer and over bank holidays.

Rooms	1 double (en suite); 1 double, 1 twin, each with separate bath: £70-£90. Singles £60-£80. Extra bed/sofabed available £10-£15 per person per night.
Meals	Dinner, 3 courses, £20. Packed lunch from £8. Pub 250 yds. Owners can cater for gluten free diets at no extra cost.
Closed	Rarely.

Judith Lappin
Penfro,
111 Main Street, Pembroke,
Pembrokeshire SA71 4DB
Tel +44 (0)1646 682753
Mobile +44 (0)7763 856181
Email info@penfro.co.uk
Web www.penfro.co.uk

Entry 669 Map 6

Pembrokeshire

Pentower

Curl up with a cat and watch the ferries – or sometimes a porpoise – coasting to Ireland; French windows open onto the terrace and a glorious vista. Mary and Tony are warm and interesting hosts; their turreted 1898 house has an easy-going atmosphere, quarry tiled floors, decorative fireplaces and an impressive staircase. Spotless bedrooms are light and airy, with large showers; the Tower Room has the views. Wake for a very good full English (or Welsh) breakfast in the tiled dining/sitting room – tuck in while admiring the panoramic view over a bay full of boats. Fishguard is a short stroll, and the stunning coastal path is nearby.

Rooms	1 double, 1 twin/double: £85-£90. Singles £55.
Meals	Packed lunch £5. Pubs/restaurants 500 yds.
Closed	Occasionally.

Tony Jacobs & Mary Geraldine Casey
Pentower,
Tower Hill, Fishguard,
Pembrokeshire SA65 9LA
Tel   +44 (0)1348 874462
Email   sales@pentower.co.uk
Web   www.pentower.co.uk

Entry 670   Map 6

Pembrokeshire

Cefn-y-Dre Country House

Geoff and Gaye want your stay to go without a hitch, and they're proud of the rich history of their house. Solid, handsome and 500 years old, Cefn-y-Dre is on the fringe of the Pembrokeshire Coast National Park with views to the Preseli Hills. The sitting room is set aside for guests, notable for its striking red chairs used during Prince Charles' investiture in 1969 – quite a talking point! Geoff is a great cook who takes pleasure in using local produce and home-grown veg from the large garden; not so long ago he trained at Ballymaloe. St David's, with its ancient cathedral, is nearby, as are some of Britain's finest beaches.

Rooms	1 double, 1 twin/double; 1 double with separate bath/shower: £79-£99. Singles £50-£70.
Meals	Dinner, 3 courses, £24.50. Pubs/restaurants 2 miles.
Closed	Rarely.

Gaye Williams & Geoff Stickler
Cefn-y-Dre Country House,
Fishguard,
Pembrokeshire SA65 9QS
Tel   +44 (0)1348 875663
Email   welcome@cefnydre.co.uk
Web   www.cefnydre.co.uk

Entry 671   Map 6

Powys

The Farm

Lose yourself in the wildlife, from a warm-hearted Welsh Marches B&B. There are just five sheep remaining now (all pets!) and your hosts have hearts of gold. Find fresh flowers on the Welsh dresser, a big dining table with a lovely garden view, breakfasts locally sourced and marmalades, jams and bread homemade. (And special diets easily catered for.) Overlooking the garden – yours to enjoy – are big bedrooms with TVs, clock-radios, tea and coffee making facilities and WiFi; one is on the ground floor in an extension, ideal for the less sprightly. Montgomery and Bishop's Castle, lovely little towns, are a must-see.

Rooms	1 double, 2 twin/doubles: £70–£85. Singles from £40.
Meals	Dinner from £16. Pubs/restaurants 2 miles.
Closed	Rarely.

Sandra & Alan Jones
The Farm,
Snead, Montgomery,
Powys SY15 6EB
Tel   +44 (0)1588 620281
Email   asj.farmsnead@btconnect.com
Web   www.thefarmsnead.co.uk

Entry 672   Map 7

Powys

The Old Vicarage

Come for vast skies, forested hills and quilted fields that stretch for miles. This Victorian vicarage is a super base: smart, welcoming, full of comforts. You get a log fire in a cosy sitting room, a small restaurant with long country views and fancy bedrooms that spoil you all the way. Chef Tim has quite a pedigree, the food is delicious, local suppliers are noted on menus, and much is grown in the garden, where chickens run free. Resist laziness and take to the hills for glorious walking and cycling: the Kerry Ridgeway is on your doorstep as is Powis Castle.

Rooms	2 doubles, 1 twin/double: £95–£120. 1 suite for 4: £150. Singles £70.
Meals	Dinner, 3 courses, £35. Packed lunch & picnics available. Pub 0.75 miles.
Closed	Rarely.

Tim & Helen Withers
The Old Vicarage,
Dolfor, Newtown, Powys SY16 4BN
Tel   +44 (0)1686 629051
Mobile   +44 (0)7753 760054
Email   tim@theoldvicaragedolfor.co.uk
Web   www.theoldvicaragedolfor.co.uk

Entry 673   Map 7

Powys

The Old Vicarage

A wide hall, deep window sills and expanses of glass have created a light and appealing home. On the edge of the hamlet, this Arts and Crafts house has spectacular views. Pat serves afternoon tea when you arrive, and breakfast is in a snug spot by the wood-burner. Bedrooms are traditional, big and blessed with homemade biscuits, tea trays and flowers; both have views across gardens, woodland and paddocks — there are acres to explore. The veg patch provides for dinner and you can enjoy a sunset drink in the walled garden. Walks are wonderful — Offa's Dyke footpath is close by — and the Hay-on-Wye festival is a 30-minute drive.

Rooms	1 double; 1 twin with separate bath: £85–£95. Singles £50–£55.
Meals	Dinner, 3 courses, £25. BYO. Pub 3 miles.
Closed	Rarely.

Patricia Birch
The Old Vicarage,
Evancoyd, Presteigne,
Powys LD8 2PA

Tel	+44 (0)1547 560951
Mobile	+44 (0)7903 859012
Email	pat.birch38@gmail.com
Web	www.oldvicaragebandb-welshborder.co.uk

Entry 674   Map 7

Powys

Pottery Cottage

Balm for urban souls searching for a retreat… This gorgeous old potter's shed, once worked in by Adam Dworski, is now a village hideaway sprinkled with beautiful objects and books. Nothing could be lovelier than sitting up in the wide bed, clouded over by Hungarian goose down and contemplating the pretty garden laid out at your feet. Hungry? Put an idle hand out for Emma's breakfast basket which bustles with local apple juice, bread and pastries, organic yogurt, fruit, Hay Deli granola. Make your own proper coffee, choose when to come and go. Stride the hills, find great pubs, return to a soak in a big tub with a glass of wine. Bliss.

Rooms	1 double (extra mattress & cot available): £70–£80.
Meals	Pub in village & pubs/restaurants 1 mile.
Closed	Rarely.

Favourite
newcomer

Emma Balch
Pottery Cottage,
Clyro, Hereford,
Powys HR3 5SB

Tel	+44 (0)1497 822931
Mobile	+44 (0)7879 373431
Email	doblemdesign@gmail.com
Web	www.potterycottageclyro.com

Entry 675   Map 7

Powys

Rhedyn

Come here if you need to remember how to relax. Such an unassuming, little place, but with real character and soul: great comfort too. Find exposed walls in the bedrooms, funky lighting, pocket sprung mattresses, lovely books to read, and calm colours; bathrooms are modern and delightfully quirky. But the real stars of this show are Muiread and Ciaran: warm, enthusiastic and engaging, with a passion for good local food and a desire for more self-sufficiency – pigs and bees are planned next. This is a totally tranquil place, with agreeable walks through the Irfon valley, and bog snorkelling too!

Rooms	3 doubles: £90.
	Singles £80.
	Dinner, B&B £73 per person.
Meals	Dinner, 3 courses, £28.
	Packed lunch £7.50.
	Pub/restaurant 1 mile.
Closed	Rarely.

Muiread & Ciaran O'Connell
Rhedyn,
Cilmery, Builth Wells,
Powys LD2 3LH
Tel   +44 (0)1982 551944
Email   info@rhedynguesthouse.co.uk
Web   www.rhedynguesthouse.co.uk

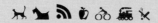

Entry 676   Map 7

Powys

Hafod Y Garreg

A unique opportunity to stay in the oldest house in Wales – a fascinating, 1402 cruck-framed hall house, built for Henry IV as a hunting lodge. Informal Annie and John have filled it with a charming mix of Venetian mirrors, Indian rugs, pewter plates, gorgeous fabrics and oak furniture. Dine by candlelight in the fabulous dining room – maybe pheasant pie with chilli jam and hazelnut mash: delicious. Bedrooms are luxurious and comfortable with Egyptian cotton bed linen. Reach the Grade II* listed house by a bumpy track across gated fields crowded with chickens, cats... a special, secluded and relaxed place.

Rooms	2 doubles: £86.
	Singles from £80.
Meals	Dinner, 3 courses, £25. BYO.
	Pubs/restaurants 2.5 miles.
Closed	Christmas.

Annie & John McKay
Hafod Y Garreg,
Erwood, Builth Wells,
Powys LD2 3TQ
Tel   +44 (0)1982 560400
Email   john-annie@hafod-y.wanadoo.co.uk
Web   www.hafodygarreg.co.uk

Entry 677   Map 7

Broomfield House

A tree-lined drive leads to this rather wonderful Georgian mansion… views sweep over the Wye valley. Peter has carried out an immaculate and traditional restoration: antiques in every corner, perfect linen, silk drapes and decanters of sherry in large sumptuous bedrooms. The suite is perfect for your honeymoon. A morning tray is brought to your room, then breakfast is served round the huge dining table: local produce, perhaps smoked salmon – the papers too. Hay-on-Wye, Golden Valley, Black Mountains and Brecon are all within an easy drive. Gather round an open fire in the elegant drawing room for drinks before dinner.

Shepherd's Hut at Argoed

Like its owners, the shepherd's hut has settled happily into a spectacular, peaceful spot with mountain views dominated by the enticing Pen y Fan peak. It's carefully designed with a big dozing bed and a corner bathroom. The wood-burner keeps the whole thing cosy and warm and there's a kettle for early morning tea at the folding table in front of broad windows that frame the mountains. Breakfast is included and served at the house until 10. The only visitor you're likely to have is a curious chicken; your neighbours: cows or sheep in the adjoining field. You've Hay to visit and miles and miles of Black Mountain walks.

Minimum stay: 2 nights. Book through Sawday's Canopy & Stars online or by phone.

Rooms	2 doubles, 2 twin/doubles, 1 four-poster: £150–£295. 1 four-poster suite for 2 with separate sitting room: £150–£295. Singles £125–£265.
Meals	Dinner, 3 courses with wine, £35. Pubs/restaurants 3 miles.
Closed	Rarely.

Rooms	Shepherd's hut for 2: £115.
Meals	Breakfast included.
Closed	Rarely.

	Peter Bond Broomfield House, Glasbury on Wye, Powys HR3 5NS
Tel	+44 (0)1497 842970
Email	info@broomfieldhse.co.uk
Web	www.broomfieldhse.co.uk

	Sawday's Canopy & Stars Shepherd's Hut at Argoed, Argoed Barns, Talachddu, Felin Fach, Powys LD3 0UG
Tel	+44 (0)117 204 7830
Email	enquiries@canopyandstars.co.uk
Web	www.canopyandstars.co.uk/ shepherdshutargoed

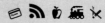

Powys

Powys

The Old Store House

Unbend here with agreeable books, chattering birds, and Peter, who asks only that you feel at home. Downstairs are a range-warmed kitchen, a sunny conservatory overlooking garden, chickens, ducks and canal, and a charmingly ramshackle sitting room with a wood-burner, sofas and a piano – no babbling TV. Bedrooms are large, light and spotless, with more books, soft goose down, armchairs and bathrooms with views. Breakfast, without haste, on scrambled eggs, local bacon and sausages, blistering coffee. Bliss – but as far from tickety boo as possible. Walk into the hills from the back door.

Children over 6 welcome.

Ty'r Chanter

Warmth, colour, children and activity: this house is huge fun. Tiggy welcomes you like family; help collect eggs, feed the lambs, drop your shoes by the fire. The farmhouse and barn are stylishly relaxed; deep sofas, tartan throws, heaps of books, views to the Brecon Beacons and Black Mountains. Bedrooms are soft, simple sanctuaries with Jo Malone bathroom treats. The two children's rooms zing with murals; toys, kids' sitting room and a sandpit it's child heaven. You can walk, fish, canoe, book-browse in Hay or stroll the estate. Homemade cakes and whisky to help yourself to: fine hospitality and Tiggy is wonderful.

Rooms	3 doubles, 1 twin: £80. Singles £40.
Meals	Packed lunch £4. Pub/restaurant 0.75 miles.
Closed	Rarely.

Rooms	3 doubles: £95. 1 twin with separate bath/shower (children's room; price per child): £20. Singles £55.
Meals	Packed lunch £8. Pub 1 mile.
Closed	Christmas.

Peter Evans
The Old Store House,
Llanfrynach,
Brecon,
Powys LD3 7LJ
Tel   +44 (0)1874 665499
Email   oldstorehouse@btconnect.com
Web   www.theoldstorehouse.co.uk

Tiggy Pettifer
Ty'r Chanter,
Gliffaes, Crickhowell,
Powys NP8 1RL
Tel   +44 (0)1874 731144
Mobile +44 (0)7802 387004
Email   tiggy@tyrchanter.com
Web   www.tyrchanter.com

Entry 680   Map 7

Entry 681   Map 7

Swansea

Blas Gwyr

Llangennith was once a well-kept secret – now walkers, riders, surfers and beach bunnies of all ages flock. Close to the bustling bay is an extended 1700s cottage with a youthful facelift. All is simple but stylish: bedrooms (two overlooking the road) are modern and matching; bathrooms and wet rooms come with warm floors and fluffy towels. Everything from the bedspread to the breakfast is local: make sure you try the laverbread. After a day at sea, fling wet gear in the drying room and linger over a coffee in the courtyard, or walk to the pub for a sun-kissed pint. Laid-back bliss.

Rooms	1 double, 1 double with sofabed, 1 twin/double; 1 suite for 2-4: £115-£125. Children from £15.
Meals	Packed lunch available. Dinner £27.50-£30 (selected weekends). Pub 150 yds.
Closed	Rarely.

Dafydd James
Blas Gwyr,
Plenty Farm, Llangennith,
Swansea SA3 1HU

Tel	+44 (0)1792 386472
Mobile	+44 (0)7974 981156
Email	info@blasgwyr.co.uk
Web	www.blasgwyr.co.uk

Entry 682   Map 2

Wrexham

Worthenbury Manor

Welcome to one half of a big country house on the border of Wales and Shropshire. Congenial, generous Ian and Elizabeth look after you wonderfully well. The guest sitting room is warmed by a log fire in winter; the dining room has listed Jacobean panelling. Choose between two comfortable bedrooms, one decorated in Georgian style, one in Jacobean, both with rich drapes, chandeliers, fresh coffee and antique four-posters. Wake refreshed for a beautifully cooked breakfast: local and home-grown produce, home-baked bread and Ian's impressive marmalades; dinner too is a treat. Visit Erddig, Chirk Castle, Powis…

Reductions on longer stays; enquire with owners.

Rooms	1 four-poster; 1 four-poster with separate bath: £60-£100. Singles £45-£70. Dinner, B&B £75-£100 per person. Extra bed/sofabed available £20-£30 per person per night.
Meals	Dinner, 3 courses, £30. Supper, 2 courses, £20. BYO. Pub/restaurant 5 miles.
Closed	24-28 December.

Elizabeth & Ian Taylor
Worthenbury Manor,
Worthenbury,
Wrexham LL13 0AW

Tel	+44 (0)1948 770342
Email	enquiries@worthenburymanor.co.uk
Web	www.worthenburymanor.co.uk

Entry 683   Map 7

Children of all ages welcome

These owners have told us that they welcome children of all ages. Please note cots and highchairs may not necessarily be available.

Quick reference indices

Alastair Sawday has been publishing books for over twenty years, finding Special Places to Stay in Britain and abroad. All our properties are inspected by us and are chosen for their charm and individuality, and with twelve titles to choose from there are plenty of places to explore. You can buy any of our books at a reader discount of 25%* on the RRP.

 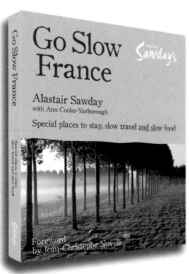

List of titles:	RRP	Discount price
British Bed & Breakfast	£15.99	£11.99
Special Places to Stay in Britain for Garden Lovers	£19.99	£14.99
British Hotels and Inns	£15.99	£11.99
Pubs & Inns of England & Wales	£15.99	£11.99
Dog-friendly Breaks in Britain	£14.99	£11.24
French Bed & Breakfast	£15.99	£11.99
French Châteaux & Hotels	£15.99	£11.99
Italy	£15.99	£11.99
Portugal	£12.99	£9.74
Spain	£15.99	£11.99
Go Slow England & Wales	£19.99	£14.99
Go Slow France	£19.99	£14.99

*postage and packaging is added to each order

How to order:
You can order online at: www.sawdays.co.uk/bookshop/
or call: **+44(0)117 204 7810**

Photo: The Old Post Office, Dorset, entry 167

Photo: Sunnybank, Yorkshire, entry 539

Alastair
Sawday's

'More than a bed
for the night...'

Britain
France
Ireland
Italy
Portugal
Spain

www.sawdays.co.uk

Self-Catering | B&B | Hotel | Pub | Canopy & Stars

Join us

TIME AWAY IS FAR TOO PRECIOUS TO
SPEND IN THE WRONG PLACE. THAT'S WHY,
BACK IN 1994, WE STARTED SAWDAY'S.

Twenty years on, we're still a family concern – and still
on a crusade to stamp out the bland and predictable,
and help our guests find truly special places to stay.

If you have one, we do hope you'll decided
to take the plunge and join us.

———

ALASTAIR & TOBY SAWDAY

"Trustworthy, friendly and helpful – with a reputation
for offering wonderful places and discerning visitors."
JULIA NAISMITH, HOLLYTREE COTTAGE

"Sawday's. Is there any other?"
SONIA HODGSON, HORRY MILL

WHY BECOME A MEMBER?

Becoming a part of our 'family' of Special Places is like being awarded a Michelin star. Our stamp of approval will tell guests that you offer a truly special experience and you will benefit from our experience, reputation and support.

A CURATED COLLECTION

Our site presents a relatively small and careful selection of Special Places which helps us to stand out like a brilliantly shining beacon.

QUALITY, NOT QUANTITY

We don't pretend (or want) to be in the same business as the sites that handle zillions of bookings a day. Using our name ensures that you attract the right kind of guests for you.

INSPECT AND RE-INSPECT

Our inspectors have an eagle-eye for the special, but absolutely no check-lists. They visit every member, see every bedroom and bathroom and, on the lucky days, eat the food.

VARIETY

From country-house hotels to city pads and funky fincas to blissful B&Bs, we genuinely delight in the individuality of our Special Places.

LOYALTY

Nearly half of our members have been with us for five years or more. We must be doing something right!

The friendly crew

GET IN TOUCH WITH OUR MEMBERSHIP TEAM...

+44 (0)117 204 7810
members@sawdays.co.uk

...OR APPLY ONLINE

sawdays.co.uk/joinus

1 Flintshire

Gwynedd

Plas Penucha

2 Swing back in time with polished parquet, tidy beams, a huge Elizabethan panelled lounge with books, leather sofas and open fire – a cosy spot for Nest's dogs and for tea in winter. Plas Penucha – 'the big house on the highest point in the parish' – has been in the family for 500 years. Airy, old-fashioned bedrooms have long views across the garden to Offa's Dyke and one has a shower in the corner. The L-shaped dining room has a genuine Arts & Crafts interior; outside, rhododendrons and a rock garden flourish. There are views to the Clywdian Hills and beyond is St Asaph, with the smallest medieval cathedral in the country.

Caerynwch

Feast your eyes on a mountain framed against brilliant skies from this Georgian home. Come for peace, space, acres of beautiful garden, woodland and burbling streams, and vast trees sheltering rhododendrons and plants collected by Andrew's botanist grandmother. Inside is unpretentious and charming with big comfy country bedrooms and those mesmerising views. Gaze at Cadair Idris from a grand-scale drawing room; cosy up in a sitting room with a wood-burner; breakfast under the gaze of the ancestors. Snowdonia and river walks beckon — and then there's the pub, a short stroll through the grounds.

Pets welcome, sleeping downstairs.

3 Rooms	1 double, 1 twin: £76. Singles £38.	
4 Meals	Dinner £19. Packed lunch £5. Pub/restaurant 2-3 miles.	
5 Closed	Rarely.	

Rooms	1 double; 1 double, 1 twin, each with separate bath/shower: £100. Singles £50.
Meals	Pub within 1 mile.
Closed	Christmas, New Year.

Nest Price
Plas Penucha,
Pen y Cefn Road, Caerwys, Mold,
Flintshire CH7 5BH
Tel   +44 (0)1352 720210
Email   nest@plaspenucha.co.uk
Web   www.plaspenucha.co.uk

Andrew & Hilary Richards
Caerynwch,
Brithdir, Dolgellau,
Gwynedd LL40 2RF
Tel   +44 (0)1341 422263
Email   richards@torrentwalkcottages.com
Web   www.torrentwalkcottages.com

6

7   Entry 658   Map 7

Entry 659   Map 7